Queen Victoria

Paula Bartley's *Queen Victoria* examines Victorian Britain from the perspective of the Queen. Victoria's personal and political actions are discussed in relation to contemporary shifts in Britain's society, politics and culture, examining to what extent they did – or did not – influence events throughout her reign.

Drawing from contemporary sources, including Queen Victoria's own diaries, as well as the most recent scholarship, the book contextualises Victoria historically by placing her in the centre of an unparalleled period of innovation and reform, in which the social and political landscape of Britain, and its growing empire, was transformed. Balancing Victoria's private and public roles, it examines the cultural paradox of the Queen's rule in relation to the changing role of women: she was a devoted wife, prolific mother and obsessive widow, who was also queen of a large empire and the Empress of India.

Marrying cultural history, gender history and other histories 'from below' with high politics, war and diplomacy, this is a concise and accessible introduction to Queen Victoria's life for students of Victorian Britain and the British Empire.

Paula Bartley has published extensively on women's history. Her previous publications include *Emmeline Pankhurst* (Routledge Historical Biographies, 2002), *Votes for Women* (2007) and *Ellen Wilkinson: From Red Suffragist to Government Minister* (2014).

ROUTLEDGE HISTORICAL BIOGRAPHIES

Series Editor: Robert Pearce

Routledge Historical Biographies provide engaging, readable and academically credible biographies written from an explicitly historical perspective. These concise and accessible accounts will bring important historical figures to life for students and general readers alike.

In the same series:

Queen Victoria

Paula Bartley

Routledge
Taylor & Francis Group

LONDON AND NEW YORK

First published 2016
by Routledge
2 Park Square, Milton Park, Abingdon, Oxon OX14 4RN

and by Routledge
711 Third Avenue, New York, NY 10017

*Routledge is an imprint of the Taylor & Francis Group,
an informa business*

British Library Cataloguing in Publication Data
A catalogue record for this book is available from the
British Library

Library of Congress Cataloging-in-Publication Data
Bartley, Paula, author.
  Queen Victoria / Paula Bartley.
    pages cm. — (Routledge historical biographies)
  Includes bibliographical references and index.
  1. Victoria, Queen of Great Britain, 1819–1901.   2. Queens—
Great Britain—Biography.   3. Great Britain—History—Victoria,
1837–1901.   I. Title.
  DA554.B26 2016
  941.081092—dc23
  [B]
  2015031871

ISBN: 978-0-415-72090-8 (hbk)
ISBN: 978-0-415-72091-5 (pbk)
ISBN: 978-1-315-64209-3 (ebk)

Typeset in Sabon
by Apex CoVantage, LLC
Printed by Ashford Colour Press Ltd.

MIX
Paper from
responsible sources
FSC® C011748

For Jonathan Dudley

Contents

Figures

Acknowledgements

My first thanks are to the series editor, Dr Robert Pearce, who commissioned *Queen Victoria*, steered me through Routledge's book proposal guidelines and edited the manuscript with style and wit. His comments were not just astute and well judged but also made with such wry humour that he even made revisions pleasurable. Thanks also to the four independent reviewers who recommended that my book proposal be accepted, and to Catherine Aitken and Laura Pilsworth at Routledge for their enduring patience, support and guidance. I would also like to thank Hamish Ironside for his extraordinarily assiduous proofreading skills; and Dr Megan Hiatt for her careful attention to detail while preparing the book for publication. Naturally, I take responsibility for any remaining errors.

I am grateful to Dr Diane Atkinson, Prof Maggie Andrews, Rosie Keep, Prof Angela V. John and Dr Kathy Stredder for their advice and encouragement, and to Cathy Loxton and Dawn Rumley for their apposite comments on early drafts of the book. Special thanks to Prof Sue Morgan for her reassuring and helpful observations on the final manuscript and to Prof Andrew August for his endorsement of the book. I should like to thank Colin and Libby Bennett for an unforgettable trip to Osborne House; and Myles and Alison, Earl and Countess of Bessborough, for sharing their knowledge of Henry Ponsonby with me. Thanks also to Dr Teresz Kleisz for helping me to understand Hungarian history.

This book could not have been written without the labours of previous biographers and historians who have written extensively on Queen Victoria, her family and her times – so thank you to all those included in my bibliography. Thanks are due to Queen Elizabeth II for giving permission for the journals of Queen Victoria to be made available online and to the Bodleian libraries for helping to fund the website and make it free of charge to all users in the United Kingdom. Thanks to all those in Britain who pay their taxes for helping to keep such institutions flourishing.

A special thanks to the Royal Archives for giving me permission to quote from the journals and to one anonymous individual for some exceedingly useful comments on my manuscript. Victoria's journal entries were accessed online at www.queenvictorias journals.org. Subsequent quotations from the journals are cited according to the guidance listed at www.queenvictoriasjournals. org/info/about.do, using the code RA VIC/MAIN/QVJ (W) followed by the date of the entry. Between 1832 and 1840 I used Lord Esher's typescripts unless otherwise stated, and from 1840 onwards, Princess Beatrice's copies. These were all accessed between February 2013 and May 2015.

My final thanks are to my fantastic Dudley family, especially Jonathan, Edmund, Kata, Réka and Dóra, who individually and collectively provided me with the love and encouragement necessary to engage in the solitary pursuit of research and writing. The book is dedicated to my husband, Jonathan, whose emotional and intellectual support continues to be a source of strength to me.

Chronology

Date	Personal events	British events	World-wide events
1819	Birth of Victoria, birth of Albert.	Peterloo massacre. Shelley's 'The Mask of Anarchy' and Scott's *Bride of Lammermoor* published. Factory Act.	
1820	Death of father, Duke of Kent; death of George III. George IV succeeded.	Cato Street conspiracy.	
1821	Coronation of George IV. Death of Queen Caroline.	*Guardian* newspaper launched.	Death of Napoleon I.
1822		Death penalty repealed for over 100 crimes. Precursor to the computer invented.	
1824		National Gallery opened. Society for the Prevention of Cruelty to Animals (SPCA) founded.	
1825	Victoria recognised as heir to the throne.	First public railway opened.	Nicolas I became Tsar.
1826	Victoria met George IV.		
1827	Prince Frederick died.	Canning appointed PM. Goderich appointed PM.	Treaty of London.
1828	Princess Feodora married.	Wellington appointed PM. London Zoo opened.	Russo-Turkish War.

1829		Catholic Emancipation Act. First Oxford–Cambridge boat race.	
1830	George IV dies. William IV succeeded.	Metropolitan police established. Grey PM. First intercity railway. Swing Riots.	Revolution in France. Louis Philippe crowned king of France. Belgian Independence movement.
1831	William IV crowned.	Factory Act forbade nightwork for those under 21. Darwin sets sail on HMS *Beagle*.	Leopold crowned first king of Belgium. Revolts in Italy.
1832	Tour of England and Wales. Victoria began journal.	Great Reform Act. Tennyson's 'Lady of Shalot'.	Greece recognised as an independent nation: Treaty of London. Bavarian prince appointed king of Greece.
1833	Princes Alexander and Ernst visited. Tour of south and west England.	Factory Act regulated hours of women and children. Slavery abolished in Britain. *Norma* opened in London.	
1834	Feodora visited.	Melbourne PM (July). Peel PM (December). Poor Law Amendment Act. House of Commons burnt down. Slavery abolished in British Empire.	Throne of Portugal seized. Palmerston sent British forces to re-instate legitimate heirs.

(continued)

(continued)

Date	Personal events	British events	World-wide events
1835	Tour of north of England. Leopold visited. Victoria confirmed. Victoria contracted typhoid.	Municipal Corporations Act. Melbourne PM (April)	English became official language of India.
1836	Princes Ferdinand and Augustus; Prince William and Alexander; Prince Ernest and Albert all visited.	Civil Marriages Act. *Pickwick Papers* serialised.	Queen Maria II of Portugal married Prince Ferdinand.
1837	Victoria celebrated 18th birthday. Death of William IV. Victoria became queen. Palace orchestra appointed.	Melbourne PM. Registration of Births, Marriages and Deaths Act. *Oliver Twist* serialised.	Rebellion in Canada.
1838	Victoria crowned.	Chartist petition. *Lucia di Lammermoor* opened in London. National Gallery moved to Trafalgar Square.	Pitcairn Islands became Crown Colony. First Anglo-Afghan war.
1839	Flora Hastings affair. Bedchamber crisis. John Conroy dismissed. Victoria proposed to Albert.	Custody of Infants Act. Rebecca riots began. First Grand National race. First telegraph sent. Anti-Corn Law League Founded.	Belgium recognised as independent country: Treaty of London. First Anglo-Afghan war. Egyptian rebellion against Ottomans. First Opium War.

1840	Victoria and Prince Albert married. Princess Victoria born. First assassination attempt. Albert appointed Regent.	Penny post established.	Canadian Act of Union. Beirut bombarded by British and Ottoman troops. British claimed New Zealand.
1841	Prince Albert Edward born.	Melbourne resigned. Peel PM. Great Western railway completed. *Punch* magazine launched.	Convention of London. United Province of Canada proclaimed. Afghan war.
1842	Lehzen leaves. Victoria, Albert and Bertie vaccinated against smallpox. Victoria's first train ride. First visit to Scotland. Second and third assassination attempts.	Mines Act. Chartist petition. Railway Act. Robert Browning's 'My Last Duchess' published. Income tax levied for the first time in peace time. Chadwick's *The Sanitary Conditions of the Labouring Poor* published.	Opium War ended, Treaty of Nanking. Webster-Ashburton Treaty.
1843	Princess Alice born. Victoria's first visit abroad.	Rebecca riots ended. Opening of Thames tunnel. *News of the World* launched. First propellor-driven steamship launched. First commercial Christmas card.	Natal became British colony.
1844	Prince Alfred born, chloroform used for his delivery. Osborne House bought.	Factory Act. Bank Charter Act. Railway Regulation Act.	

(continued)

(continued)

Date	Personal events	British events	World-wide events
1845	Foundations laid for new Osborne House. Victoria visited Albert's birth-place.	Irish potato blight. Increase in Maynooth Grant. Last British duel fought. Disraeli's *Sybil* published.	First Anglo-Sikh War.
1846	Koh-i-Noor diamond acquired. Princess Helena born.	Repeal of Corn Laws. Peel resigned. Russell PM. Palmerston foreign secretary.	Oregon Treaty. Treaty of Lahore.
1847	New education system devised for royal children.	Ten Hours Act. Thackeray's *Vanity Fair* serialised. Charlotte Brontë's *Jane Eyre* published. Emily Brontë's *Wuthering Heights* published. Chloroform first used as anaesthetic.	
1848	Princess Louise born. Charles Kean appointed director of Windsor Castle theatricals. First visit to Balmoral. Royal family retreated to Osborne.	Habeus corpus suspended in Ireland. Revival of Chartism. Cholera epidemic. Public Health Act.	European revolutions. Spanish marriages. First Schleswig-Holstein war. First German National Assembly. Californian Gold rush. French royal family given asylum in Britain.
1849	Fourth assassination attempt. Victoria and Albert visited Ireland. Albert devised rigorous educational programme for Bertie.		Revolutions crushed.

Year			
1850	Prince Arthur born. Fifth assassination attempt. Brighton Royal Pavilion sold.	Haynau incident. Factory Act. Tennyson appointed Poet Laureate. Peel died. Public Library Act.	Pope issued Bull. Don Pacifico incident. Colony of Victoria, Australia created.
1851	Great Exhibition	Ecclesiastical Titles Act. Kossuth incident. Palmerston resigned as Foreign Secretary. Mayhew's *London Labour and the London Poor* published.	Coup d'état Louis Napoleon. Australian Gold Rush began.
1852	Balmoral bought. Victoria and Albert Museum opened.	Russell resigned. Earl of Derby PM (February). Millais's *Ophelia* exhibited. Death of Wellington. First free public library opened. First pillar box erected. New Houses of Parliament opened. Lord Aberdeen PM (December).	Harriet Beecher Stowe's *Uncle Tom's Cabin* published. London Protocol established independence of Schleswig-Holstein.
1853	Prince Leopold born. Swiss Cottage built at Osborne House. Foundations laid for Balmoral.		
1854	Victoria bought Frith's *Ramsgate Sands*. Crimean medal created.	John Snow established cause of cholera. Elizabeth Gaskell's *North and South* serialised. Florence Nightingale went to Crimea.	Crimean War began. British defeated Russians at Battle of Alma. Battle of Balaclava. Charge of the Light Brigade. Siege of Sebastopol. Battle of Inkerman.

(continued)

(continued)

Date	Personal events	British events	World-wide events
1855	Princess Victoria engaged to Prince Frederick of Prussia.	Palmerston PM. Abolition of Stamp Duty. *Daily Telegraph* launched. *Little Dorrit* serialised.	Sebastopol captured. Livingstone saw Victoria Falls.
1856	Prince Alfred sent away to study. Victoria gave audience to Florence Nightingale.	Mass production of steel began. County and Borough Police Act.	Crimean War ended. Peace of Paris. Second Opium War. Serbia and Romania became independent.
1857	Princess Beatrice born. Victoria awarded first Victoria Cross. V&A Museum moved to Kensington. Albert made Prince Consort.	Matrimonial Causes (Divorce) Act. Thomas Hughes's *Tom Brown's Schooldays* published.	Indian Mutiny. Cawnpore massacre. Relief of Lucknow.
1858	Princess Victoria married Prince Frederick. Prince Alfred passes naval exams.	The Great Stink. Public Health Act. Derby PM. Jewish Disabilities Act. First transatlantic telegraph. Hallé orchestra founded.	Government of India Act. Orsini attempted to assassinate Louis Napoleon.
1859	Victoria's first grandchild born. He later became Kaiser Wilhelm.	Derby resigned. Palmerston appointed PM. Peaceful picketing allowed. J.S. Mill's *On Liberty*, George Eliot's *Adam Bede*, Dickens's *Tale of Two Cities*, Wilkie Collins's *Woman in White*, Darwin's *Origin of Species* published.	Napoleon III declared war on Austria. Second Italian war of independence. Treaty of Villafranca.

1860	Granddaughter Charlotte born.	Food and Drugs Act.
1861	Death of Victoria's mother, Duchess of Kent. Death of Albert.	First colour photograph. Mrs Beeton's *Household Management* published.	American Civil War began.
1862	Foundation stone for Royal Mausoleum laid. Princess Alice married Prince Louis of Hesse. Grandson Henry born.	Ladies Sanitary Association founded. Christina Rossetti's poem 'Goblin Market' published. Charles Kingsley's *The Water Babies* serialised.	
1863	Prince of Wales married Princess Alexandra of Denmark. Birth of granddaughter Victoria.	London Underground opened. Football Association formed.	Schleswig-Holstein question. Polish revolted against Russia. Māori war. First Ashanti war.
1864	Grandson Albert Edward, first son of Bertie, born. Birth of granddaughter Elizabeth.	First Contagious Diseases Act.	First Geneva Convention signed. Schleswig-Holstein invaded.
1865	Birth of grandson Prince George, later George V. John Brown appointed Queen's highland servant.	Elizabeth Garrett Anderson qualified as first English doctor. Russell PM. Lewis Carroll's *Alice in Wonderland* published. Death of Palmerston. Lister established antiseptic surgery.	Abraham Lincoln assassinated. Jamaica revolt.

(continued)

(continued)

Date	Personal events	British events	World-wide events
1866	Prince Alfred created Duke of Edinburgh. Princess Helena married Prince Christian of Schleswig-Holstein-Sonderburg-Augustenburg. Birth of granddaughters Victoria and Irene.	Derby PM. Sanitary Act.	Austro-Prussian War.
1867	Birth of granddaugher Louise and grandson Christian.	Dynamite patented in Britain. Second Reform Act. Bagehot's *English Constitution* published.	Canada became British Dominion. Abyssinian war.
1868	*Leaves from the Journal of Our Life in the Highlands* published. Attempt on life of Prince Alfred. Birth of granddaughter Victoria.	Disraeli PM (February). Last public hanging in England. Gladstone PM (December). National Union of Women's Suffrage Societies founded.	Māori war in New Zealand.
1869	Birth of granddaughter Maud, later Queen of Norway. Birth of grandson Albert.	Disestablishment of Irish Church Act. Girton College founded.	Dual Austro-Hungarian monarchy created. Suez Canal opened.
1870	Birth of granddaughters Sophie and Helena.	Education Act. Death of Charles Dickens. Irish Land Act. Married Women's Property Act. Cardwell's Army Reforms begin. Civil Service Reforms.	Franco-Prussian War. Napoleon defeated. Siege of Paris Commune. Napoleon III given asylum in Britain.

1871	Princess Louise married Marquis of Lorne. Prince of Wales contracted typhoid.	Edward Lear's 'The Owl and the Pussy-cat' published. First Rugby Union international. Royal Albert Hall opened. University Test Act. Trade Union Act. Abolition of the purchase of Commissions. Republican Clubs founded.	German union proclaimed. Paris Commune.
1872	Thanksgiving for Prince of Wales' recovery. Fifth assassination attempt on Victoria. Albert Memorial unveiled. Granddaughter Margaret born. Birth of granddaughters Marie and Alix, who would marry Nicolas, Tsar.	Secret ballot. First Football Association Cup Final. Licensing Act. Public Health Act.	
1873	Victoria gave audience to Shah of Persia.	Judicature Act.	Second Ashanti War.
1874	Prince Alfred married Grand Duchess Marie Alexandrovna of Russia. Birth of grandson Alfred and granddaughter Mary.	Thomas Hardy's *Far from the Madding Crowd* serialised. Disraeli PM. Licensing Act. Public Worship Regulation Act.	

(continued)

(continued)

Date	Personal events	British events	World-wide events
1875	Prince of Wales toured India. Birth of granddaughter Marie, who later married the King of Romania.	Climbing Boys Act. Artisans Dwelling Act. Peaceful picketing allowed. Public Health Act. Sale of Food and Drugs Act. First man swam English Channel.	Disraeli purchased shares in Suez Canal. Bosnia-Herzegovina rebelled against Ottoman Empire.
1876	Victoria awarded title of Empress of India. Birth of granddaughter Victoria.	Education Act. Merchant Shipping Act. Disraeli created Earl of Beaconsfield.	Alexander Graham Bell patented telephone. Bulgarian massacres.
1877		First Wimbledon tournament. Anna Sewell's *Black Beauty* published. Annie Besant and Charles Bradlaugh published pamphlet on birth control.	Russia declared war on Ottoman Empire. Transvaal annexed.
1878	Death of Princess Alice.	Gilbert and Sullivan's opera *HMS Pinafore* opened. Factory and Workshop Act.	Thomas Edison patented the phonograph. Congress of Berlin. Treaty of San Stefano. Afghan war.
1879	Prince Arthur married Princess Louise of Prussia.	Electric light bulb patented. Irish Land League formed.	Zulu War.
1880	Princess Alice died of diptheria.	Gladstone PM. Employers' Liability Act. First Eisteddfod Association.	Henry James's *Portrait of a Lady* published. First Boer War.
1881	Death of Disraeli.	Natural History Museum opened. Irish Land Act. Education Act made school compulsory up to ten.	Assassination of Tsar Alexander III. Anti-foreign riots in Egypt. Boers attacked British army.

1882	Sixth assassination attempt. Prince Leopold married Princess Helen of Waldeck-Pyrmont. Prince Arthur awarded medal for gallantry. Birth of granddaughter Margaret, who later married the Crown Prince of Sweden.	The Ashes Cricket began. Married Women's Property Act. Phoenix Park murders. Coercion Act.	Tchaikovsky's 1812 *Overture* performed. Egyptian rebellion defeated.
1883	John Brown died. Birth of grandson Arthur and granddaughter Alice.	Robert Louis Stevenson's *Treasure Island* published. Corrupt and Illegal Practices Act.	
1884	Death of Leopold. Birth of grandson Charles. More *Leaves from a Journal* published.	First part of *Oxford English Dictionary* published. Third Reform Act.	General Gordon and army sent to Khartoum. Siege of Khartoum. Convention of London returned independence to Boers.
1885	Princess Beatrice married Prince Henry of Battenburg.	Modern bicycle invented. Salisbury PM. Redistribution Act. Gladstone converted to Home Rule.	Death of General Gordon.
1886	Birth of granddaughter Victoria and grandson Alexander.	First motor car patented. Liberal Party split. Liberal Unionists founded. Gladstone PM (February). First Irish Home Rule Bill. Salisbury PM (July).	Berlin conference. Gold discovered in Transvaal.

(continued)

(continued)

Date	Personal events	British events	World-wide events
1887	Golden Jubilee. Arrival of Abdul Karim. Birth of granddaughter Victoria, later Queen of Spain.	Redistribution Act. Independent Labour Party founded. Criminal Law Act.	
1888		Contagious Diseases Acts repealed. Match-girls' strike. County Councils Act.	Prince Frederick crowned German Emperor. Death of Frederick, Wilhelm II crowned. First Kodak camera patented.
1889	Victoria became patron of newly created National Society for the Prevention of Cruelty to Children. Birth of grandson Leopold.	Prevention of Cruelty to Children Act. London Dock Strike.	
1890		Oscar Wilde's *The Picture Of Dorian Gray* published.	Bismarck resigned as German Chancellor.
1891	Death of Prince Albert Victor, Bertie's eldest son. Birth of grandson Maurice.	Fee Grant Act made education free. Death of Charles Parnell.	Revolt in Manipur, India.
1892	Death of son-in-law Prince Louis.	Gladstone PM.	
1893	Prince George, son of Prince of Wales, married Mary of Teck. Prince Alfred appointed Duke of Saxe-Coburg and Gotha.	Elementary Education Act for blind and deaf children. Defeat of second Irish Home Rule Bill.	Third Ashanti war.

1894	Birth of Prince Edward, eldest son of Prince George, the heir to the throne. Alexandra, Victoria's granddaughter, married Prince Nicolas of Russia.	Rosebery PM. Rudyard Kipling's *Jungle Book* published. Local Government Act. Death duties introduced.	Olympic Games re-established. Nicolas appointed Tsar.
1895	Prince Albert George, second son of Prince of Wales, born.	H.G. Wells's *Time Machine* published. Salisbury PM. First car journey in Britain.	Renewed tensions in the Balkans. Ashanti war. Jameson raid; rebellion in Transvaal.
1896			Nicolas and Alexandra crowned tsar and tsarina. First modern Olympic Games held in Athens. Anglo- Zanzibar War.
1897	Diamond Jubilee.	First wireless message sent. Bram Stoker's *Dracula* published. National Union of Women's Suffrage Societies founded. Workmen's Compensation Act.	Fashoda incident. War between Ottoman Empire and Greece.
1898		Death of Gladstone.	Battle of Omdurman. George Curzon appointed Viceroy of India.
1899			Second Anglo-Boer War. Kimberley, Ladysmith and Mafeking relieved. Boxer Rebellion.
1900	Death of Prince Alfred. Victoria visited Ireland.		
1901	Death of Queen Victoria.		

Introduction

On 28 March 1819, a seven-months-pregnant German princess left her home in Amorbach, Bavaria, for a 427-mile horse-drawn coach journey to England. She travelled with her husband, her daughter from a previous marriage, a lady-in-waiting, a midwife, a doctor, a governess, cooks, servants, two lapdogs and a cage of birds. The group trekked across the bumpy pot-holed roads of Europe in an assorted caravan of post-chaises, barouches and baggage carts and arrived in Calais on 18 April. Here they waited until the weather was fair enough for them to cross the Channel. A month later, safely installed in Kensington Palace, the Princess gave birth to a baby daughter, a 'pretty little Princess, as plump as a partridge'. The baby was delivered by a female obstetrician, was breastfed by her mother and vaccinated against smallpox. Eighteen years later, in 1837, this daughter was crowned Victoria, Queen of Great Britain.

Britain in 1819

Victoria was born into a Britain where most people still lived and worked in the country. But it was a countryside in flux. The Enclosure Acts of the eighteenth century had broken up most of the old open fields and shared commons, land which was then hedged, ditched and fenced. Most small farmers could not afford the costs of these transformations so were forced to sell, sometimes becoming landless labourers, sometimes moving to the new towns. Life may have been harsh for the newly dispossessed smallholders but the enclosures allowed wealthier farmers to buy more land, and to introduce new methods of farming, new machinery and new ways of breeding pedigree herds. As a result, food production increased substantially, which led in turn to a dramatic growth in population. Families in 1819 were large: giving birth to nine children, as Queen Victoria would later do, was not unusual.

In other respects, too, Britain was undergoing momentous change as technological developments transformed the way in which people lived and worked. Cotton replaced wool as the material of choice. It was cheaper to produce, easier to keep clean and comfortable to wear. More and more workshops, factories, mills and mines used water and steam power rather than human muscle to make cotton cloth. This resulted in factories increasing in size as the installation of large, heavy and expensive machinery made it necessary to employ more than just a few people. Soon these new towns and cities became densely populated and exceedingly dirty as the coal-fired steam factories polluted the air people breathed and turned buildings black. These new factory workers needed to live somewhere, so houses were quickly – and often shoddily – built to accommodate them. Back-to-back houses were the norm in industrial cities. Most people did not have an inside lavatory let alone a bathroom: they used earth closets outside. Many families shared one earth closet – in one factory town about 7,000 people shared 33 such closets – which frequently overflowed into the street. Not surprisingly, health problems such as cholera, typhoid and other related diseases were the results, all caused by poor sanitation. These types of illnesses affected all classes: Queen Victoria and her eldest son, Bertie, the Prince of Wales, became seriously ill from typhoid; many believe Prince Albert died from it.

In 1819 the Factory Act forbade children to work under the age of nine but the Act was unenforceable and owners generally ignored it. Conditions in the factories were often harsh. Every textile factory was damp, dusty and noisy: many workers stood in their bare feet in puddles of water; fluff and cotton dust was everywhere; and the noise of the weaving and spinning machines was deafening. In addition, factory workers were regimented and subjected to petty rules; many employers fined their workers to make sure they behaved themselves and worked hard. Finable offences at Strutts Mill in Belper included 'idleness and looking thro' window; noisy behaviour; being off with a pretence of being ill; and riding on each other's back'. Children worked as 'scavengers' picking up the bits of thread and cotton underneath the machines or as 'piecers', joining together the ends of broken thread. The textile industry depended on slave-grown cotton to provide the raw materials to make its cloth. In 1807 the British government abolished the slave trade but slavery remained widespread at the time of Victoria's birth.

Textile factories relied on coal to power the new machines. In 1819, coal mines employed men, women and children: the male collier hewed the coal; women, harnessed like animals, carried it to the pit-brow; and children worked as trappers, opening and shutting the underground doors for ventilation. Hours were long and the work was arduous and dangerous. Explosions, roof falls and accidents were common. When she was 13 years old, Princess Victoria wrote of having just 'passed through a town where all coal mines are . . . The men, women and children . . . are all black. But I can not . . . give an idea of its strange and extraordinary appearance. The country is very desolate every where.'[1]

Britain had changed spectacularly in the period just before Victoria's birth but it was to experience more unprecedented technological, political, economic and social change throughout the nineteenth century. Such dramatic changes posed challenges to government as it sought to ameliorate or contain the social dislocation which ensued. When she became queen, Victoria would need high levels of political skill to handle the changing needs and demands of her subjects brought on by this progressively accelerating industrialisation.

Government and politics

When Victoria was born, a small elite ruled Britain. At the top of the hierarchy was the Crown, represented by 'mad' George III, but because of the King's incapacity his disreputable and profligate son, George, became the Prince Regent, governing in place of his father. The Prince Regent created a world of such unbridled extravagance and luxury for himself that he was nicknamed Falstaff after the notoriously dissipated – yet

attractive – character in Shakespeare's *Henry IV* plays. In 1820
King George III died and his son replaced him as King George IV.
British sovereigns were not absolute rulers; they were constitutional monarchs empowered to rule according to an unwritten
constitution, not by divine right.

The United Kingdom, unlike the United States and many other
countries, has no single written constitution. Instead, the British
constitution is a matter of custom, expectation and usage. It is
uncodified, incremental and embodied in Parliamentary laws,
court judgements and treaties, all of which have been pieced
together over time. The real beginning of constitutional monarchy
dates back to the Magna Carta 1215 when King John, under
pressure from his barons, agreed that sovereigns must rule by
law, not by personal inclination. In 1689 these principles were
reinforced and developed when the British parliament invited
William of Orange and Mary to become joint sovereigns after
King James II fled the country. William and Mary's claim to the
throne was therefore not directly hereditary since it depended on
an Act of Parliament for its legitimacy. This Act established the
principle that monarchs owed their position to parliament as
much as to inherited right. In addition, the 'Glorious Revolution'
confirmed parliament as the chief law-making body; from then
on the supreme power in Britain was parliament not the sovereign.
The coronation oath, where the king or queen promises to govern
according to the law, reinforces this principle. As queen, Victoria
would object to any further strengthening of the parliamentary
system, particularly if it affected her constitutional rights.

In 1819 parliament was composed of an unelected House of
Lords and an elected House of Commons. The main political
parties, the Whigs (Liberals) and the Tories (Conservatives), consisted largely of male Anglican aristocrats: Catholics, Quakers
and Jews could not become MPs.[2] Whigs had helped engineer
the 1689 Revolution and were strong supporters of the Hanove-
rians when that dynasty succeeded to the British throne. Princess
Victoria's parents were both Whigs: she was surrounded by Whigs
in her youth and throughout her life maintained that she held to
Whig principles. Whigs believed that monarchs must govern with
the consent of the nation and that ultimately sovereignty rested
with the people, principles that Queen Victoria would often find

hard to respect. Naturally, the Whigs sought to extend the franchise in order to strengthen parliament, and their own influence, even more. They were also committed to the defence of liberties and religious toleration. In contrast, the ideological hallmarks of the Tories were the principles of divine monarchical right, hereditary succession and commitment to the Anglican Church. Not surprisingly, a large number of Tories opposed the 1689 Revolution, were against any extension of democracy and tended to squash radicalism wherever and whenever they could.[3]

At the time, the state was small with the government mainly focusing on defence, the control of trade through customs and excise, and the maintenance of law and order. Britain was a country under pressure. The triple challenges of a population explosion, industrialisation and urbanisation had created multi-layered tensions, particularly in vulnerable areas. In 1815, after Napoleon was defeated at the Battle of Waterloo, the demobilisation of hundreds of thousands of soldiers – who had no pension or government support – led to increased unemployment and deepening distress for the very poor. And when the government passed the Corn Law Act 1815, which banned the import of foreign corn until the price of British corn had reached £4 a quarter, the poorer section of society which relied on bread as their staple diet suffered. Victoria's birth coincided with a time of significant poverty and suffering for the working class; in contrast, there appeared to be a marked escalation of privilege and prosperity for the upper classes.

In August 1819, just a few months after the birth of Princess Victoria, a meeting was held in St Peter's Fields, Manchester to call for parliamentary reform. At the time only a small minority of men – and no women – were allowed to vote. The meeting was broken up by a voluntary cavalry force, the Manchester Yeomanry, and at least 11 people were killed and 400 injured in the mêlée. It was soon called the Peterloo Massacre. The English Romantic poet, Percy Bysshe Shelley, wrote *England in 1819* in response to this event. The poem is politically radical: it encapsulates the anger of people against their royal family and what was considered to be a perfidious government. It talks of an 'old, mad blind, despised and dying king, . . . Rulers who neither see, nor feel, nor know, but leech-like to their fainting country cling. . . . A people starved and stabbed.' In the same year Shelley also wrote 'The Mask of Anarchy', a poem which has been described as the greatest political poem ever written in English and one often quoted by Gandhi in his campaigns against the British in India. 'The Mask of Anarchy' is an anthem to freedom, liberty and equality, and ends with an exhortation to the people to 'Rise Like Lions after slumber' against injustice, as 'ye are many – they are few'. Many people agreed with Shelley and did indeed 'rise like lions'. As queen, Victoria would face periods of social and political unrest and be forced to accept the reforms brought in by her government in response to this turbulence.

Censorship, both overt and covert, was common. Sometimes political writers such as Shelley found it difficult to find a publisher;[4] sometimes publishers were prosecuted for printing revolutionary texts. In October 1819 Richard Carlile was convicted of blasphemy and seditious libel, and sent to prison for publishing Tom Paine's *The Age of Reason*, a book that challenged institutionalised religion and the legitimacy of the Bible. The book was a best-seller in the United States. Of course, not all art was political: in the same year John Keats wrote 'La Belle Dame sans Merci', a love ballad drawn from medieval tales, and Walter Scott's historical novel *The Bride of Lammermoor*, probably now better known as Donizetti's dramatic opera *Lucia di Lammermoor*, was published. Walter Scott was to become one of Queen Victoria's favourite novelists, and the opera a much treasured piece of music. The art and music world was thriving too. On 23 April 1819, to co-incide with his birthday and the birthday of the Prince Regent, the best-loved British artist, J. M. W. Turner, exhibited his painting *Richmond Hill*. In the same year, Rossini had four of his operas performed in London. Britain seemed to be the cultural capital of the world. Certainly, at the time of Victoria's birth, Britain was the world's greatest power. It had the largest navy, the biggest share of the world's trade, the most developed industry and London as the world's financial capital. In 1837 Victoria would be queen of it all.

Historiography

Queen Victoria is one of the most studied women in history – over 500 books have been published on her life – so that biographies sometimes read like a historical tiered cake, each author stacking ever more obscure facts onto previous layers and often repeating the same old facts expressed slightly differently. New books about Queen Victoria appear regularly, often written by biographers rather than historians, often emphasising the monarch's personal lifestyle at the expense of her political influence and often aimed primarily to entertain general readers. There are psychological biographies, literary biographies, chatty biographies, biographies that deal solely with Victoria's family, her prime ministers, or her courtiers.[5] There are books about young Victoria, married Victoria, widowed Victoria and even imperial Victoria. There are, commented the historian Fassiotto, 'so many Victorias. Old Victorias, dignified Victorias, charming Victorias, angry Victorias, Victorias in white satin and Victorias in black silk'.[6]

Lytton Strachey, often regarded as the father of modern biography, wrote the first scholarly biography, *Queen Victoria*.[7] For a man with a fondness for taking a rude and irreverent approach to his subjects, Strachey's book is strangely adulatory; it also focuses on the Queen's early life and pays scant attention to her later reign. Other biographers have written exhaustive cradle-to-grave narratives. Elizabeth Longford's long, authoritative, sympathetic, yet unsentimental biography *Victoria*[8] remains the best. However, her avoidance of sexually contentious issues and her minimal treatment of the Queen's constitutional role are drawbacks to an otherwise splendid book. Nonetheless, it remains, as Giles St Aubyn notes, 'the envy and despair of those who venture to follow her'.[9] Cecil Woodham-Smith's superb, sympathetic *Queen Victoria: Her Life and Times, Volume One 1819–1861*[10] sets the life of Victoria within the history of the period exceptionally well but stops at the death of Albert. Stanley Weintraub's best-selling scholarly, descriptive and readable *Victoria: Biography of a Queen*[11] is less reverential, providing a life-like portrait which is both critical and sympathetic. Yet even so, the historical background to her reign remains slight and the book is of a length which is off-putting to many. Later interpretations such as Christopher Hibbert's *Queen Victoria*[12] paint a different portrait of the monarch as a shy, diffident and vulnerable yet sensual person rather than the rather capricious, censorious and morally repressive one of popular imagination. A. N. Wilson's *Victoria*[13] creates a fresher, yet sympathetic, Victoria for the twenty-first century.

Wilson draws on new evidence from German archives to enrich his portrait of the Queen as an unconventional, volatile yet kindly and unsnobbish woman. His witty biography is an enjoyable and captivating read, full of gossipy anecdotes about royal life, but as with other accounts the focus remains on the personal, rather than the political story.

Other writers have written shorter and differently focused biographies. Frank Hardie's *The Political Influence of Queen Victoria, 1861–1901*[14] was the first to challenge the myth that Queen Victoria took little interest in politics. On the contrary, he argues, the Queen had a pervasive influence particularly over foreign policy, the Church and legislation. Hardie provides a frank exposition of Victoria's behind-the-scenes royal influence, revealing how the Queen promoted legislation, campaigned and intrigued against policies of which she disapproved and tried to influence the composition of governments. Throughout her life, he argued, she preferred to take an active role in government rather than take part in ceremonial occasions. Queen Victoria wanted to rule not just reign.

Some have sought to interpret Victoria theoretically. Dorothy Thompson's *Queen Victoria*[15] analyses the role of the monarch through the prism of gender, arguing that the presence of a woman in the highest political spheres affected the lives of all her subjects. Thompson's feminist leanings, however, make her a little too sympathetic towards the monarch and she has a tendency to overlook the Queen's obvious failings. The gender theme is developed by Adrienne Munich's *Queen Victoria's Secrets*,[16] which is a challenging and thought-provoking exploration of the influence of Victoria on cultural history. It is, however, more a compendium of how Victorians saw Victoria rather than a biography. Others have employed the analytical tools of cultural studies. John Plunkett's scholarly *Queen Victoria: First Media Monarch*,[17] examines the role of the media in Queen Victoria's reign and analyses how the development of popular media helped re-invent the monarchy and make it more popular.

There has been a recent shift in biographical writing, that which examines particular aspects of Victoria's private life: Lynne Vallone's *Becoming Victoria*[18] and Kate Williams's *Becoming Queen*,[19] for example, both focus on the Queen's emotional and psychological early life. Others have inspected Victoria's relationships with significant others. Richard Hough's *Victoria and Albert*[20] and Helen Rappaport's *Magnificent Obsession: Victoria, Albert and the Death That Changed the Monarchy*[21] chronicle the marriage of Queen Victoria and Prince Albert. John Van Der Kiste's *Sons, Servants and Statesmen*[22] looks at how the men in Victoria's life influenced and affected her; Shrabani Basu's *Victoria and Abdul*[23] narrows this further by examining how a young Indian immigrant came to play a central role in the Queen's life. Some historians have focused on certain themes. Barrie Charles's *Kill the Queen*[24] and Paul Thomas Murphy's *Shooting Victoria*[25] both examine the eight assassination attempts on Victoria by respectively a public house waiter, an unemployed carpenter, a news vendor, a navvy, an army officer, a clerk, an artist and some Irish nationalists. Tony Rennel's *The Death of Queen Victoria*[26] traces her dying days through to her funeral. However, the narrow focus of such books ignores or minimises Victoria's greater and broader life. In addition the cult of royal personality which is sometimes promoted within these books tends to eulogise the Queen and/or abstract her from her historical context.

Despite the plethora of books about Queen Victoria, she has received little attention by academic historians. Walter L. Arnstein's *Queen Victoria*[27] book is a succinct and engaging introduction to the *period* in that it provides a social, cultural, religious and political context for the Queen. The main drawback to this book is that Victoria remains a backdrop to a history of the period rather than a central figure – there is too much of a historical framework and not enough about what Victoria thought, felt and did. Certainly, Arnstein raises some interesting questions about the Queen but these are located in the last few pages rather than incorporated in his general narrative. More importantly, Queen Victoria's journals were not available online when Arnstein researched his book and their absence weakens it.

Perhaps the best way of discovering the politics of Queen Victoria is through the biographies and writings of her ministers. For example, the essential first point of reference for readers who want to trace Victoria's attitude towards the Crimean War is David Brown's *Palmerston: A Biography*,[28] which as well as a statesman-like life of the prime minister is an impressive study of mid-Victorian politics. It is a meticulously researched erudite chronicle which brings to life Palmerston's disagreements with the Queen over foreign policy. Historians can also rely on Queen Victoria's private secretaries and other key staff members who published their memoirs for an insight into Victoria's attitudes and convictions. Charles Greville, for example, was clerk to the Privy Council, which brought him into contact with all the leading politicians as well as Queen Victoria. His *Greville Memoirs, 1814–1861*[29] provide an acerbically refreshing insight into the personal opinions of Queen Victoria. Similarly, the publication of a selection of Henry Ponsonby's letters to the Queen and various officials offer a taste of what it was like to act as private secretary to Queen Victoria.[30] Prince Albert is well known for his authority over the Queen and biographies such as Robert Rhodes James's *Albert, Prince Consort*[31] and Edgar Feuchtwanger's *Albert and Victoria, The Rise and Fall of the House of Saxe-Coburg-Gotha*[32] help us understand quite how much Albert influenced the Queen and British politics.

Victoria left an archival treasure trove of material for biographers and historians. By the time of her death she had written millions of words, often confiding her opinions and emotions as well as writing about the important events and people of the time. At the age of 13 she began keeping a diary – or journal as it is sometimes called – which she kept until a few days before she died. The journal filled 122 volumes. But the Queen, knowing that her diaries would be made public, appointed her youngest daughter Beatrice as literary executor. It is well known that Beatrice censored the journal, copied out the parts she felt appropriate and burnt the rest – a remarkable case of historical vandalism. Victoria also wrote a great many letters and telegrams to her officials, her family and her friends. A collection of Victoria's letters, published between 1907 and 1930, consists of nine volumes of over 600 pages each. These letters were heavily edited as several hundred volumes would need to be printed if the entire range of the Queen's letters were published. As with the journals, much was destroyed. Victoria's eldest son, Bertie, destroyed letters from the Queen to Lord Granville, all the correspondence in the Flora Hastings affair, all the letters to Disraeli if they concerned the family and all the correspondence between the Munshi and his mother.

Themes and discussions

In this book, Queen Victoria's thoughts, feelings and actions, as revealed in her journals and letters, will be used to shed light on the contemporary economic, social, religious, cultural and political history and to explore how Queen Victoria's views did – or did not – reflect the period in which she lived. *Queen Victoria* will be a historical and political biography rather than a personal and literary one and as such will place Victoria in her own contemporary context more firmly than those biographies which have tended to isolate the Queen from her environment. This allows topics such as Victoria's role in politics to be addressed, a subject often neglected or underplayed in many biographies. It will take a chronological approach, although themes are highlighted and examined analytically within that chronology.

Queen Victoria was not like the other three queens regnant – Mary Tudor (1553–8), Elizabeth I (1558–1603) and Anne (1702–14) – even reigning longer than all the previous queens put together. Each queen faced her own political difficulties: Queen Victoria's was her changing constitutional role. During Victoria's reign, the distribution of political power gradually yet significantly shifted away from the monarch and the aristocracy to parliament and the people. This, and the vast and transforming social, economic and political changes that were already underway, would pose challenges to any monarch, even one with vast experience. Numerous biographies of Queen Victoria have helped cultivate a raft of taken-for-granted myths about her. This book will use both contemporary sources and published work to challenge the veracity of such myths. For example, it is often held that Victoria withdrew from political life when Albert died, a belief that is not borne out by the evidence.

The first chapter will examine assess the extent to which Victoria was prepared for her future role as queen. Certainly, the traces of an older Victoria are apparent in her younger years. For example, when her mother and John Conroy tried to force the young Princess to sign away her rights, Victoria showed an obstinacy and resolve that became familiar throughout her reign. Her Germanic upbringing, and her love of her German relatives, would generally shape Victoria's outlook: in future years political matters would usually turn out to be personal ones, especially in situations concerning Germany.

Victoria ascended the throne with little preparation and relied upon her first prime minister, Lord Melbourne, to guide her through the intricacies of government. Chapter 2 will examine the constitutional constraints and freedoms of the young Queen and the ways in which she tried to resist the checks placed upon her. In these years, Victoria's character and style of reigning become evident: she tended to respond instantaneously rather than carefully thinking through the possible outcomes of her decisions. Throughout her life she remained passionate rather than reserved, never able to camouflage her feelings: warm and demonstrative to those she loved; cool and distant to those she did not. In particular, possibly because Victoria was an only – and lonely – child, she placed a great significance on her wider family connections. These family relationships often swayed her views of European politics making it difficult for the Queen to remain politically dispassionate, an increasingly essential component of being a sovereign in a new democratic age. At the beginning of her reign, the young Victoria enjoyed huge popularity, a popularity which rapidly evaporated in the light of her all-too-obvious political inexperience and partisanship.

Queen Victoria was also a young woman, a daughter, a wife and a mother in an age in which each of those roles conflicted with the idea of taking charge of one of the world's leading countries. Recent histories have shown that Victoria was a sensual, stubborn, emotional and hot-tempered young woman who found it hard to compromise. Chapter 3 will discuss Victoria's sexuality within nineteenth-century norms, chart her stormy relationship with Albert and suggest that far from being a subservient wife to her husband, Victoria was (initially at least) obstreperously single-minded. Victoria and Albert's first child, Victoria Adelaide, was born on 21 November 1840. Eight other children followed. The book will examine how Victoria responded to pregnancy and childbirth in the light of general female reactions and practices of the time.

By early 1841, Melbourne's government was under threat, he was defeated on a vote of no confidence and Robert Peel became prime minister, followed by Russell, Derby and Aberdeen. Chapter 4 will discuss the turbulent years of the 1840s. For example, Chartism and the Irish potato famine and its consequences dominated the political debate. In April 1848, Queen Victoria and her family, fearful of Chartist and Irish nationalist uprisings, left London for the safety of Osborne House, Isle of Wight. Revolutions spread across mainland Europe. Victoria disapproved of the insurrections whatever their cause: in France against the corrupt government of Louise Philippe, in Italy for unification, in Austria against Metternich, in Hungary against the Austrian Empire, and in Germany for liberal nationalism.

As the Queen grew in political and diplomatic confidence, Lord Palmerston, foreign secretary, began to exasperate Victoria: she thought him too impetuous, too rude and too undiplomatic. More importantly, the two disagreed over politics. Queen Victoria loathed revolutions and revolutionaries; in contrast, Palmerston despised autocratic sovereigns and sympathised with those who wanted an increase in democracy. Victoria regularly tried to dismiss him but at first failed to do so because Palmerston's popularity was too great – the fact that she tried to do so was detrimental to the health of the constitution.

Meanwhile, as Chapter 5 will show, Queen Victoria's family grew in size. Her ninth and last child, Beatrice, was born in 1857: Victoria was 38 years old. The Queen, some historians claim, hated being pregnant, suffered from post-natal depression, viewed breastfeeding with disgust, thought new-born babies ugly, was a poor mother and left household affairs to Albert. These popular assumptions will be questioned: using Queen Victoria's journals, it will be suggested that she was a better mother than has often been supposed. In 1858 her eldest daughter, Vicky, was married at the age of 17 to Prince Frederick William, heir to the throne of Prussia. It was a dynastic marriage encouraged by both parents who hoped to influence German politics through the medium of their daughter: Victoria often longed for governments to trust her extended family networks and to frame its foreign policy accordingly.

By 1851 the Queen had come to loathe Palmerston's style of politics and thought his foreign policy much too cavalier for comfort. She and Albert nicknamed him 'Pilgerstein'. Victoria tried again and again to dismiss her foreign secretary, and she was eventually victorious in December 1851 when Palmerston was removed from office. Palmerston's subsequent absence from overseeing foreign policy co-incided with what was to be one of the century's biggest international flash-points: Russian expansion in the Ottoman-controlled Crimea. Chapter 6 will argue that Queen Victoria's engineering of Palmerston's dismissal helped the escalation of the crisis. Palmerston had wanted to check Russian aggression towards the Ottoman Empire; in contrast, the Queen was initially pro-Russian.

Queen Victoria is generally remembered as a ruler who, once widowed, withdrew from public life. Albert's death, as is well known, devastated Victoria: her court never went out of mourning. This phase of political seclusion – the Queen only opened parliament seven times in this period – meant that the rise of a popular republican movement grew apace. It is said that a Scottish servant, John Brown, rescued her from her doleful self. Rumours of their relationship were rife and historians differ as to whether an affair actually took place.

Apart from a brief spell when Prince Albert died, Queen Victoria took a great interest in politics: she interfered in ministerial decisions, made her views known about reforming legislation and kept demanding that Britain maintain its role as a strong imperial power. Indeed from 1861, as Chapter 7 will demonstrate, it is possible to chart more accurately the political influence of the Queen upon government policy and her changing relationships with her ministers, particularly those of Palmerston, Russell and the two diametrically opposed characters, Gladstone and Disraeli. *Queen Victoria* will chart how and why the Queen's view of Disraeli shifted from one of animosity to one of friendship: in 1844 Queen Victoria referred to 'obnoxious Mr Disraeli',[33] accusing him of being 'very troublesome' and with a 'bad character',[34] yet she later thought him a good friend.

In December 1868, William Gladstone became Queen Victoria's eighth prime minister. It is well known that the Queen disliked her precise and exacting prime minister, complaining that he spoke to her as if he were addressing a public meeting. However, Chapter 8 will argue that Gladstone was perhaps the first prime minister to treat his sovereign as a competent and intelligent head of state. He never charmed or flattered, much preferring to speak to the Queen as an intellectual equal. In striking contrast, Disraeli sweet-talked his sovereign, famously maintaining that 'everyone likes flattery; and when you come to Royalty you should lay it on with a trowel'. Gladstone would have considered such a comment much too disrespectful. However, Disraeli found favour with the Queen precisely because he treated her as a gentleman might treat a lady in the nineteenth century: too intellectually inconsequential and frivolous to be taken seriously. Marie Louise, one of Queen Victoria's granddaughters, spoke about the differences between Gladstone and Disraeli: 'After sitting next to Mr Gladstone I thought he was the cleverest man in England. But after sitting next to Mr Disraeli I felt I was the cleverest woman in England.'

Queen Victoria disliked Gladstone and disapproved of most of his parliamentary programmes, particularly his emerging views on the Irish question and his attitude towards the Ottoman Empire. During the 1870s Victoria's popularity dipped to its lowest point while Republicanism reached its peak. Gradually Queen Victoria's reputation improved under Gladstone's guiding hand but it took Disraeli's interventions to salvage it completely. In 1877 Disraeli – reluctantly and under duress – proclaimed Victoria Empress of India, a popular move which helped reverse the negative feelings which had been growing about monarchy. Disraeli's indulgence towards the Queen increased her political confidence and she became more and more prepared to insist that her demands be met.

In 1887 Queen Victoria celebrated her Golden Jubilee, often considered one of the high points of monarchical popularity. Here, Queen Victoria was forced to conquer her reclusive tendencies because of the public desire for royal pageantry and ostentatiously grand ceremonies. Since the death of Albert, Victoria had craved a quiet isolated life, well away from the public gaze even if this meant growing unpopularity. This did not mean that she had no wish to govern. Far from it. As she grew older and more assertive, the Queen interfered more and more, often trying to undermine constitutional changes, particularly whenever Gladstone was prime minister. The years between 1880 and 1892, as Chapter 9 will demonstrate, were marked by the continuing crisis of Ireland, franchise reform, problems in the Middle East and the collapse of the Liberal Party. Queen Victoria had opinions on all these and was prepared to voice them to her governments. More significantly, when her views were not listened to by the Liberal government, she expressed them to the Conservative opposition, whether or not it was constitutionally proper to do so.

In July 1892 Victoria reluctantly appointed Gladstone as prime minister. Chapter 10 introduces his fourth, and last, premiership. Predictably, the two protagonists clashed once more, particularly over Irish Home Rule. Gladstone wanted to repeal the Act of Union with Ireland and establish a parliament in Dublin responsible for domestic affairs, whereas Victoria abhorred the idea. The Queen even wrote to the leader of the opposition asking him to contest it. In her letter the Queen included copies of correspondence between Gladstone and herself, arguably a serious breach of the constitution.

In March 1894, Rosebery replaced Gladstone as Liberal prime minister. Queen Victoria initially welcomed his appointment, particularly when he jettisoned Home Rule, but soon the two disagreed. Rosebery was after all a Liberal, and he held many Liberal beliefs which the Queen disliked. Tensions grew when Rosebery pressed for reform of the House of Lords, a policy which the Queen tried to undermine by consulting with the Conservative leadership and thus – yet again – testing monarchical constitutional boundaries.

In June 1895 Queen Victoria appointed her last prime minister, Lord Salisbury. By now she had reigned longer than any other British sovereign. Her Diamond Jubilee confirmed her status as a 'national treasure'; Republicanism had been emphatically vanquished. The ageing queen continued to be attentive to foreign affairs, and when her life ended she was worrying about the Boer War. She was 81 years old.

Notes

1 RA VIC/MAIN/QVJ (W) August 2nd 1832.
2 Catholics were allowed to sit as MPs in 1829; Quakers in 1832 and Jews in 1858.
3 See Frank O'Gorman and Peter Fraser, 'Party Politics in the Early Nineteenth Century, 1812–32', *English Historical Review*, January 1987.

4 'The Mask of Anarchy' was not published until 1832 because of censorship.
5 See Michael Eugene Fassiotto, *Finding Victorias/Reading Biographies*, PhD, University of Hawaii, 1992.
6 Ibid.
7 Chatto and Windus, 1921.
8 Abacus, 1965.
9 Giles St Aubyn, *Queen Victoria*, Sinclair-Stevenson, 1991, p. 623.
10 Hamish Hamilton, 1972.
11 Unwin, 1986.
12 Harper Collins, 2000.
13 Atlantic, 2014.
14 Frank Cass, 1935.
15 Virago, 1990.
16 Columbia University Press, 1996.
17 OUP, 2003.
18 Yale University Press, 2001.
19 Arrow, 2009.
20 Macmillan, 1996.
21 Windmill Books, 2012.
22 Sutton, 2006.
23 The History Press, 2011.
24 Amberley, 2012.
25 Pegasus Books, 2012.
26 Viking, 2001.
27 Palgrave Macmillan, 2003.
28 Yale University Press, 2010.
29 Macmillan, 1936.
30 Arthur Ponsonby, *Henry Ponsonby, Queen Victoria's Private Secretary, His Life from his Letters*, Macmillan and Co, 1943; Sir John Ponsonby, *The Ponsonby Family*, The Medici Society, 2009.
31 Hamish Hamilton, 1983.
32 Continuum, 2006.
33 RA VIC/MAIN/QVJ (W) June 17th 1844.
34 Ibid. June 18th 1844.

1 Becoming Victoria: 1819–1837

Victoria was not born to be queen; at birth she was only fifth in line of succession to the throne. Her father, Edward, and his elder brothers – George, Frederick and William – all took precedence over her. However, a series of childless marriages and premature deaths brought the young Victoria closer and closer to the crown. The reigning monarch in 1819, King George III, had 15 children – nine sons and six daughters – enough offspring one might suppose to provide several potential heirs to be sovereign. But extraordinary as it may seem, only his eldest son, Prince George, had ever produced a legitimate child: Princess Charlotte. In 1817, Charlotte died unexpectedly in childbirth and her death precipitated a succession crisis. Who was to inherit the British throne? King George had 12 surviving children but no officially authorised grandchildren. Quite a few of his sons were fertile: between them they had fathered 56 children, but there was one major problem – not one was legitimate.

Her 'wicked uncles', as Queen Victoria was later to term them, were mostly notorious adulterers, spendthrifts, heavy drinkers, gluttons and selfish individuals with a fondness for excessive pleasure. Not one of them benefitted from a stable marital relationship. At the time of Charlotte's death in 1817, the King's two eldest sons – Prince George and Prince Frederick – were both separated from their wives and had no living legitimate children. The third in line to the throne, Prince William, had ten children but was still unmarried; the fourth in line, Prince Edward, was single too. The remaining princes – Ernest, Augustus and Adolphus – were either unmarried or had not yet fathered a child. Suddenly, the royal succession looked insecure. Consequently, all the unmarried dukes, realising that they might well father the heir to the throne, all rushed to get married.

Prince William cast off his long-term mistress and mother of his illegitimate children to marry a bride 25 years his junior in the hope that he could father a legally eligible child. The youngest son, Prince Adolphus, copied his older brother and got wed. The 50-year-old Prince Edward, Duke of Kent, also recognised the possibility of begetting an heir to the British throne and quickly set about getting married. His wife, Princess Victoire, was an impecunious 31-year-old widow with a 14-year-old son and an 11-year-old daughter, but she was well connected, being the daughter of Francis, Duke of Saxe Coburg-Saalfeld, and sister of Prince Leopold who had married Princess Charlotte, the late heir to the British throne. More importantly, Victoire was fertile.

Shortly after their marriage, Prince Edward and Princess Victoire – the Duke and Duchess of Kent – left England for Germany where they settled in a rambling old house in Amorbach with his wife's children, Charles and Feodora. Soon Victoire became pregnant. The Duke, concerned that the British might challenge the legitimacy of his future offspring, returned to England with his very pregnant wife, his step-children and his servants to take up residence in Kensington Palace.

Prince George, who had been Prince Regent since 1811, disliked the idea of his younger brother's daughter becoming the next British monarch and made life uncomfortable for the new baby and her parents. When the date for the still unnamed baby's christening was set for 24 June 1819, George acted petulantly. He refused to permit a large christening ceremony and insisted that the child be christened in a small private service at Kensington Palace. No foreign dignitaries were invited and only eight guests allowed. Court regalia and evening dress was banned: the Prince Regent insisted on a low-key ceremony more suited for a minor royal than a likely heir to the throne. The Prince Regent's behaviour worsened. The night before the christening George objected to the proposed names of the infant and informed the frustrated parents that he would let them know which names to call their young baby the next day. Prince Edward and Victoire wanted to name their daughter Victoire Georgiana Alexandrina Charlotte Augusta after her mother and the four people – the Prince Regent, the Tsar of Russia, the Queen of Wurttemberg and the Dowager Duchess of Saxe-Coburg Saalfeld – who were godparents. The Prince Regent procrastinated. The parents brought the baby girl into the chapel; the Archbishop of Canterbury held the infant over the baptismal font – and waited patiently for a name. Eventually the Regent, after a sadistically measured waiting time, agreed that the baby could be called Alexandrina, after the Tsar, and only after protests from the father and tears of the mother did he allow the name Victoria to be added. The upshot of this humiliation and other such indignities resulted in the Duchess loathing the royal court. She would in future make every effort to keep her young daughter from it, with the unintended consequence of Victoria not being fully prepared for life as a queen.

In December 1819 the impoverished Duke and Duchess of Kent, struggling to remain solvent, left the Palace with their baby daughter to move to a damp farmhouse in Sidmouth, Devon. They arrived on Christmas Day. The Duke went out for a walk, got wet and caught a cold which developed into pneumonia. His doctors bled him, cupped him and put leeches on his body, but the Duke, weakened by losing more than six pints of blood by these invasive procedures, grew more feverish. He died on 23 January 1820, leaving a 32-year-old widow who spoke little English, an 8-month-old daughter and a mountain of debts. However, it left little Vickelchen, as her mother called her, fourth in line to the throne.

Six days later, on 29 January 1820, the ailing King, the mentally unstable George III, died. Victoria's uncle, the Prince Regent, was crowned King George IV and the young Princess moved up another notch in the monarchical tree to third place. King George IV reigned for ten years, but on 26 June 1830 he too died, leaving no heir. Meanwhile, in 1827 the next in line, Prince Frederick, had died of dropsy and cardio-vascular disease, leaving Prince William as future heir. In 1830 William IV was crowned king. He had no legitimate children, so Victoria, now aged 11, became heir to the British throne. Her rise in the accession, so like the stuff of comedy, had been one of those unexpected and accidental acts of fate.

Bringing up Drina

For someone who was to become queen of the United Kingdom and its colonies, Victoria was not brought up in luxurious surroundings. When the Duke of Kent died, the Duchess moved her family back to Kensington Palace. The Palace contained a number of spacious and opulent apartments, yet the baby Princess, her mother and step-sister were allocated gloomy, barely furnished, cockroach-infested rooms. The Duchess and her daughter were forced to live frugally: Queen Victoria's later parsimony can be attributed to these earlier straightened circumstances, especially when she was taught not to spend over the limit of her meagre pocket money. The family were only saved from penury because Victoria's Uncle Leopold gave his sister Victoire an allowance of £3,000 a year from the £50,000 he received from the British tax-payer as husband of the late Princess Charlotte. He also became a surrogate father to Victoria. Historians tend to agree that because Victoria's father died when she was a baby, she sought a father-figure for most of her younger life. Victoria thought Uncle Leopold was 'so clever, so mild, and so prudent, he alone can give me good advice on everything. His advice is perfect. He is indeed . . . "solo padre"! for he is indeed like my real father, as I have none.'[1] The two wrote to each other regularly. Victoria, soon nicknamed Drina, a diminutive of Alexandrina, lived a secluded life with her mother, her half-sister Feodora, her half-brother Charles and a largely German-speaking household. This Germanic influence shaped young Victoria, causing problems in later life when the need for political objectivity clashed with her deep-seated sentiments.

Princess Victoria was an only child with both the negative and the positive traits associated with this. Only children are often thought to be 'spoiled, selfish brats' and perhaps Victoria was no exception. Certainly, this rather plump toddler with big blue eyes and a sloping Hanoverian chin received a lot of attention. Her mother, with no other small child or husband to cherish, focused on her daughter so exclusively that Victoria got used to being the centre of the world. Maybe as a result, she became bossy: she would be uncompromisingly autocratic, over-confident, self-opinionated and arrogant. Most importantly, Victoria was neither encouraged nor taught to be submissive as most girls were; on the contrary, her assertive traits were encouraged as they were thought to be essential qualities of monarchy.

It is sometimes alleged that Victoria had an unhappy childhood, experiencing little joy or fun in her life. Such an upbringing, it is thought, led to a seriously minded, no-fun queen who was never amused. Yet as a child, the Princess enjoyed playing with her dolls, doing jig-saws, playing billiards and playing shuttlecock. Like most young children, she loved blowing soap bubbles. She adored her pet dog, Dash, saying that 'Dear little Dashy is quite my playfellow, for he is so fond of playing at ball, and of barking and jumping.'[2] When she was in her early teens, Victoria took delight in dressing up after dinner, sometimes appearing as a nun, an Italian brigand's wife, a Turkish lady, or an old Turkish lawyer, 'to amuse Mamma'. Once the young princess spoke of dressing 'myself as a Turkish lady. A red scarf and a white shawl made the turban with a dark blue one and a bright red one for the dress and large hanging white sleeves. I remained so for the rest of the evening.'[3] She played other games with the ladies after dinner; the gentlemen never returned until the young Princess had gone to bed. Victoria loved to play Hen and her Chickens, Puss in the Corner, Blind Man's Bluff and Forfeits. On one occasion, the penalty or Forfeit was for two people to dance a minuet blindfold: Victoria spoke of how she and one of the ladies did so with 'great enjoyment'.

Victoria, like many upper-class girls, was introduced to high culture early on in her life. Many of Victoria's diary entries as a young teenager record her many visits to the theatre and the opera. There was no way Victoria would have been able to watch football, see cock-fighting or dog-, bear- or bull-baiting,[4] a boxing match or engage in other low brow entertainments. At an early age, Victoria's likes and dislikes were unambiguous, unmistakeable and instantly recognisable. When she enjoyed an event, she recorded in her journal that she was 'amused': but her amusement ranged from a plain 'I was amused', through to 'I was <u>much</u>

amused', 'I was <u>very much amused</u>' to the highest praise of the triple underlined, '<u>I was very much amused indeed</u>'. On New Year's Eve 1833 she went to see the *Barber of Seville* 'so well known that I need not describe it. . . . I was very much amused.'[5] Victoria's favourite opera singer was not much older than she was: Giulia Grisi, a beautiful 19-year-old Italian singer whose brilliant dramatic voice established her as the leading soprano for over 30 years. The Princess's journal was full of comments that Signora Giulietta Grisi '<u>sung</u> and <u>acted</u> <u>quite beautifully</u>! And looked lovely. . . . I was <u>*very much amused indeed*</u>.'[6] Victoria adored the ballet too. She delighted in seeing the *Maid of Cashmere*, saying of the lead dancer, Duvemay, 'who danced and acted <u>quite beautifully</u>, with <u>so much grace and feeling</u>; she looked likewise <u>quite lovely</u>. . . . I was <u>very much amused</u>.'[7] Victoria did not enjoy every performance. When she visited Drury Lane to see *The Chevy Chase* she thought it a 'stupid affair . . . Really the vulgarity of Mrs Humby was quite atrocious. The plot which to my astonishment . . . was the most stupid and vulgar nonsense that can be imagined. . . . I was not much amused.'[8]

Formal education took place at home. In 1824, when Victoria was five years old, her mother appointed a German governess, Louise Lehzen, the clever, well-educated daughter of a German Lutheran pastor, as her tutor. Lehzen quickly established a firm yet loving relationship with her young charge. As well as being responsible for her education, Lehzen gave the young Princess the unconditional love she desired, helped her control her moods and tantrums and encouraged her to grow up.[9] Lehzen also consolidated the Germanic sentiments already prevailing in the royal household.

At the time, it was expected that girls of all social classes would get married and raise a family. Education was not considered so important. Upper-class and aristocratic young ladies were expected to be able to play a few tunes on the piano, to sing, to dance the minuet, to draw a simple sketch, to sew a delicate sampler and sometimes to speak a little French. These accomplishments helped them achieve the ideal of the perfect educated woman: a decorative, poised and empty-headed companion for a future husband. Victoria, as a young female, learned the traditional female accomplishments. Dancing teachers, drawing masters, singing and music coaches and riding instructors were appointed to teach her how to dance elegantly, paint a pretty picture, sing in tune, play the piano and ride with confidence. One of the best-known opera singers, Luigu Lablache, gave her singing lessons. On 19 April 1836, aged 15, when she had her first lesson with him, Victoria was nervous and sang Mozart's 'Or che in cielo' 'in fear and trembling'.[10] Fortunately Lablache praised her and so she was 'very much pleased' with her lesson. A few months later, Victoria no longer sang in 'fear and trembling . . . I cared not now what I sing before him'.[11] She clearly enjoyed her lessons and continued to employ Lablache for the next 20 years.

In the spring of 1830, when it became clear that George IV was dying and leaving no heir and that the next king, William IV, had still not fathered any legitimate children, Victoria's mother re-focused her 11-year-old daughter's education. Victoria learned to be disciplined and diligent. Every day was structured. Each morning she was woken at 7am, ate breakfast at 8:30am and went to bed at 8:30pm most nights. As well as traditional skills, the young Princess studied economics, geography, history, astronomy, mathematics and politics. Victoria, already fluent in English and German, became adept in Latin, Italian and French too. In addition, elocution lessons taught Victoria to speak clearly: her voice was thought to be one of her greatest assets.

In June 1831, Victoria's Uncle Leopold left England to become King of Belgium, leaving no influential figure to challenge her mother's authority. Victoria was devastated. She not only missed her confidante but also it left the 12-year-old Princess under the sole control of her mother and Sir John Conroy, a British army officer appointed to take charge of her mother's affairs. Victoria grew to hate Conroy, partly because he tried to play the role of husband and step-father rather than secretary or servant and partly because she was jealous of the close relationship Conroy enjoyed with her mother. The Duchess, encouraged by Conroy, hoped that her daughter would ascend the throne before she was 18, thus allowing herself to become Regent of Britain. In this way, the Duchess would rule Britain, making her wealthy, formidably powerful and no longer dependent on her relatives for their goodwill and financial help.

Together the Duchess and Conroy invented the 'Kensington System', a strict system designed to make Victoria dependent on the two of them. She was secluded from other children, effectively barred from seeing her other relatives and placed under close surveillance. Her only youthful companions were Conroy's daughters but Victoria was never left alone. She was not allowed to see anyone – child or adult – without a third person being present. She even slept in her mother's bedroom, guarded by her governess until her mother retired for the night.

Victoria was taught to be an exemplary, morally upright young woman. The Duchess carefully shielded her daughter's charming innocence from the potentially malign influence of her British male relatives and from any intimacy with her Fitzclarence cousins.[12] Victoria's mother disapproved of King William IV's illegitimate offspring and objected to them living openly in the Palace with their father rather than hidden away in a private villa. Nonetheless, King William and Queen Adelaide were both very fond of their niece and wanted to introduce her to court life in preparation for her future life as a monarch. Victoria's mother conversely wanted to ensure that her daughter remained morally uncontaminated, so steadfastly kept her away from court functions and prevented her from visiting the King and Queen. There were dangers in this approach as well as benefits: in future, Victoria would be intimidated by formal courtly manners and be awkward and diffident in initiating conversation at Palace functions.

For her part, the Duchess created her own 'courtly' training regime and implemented it. In order to make Victoria hold herself erect, a bunch of holly was placed directly under her chin – naturally, the young Princess hated what she called the 'holly days'. In later years Victoria maintained that she had 'led a very unhappy life as a child – had no scope for my very violent feelings of affection – had no brothers and sisters to live with – never had a father – from my unfortunate circumstances was not on a comfortable or at all intimate or confidential footing with my mother'.[13] The relationship between Victoria and her mother was problematic during the teenage years: girls like Victoria want their mothers to love them unconditionally, and mothers like the Duchess want to help their daughters grow into reasonable and effective adults. Conflict was largely inevitable, especially as Victoria, like many teenagers, had strong emotions, was over-sensitive and often moody, angry and irritable. The Duchess, because she was accessible and because Victoria felt secure and safe with her mother, found herself the target of teenage resentment. Rows between Victoria and her mother were common. Not until she reached her mid-twenties, when Victoria was safely married and had had some of her own children, did she begin to value and respect her mother.

A royal progress

The Duchess, who refused to let her daughter visit the court, still wanted to let the British people know about her daughter and her place in the royal hierarchy. On 1 August 1832, the 13-year-old Victoria was taken on an expedition across the middle of England to Wales. On that day Victoria wrote her first entry into a journal she would keep for the rest of her life. 'This book, Mamma gave me, that I might write the journal of my journey to Wales.'[14] Her early entries, probably read by both her mother and her governess, rarely include negative comments. The world, according to Victoria's journal, was very rosy indeed.

The tour lasted over three months. On the second day of her tour, Victoria visited the Black Country in the West Midlands. In her journal, possibly guided by Lehzen, the 13-year-old Victoria wrote that the 'country is very desolate everywhere; . . . the grass is quite blasted and black. I just now see an extraordinary building flaming with fire. The country continues black, engines flaming, coals in abundance, everywhere, smoking and burning coal heaps, intermingled with wretched huts and little ragged children.'[15] Lehzen encouraged her young charge to read the evangelical texts of Hannah More and Maria Edgworth and urged Victoria to understand the 'real world' of working people. Such journeys of course helped the Princess gain a more realistic impression of the country over which she would reign.

Victoria's mother, influenced by John Conroy, had less elevated reasons for the journeys. The Duchess wanted to show off the young Princess to the British public. Each time the party visited a place, they were greeted majestically: troops of Yeomanry paid their respects; guns saluted; sometimes bands played; and flags, flowers and bunting festooned buildings. At Conway, charity children 'strewed the paths with flowers and walked two by two before us'.[16] In addition, many adults came out to see the young Princess Victoria and her entourage. The *Caernarfon Herald* reported that 'at 4 o'clock the Royal cavalcade arrived in five carriages and with some horses and were welcomed by hundreds assembled before, in intense anxiety, with hearty and enthusiastic huzzas, which made the welkin reverberate to their loyal and unfeigned vociferations of devotedness and respect'.[17] 'Nothing', according to *The Times*, could exceed the 'enthusiasm of the inhabitants in their endeavours to give all possible éclat to the visit of the Duchess of Kent and the Princess Victoria. The shops were closed. The houses, windows, and even the posts were tastefully decorated with laurel and garlands of flowers, interspersed with flags.'[18] Here Victoria laid her first stone – for a school for boys. She was given a 'small trowel with mortar with which I smeared the stone which was there, then I beat the stone thrice with a wooden hammer.'[19] These trips were preparation for a public role in later life: as queen, Victoria would be expected to lay stones, unveil statues, open buildings and appear regularly in public.

Fortunately for the lively high-spirited teenager, the journey was sometimes more fun. On 29 September 1832, Victoria went to the Rural Sports at Plas Newydd where she saw competitors 'donkey racing, climbing up a greasy pole for a live duck at the top, jumping in sacks, running with wheel-barrows blindfolded, and chasing after a pig with its tail soaped, the right hand tied behind'.[20] Nothing, she noted in her journal, could be 'more ridiculous or amusing'. Victoria took no part in such activities. These kinds of games, common to country fairs, were thought inappropriate for a young royal so the spirited and lively Princess could only watch. Victoria loved horse riding – fast. At Plas Newydd she 'galloped over a green field . . . Rosa went an enormous rate; she literally flew'.[21] At Pitchford, Shropshire she walked out to see the hunt and saw them off. She was excited by the hunt and completely unperturbed by the bloodshed, writing that:

> it was an immense field of horsemen, who in their red jackets and black hats looked lively and gave an animating appearance

to the whole. They had a large pack of hounds . . . we saw the fox dash past and all the people and hounds after him, the hounds in full cry. The hounds killed him in a wood close by. The huntsman . . . cutting off the brush . . . brought it to me. Then the huntsman cut off for themselves the ears and 4 paws, and lastly they threw it to the dogs, who tore it from side to side until there was nothing left.[22]

Victoria became a good horsewoman, an attribute which was much-admired when she later addressed her troops on horseback. The teenager enjoyed spectacle too. When the group visited Chatsworth there were fireworks: rockets, wheels, windmills and red and blue lights; Victoria enjoyed seeing 'a temple and my name in stars and a crown'.[23]

The trip had been a huge success: Princess Victoria had made a good impression on the British public. As a result, in summer 1833, another royal tour took place to the south and west of England: Portsmouth, Plymouth, Torquay, Exeter, Weymouth, Dorset and the Isle of Wight. On 1 August they arrived at Torquay, which Victoria thought 'a beautiful place; it looks more like some Italian town than an English port'.[24] The inhabitants of Torquay were 'honoured with a Visit . . . immediately the Royal Standard was hoisted and a royal salute was fired'.[25] At Plymouth, they reviewed the regiments; at Dartmouth, Victoria 'was most enthusiastically received by the assembled inhabitants. . . . As she passed salutes were fired . . . Boats, to the number of several hundreds, thronged with inhabitants, floated on the tide, and bands of music and deafening cheers welcomed the approach of the royal visitors.'[26]

In 1835, Princess Victoria, her mother and their entourage all journeyed north. The royal company visited the York Music Festival. At York Minster, the 'assembled thousands rose . . . and such was the enthusiasm of the moment that the sanctity of the temple was forgotten, and a simultaneous burst of applause escaped from the audience as their Royal Highnesses entered'.[27] At Leeds, a town with a radical heritage which rarely took notice of royal visits, huge crowds arrived to see Victoria and the royal party. Early in the day roads leading to Chapel Allerton were crowded with spectators, some roads were impassable and the windows of houses were full of people eager for a glimpse of the young

Princess.[28] In Lynn, Norfolk, a vast crowd unyoked the horses and pulled the coach containing the Princess and her mother through the town. Victoria later commented that 'the people, of whom there was a dense mass, insisted on dragging us through the town and in spite of every effort which was tried to prevent them from so doing, they obstinately persisted. . . . I could see nothing of the town; I only saw one living dense mass of human beings!'[29] The horses were eventually reattached to their carriage but by this time Victoria was 'well-nigh dead by the heat of this long and tiresome day'. At each town, Victoria and mother had to listen to speeches by the various dignitaries. Victoria thought them all very kind and well meant but confided that truly 'these addresses are really ein wenig, sehr langweilig [a little too boring]'.[30] In a later letter to Lord John Russell, Victoria described her loathing of being a 'spectacle' to be gazed at.[31] These parades and pageants were increasingly seen as an essential part of monarchical duty, but in later life Victoria would do her best to avoid such events.

William IV disapproved of these journeys. In his opinion, they were too much like royal progresses, where crowned sovereigns showed themselves off to their subjects, rather than a trip around Britain. The journeys of Victoria and the Duchess, the King believed, undermined his authority by portraying Victoria as having more power than she possessed. Arguably, Victoria's carriage drawn by grey horses with post boys in 'pink silk jackets, with black hats, and the horses have pink silk reigns with bunches of artificial flowers'[32] represented more of a royal procession than a family outing. Victoria too disliked these journeys and wanted them to stop, citing the King's objections to them. She suffered from sickness, stomach upsets and headaches as well as an intense loathing of Conroy – she called him 'a monster and devil incarnate'. However, her mother took no notice and insisted that Victoria continue the tours: she was after all destined to be queen.

After this latest journey, Victoria, her mother, Conroy and Lehzen went to the popular resort of Ramsgate for a holiday, just as they had since the Princess was four years old. On 6 October 1835, Victoria became ill. The doctors initially thought her illness psychosomatic and ignored her symptoms. Later, typhoid – a bacterial disease transmitted by infected food or water and often fatal – was diagnosed. When she was dangerously ill in bed and thought to be much too weak to resist, Conroy and her mother tried to force her to sign a document making Conroy her private secretary when she came to the throne. Her mother, Conroy and his daughters, and her mother's lady-in-waiting Lady Flora Hastings threatened and pleaded for Victoria to sign the document. Fortunately, Lehzen protected her young charge from this psychological warfare and Conroy left humiliated. Five weeks later, after having lost much of her hair, the much diminished Victoria began to recover. She never referred to the event in her daily journal but a few months later wrote:

> I quite forgot to mention that after my illness at Ramsgate I lost my hair frightfully, so that I was literally now getting bald; the comb-tray was full every morning with my hair; as a last and desperate refuge Lehzen, with Mama's and my consent, cut off half and even more of my back hair, once so thick. . . . there is just enough left to be able to tie it and made a small puff; I wear a false plait of course.[33]

Undoubtedly, the young Princess had been very seriously ill yet even at her weakest she refused to be bullied, showing an obstinacy that many of her future ministers would find exasperating. Moreover, Victoria never forgot, or forgave, the attempts of her mother, Conroy and Lady Flora to coerce her into signing away her rights. As queen, Victoria would fight equally untiringly to defend and retain what she considered her royal prerogatives – her monarchical rights – whenever they were threatened.

As she got older, Victoria, in common with other aristocratic and upper-class girls, was expected to be involved in charitable work. In August 1836, now aged 17, Victoria visited the Victoria Asylum set up by one of her future maids of honour for poor homeless girls under the age of 15. When they have 'become quite good, and can read, write and do work of all kinds necessary for a house, they are sent abroad, mostly to the Cape of Good Hope where they are apprentices and become excellent servants'. Victoria was told the story of one little girl:

> a pretty black-eyed girl, 11 years old, called Ellen Ford, who was received two month ago, from Newgate, and who boasted

she could steal and tell lies better than anybody. She had been but two or three days in the school, and she got over 3 high walls, and stole a sheet; she was caught and brought back again . . . the girl was put in solitary confinement for that night and taken out the next morning; and ever since she has been a perfectly good girl.[34]

One senses that the young Princess enjoyed the waywardness of Ellen Ford more than she did the punishment and transformation of the rebellious young girl. She might have even remembered her own confession in her Good Behaviour Book as a mischievous 13 year old when she had been 'VERY VERY VERY VERY HORRIBLY NAUGHTY!!!!', which she had underlined four times.[35] Until she was widowed, Victoria's natural temperament was always being quashed by one adult or another.

Towards marriage

One of the traditional functions of a monarch was to establish a dynasty. Princess Victoria, the future queen, needed a husband to father her children and make the British throne secure: no one wanted a revival of the debacle which followed the death of George III. In addition, there was widespread fear that her notoriously profligate and unpopular uncle, Prince Ernest, Duke of Cumberland, might inherit the throne if Victoria did not produce an heir. It was considered inappropriate for the future queen to marry a subject; it would have to be a European royal. Her mother and her uncle Leopold favoured a German prince, preferably one of their kinsmen; King William IV who disliked the idea of Victoria marrying one of her mother's relatives, favoured a Dutch one. Each hoped, with equally flawed justification, that the future Queen would be moulded by a husband chosen by themselves, and thus obliquely command authority over Britain. Politicians, the press and most of Britain also thought it vital for the Queen to marry the right man. He would, after all, be marrying the most powerful woman in the world, and through his marriage would be able to influence British politics, positively – or negatively.

Visitors, especially young ones, to Kensington Palace were always a welcome diversion from the interminable boredom that

Victoria faced with her mother, her tutors and the band of sycophants that surrounded her. Undoubtedly, the young Princess was
lonely. On 16 June 1833, a few weeks after Victoria's fourteenth
birthday, two cousins, Princes Alexander and Ernst Württemberg,
son of her mother's sister Antoinette, came to stay. Victoria noted
that 'they are both extremely tall, Alexander is very handsome,
and Ernst has a very kind expression. They are both extremely
amiable.'[36] The Princess was delighted by their youthful exuber-
ance. When they left she was 'very very sorry' as the two were
so agreeable and so amiable. In a charming journal entry she
wrote that she would miss them 'at breakfast, at luncheon, at
dinner, riding, sailing, driving, walking, in fact everywhere'.[37]

Towards her sixteenth birthday, young men began to arrive, this
time as likely suitors. Victoria may have been short (she was 4'11",
i.e. a little less than 150 cm) and slightly plump with a receding
chin, but as heiress to the British throne, she was the best catch in
the world. On 15 March, Uncle Ferdinand with his sons, Ferdinand
and Augustus, arrived. Ferdinand was on his way to marry the
young Queen of Portugal. Victoria described Ferdinand as a

> very slight figure, rather fair hair, beautiful dark brown eyes,
> a fine nose, and a very sweet mouth. . . . Augustus is as tall
> and by far stouter. . . . At first, I thought him handsomer
> than Ferdinand, but not afterwards. . . . Ferdinand speaks
> through his nose and in a slow and funny way which at first
> is against him but soon wears off. . . . During the evening,
> Ferdinand came and sat near me and talks so dearly and so
> sensibly. I do so love him.[38]

The cousins were, at that particular moment, Victoria's favourites. She thought that they were 'not like Cousins, but brothers'.
She missed them both when they left, especially at dances since
Victoria was only allowed to waltz and galop (an early version
of the polka) with other royals. Etiquette forbade her to dance
with lesser mortals if it meant too much physical contact or if it
was too lively. Even so, the dances did not spark off romance;
the two boy cousins were friends but no more.

King William IV, in an attempt to thwart the plans of Victoria's
mother to marry her daughter into German nobility, encouraged

the Dutch Prince of Orange and his sons, William and Alexander, to visit. On 12 May 1836 the two arrived at 4pm. Victoria made no positive comment about them in her journal and wrote to her Uncle Leopold that she thought the two very plain, and looked dull, heavy and frightened. The King's hopes were dashed, seemingly through lack of interest.

Soon after, another couple of German cousins arrived: Ernest and Albert. Ernest, aged 17, was due to inherit his father's throne of Saxe-Coburg-Gotha while the 16-year-old Albert was being positioned to be Victoria's husband. It was a Coburg conspiracy: the Duchess and her two brothers Leopold and Ernest (Albert's father) all wanted Victoria to marry her first cousin. It would keep Britain Germanic, and keep the British throne in the Coburg family. Their joint plan seemed bound for success; Victoria's first impressions of Albert were positive. Albert, she thought,

> is extremely handsome; his hair is about the same colour as mine; his eyes are large and blue, and he has a beautiful nose, and very sweet mouth with fine teeth; but the charm of his countenance is his expression, which is most delightful; c'est a la fois, [that is both] full of goodness and sweetness, and very clever and intelligent.[39]

The more she knew them, the better she liked them. She commented later that they were so natural, so kind, so very good and so well instructed and informed. In her view they were 'so well bred, so truly merry and quite like children and yet very grown up in their manners and conversation'.[40] When the young Princess had breakfast with them on the last day of their visit she spoke of

> dearest, beloved Cousins, whom I <u>do</u> love so <u>very very</u> dearly; <u>much more dearly</u> than any other Cousins in the <u>world.</u> Dearly as I love Ferdinand, and also good Augustus, I love Ernest and Albert <u>more</u> than them, oh yes, <u>much more</u>. . . . When I think that I shall not see my dear Cousins' dear kind faces, any more at breakfast, at dinner, nowhere, and that we shall have no more merry breakfasts, no more of those delightful walks, no more merry dinners, no more

happy evenings . . . it makes me quite miserable! Oh me!
I cannot hardly think of all this today without shedding tears,
it makes me quite sick at heart![41]

Certainly, it seemed as if Victoria's mother's stratagem was
working.

In September 1836, shortly after Albert's visit, Victoria's uncle
King Leopold arrived in England. The press was suspicious of
his motives, particularly because Victoria would come of age the
following year. Leopold's visit, it was believed, was of a political-
matrimonial character rather than a social occasion. Newspapers
disapproved of his possible meddling in British affairs, and disliked
the thought of too much Germanic influence. 'There will arise',
one newspaper reported,

> many serious considerations in the mind of every thinking
> Englishman with regard to a matrimonial alliance for her, who,
> if she lives, must be our future Queen. . . . Far be it from us
> to suggest or insinuate that anything like intrigue is going
> forward . . . for the promotion of selfish family views, or of
> foreign interests remote from those of the principal party her-
> self. . . . But still the people of England do not like the appear-
> ance of designing or meddling motives. . . . and . . . would
> be revolted by the suspicion that the destiny of her whole life
> had been pre-disposed of by a clandestine family caucus held
> on one side of the House only, and that the side which was
> not *English*.[42]

The *Derby Mercury* believed that the 'rose of England must
not therefore be approached by any tainted hand . . . What right
has Leopold of Belgium to interfere with the marital responsibilities of a Princess who only has the misfortune to be related
to him?'[43]

A month earlier, tensions had erupted between the King and
the Duchess. William IV had visited Kensington Palace only to
find that his sister-in-law, without his knowledge and certainly
without his permission, had requisitioned new apartments for
herself and her daughter. The King was livid. A few days later,
the Duchess and Victoria were invited to William IV's birthday.

During his birthday dinner, the King gave vent to his fury before 115 guests who included nobles, politicians and other influential figures. In his tirade he ranted that he hoped his 'life may be spared for nine months longer. . . . I should then have the satisfaction of leaving the royal authority to the personal exercise of . . . the heiress presumptive of the Crown, and not in the hands of a person who is surrounded by evil advisors and who is herself incompetent to act with propriety'.[44] Victoria burst into tears; the Duchess sat immobile, once more humiliated by a royal senior to herself.

On 18 May 1837, with Victoria approaching 18, William wrote to his niece saying that he would ask parliament to award her an income of £10,000 a year. The King wanted his niece and heir to the throne to have money of her own. Victoria, bullied by her mother and Conroy, wrote a letter drafted by the two declining it. King Leopold, aghast at the control Conroy exerted over his sister and ultimately his niece, sent Baron Stockmar to Britain to undermine Conroy's influence and provide useful advice. Soon Baron Stockmar began to have 'long and important' conversations with the Princess.

The Germanic influence was strong. Stockmar, Lehzen and King Leopold all offered advice, something which the somewhat xenophobic British disapproved of since they feared excessive German control. All three held no official government post, wielding their authority through personal relationships. Baron Stockmar, King Leopold's private secretary, had been sent by her uncle to teach and advise Victoria. Uncle Leopold reassured his niece that Stockmar 'will never press anything, never plague you with anything, without the thorough conviction that it is indispensable for your welfare. I can guarantee his independence of mind and disinterestedness.'[45] Victoria approved and replied to her uncle that she was 'happy and thankful' to have Stockmar advise her for 'he has <u>been</u>, and <u>is</u>, of the greatest possible use, and be assured, dearest Uncle, that he possesses <u>my most entire confidence</u>'.[46] For the next few years, he taught Victoria about constitutional proprieties and tried, often unsuccessfully, to persuade her to believe that the Crown should be above party politics.

On 24 May 1837, Victoria reached her eighteenth birthday. At 7am, a party of 37 gentlemen in full dress serenaded her; later that morning she received her friends and family; in the afternoon the nobility; at 4pm she went in an open carriage to Hyde Park and walked around Kensington Gardens; in the evening, Victoria attended a ball in her honour at St James's Palace. Most of the country celebrated her coming of age: Victoria could now reign in her own right, without the need for a guardian. Fetes were held across the United Kingdom: a grand dinner was held in Ramsgate, roast beef and plum puddings were given to 900 children in Margate and a ball was held in Leamington Spa. The usual bad poems were written. 'Youth is around thee, Lady of the Ocean, Ocean that is thy kingdom and thy home, Where not a heart but kindles with emotion, Dreaming of honoured years that are to come.'[47] King William IV rejoiced: the Princess no longer needed a regent and he could now give in to his illness. Three weeks later, on 15 June 1837, the news of the King's health was so bad that Victoria had her lessons cancelled.

At 6am on 20 June 1837, the Duchess woke her daughter. Victoria got out of bed and, still in her dressing gown, went to her sitting room to meet the Archbishop of Canterbury and the Lord Chamberlain. Here, she was told that the King, William IV, had died: Victoria, aged 18, was Queen of Great Britain and its empire, and the most powerful woman in the world. In her journal, written later that day, she wrote 'I shall do my utmost to fulfil my duty towards my country. I am very young and perhaps in many, though not in all things, inexperienced, but I am sure, that very few have more real good will and more real desire to do what is fit and right than I have.'[48] Lytton Strachey observed that after 'years of emptiness and dullness and suppression, she had come suddenly, in the heyday of youth, into freedom and power'.[49] Her new subjects were more concerned about her youth, her inexperience and 'the novel circumstance of a female reign'.[50]

Notes

1 RA VIC/MAIN/QVJ (W) September 16th 1836.
2 Ibid. March 14th 1833.
3 Ibid. December 5th 1832.
4 Blood sports, apart from those such as fox hunting which involved wild animals, were banned in 1835.

5 RA VIC/MAIN/QVJ (W) December 31st 1832.
6 Ibid. April 19th 1834. Victoria had just seen Grisi performing in *Anne Boleyn*.
7 Ibid. March 19th 1833.
8 Ibid. March 3rd 1836.
9 Arnstein, *Queen Victoria*, p. 24.
10 RA VIC/MAIN/QVJ (W) April 19th 1836.
11 Ibid. August 2nd 1836.
12 King William IV, when Duke of Clarence, had given his sons and daughters the surname Fitzclarence. Fitz is an Anglo-Norman word meaning 'son of'. It was later adopted as a prefix for the illegitimate children of royalty.
13 Victoria to the Princess Royal, June 9th 1858, quoted in Roger Fulford, *Dearest Child, Private Correspondence of Queen Victoria and the Crown Princess of Prussia, 1858–1861*, Evans, 1964, p. 112.
14 RA VIC/MAIN/QVJ (W) July 31st 1832.
15 Ibid. August 2nd 1832.
16 Ibid. August 13th 1832.
17 *Caernarfon Herald* quoted in *The Times*, September 5th 1832.
18 *The Times*, October 22nd 1832.
19 RA VIC/MAIN/QVJ (W) October 13th 1832.
20 Ibid. September 29th 1832.
21 Ibid. October 14th 1832.
22 Ibid. October 31st 1832.
23 Ibid. October 22nd 1832.
24 Ibid. August 1st 1833.
25 *Plymouth and Cornish Advertiser*, August 8th 1833.
26 *The Standard*, August 9th 1833.
27 *The Morning Post*, September 10th 1835.
28 *The Leeds Mercury*, September 19th 1835.
29 RA VIC/MAIN/QVJ (W) September 22nd 1835.
30 Ibid. September 23rd 1835.
31 Yvonne Ward, *Censoring Queen Victoria*, Oneworld Publications, 2014, p. 94.
32 RA VIC/MAIN/QVJ (W) October 27th 1832.
33 Ibid. January 25th 1836.
34 Ibid. August 3rd 1836.
35 Quoted in Williams, *Becoming Queen*, p. 213.
36 RA VIC/MAIN/QVJ (W) June 16th 1833.
37 Ibid. July 13th 1833.
38 Ibid. March 17th 1836.
39 Ibid. May 18th 1836.
40 Ibid. May 21st 1836.
41 Ibid. June 10th 1836.
42 *The Belfast News-Letter*, September 23rd 1836.
43 *The Derby Mercury*, October 26th 1836.

44 Quoted in Williams, *Becoming Queen*, p. 246.
45 Leopold to Queen Victoria, June 30th 1837. Unless otherwise stated, the quotations from letters have been taken from the collections of letters edited either by Buckle or by Benson and Esher.
46 Victoria to Leopold, June 19th 1837.
47 Miss Lindon's 'Birthday Tribute' quoted in *The Derby Mercury*, May 24th 1837.
48 RA VIC/MAIN/QVJ (W) June 20th 1837.
49 Strachey, *Queen Victoria*, p. 33.
50 *The Aberdeen Journal*, June 28th 1837.

2 The young queen: 1837–1840

At 9am on 20 June 1837, Queen Victoria received her first prime minister, Lord Melbourne. Two and a half hours later, she held her first Privy Council: a 100-strong gentlemanly body of advisors mostly made up of senior politicians, lords, bishops and generals. Victoria walked into the room unaccompanied, without any female attendants, bowed to the Lords, took her seat and read her speech in a clear, distinct and audible voice, acquitting herself 'with a self-possession and a modesty which astonished and grati- fied all who witnessed the scene'.[1] The new fresh-faced queen was virtually unknown as a result of her mother's policy of keep- ing her in obscurity: protecting her daughter, that is, from the loose morals of the court. 'Think', Victoria confided later, 'what it was for me, a girl of 18 all alone, not brought up in court – but very humbly at Kensington Palace.'[2] Most people noted 'the contrast between Queen Victoria and her uncles. The nasty old men, debauched and selfish, pig-headed and ridiculous, with their perpetual burden of debts, confusions, and disreputabilities – they had vanished like the snows of winter, and here at last, crowned and radiant, was the spring'.[3] She had, said one courtier, suc- ceeded 'an imbecile . . . a profligate . . . and a buffoon'.[4] In gen- eral, the British public welcomed the accession of a young monarch as a breath of royal fresh air who would turn the monarchy into 'a beneficent institution'. One newspaper commented that no other sovereign enjoyed such a brilliant prospect for she 'appears in it as the rainbow of a blessed promise. The young Queen of England has not a prejudice or an enmity to encounter, except, perhaps in the lowest dregs.'[5] It was hoped that the new queen would do more for her subjects than any monarch in history, making the weight of people's expectations a heavy burden for a teenager to bear.

A year and eight days later, on 28 June 1838, Victoria was crowned queen. There is nothing calculated to establish devotion to a monarchy more than a birth, a marriage – or a coronation. The coronation provided an opportunity for the country to rejoice at the sight of a young queen, untainted by the degeneracy of previous royals, rejuvenating the country's monarchy and with it the nation. The government allocated £200,000 to the event, medals were struck, poems, songs and hymns written, coronation ribbons woven and the longest ever state procession since 1660 took the Queen from Buckingham Palace, via Hyde Park Corner, Pall Mall, Charing Cross and Whitehall to Westminster Abbey. The organisers erected platforms along the route so that people could view the regal pageant. It was designed to be a public spectacle and the population responded with enthusiasm. Britain was coronation mad. There never was anything, said one commentator, 'seen like the state of this town; it is as if the population had been on a sudden quintupled; the uproar, the confusion, the crowd, the noise, are indescribable. Horsemen, footmen, carriages squeezed, jammed, intermingled . . . the town all mob, thronging, bustling, gaping, and gazing at everything . . . the railroads loaded with arriving multitudes.[6] Queen Victoria feared 'the people would be crushed, in consequence of the tremendous rush and pressure'.[7] Not everyone welcomed such a public event. One lord expressed 'horror at the notion of a young girl being exposed to the gaze of the populace, a violation of feminine delicacy'.[8] Women, the noble lord believed, should be at home hidden away, not paraded in front of multitudes.

At dawn, a 21-gun salute ushered in the coronation day. Fortunately, the weather was un-British, fine and rain free. From the first glimpse of morning, one paper reported 'the usual quietude of the streets was broken by the rattle of carriages and the busy hum of thronging multitudes anxiously hastening to take possession of places secured for a view of the ceremony of the day'.[9] At 10am, the Queen left Buckingham Palace in the state coach to the tune of the *National Anthem*. She was escorted by trumpeters and life-guards, members of the royal family, military officials and the carriages of foreign ambassadors. It was hoped that the new queen would inaugurate a new ceremonial style of monarchy which in turn would generate an era of royal popularity.

An hour and a half later, the Queen reached the Abbey door, having delighted the huge numbers of her subjects by her participation in the splendid procession. The more aristocratic of her subjects, wearing their robes and diamonds, waited inside. There was a strict dress etiquette: all peers wore their crimson velvet edged with miniver and ermine according to their rank: dukes were allowed four rows of ermine, marquesses three and a half rows and mere barons only two rows.[10] The Abbey glittered and glistened, particularly the peeresses, who twinkled with diamonds. The feminist radical Harriet Martineau said that she 'had never before seen the full effect of diamonds. As the light travelled each peeress shone like a rainbow . . . Prince Esterhazy crossing a bar of sunshine was the most prodigious rainbow of all. He was covered with diamonds and pearls, and as he dangled his hat it cast a dancing radiance all round.'[11] Diamonds even sparkled from the heels of Esterhazy's shoes.

The Queen, dressed for the journey in robes of delicate gold tissue and a crimson mantle, changed into her coronation vestments and proceeded up the Abbey. There had been no rehearsal for this auspicious event – the Queen merely visiting the day before to try out the thrones (they were too low and had to be changed) – and the coronation was a bit ramshackle by today's well-rehearsed standards. The different actors in the ceremony had neglected to practise their roles and were very imperfect in their parts, consequently there was 'a continual difficulty and embarrassment, and the Queen never knew what she was to do next'.[12] The officiating clergy were unsure of coronation procedure, the Archbishop forced a ceremonial ring on to the wrong finger of the Queen and an aged lord fell down the steps to the throne.

The disorganised nature of the coronation remained private: newspapers merely reporting that the event united 'all classes, ranks, ages, and conditions'.[13] Moreover, it only cost £70,000, well under budget, as compared to George IV's, which had cost £243,000. Across the country, people celebrated; it was to be the most widely shared public event until the jubilees. There were dinners for the poor, pony races, grinning matches and a ball in Bury Edmunds; processions in Oldham; special firework displays in Canterbury, Edinburgh and Torquay; a 2'6", 214lb Victoria pudding cooked in Brighton; boat races, flower shows and archery in Belfast;[14] and a shilling given to all the poor in Arundel. London was illuminated by oil lamps and fireworks and there was 'scarcely a house in any of the principal streets but what was brilliantly lighted up, crowns, stars, and the letters V.R. meeting the eye in every direction'.[15] The young Queen, touched by 'the enthusiasm, affection and loyalty' of her people, felt overjoyed at being queen of such a nation and insisted that she would always remember the day as the proudest of her life.[16]

The young Queen would need more than pride and self-possession. Political by definition of her role and powers, she was at the apex of the constitutional structure. The Royal Prerogative, that is, the special rights and powers of the Crown, meant that Victoria automatically became commander in chief of the armed forces; enjoyed the right to appoint ministers and diplomats, to bestow knighthoods and other honours, to choose bishops and archbishops, and to appoint the colonial governors. During her reign, she would appoint ten prime ministers, 15 foreign secretaries, 11 lord chancellors, six army commanders, and five archbishops of Canterbury. As Walter Bagehot later noted in his classic book *The English Constitution* (1867), the Queen also had the power to declare war, to make peace, negotiate treaties, disband the army, dismiss all sailors, sell off all warships, make every parish a university and pardon all offenders. It seemed a frightening prospect for both Britain and her friends and allies abroad: an untested, naïve and inexperienced teenager at the head of the most powerful country in the world. 'The reign of Queen Victoria', reported one local newspaper 'will form one of the brightest or one of the saddest pages in English history.'[17]

The Queen enjoyed numerous prerogatives but she could not exercise them freely. Victoria, unlike many of the crowned heads of her European family, was not an absolute monarch since her authority was limited by her constitutional status. Laws such as the Bill of Rights 1689[18] and the Act of Settlement 1701[19] had restricted the special rights and powers of the sovereign. Naturally, in her coronation oath Queen Victoria promised to govern according to the statutes in parliament, and the laws and customs of the same. For example, although monarchs had the theoretical right to refuse to sign a parliamentary bill no monarch since Queen Anne had actually exercised the royal veto.

More importantly, the 1832 Great Reform Act[20] marked a decisive shift in monarchical power, a power which would be further eroded throughout the nineteenth century. Until the Act, monarchs were generally able to choose their own prime minister, who in turn could be sure to win an election; he had, after all, the confidence of the reigning monarch who had patronage to bestow. Prior to the 1832 Act, and indeed until 1918, the electorate consisted only of men: women were not allowed to vote. Moreover, the electorate was small, corruptible and easily swayed, allowing a sovereign to influence the outcome of an election and manage the House of Commons through a party of 'the King's friends'. These friends consisted of small factions and groups easily manipulated by the sovereign with the gifts of patronage. However, the Great Reform Act, which basically enfranchised the male middle class, began to establish the sovereignty of the people. After 1832, the Crown's power to appoint a prime minister without consulting parliament was undermined for unless the minister enjoyed support in the House of Commons he could not survive. Indeed, Victoria's reign symbolised the change from 'the concept of government as the King's government to government as party government'.[21] By the time Victoria was crowned, ministers depended on their parliamentary majorities, rather than the monarch, for their preservation. Ministers appointed by the sovereign could no longer be sure of electoral support and the Crown could no longer manoeuvre the various factions and groups within parliament. Gradually, throughout Victoria's reign, the Crown lost influence as the elected House of Commons became more and more identified with the nation. Certainly, the Queen, crowned five years after the Great Reform Act, was to become incrementally less powerful than her predecessors.

In addition, as Britain became more democratic, the roles of head of state and head of government became separated. Victoria's task in this new democratic era was to be politically impartial, leaving the elected parliament and its parties to govern. In theory, the Crown's constitutional prerogative of appointing ministers remained, in practice Queen Victoria could only appoint those who enjoyed support in the House of Commons. As the monarch's role as head of government diminished, it began to be replaced by a new role as head of state. Here the sovereign was cast in a ceremonial and symbolic role rather than an executive one. The country and the government expected Queen Victoria to reign not rule. Unfortunately, the Queen never really adapted to this new situation: she regularly tried to take an executive role in government affairs and all too often declined to carry out her ceremonial duties.[22] At the beginning of Victoria's reign, the party system was still rudimentary and there was often leeway for the monarch to get her way; however, as parties became better organised, this latitude diminished.

The extent of the new Queen's popularity is difficult to ascertain but it is safe to say that Victoria's accession to the throne was widely welcomed. Parliament was pleased and awarded the Queen an annuity of £385,000. Victoria also enjoyed revenues from the Duchy of Lancaster, which amounted to over £27,000 a year. After the expenses of her household, there was a surplus of £95,000 a year. This enabled the Queen to pay off her father's debts, and then save; after her years of relative impoverishment she was determined to be financially secure.

Victoria, swept up by the sheer business of the first few days of her reign, commented excitedly in her journal with all the artlessness of her youth that she 'really have immensely to do [*sic*] . . . but I like it very much.'[23] She had 'so many communications from the Ministers, and from me to them, and I get so many papers to sign every day, that I always have a very great deal to do . . . I delight in this work'.[24] In the first few days of her reign she made decisions on a court martial and conferred on the Grand Cross of the Bath to the Earl of Durham, knighting him with the Sword of State which is 'so enormously heavy that Lord Melbourne was obliged to hold it for me, and I only inclined it. I then put the ribbon over his shoulder.'[25] In addition, the young Queen was introduced to her foreign ambassadors and ministers; received homage from the Bishop of Norwich; received various foreign ambassadors from France and Russia – Count Orloff of Russia presented her with the Order of St Catherine set in diamonds; chose over twenty ladies of the bedchamber from the aristocratic list; and attended levees and audiences. On one occasion, she had her 'hand kissed nearly <u>3,000</u> times'.[26] It was mostly ceremonial, rather than governmental, work.

Almost immediately, Victoria punished her mother and John Conroy. On the first night of her reign, like a petulant teenager, Queen Victoria took revenge on her mother's controlling behaviour by moving her mother's bed from her room and sleeping alone. Within a month of ascending the throne, Queen Victoria moved out of Kensington Palace to Buckingham Palace. Her mother, still out of favour, was given a suite of rooms separate from her daughter. Conroy was banned from the court. In 1839, after considerable negotiation, Victoria got rid of John Conroy by giving him a baronetcy and a pension of £3,000 a year. Victoria enjoyed her *schadenfreude* moment, Baroness Lehzen was triumphant and Stockmar took up residence in the Palace.

The Germanic influence was potent. Victoria adored and perhaps feared her governess, friend and advisor Baroness Lehzen. Victoria had rebelled against the authority of her mother but she was still a teenager and still relied on adults to guide her. Her journals are unwaveringly flattering about her new protector, possibly because Lehzen still read them. 'My beloved and faithful Lehzen' Victoria would write, 'I cannot sufficiently praise; no words can express what she has <u>done, what</u> she has <u>endured</u> for me!! I can <u>never never</u> recompense her sufficiently for <u>all, all</u> what she has <u>borne</u> and <u>done</u> for me these 13 years!'[27] The Queen called Lehzen 'Mother', 'for that she <u>ever has been</u> and <u>is</u> and friend, my <u>angelic</u> dearest beloved <u>Lehzen</u>, whom I love <u>so</u> very <u>dearly</u> . . . and without whom I could not <u>exist</u>.'[28] Others took a dimmer view of Lehzen, viewing her as a manipulative intriguer; Albert was to call her 'the old hag'.

Uncle Leopold, now King of Belgium, enjoyed giving his niece advice. Frequent letters arrived, encouraging, educating and sometimes prescribing how to rule. Leopold wanted Victoria to depend on his former secretary, Baron Stockmar from Coburg, for guidance. He advised his niece to keep her mind cool and easy and not to be alarmed at the prospect of being queen as 'aid will not be wanting, and the great thing is that you should have some honest people about you who have your welfare really at heart. Stockmar will be in this respect all we can wish.'[29] Victoria was encouraged to be 'courageous, firm and honest, as you have been till now . . . you have at your command Stockmar, whose judgment, heart and character offer all the guarantees we can wish for. . . . My object is that you should be no one's tool'[30] – except of course his own. Leopold recommended that Victoria take her time in making decisions and that 'whenever a question is of some importance, it should not be decided on the day when it is submitted to you . . . when a Minister brings his box and the papers, get him to explain them. . . . Then you will keep the papers, either to think yourself upon it or to consult somebody.'[31] Leopold knew how impetuous his young niece could be but Victoria took her uncles's advice. In her early reign, she depended on Stockmar's guidance and rarely gave an immediate response to ministerial questions. Her uncle counselled his niece to study history, international law, political economy, classic studies, physical science. Once more, Stockmar 'would have the immense advantage, for so young a Queen, to be a living dictionary of all matters scientific and political'.[32] In addition, Leopold taught his niece some Machiavellian tactics. He told Victoria that foreign spies always read confidential documents and if she wanted to bring a particular policy to the attention of a foreign government, then she should deliberately write about it in a despatch. In future years, Queen Victoria would often engage in secretive, and some would say devious, negotiations. Moreover, Victoria's early dependence on dominant clever men laid the foundations for her future relationships with politicians, and even with Albert.

Victoria was blessed with a work ethic, making it 'the greatest pleasure to do my duty for my country and my people, and no fatigue, however great, will be burdensome to me if it is for the welfare of the nation'.[33] The day's routine was unwavering. Each morning, taking her Uncle Leopold's advice, Victoria devoted herself to business matters. It was a schedule she would keep all her life, a direct contrast to George IV, whose heavy drinking and indulgent lifestyle caused him to take to his bed and stay there for days on end.

Victoria and Melbourne: 1837–1841

Many hoped that the new young Queen might break royal tradition and remain above party politics. This wish was not, and never would be, granted. At her accession, Victoria was a fervent Whig, surrounded by people from a small aristocratic Whiggish circle. Hers was a Whig family: her mother, her late father, Baroness Lehzen and Prince Leopold were all Whig supporters. The teenage Queen Victoria's first prime minister, Viscount Melbourne, was a member of the ruling Whig faction in parliament. The Whigs were not a party in the modern conventional sense, they were rather a group of MPs who stood for constitutional monarchy and the reduction of crown patronage, who had a commitment to reform and who tended to favour the merchant, banking and industrialist class rather than the landed aristocracy. The hope that Victoria might be a dispassionate, impartial – and above all – constitutional monarch was dashed almost immediately she became queen, and was undermined further by her increasing reliance on Melbourne. The Queen was an impressionable 18 year old whereas Melbourne was 58 years old, well versed in politics, sophisticated, clever and urbane, thus making the intellectual and emotional relationship somewhat unbalanced. Melbourne, as much a father figure as a prime minister, became Victoria's mentor, friend and confidante, and this personal rapport propelled Victoria towards Whig politics even more. The two met socially, not just politically: Melbourne went out riding with the Queen, usually joined her for lunch or dinner, and regularly stayed at Windsor. They frequently spent six hours or more together and met almost every day, more than was considered appropriate for even a sociable prime minister, and led to the young Queen being dubbed 'Mrs Melbourne'. Lord Greville, a senior civil servant who was often at court, thought the Queen relied much too much on Melbourne, who treated her with 'unbounded consideration and respect, consults her tastes and her wishes, and he puts her at her ease by his frank and natural manners, while he amuses her by the quaint, queer, epigrammatic turn of his mind, and his varied knowledge upon all subjects. . . . Her reliance upon Melbourne's advice extends at present to subjects quite beside his constitutional functions.'[34]

Victoria shared her intimate secrets with her prime minister, telling him of how shy she felt, of how she never knew what to say, of how she often felt awkward, and of her 'great nervousness' which she feared she would never get over when speaking in public.[35] She discussed with Melbourne whether couples should get to know each other before marriage, commenting that 'if people knew each other better there never would be any marriages at all'.[36] The two spoke frankly, even discussing Melbourne's bowel movements and their respective bedtime habits. For much of the time, Victoria preferred to gossip with Melbourne rather than discuss affairs of state. The two enjoyed chatting about inconsequential matters. They discussed how someone had a peculiar way of eating a potato, of another of having a fidgety temper, of how one lord's elopement had killed his sister, of how a foreigner thought the English danced too slowly, of the peevishness of some of the peers, and of who hated whom. The two dissected the characters of acquaintances, spoke of how one lady was a 'great goose', of someone else's beauty, of the 'unquietness' of another, of people's jealousy of a beautiful lady, of which men had mistresses. Lady Cecil Copley, Victoria pronounced, 'was one of those clever, strange, wild people who would do anything. "Like her" Lord Melbourne said, looking at Miss Dillon; I said I thought she would never do anything of that kind, for that she was too good for that; he said, "I hope not!".'[37] Victoria declared to Melbourne that Lady Stanhope was 'undisguisedly jealous of everybody' and had no more sense than a donkey and told him that the Bishop of Chester was called Crumpet 'because his face is said to be in the shape of a crumpet, like dough'.[38] She confided that she was utterly astonished at the talkativeness of Lord Palmerston and of the Duke of Cambridge who 'talks quite immensely and in such a loud excited manner'.[39] The fun that the young sovereign enjoyed with Melbourne was evident and there is no suggestion here of a serious, moralistic, disapproving monarch who was never amused. More significantly, Melbourne acted as a friend and confidante more than a prime minister, taking on a role which would have serious repercussions later on.

In addition, Melbourne helped Victoria cope with the negative and volatile relationship she had with her mother. It was not actually dysfunctional but more akin to the predictable cycle of a mother–daughter relationship. In her late adolescence, Victoria was determined to build her own identity, and she resented what she considered her mother's controlling and domineering behaviour. When her mother offered suggestions, Victoria thought her intrusive and interfering. She complained to Melbourne about the excessive tyranny of her mother and about her 'former dreadful and inconceivable torments' when she was at Ramsgate.[40] Melbourne was told about 'all I underwent there; their (Ma and JC) attempts (when I was still very ill) to make me promise beforehand (about letting John Conroy be Private Secretary) . . . Spoke at great length about all this and many more sad scenes and events.'[41] Melbourne diplomatically listened, advised the Queen on what to say, and drafted her responses. Just after she became queen, Victoria wrote in her journal that Melbourne was a most truly honest, straightforward and noble-minded man who she was 'most fortunate to have at the head of the Government; a man in whom I can safely place confidence.'[42] This perception of Melbourne remained with her throughout his premiership and quite undermined any idea that Victoria might be an impartial monarch. Over the next few years, Melbourne flattered her, controlled her intemperate nature, curbed her intolerance and her tendency to narrow-mindedness – and often gave her unsound advice.

There were downsides to this relationship. Melbourne's manner to the Queen, observed Greville, and hers to him, were embarrassing: 'his, so parental and anxious, but always so respectful and deferential; hers, indicative of such entire confidence, such pleasure in his society. She is continually talking to him . . . he always sits next her at dinner'.[43] It was not a relationship expected between sovereign and prime minister. Moreover, he prophesised that if 'Melbourne should be compelled to resign, her privation will be the more bitter on account of the exclusiveness of her intimacy with him'.[44]

More importantly, the strong relationship between the Queen and her premier was detrimental to the development of constitutional monarchy. The Queen admired Melbourne even though his government was thought 'miserably weak, dragging on a sickly existence . . . and so incapable of standing, on any great principles, that at last they have, or appear to have, none to stand on'.[45] Between 1837 and 1840 the Whigs were too politically frail, and Melbourne too indolent, to carry out important measures. In reality, and only with the support of the Queen and the Irish MPs, were Melbourne and his party – just about – able to cling to office.

A weak government cannot deliver a programme of reform, so only minor changes were made, mostly tidying up legislation of the previous Whig government. There was a Municipal Corporations Act; a Marriage Act that gave people the right to marry in a local register office; and a Chimney Sweeps Act that raised the minimum age of apprenticeship to 16. In addition, there were various Acts to abolish the death penalty for a number of statutory offences – forgery, piracy, shooting, stabbing and for having or procuring an abortion – and replacing it with transportation for life; a Slave Compensation Act which compensated former slave owners for the loss of their freed slaves; and a Custody of Infants Act which allowed mothers custody of their children up to the age of seven, and for the right of access to older children. The Queen thought the Custody of Infants Act a good thing and criticised one lord who 'wanted to exclude Roman Catholic women from having the same, which I do think too atrocious'.[46]

At the time of the Queen's accession, only a tiny percentage of men were able to take part in the parliamentary process. Women still did not have the vote. Even so, the Queen had no wish to widen the franchise further. In 1838, a Chartist petition put forward six demands, including a vote for every man over the age of 21, a secret ballot, annual parliaments, equal electoral districts, the abolition of property qualifications for MPs and payment for MPs. The Queen paid little attention to it. A year later, after a widespread national campaign, the Chartists took a large petition to parliament only to have parliament refuse to accept it. Several outbreaks of violence occurred. In November 1839 one of the most serious outbursts occurred in Newport, Monmouthshire, when a crowd of about 20,000, large numbers of whom were armed with rifles, marched on the town. The Mayor called out the troops: a violent and bloody battle took place and about 22 Chartists died in the fracas. The main leaders of the march were found guilty of high treason and sentenced to be hanged, drawn and quartered. Queen Victoria had little sympathy for the rebels and rejected a petition to pardon them. In her view, riots were a precursor of revolution. In the end, after a nationwide petitioning campaign and direct lobbying of Melbourne, the government commuted the sentence. The Queen, possibly in protest, invited the Mayor of Newport, who had suppressed the demonstration, to dine at the Palace, 'thanked him for his services and said he had set an excellent example to . . . the country'.[47] He was also knighted.

Britain may have been the workshop of the world but the exploited majority who helped create this wealth went unrewarded. The 1833 Factory Act made it illegal to employ children under the age of nine and restricted the hours of children between 9 and 13 years of age. Nevertheless, conditions in factories remained abominable: children were beaten, malnourished and often worked on unguarded machines. Accidents were common. Melbourne informed the Queen that the accounts of factory children were 'greatly exaggerated . . . He says it's better children should work than be idle and starve.'[48] The British cotton industry depended on slave-grown cotton for its factories. Britain abolished the slave trade in 1807 and slavery in 1833. However, the notorious 'apprenticeship' system replaced it. In this egregious system, former slaves had few rights and remained subject to the same punishments they had endured as slaves. In 1838, an Amendment to the Abolition of Slavery Act made it unlawful for female apprentices to be placed on a treadmill, in a penal gang, in chains, or to be punished by whipping, beating or cutting off her hair. It also forbade the whipping or beating of male slaves. Queen Victoria noted in her journal that 'I must just observe that the necessity of this Act shows how shockingly cruel and cheating the Masters are'.[49]

Political crises

On 24 Friday, May 1839, Victoria wrote in her journal that 'this day I go out of my teens and become 20!'[50] A sweet enough entry in her journal but her juvenile naivety was evident. At first, the young, attractive and vivacious queen had enchanted her loyal subjects. This changed dramatically in early 1839 when she became embroiled in two political scandals, one regarding the private life of a Tory lady-in-waiting, the other concerning her manipulation of government. An older, wiser queen might have avoided such injudicious scandals: they were the blunders of an immature, egocentric and opinionated girl.

The Queen's popularity plummeted when she became embroiled in the first of these episodes. It concerned Lady Flora Hastings, a single woman from an aristocratic and powerful Tory family and one of her mother's ladies-in-waiting. Lady Flora's stomach was seen to swell: Victoria and Lehzen had no doubt 'that she is – to use the plain words – <u>with child</u>!! . . . the horrid cause of all this is the Monster and demon Incarnate',[51] that is, the detested John Conroy. Interestingly, at a time in history when girls were kept in sexual ignorance, Victoria seemed very knowledgeable about pregnancy and its causes. She certainly appeared scandalised by a young, unmarried, aristocratic lady being pregnant and asked Melbourne to sort it out. Victoria's attitude towards Lady Flora suggests a young woman of strong moral rectitude but, in reality, it was more a malicious revenge against her mother and her mothers' ladies-in-waiting. Victoria loathed Flora Hastings and her Tory politics, regarding her as a spy of John Conroy. Indeed Queen Victoria never forgave Lady Flora for giving support to Conroy when he harassed the young Princess at Ramsgate.

Victoria's hasty accusations were shown to be false. When Lady Flora was eventually medically examined, it was found that she had advanced cancer of the liver. Soon the slanders experienced by Lady Flora filled the newspapers, especially after Flora's mother, Lady Hastings, published her letters to Melbourne. These letters showed the Queen in a distinctly unfavourable light. Queen Victoria was furious that the 'wicked old foolish woman Lady Hastings has had her whole correspondence with Lord Melbourne published in the Morning Post . . . I could have and would have wished to have hanged the Editor and the whole Hastings family for their infamy.'[52] She never blamed herself for the slanderous gossip. Lady Flora died on 5 July, a few months after the scandal first broke. Lytton Strachey observed that 'the tide of opinion turned violently against the queen and her advisers; high society was disgusted by all this washing of dirty linen in Buckingham Palace; the public at large was indignant at the ill-treatment of Lady Flora'.[53] The young queen's popularity began to evaporate; she was publicly insulted, hissed at during Royal Ascot and when she sent a representative to the funeral of Lady Flora, the carriage was stoned. The Queen 'used to ecstatic huzzas from

Parliament and the newspapers reacted violently against the unexpected hostility'.[54] Rather than stand back and reflect on the loss
of her popularity, the Queen attacked the Tories. The Tories, she
later told Prince Albert, 'really are very astonishing; as they cannot and dare not attack us in Parliament, they do everything that
they can to be personally rude to me'.[55] Once more, Queen
Victoria's partiality was disturbingly evident, leading Tories to
accuse her of acting as the queen of the Whigs, not as queen of
Britain. Certainly Victoria appeared to be too young and inexperienced to realise that she had brought the Crown into
disrepute.

Meanwhile, a second scandal began in May 1839 when Melbourne's majority was whittled down to five and he was forced
to resign. For Victoria, 'the state of agony, grief and despair into
which this placed me, may be easier imagined than described.
All, all my happiness gone! . . . I felt quite in despair and did
nothing but cry.'[56] In her view, Melbourne had the

> 'confidence of the Crown', God knows! No Minister, no
> friend, ever possessed it so unboundedly as this truly excellent
> Lord Melbourne possesses mine! But I am but a poor helpless
> girl, who clings to him for support and protection, – and the
> thought of all all my happiness being possibly at stake, so
> completely overcame me, that I burst into tears, and remained
> crying for some time.[57]

When the Queen insisted that she hated the Tories, Melbourne
tried to restrain such bigotry by telling Victoria that she 'should
have no dislikes, you should treat them all as a pack of cards'.[58]
The Queen valued her friendship with Melbourne, ignored the
political convention that monarchs should not fraternise with
former party leaders and invited him to dinner as usual, an invi-
tation Melbourne sensibly refused. He wrote to Victoria saying
that it would be unwise to 'dine with your Majesty . . . It would
create feeling, possibly lead to remonstrance, and throw a doubt
upon the fairness and integrity of your Majesty's conduct.'[59] Once
more, Queen Victoria disregarded his advice and continued to
write to Melbourne, thus imperilling her own position and that
of the Crown. Victoria needed to learn that a queen's personal

view of politics and politicians should be judiciously exercised or else kept well hidden.

Melbourne advised the Queen to send for the Duke of Wellington, a former Conservative prime minister and commander-in-chief of the army. When he arrived, Wellington refused office and so Robert Peel was summoned. Peel was very different from Victoria's previous experience of a charming, sophisticated and light-hearted prime minister: the young Queen thought Peel a cold, odd man and confided to Melbourne that 'I don't like his manner'.[60] Peel was in a difficult position for he was trying to form a government with a minority in the House of Commons and needed the support of his sovereign. His anxiety increased when he asked the Queen to replace some of her Whig ladies-in-waiting – in effect royal personal assistants – with those of a Tory persuasion to reflect the governing party and royal confidence in his ministry. Victoria – angry, upset, reckless, prejudiced, immature and politically inexperienced – refused. Melbourne was partly to blame. When Victoria ascended the throne, he had recommended a number of ladies-in-waiting, all of whom were related either to himself or to his Whig colleagues. The mistress of the robes and the ladies of the bedchamber were all Whigs.[61] Naturally, Victoria formed strong attachments to them and did not wish to replace them with other, inimical, political appointments. However, Peel did not wish to create 'the impression that the confidence of the Queen was bestowed on his enemies and not himself'.[62]

Queen Victoria, acting more like a young head-strong girl who had had her wish thwarted rather than a reigning monarch, complained to Melbourne. Peel, she claimed, 'has behaved very ill, he insisted on my giving up my Ladies, to which I replied that I never would consent, and I never saw a man so frightened . . . Keep yourself in readiness, for you may soon be wanted.'[63] The crisis lasted four days, encouraged by Melbourne who met regularly with the Queen and wrote to her daily. He recommended that she write to Peel saying 'the Queen having considered the proposal made to her yesterday by Sir Robert Peel to remove the Ladies of her Bedchamber, cannot consent to adopt a course which she conceives to be contrary to usage, and which is repugnant to her feelings'.[64] The Queen wrote exactly as suggested. She won the battle. Peel resigned and Melbourne returned for a further two years, still with a small majority and still leading a rather unstable government.

The Queen's behaviour over what was termed the 'bedchamber crisis' drew forth an enthusiastic burst of loyalty from the Whigs. The Whig papers denounced Peel, maintaining that

> the attempt of Sir Robert Peel to 'ride roughshod through the Queen's Palace' has roused a spirit in her MAJESTY which has blighted the full-blown hopes of the Tories. In her resistance to the unbecoming dictation of the Tory leader, QUEEN Victoria will have the cordial approbation and sympathy of her subjects, both male and female . . . To carry the political changes into the inner apartments of a female sovereign, to insist on the removal of her female attendants, her chosen friends, is nothing less than tyranny.[65]

In contrast, the Tories 'gnashed their teeth with rage'.[66] Traditionally, Tories were strong royalists, loyal to the monarch, but the young Queen tested their values severely. Lord Greville observed that 'among other bad signs of these times, one is the decay of loyalty in the Tory party'. They seemed 'not to care one straw for the Crown, its dignity, or its authority, because the head on which it is placed does not nod with benignity to them'.[67] Speeches against the Queen were common. According to Greville, 'the Tories, the professors and protectors of Conservative principles, the abhorrers of changes, who would not have so much as a finger laid upon the integrity of the Constitution, are ready to roll the Crown in the dirt, and trample it under their feet'.[68] The Times newspaper, generally strongly monarchist but also strongly Tory, complained that the female clique at the palace 'have done their Royal mistress such unmerited and almost irreparable mischief. Here, then, is an Administration about to attempt to resume office – the country against them; the House of Lords against them; not possessing the confidence of the house of Commons; but supported by a female "array" of petticoat influence at the Palace'.[69]

The damage to the Queen's reputation was severe. 'It is a high trial to our institutions' complained Greville, when the wishes of a 19-year-old queen could overturn a great ministry. The Whigs had resigned because they no longer enjoyed parliamentary support, yet they remained in office 'for the purpose of enabling the Queen to exercise her pleasure without any control or interference'.[70] The whole affair was seen as 'utterly anomalous and unprecedented and a course as dangerous as unconstitutional'.[71]

It may have seemed a victory for the Queen but it was to be the last time a British monarch was able to block the formation of a government. Victoria had won but at a cost to her popularity. The crisis lasted four days, days which cast a long shadow over the Queen and her government. The impropriety of continuing to deal with a previous government, combined with the Queen's obvious hostility to the incoming one was unsound practice. Victoria may have triumphed but her popularity had disappeared in a flash.

Palmerston and foreign policy: 1837–1841

Queen Victoria took a greater interest in foreign policy than in domestic, especially in matters affecting the interests of her extended family. Her first foreign secretary, the Whig politician Lord Palmerston (1784–1865), is remembered both for his robust foreign policy during a period when Britain was at its most powerful and for his disagreements with the Queen. This was not always the case. In the early years of her reign, Queen Victoria simply approved of whatever her foreign secretary recommended, often asking him for advice on how to compose official letters or even who to invite for state dinners. Encouraged by the rapport he enjoyed with his sovereign, Palmerston began to send off dispatches to foreign governments without seeking royal approval, a practice that in future years would cause increasing tensions between himself and his – by now less impressionable – young sovereign.

In Palmerston's view, the main aim of foreign policy was to safeguard the interests of Britain in the world, keep the balance of power in Europe, and advance the cause of constitutional monarchy whenever possible; in contrast, Queen Victoria grew to believe that foreign policy should help protect her royal relatives against revolutionary republicanism. Under Palmerston's aegis, Britain's imperialist expansion continued unabated: the first Anglo-Afghan war occurred between 1839 and 1842; Beirut and Acre were attacked; the British East India Company captured Aden; unrest in British Canada led to the establishment of the Province of Canada; and New Zealand was colonised; David Livingstone left for Africa and the construction of Nelson's column in Trafalgar Square was begun.

At first, relationships between Queen Victoria and Palmerston were cordial even though she disapproved of his character. Palmerston was well known as a notorious philanderer who had fathered several illegitimate children. During a visit to Windsor in 1839, he outraged the Queen by entering the bedroom of one of Victoria's ladies-in-waiting, locking the door behind him and placing furniture in front of the other. The lady in question jumped out of bed and called for help. Victoria never forgave Palmerston's sexual incontinence.

One of the first diplomatic incidents that the Queen and Palmerston faced was over the question of Belgium. Victoria, largely because of her relationship with her Uncle Leopold, was personally anxious about a crisis in Belgium, a country originally ruled by the Netherlands. In August 1830, the Belgians had risen up against their Dutch masters and declared their independence. A conference of major European powers, including Britain, France and Prussia, recognised Belgian independence, established the borders of the new state and decided on Leopold, Victoria's uncle, as Belgium's first monarch. The Dutch were unhappy about this and in August 1831 invaded Belgium, only to be repelled by the French army. Seven years later, in 1838, the newly created Belgium remained in danger of again being annexed by the Netherlands. Leopold asked his niece to put pressure on her ministers to protect Belgian interests; he had no scruples in using his kinship with Victoria to further the cause of his newly created kingdom. Queen Victoria found herself placed in a difficult situation, trying to balance family loyalty and national duty. Acting with due constitutional propriety, she showed Leopold's letters to Melbourne who drafted her response. 'My Ministers' she wrote to Leopold 'should, as far as it may not conflict with the interests or engagements of this country, do everything in their power to promote the prosperity and welfare of your Kingdom.'[72] Victoria couched her letters in diplomatic language, interspersing formality with affectionate phrases such as 'dear Uncle', and 'I love you tenderly'. At the same time, Victoria warned her uncle that in future she would not touch upon political matters in her letters, as she did not want to 'change our present delightful and familiar correspondence into a formal and stiff discussion upon political matters'.[73] Leopold had been warned. Nonetheless, Victoria put pressure on her government to protect Belgium. She told a senior royal naval officer, Lord Seymour,[74] who wanted to blockade Belgium that it 'would be so awkward for me to do; and that Uncle would never forgive me for it. Talked of the Inconvenience of Sovereigns being related.'[75]

In 1839, a Treaty of London, mainly instigated by Palmerston, settled the conflict when all the European powers, including the Netherlands, recognised Belgium as an independent country and guaranteed Belgian neutrality. In the early twentieth century, this treaty would have momentous significance, far greater than ever expected by those who signed it. In 1914 when the German army invaded Belgium, Britain declared war on Germany because it had violated Belgium neutrality. Germany was surprised. Its Chancellor Bethmann Hollweg could not understand why this 'mere scrap of paper' signed so long ago had precipitated Britain's entry into the Great War.

Queen Victoria and Palmerston were equally concerned about the Turkish Ottoman Empire but for different reasons. Victoria feared the breakdown of family relationships whereas Palmerston feared the breakup of that empire. The Ottoman Empire was a multinational, multireligious empire that ruled over much of southeast Europe, western Asia, the Middle East, Egypt and other parts of north Africa. It also controlled the Caucasus, which today consists of parts of Georgia, Azerbaijan, Armenia and Ossetia and parts of Russia. By the nineteenth century, the Ottoman Empire was in decline, weakened by internal dissension and demands for independence by the subjugated countries. The Russian tsar dubbed it the 'sick man of Europe'. In 1839, the Egyptians, led by Mehmet Ali, challenged Ottoman authority and war broke out between the two. The Egyptian army made very rapid progress and soon threatened the existence of the Ottoman Empire by invading Syria. Palmerston, fearing that the breakup of the

empire would threaten the whole region and lead to land grab-
bing by Russia and France, persuaded the great powers, that is,
France, Russia, Prussia and Austria, to sign a treaty pledging to
maintain the integrity of the Ottomans. However, when conflict
seemed likely, France refused to be involved in any coercive action
against Egypt. In the end, Palmerston excluded France from the
negotiations and signed a secret treaty with Austria, Russia and
Prussia guaranteeing hereditary rule in Egypt in return for its
withdrawal from the occupied countries. France was furious at
Britain's secret diplomacy and immediately threatened war while
Egypt, counting on France's support, refused to evacuate its
captured territories.

It was a complicated situation. Victoria's uncle Leopold was
married to a French princess, so the Queen was as much worried
about family ramifications as she was about the stability of the
Ottoman Empire. She became especially anxious when the British
and the other powers intervened with force, bombarded Beirut
and Acre and deposed the Egyptian Mehmet Ali. The French,
furious both at Britain's secret diplomacy and at Egypt's humiliation, became so belligerent that a European war seemed likely.
The French prime minister called up reserves, strengthened the
French fleet, fortified Paris and threatened war.[76] Victoria confessed
that she was 'in a great state of nervousness and alarm, on
account of Leopold; terrified at Palmerston's audacity, amazed at
his confidence, and trembling lest her uncle should be exposed
to all the dangers and difficulties in which he would be placed
by a war between his niece and his father-in-law', the King of
France.[77] The Queen urged a reluctant Palmerston to compromise
with the French 'for she hears constantly from Leopold, who is
mad with fright, and who imparts all his fears to her'.[78] In 1841,
the powers reached an agreement – the Convention of London –
and Mehmet Ali was re-instated. Nonetheless, the British and French
relationship remained strained. Victoria helped ease the tensions
by inviting the French ambassador, Guizot, to the Palace: she was
beginning to learn the art of diplomacy. Guizot was placed next
to the Queen at dinner, a significant honour, and Victoria used the
opportunity to tell him 'that I hoped he knew how much I had
"á cour" to see matters put right with France and that I hoped
he would do all in his power to bring this about'.[79] Fortunately,

possibly helped by the Queen's diplomacy, Britain and France renewed their friendship.

Queen Victoria was particularly interested in Canadian politics. Her late father, Prince Edward, had spent nearly ten years in Quebec as an officer in the British army. He had arrived in 1791 to witness the country divided into a British Upper and a French Lower Canada, each with its own governor, council and House of Representatives, but all ruled by Britain. In 1837, just as Victoria ascended the throne, both Upper and Lower Canada rebelled against the British colonial government: in Lower Canada, the rebellion was an expression of French Canadian nationalism against British rule; in Upper Canada, the rebellion was largely led by republicans of American heritage who objected to the oligarchic rule of the British. Strong measures were taken for the repression of the insurrection. 'This is joyous news indeed!' wrote the Queen in her journal when the insurrection was put down.[80] However, the underlying problem remained. Queen Victoria made it clear that she favoured a united Canada; in 1814 her father had proposed a similar scheme. In 1840, the Act of Union was passed and in 1841 the United Province of Canada came into being. Today in Canada, Queen Victoria is linked to the birth of the united nation. She is called the 'Mother of Confederation' and has more streets, parks and other places named after her than any other individual.

At this time, too, the Queen and Palmerston were dealing with the First Opium War (1839–42) between Britain and China, and largely because no relative was involved, Victoria was more dispassionate. In the early nineteenth century, the technologically advanced and militarily superior Britain forced China to trade on unequal terms. In return for selling silver, silk and other goods, the Chinese received opium as payment. Victoria knew about 'the danger of this opium-smoking which produces a delightful intoxication at first, and dreadful suffering afterwards'[81] but she never asked that the trade be stopped. The Chinese Emperor, exasperated by the trade imbalance and the fact that his people were becoming addicted to the drug, ordered the seizure of opium and forbade the trade. Victoria knew also that 'opium is prohibited to be imported into China . . . and our people smuggle it in, in quantities, which the people buy' yet again raised no objection.[82]

In order to settle the question, Palmerston sent warships to China, the Chinese were forced to accept the opium trade and Hong Kong came under British rule. Victoria's government had put another notch in its imperial belt.

Queen Victoria came to the throne full of youthful optimism, determined to be a monarch who would do her utmost for her country. A number of defining characteristics were beginning to take shape: throughout her life Victoria's responses would tend to be emotional rather than rational and would often be based on the perceived needs of friends and family rather than objective realities. In particular, Victoria's family relationships often shaped her views of European politics, which led to a partisanship that made disagreements with her ministers predictable. At first, the British cherished their young sovereign. The Queen's hard work, high moral standards and charming naivety were welcomed after the lifestyles of the two most recent sovereigns. However, the Queen soon learned that royal popularity can be ephemeral. The Queen's unreflective behaviour over the Flora Hastings affair and her role in the bedchamber crisis damaged her status, especially among Tories whose fealty to the monarchy was usually beyond doubt. Politically, the sovereign had a lot to learn.

Notes

1 *Caledonian Mercury*, July 1st 1837, p. 5.
2 Victoria to the Princess Royal, March 15th 1858, quoted in Fulford, *Dearest Child*, p. 76.
3 Strachey, *Queen Victoria*, p. 26.
4 Sir Sidney Lee, quoted in Frank Prochaska, *The Republic of Britain, 1760 to 2000*, 2000, Allen Lane, p. 65.
5 *Caledonian Mercury*, July 1st 1837, p. 5.
6 Greville, *Greville Memoirs*, June 29th, 1838.
7 RA VIC/MAIN/QVJ (W) June 28th 1838 (Princess Beatrice's copies).
8 RA VIC/MAIN/QVJ (W) 'Queen Victoria's Coronation' by Sir Roy Strong (essay).
9 *The London Dispatch and People's Political and Social Reformer*, July 1st 1838.
10 *Ipswich Journal*, Saturday April 14th 1838, p. 5.
11 Harriet Martineau, quoted in Sarah Tyler, *Life of Her Gracious Majesty*, Virtue & Co., 1901, p. 1488.
12 Greville, *Greville Memoirs*, June 29th 1838.
13 *The Morning Post*, June 29th 1838, p. 8.

14 Ibid.
15 *The Bristol Mercury*, June 30th 1838.
16 RA VIC/MAIN/QVJ (W), June 28th 1838.
17 *The Essex Standard, and Colchester, Chelmsford, Maldon, Harwich, and General County Advertiser*, June 23rd 1837, p. 5.
18 This laid down limits on the power of the Crown and set out the rights of parliament, including the requirement to hold regular elections.
19 This Act secured the Protestant succession by prohibiting Roman Catholics, or anyone who married a Catholic, from being crowned. It further limited the power of the monarch in respect to parliament and established judicial independence.
20 The 1832 Act extended the male franchise from about 366,000 to 650,000, eliminated rotten and pocket boroughs, created new constituencies (e.g. Manchester), and instituted voter registration.
21 Robert Blake, *The Prime Ministers*, George Allen and Unwin, 1975, p. 13.
22 RA VIC/MAIN/QVJ (W) September 6th 1844.
23 Ibid. June 24th 1837.
24 Ibid. July 1st 1837.
25 Ibid. June 27th 1837.
26 Ibid. July 19th 1837.
27 Ibid. July 2nd 1837.
28 Ibid. February 4th 1838.
29 Leopold to Victoria, June 7th 1837.
30 Ibid. June 15th 1837.
31 Ibid. June 27th 1837.
32 Ibid. June 30th 1837.
33 Victoria to Leopold June 25th 1837.
34 Greville, *Greville Memoirs*, August 30th 1837, p. 584.
35 RA VIC/MAIN/QVJ (W) December 26th 1837.
36 Ibid. May 20th 1838.
37 Ibid. May 23rd 1838.
38 Ibid. March 10th 1839.
39 Ibid. September 10th 1837.
40 Ibid. February 26th 1838.
41 Ibid. February 26th 1838.
42 Ibid. July 2nd 1837.
43 Greville, *Greville Memoirs*, September 12th 1838.
44 Ibid. December 15th 1838.
45 Ibid. August 15th 1839.
46 RA VIC/MAIN/QVJ (W) August 3rd 1839.
47 Ibid. December 9th 1839.
48 Ibid. August 20th 1838.
49 Ibid. March 13th 1838.
50 Ibid. May 24th 1839.
51 Ibid. February 2nd 1839.
52 Ibid. April 16th 1839.

53 Strachey, *Queen Victoria*, p. 40.
54 Rhodes James, *Albert, Prince Consort*, p. 72.
55 Victoria to Albert, January 21st 1840.
56 RA VIC/MAIN/QVJ (W) May 7th 1839.
57 Ibid. March 22nd 1839.
58 Ibid. March 22nd 1839.
59 Melbourne to Victoria, May 8th 1839.
60 Victoria to Melbourne, May 8th 1839.
61 The mistress of the robes is the senior lady of the royal household, responsible for the queen's clothes and jewelry and who attends the queen at all state ceremonies: they were all, and still are today, duchesses.
62 Woodham-Smith, *Queen Victoria*, p. 173.
63 RA VIC/MAIN/QVJ (W) May 9th 1839.
64 Melbourne to Victoria, May 10th 1839.
65 *The Leeds Mercury*, May 14th 1839.
66 *The Morning Chronicle*, May 18th 1839.
67 Greville, *Greville Memoirs*, September 5th 1839.
68 Ibid. November 8th 1839.
69 *The Times*, May 11th 1839, p. 4.
70 Greville, *Greville Memoirs*, May 12th 1839.
71 Ibid. May 12th 1839.
72 Victoria to Leopold, June 10th 1838.
73 Ibid. December 5th 1838.
74 In 1841, Seymour was appointed Third Naval Lord and in 1866 became Admiral of the Fleet.
75 RA VIC/MAIN/QVJ (W) February 1st 1839.
76 William L. Langer, *Political and Social Upheaval, 1832–1852*, Harper Torchbooks, 1969, p. 303.
77 Greville, *Greville Memoirs*, September 26th 1840.
78 Ibid. October 17th 1840.
79 RA VIC/MAIN/QVJ (W) October 22nd 1840.
80 Ibid. December 8th 1838.
81 Ibid. September 24th 1839.
82 Ibid. October 23rd 1839.

3   Leisure, love and family: 1837–1844

On Friday 28 April 1837, Queen Victoria attended the opening of the National Gallery, a museum that today houses some of the finest European painting. She enjoyed the 'exquisite Landseers, and many other fine ones which I shall enumerate when we go again'.[1] British art was flourishing: heroic paintings such as J. M. W. Turner's painting of HMS *Temeraire* (this ship had fought in the Battle of Trafalgar; in 2005 the painting was voted Britain's favourite) were later exhibited. Novels with a social purpose such as Charles Dickens's *Oliver Twist* and Disraeli's *Coninsby* were published, and poetry such as Elizabeth Barrett Browning's *Seraphim and Other Poems* and Tennyson's 'Morte D'Arthur' was printed. New leisure activities, now considered part of the British establishment, emerged: the London Hippodrome opened; the first Grand National run at Aintree and the Henley Regatta boat race began. Philanthropy increased: the Sisters of Mercy established the first Roman Catholic convent since the Reformation; England's first public park, the Derby Arboretum, was financed by a rich factory owner, Joseph Strutt, and Britain's first polytechnic opened in Regent Street. And fresh flavours were created: Lea and Perrin's English sauce was first made – in Worcester. The years between 1837 and 1844 also marked a time of notable British innovations. The railway and shipping age was launched and with it the age of mass communication: Euston Station opened and the new line from London to Birmingham ran its first train; the first transatlantic steam passenger ship made its maiden voyage; the world's first electric telegraph was sent and the world's first postage stamp was issued.

Amusing Victoria

Queen Victoria generally conformed to middle-class conventions: hosting dinners or visiting the theatre and opera. Lord Melbourne spent large parts of the day and most evenings with the Queen. This urbane, cultured and erudite man, used to attending some of the dazzling salons of the great Whig hostesses, must have been exceedingly bored. Evenings at the Palace were tedious by the entertainment standards of the day. It was traditional for men to withdraw to another room after dinner, smoke a few cigarettes and drink considerable amounts of alcohol but the young Queen would not allow her gentlemen – and particularly Melbourne – to remain in another room for long. Soon the court frowned on drunkenness and sober men became less fun. Etiquette was formal and stuffy. One guest, remarked that 'when we went into the drawing-room, and huddled about the door in the sort of half-shy, half-awkward way people do, the queen advanced to meet us, and spoke to everybody in succession. . . . Nobody expects from her any clever, amusing or interesting talk . . . The whole thing seemed to be dull.'[2] The Queen was perceived as natural, good-humoured and cheerful, but she was still Queen, 'and by her must the social habits and the tone of conversation be regulated, and for this she is too young and inexperienced. . . . such conversation as can be found . . . really is, very up-hill work'.[3] Guests did not, and still do not, initiate conversation with the Crown; they depend on the monarch to ask the right sort of questions, or introduce topics of interest. Victoria, still a teenager and unschooled in courtly manners, did not have the sophistication, the education or the skill to make the Palace a stimulating environment.

Instead, Victoria enjoyed playing games of German tactics, ecarte, draughts and chess. She boasted that 'after dinner I played two games of chess with Lord Conyngham and beat him both times, without any assistance of which I am very proud',[4] a typical youthful brag which suggests the dullness of court life. Queen Victoria loved to dance, yet etiquette forbade her to dance intimate or lively dances such as waltzes and gallops: men were forbidden to touch the royal waist. She was allowed to dance the quadrille if she danced with nobility. As with many young women, the young queen loved ballet, often commenting on performances in her journal. Victoria spoke of one dancer who 'did some wonderful things on her toes, and is certainly a fine dancer, but has no grace, and does pirouette so dreadfully; her gigantic sister flings those two long legs of hers dreadfully about'.[5] In January 1838, Victoria read Walter Scott's *Bride of Lammermoor*, a story based in the Lammermuir Hills of south-east Scotland which perhaps awakened Victoria's love for the country.

Royals have always patronised the arts: Victoria was to be no exception. She was a keen theatre-goer, and admired the actor Charles Kean's performances, believing that his Hamlet, a 'very difficult, and I may almost say incomprehensible character, is admirable; his delivery of all the fine long speeches quite beautiful; he is excessively graceful and all his actions and attitudes are good'.[6] She also thought his Richard III impressive:

> the House was crammed to the ceiling; and the applause was tremendous when Kean came on; he was unable to make himself heard for at least five minutes . . . It would be impossible for me to attempt to describe the <u>admirable</u> manner in which Kean delineated the ferocious and fiend-like Richard. It was quite a <u>triumph</u> . . . All the other parts were very badly acted, and the three women were <u>quite</u> <u>detestable</u>.[7]

Theatres were unheated and sometimes it was so cold that the Queen sat 'the whole time in my fur cloak'.[8] In 1848, the Queen made Charles Kean director of her private theatricals at Windsor Castle, further helping his career and that of theatres more generally. Certainly, royal patronage of the theatre helped shift its image as a shabby lower-class entertainment with a reputation for disorderly and disreputable behaviour. In the nineteenth century, theatre became respectable.

Victoria preferred opera to theatre, thinking it less taxing on the intellect. Her favourites were all Italian: operas by Bellini, Donizetti, Rossini, all composers with seemingly effortless gifts for sweet-toned melodies, repetitive rhythmic music and emotionally charged theatrical scenes. Their operatic characters were usually larger than life individuals whose inappropriate love affairs led them ineluctably to personal destruction. In Victoria's opinion, *Lucia di Lammermoor*, a melodramatic story about an emotionally fragile heroine thwarted in love, was 'decidedly one of Donizetti's best operas; it is full of the most beautiful and touching melodies'.[9] In 1837, her favourite opera singer was Giulia Grisi, a soprano whose dramatic gifts and exquisite voice entranced audiences. On a visit to Rossini's *Semiramide*, an opera set in Babylon and based on Voltaire's play, she wrote that 'no words of any kind can do justice to Grisi; both for her acting and singing were throughout splendid. No tragic actress of any kind could have acted, better, with more feeling, pathos, dignity, and spirit . . . I wish I could say the same of poor Albertazzi, who was as inanimate, tame and devoid of feeling as Grisi was splendid.'[10] Certainly, criticism was coruscating if Victoria disapproved. 'Ricci's Scarammuccia, the story of which is stupid and tiresome and the music mediocre . . . Belinni as Tomasco was very outré and vulgar.' Undoubtedly, the Queen's enthusiasm for music, as with the theatre, improved its standing in Britain, especially when over the period of her reign Victoria knighted 20 musicians.

Shortly after her succession to the throne, Victoria employed her own palace orchestra consisting of 16 wind instruments and a drum, a 'delicious treat' for her as she could hear it quietly and without fuss. Singers were invited to the Palace and the Queen regularly commented on their performances in her journals. She once wrote of how 'Poor Pasta' looked very old, and was very ill-dressed and sang out of tune; on her favourite little Grisi who had grown exceedingly fat, on M de Melcy who had beautiful small features, very fine dark eyes, dark hair, moustaches and whiskers.[11] The young Queen enjoyed singing arias from her favourite operas at home. From an early age she had had singing lessons with a music master and later on lessons from the Italian tenor Luigi Lablache when he visited London, sometimes singing the challenging aria 'Casta Diva' from Bellini's *Norma*, yet another melodrama about failed love. As with most upper-class young girls, Victoria knew how to play the piano and sing, but unlike many, she was a proficient pianist with a good voice.

Queen Victoria also patronised painters. She was a competent amateur artist, receiving lessons from the age of eight from the royal academician Richard Westall, and later from Edward Lear, William Leighton Leitch and Edwin Landseer. Her early lessons consisted of copying other drawings, but later on, she sketched people she knew and the surrounding landscape. This training in factual representation undoubtedly influenced her preferences for paintings that reflected a near photographic reality rather than ones which arose from the imagination. Her patronage of Edwin Landseer, 'an unassuming, pleasing and very young looking man, with fair hair',[12] made him a very rich man with his paintings selling for as much as £7,000. His first commissioned royal painting depicted the Queen on her favourite horse – a romantic, rather idealised portrait. Landseer went on to produce many other, similarly sentimental, portraits of the Queen, her family, favoured servants and her pets. The more innovative painters – such as the later Pre-Raphaelites or Impressionists – were never invited to paint the Queen: throughout her reign, she retained her preference for representational art.

Victoria enjoyed less serious pursuits too. She continued to be keen on horse riding, writing in her journal 'I mounted in the garden just under the terrace in order that nobody should know I was going to ride out. I rode my dear favourite Tartar who went perfectly and <u>most delightfully</u>, never shying, never starting through all the <u>very</u> noisy streets, rattling omnibuses – carts – carriages – &c., &c.'[13] On one occasion she cantered down Constitution Hill and St James' Park, along Pall Mall, up Regent Street and up to Hampstead, across the Heath and came home by the Paddington Canal.[14] Her mother disapproved of her daughter riding through the streets: these were public spaces and, by her actions, Victoria became too much of a public woman with all the negative associations that that represented. The Queen took no notice. On her accession to the throne, against the advice of her courtiers and politicians, she reviewed her troops on horseback, riding between two male officers. No ladies accompanied her. As Queen, Victoria felt comfortable to break the conventional codes that applied to other nineteenth-century females.

Victoria was partial to a bit of flamboyance and panache. She was entranced by Lion tamers and visited one show seven times, even commissioning Landseer to paint the animals. She spoke excitedly of seeing a lion and a lioness, a tiger and two cheetahs on stage and of how the lion tamer remained about a quarter of an hour with each animal who 'all seem actuated by the most awful fear of him; . . . he seems to handle them excessively roughly; beating them, and pinching them, and he puts his hands between their teeth . . . he takes them by their paws, throws them down, makes them roar'.[15] On one occasion Victoria asked to go inside the lion cage but her courtiers persuaded her otherwise.

All too often, civic duties took precedence. On 9 November 1837, Victoria attended the Mayor's dinner. Throughout her progress to the city, she

> met with the <u>most</u> <u>gratifying, affectionate, hearty</u> and <u>brilliant</u> reception . . . the streets being <u>immensely crowded</u> as were also the windows, houses, churches, balconies, every-where . . . I cannot say <u>how</u> gratified, and <u>how</u> <u>touched</u> I am by the very <u>brilliant, affectionate, cordial,</u> <u>enthusiastic</u> and <u>unanimous</u> reception I met with in this the <u>greatest</u> Metrop-olis in the <u>World</u>; there was not a discontented look, not a sign of displeasure, – all loyalty, affection and loud greeting from the immense multitude I passed through; and no disorder whatever. I feel <u>deeply grateful</u> for this display of affection and unfeigned loyalty and <u>attachment</u> from my good people. It is much more than I deserve, and I shall do my utmost to render myself worthy of all this love and affection.[16]

The most important ceremonial ritual of the Queen was the opening of parliament. On her first State opening, the 'bustle and excitement that prevailed in the neighbourhood was great' as crowds lined the route from Buckingham Palace to the House of Lords all keen to catch a glimpse of the state carriage with the young Queen inside. The Queen, according to the *Blackburn Standard*, was cheered 'during the whole of her progress to the House. From the tops of houses, from the windows and balconies in Pall-Mall, her Majesty was saluted as she passed along, with waving of handkerchiefs, flags and banners'.[17] Dressed in a 'splen-did white robe' with the riband of the Garter across her shoulder and sparkling with diamonds, Queen Victoria arrived at the House of Lords. All the seats were filled. The Queen read the Speech 'in an audible and most distinct manner',[18] a difficult feat with so many hundreds of peers, peeresses, MPs and visitors straining to hear. She was delighted when she heard that 'people were pleased to say I read well . . . Good, kind Lord Melbourne was quite touched to tears.'[19] The first real test for the young sovereign had been accomplished with sufficient pomp and splendour to keep her subjects contented.

Victoria and Albert

The young Queen knew it was her duty to marry and have children since the Crown would never be stable without a successor. The court, the country and parliament were all desperate for an heir because if Victoria died childless, her notoriously scandalous Uncle Ernest, the Duke of Cumberland, would succeed. Rumours even circulated that he had murdered his valet and fathered a son by his sister. Victoria insisted that her husband be someone she loved, rather than a diplomatic choice imposed on her by the needs of the country. At the time, it was inconceivable for the Queen to marry someone from the British nobility, as he would be a subject, not an equal. It would have to be a foreign prince: Albert seemed the best choice.

When she first became Queen, Victoria was in no rush to marry. King Leopold's great wish was that she should wed Prince Albert but the Queen relished her new-found independence. When Victoria discussed the various eligible princes with Melbourne, she insisted that 'not one, for one reason or another, would do . . . I dread the thought of marrying, being so accustomed to having my own way.'[20] She was also having fun. Her Uncle Leopold suggested that Albert visit again – with obvious intentions – prompting Victoria to reply that her uncle must understand that there was no engagement between them. Most of German royalty wanted a match between Victoria and Albert; indeed, Albert was trained from childhood to be the husband of the heiress presumptive to the throne of England. It was not an arranged marriage in the conventional sense, yet it was a family match. Prince Albert was Victoria's cousin and the family, especially the Duchess of Kent and King Leopold, all longed for it. Nevertheless, unlike most girls who had to wait to be asked for their hand in marriage, it was Prince Albert rather than Queen Victoria who had to do the waiting. The gender roles were reversed: in 1839, the Prince, worried about his marital prospects, told his Uncle Leopold that his life would be impossible if the Queen did not wish to marry him for he would be too old to begin a new career and all the other available princesses would have already married. But he had to wait. Victoria – royal prerogative demanded it – had to ask for Albert's hand in marriage, something she later said made her more nervous than speaking at her Privy Council.

Before Albert visited England to meet the Queen, and perhaps expect a proposal, Victoria wrote to her Uncle Leopold asking him to 'consult Stockmar with respect to the finishing of Albert's education; he knows best my feelings and wishes on that subject'.[21] Victoria arranged for the faithful Stockmar to accompany Albert to Italy, asking him to send his thoughts about the Prince's personality, character and development. Stockmar, in effect, was vetting him for a future role as consort to the Queen of England.

When Victoria saw Albert, all her doubts about marriage evaporated. She fell in love. She confided to her journal that it was 'with some emotion that I beheld Albert – who is beautiful'. She spoke to Melbourne about Albert's 'fine figure', and that her 'heart is quite going'.[22] Melbourne was the first to be told that Victoria had made up her mind to marry Albert, whom she now adored. She asked Melbourne 'if I hadn't better tell Albert of my decision soon, in which Lord M agreed; how? I asked, for that on general such things were done the other way – which made Lord M and me laugh very much.'[23] Eventually Victoria sent for Albert and after a few minutes Victoria said 'it would make me too happy if he would consent to what I wished (to marry me); we embraced each other over and over again'.[24]

The arrangement was kept secret until the council was summoned to declare the Queen's marriage. About 80 privy councillors were present when the 'Queen came in, attired in a plain morning-gown, but wearing a bracelet containing Prince Albert's picture. She read the declaration in a clear, sonorous, sweet-toned voice, but her hands trembled so excessively that I wonder she was able to read the paper which she held.'[25] One courtier confided that he 'cannot describe with what a mixture of self-possession and feminine delicacy she read the paper. Her voice, which is naturally beautiful, was clear and untroubled; and her eye was bright and calm, neither bold nor downcast, but firm and soft.'[26] The Duchess of Gloucester asked the Queen whether she was nervous in making the declaration, to which the Queen replied, 'Yes; but I did a much more nervous thing a little while ago . . . I proposed to Prince Albert.'[27]

Not all of the Queen's subjects approved of Albert as a husband since they disliked the idea of the younger son of a dissolute and penniless German prince being provided with an income by the British people. One popular song spoke of how Albert 'comes to take, for better or for worse, England's fat Queen and England's fatter purse'. The British parliament had a great many members for whom the bedchamber crisis and the Hastings affair still rankled. All of them remembered the misplaced generosity provided to Prince Leopold, and refused to give Albert a peerage, a rank in the army or a generous allowance. Melbourne, who had proposed an annuity of £50,000, had to accept parliament decreasing it to £30,000, a humiliation for the Queen and her prospective husband.

The Queen's obstinacy, and perhaps Melbourne's dominance over her, can be seen in the way Victoria treated Albert before marriage. She insisted that she choose Albert's advisors, appointing his private secretary against his wishes and stipulating that his household consist of Whigs. Victoria even chose Albert's doctor. Undoubtedly, she was selfish and stubborn over the choice of Albert's advisors – Albert wrote to her pleading that he be allowed to choose his own gentlemen of the household for two main reasons. First, he expressed concern about the political persuasions of Victoria's choice, as he believed that the Crown should be above party politics and therefore he needed to choose his staff from an equal measure of Whigs and Tories. Second, he pleaded:

> I am leaving my home with all its associations, all my bosom friends, and going to a country in which everything is new and strange to me – men, language, customs, modes of life, position. Except yourself I have no one to confide in. And is it not even to be conceded to me that the two or three persons who are to have the charge of my private affairs should be persons who already command my confidence?[28]

Victoria obstinately and unsympathetically refused; Albert was forced to submit.

Marrying Albert

The morning of Monday 10 February 1840 had only just dawned when the flags were hoisted and the bells of all the main churches rang out over London. By 6am, despite heavy rain, the Mall and the space outside Buckingham Palace were full of people hoping to catch a glimpse of the royal wedding.[29] Meanwhile, Queen Victoria was looking forward to being married, commenting in her journal that this was the 'last time I slept alone'.[30] She had, some thought, showed a lack of decorum by inviting Albert to stay at the Palace the night before the wedding. But Victoria had been brought up by Germans and had no time for English superstitions. She even met 'precious Albert for the last time alone, as my Bridegroom' on the morning of their wedding. Her ladies-in-waiting helped put on her wedding outfit, a gown of white satin with a deep train of Honiton lace, a diamond necklace and earrings and a sapphire brooch given to her by Albert; the Prince wore a field-marshal's uniform with large rosettes of white satin on his shoulders.

On her wedding day, the 20-year-old Victoria wanted to be treated as a wife and bride not a queen. The wedding vows made in the Chapel Royal, St James's Palace, had the same phrasing as the humblest of her subjects: Victoria promised to 'love, honour and obey'. She could, but chose not to, omit the word 'obey': the Queen considered men were meant to rule, women to submit. Yet, apart from this phrasing, Victoria shared little else with other women, for once they were married her female subjects lost their legal status. The law stipulated that husband and wife were one, and that the 'one' was the husband. Women were considered to be the property of their husband who also owned the home and everything within it, all their earnings, their belongings, clothes, stocks, shares and money. Husbands could dispose of this wealth as they thought fit. Moreover, wives could not sue, sign contracts, run a business or make a will without the permission of their husbands. Victoria, unlike the rest of women in nineteenth-century Britain, did not take the name of her husband, nor did she give him her property. She was queen and all other legal formalities were subservient to the constitutional prerogatives of that role.[31]

Victoria and Albert's wedding was a demonstration of love and respectability. This was not always the case with royal weddings. In 1795, the Prince of Wales, later to be King George IV, was blind drunk at his wedding to Caroline and spent the first night of his honeymoon lying on the floor in an alcoholic stupor. Victoria and Albert's wedding marked a new royal propriety. The ceremony was a spectacle that inaugurated an unsullied custom of royal ritual and symbolism as the young and morally upright Victoria and Albert processed to and from Buckingham Palace for all the thousands of crowds who came to glimpse the obviously happy bride and groom. It was, Eric Hobsbawm observes, the invention of tradition.[32] In a rare outpouring of British emotion, the country celebrated: London theatres put on free plays, treats were given to children of every parish, and workhouse inhabitants received better meals than usual. In the evening, London was illuminated with crowns, stars or the initials V. A.; in Leicester Square, a very large and handsome crown was brightly lit up by gas. At the palace, the couple presided over their wedding breakfast that included a wedding cake nine feet wide and sixteen inches high. It was the wedding of the century with the British demonstrating a new taste for pageantry and the magic of a royal wedding. This event, as with the coronation, strengthened the idea of a ceremonial monarchy with its public parade of regal colours, its procession of crowns and coronets, its display of flags, its gun salutes, its national celebrations, rather than a monarchy with any real ruling power. A new age of a theatrical monarchy began with the Queen and Albert playing their parts: they were the stars in a royal performance. The two represented what David Cannadine calls the symbolic affirmation of national greatness.[33]

Married life

Victoria and the Victorians used to be synonymous with sexual repression: the phrase that Victoria and women more generally were expected to 'lie back and think of England' is a well-worn cliché. Women were thought to have little sexual appetite. A leading physician, William Acton, claimed that as a general rule, 'a modest woman seldom desires any sexual gratification for herself. She submits to her husband's embraces, but principally to gratify him; and, were it not for the desire of maternity, would far rather be relieved from his attentions.'[34] Sexual desire in women, Acton believed, was a sign of nymphomania or of a tendency towards prostitution. This interpretation held sway until historians challenged the myth, and with it the notion of Victoria being non-sexual. For the eroticism between Victoria and Albert was unmistakeable. The newly wedded wife wrote in her journal that 'we both went to bed; (of course in one bed) to lie by his side, and in his arms, and on his dear bosom, and be called by names of tenderness, I have never heard used to me before – was bliss beyond belief! Oh! This was the happiest day in my life.'[35] A joy-fully sensuous Victoria recorded the first few days of her married life. 'When day dawned (for we did not sleep much)' she wrote 'and I beheld that beautiful angelic face by my side, it was more than I can express! He does look so beautiful in his shirt only.'[36] When she found Albert asleep on the sofa, she 'woke him with a kiss. He took me in his arms (in bed) and kissed me again and again, and we fell asleep arm in arm, and woke so again.'[37] The next day, her 'dearest Albert put on my stockings for me. I went in and saw him shave.'[38] The two may have been mutually incom-patible in personality – Victoria was a bubbly, extroverted, emo-tional and fun-loving night owl whereas Albert was an introverted, cerebral lark – but their strong mutual physical attraction and active sex life kept them close. The couple bought a lot of erotic art: on Albert's thirty-first birthday, Victoria gave him a markedly sensual painting of voluptuous naked women bathing in a stream.[39] It was hung opposite their writing desks in the Queen's sitting room at Osborne House. When advised after the birth of her last child, Beatrice, that she should have no more children, Victoria is reputed to have said, 'Oh Doctor, can I have no more fun in bed?'

Unfortunately, there were three people in the marriage: Queen Victoria, Prince Albert – and Baroness Lehzen. From the outset, relations between Albert and Lehzen were frosty, not helped by the latter's continuing attempts to take Victoria's side in any marital argument and thus inadvertently undermining the Royal Prince. Albert, not wishing to confront two challenging females on a daily basis, wanted to weaken, and ultimately end, the close and mutually supportive relationship the two women enjoyed. His plan was to dismiss 'the old hag'. He regarded her as too powerful a figure, responsible for the breach between Victoria and her mother. The Queen, whose self-esteem was regularly boosted by Lehzen's unconditional love, defended her beloved governess from Albert's criticisms and heated arguments regularly broke out between the married couple. The first time Victoria and Lehzen separated, the Queen confided to her journal that she was 'feeling a little low, at my 1st real separation from my dear Lehzen, which, since my 5th year, has never occurred before'.[40] Eventually, in July 1842 Victoria conceded defeat and agreed that Lehzen could retire to Hanover with a hefty pension. Albert

> told me he had seen Lehzen, who had expressed the wish to go to Germany in 2 months time. . . . Naturally I was rather upset, though I feel sure it is for our and her best. . . . I went to see my dear good Lehzen and found her very cheerful, saying she felt it was necessary for her health to go away. Felt rather bewildered and low, at what had taken place, and naturally the thought of the coming separation from my dear Lehzen, whom I love so much, made me feel very sad.[41]

Victoria, who had nobody else to confide in, would be isolated and forced to rely solely on Albert for her emotional and psychological health. Albert was delighted. He had removed the one woman who might have seriously limited his power over his wife.

Queen Victoria adored her husband. The tenderness of their relationship can be seen in the following excerpt from her journal:

> It was as hot as in the middle of July, with a light blue sky and not a cloud to be seen, – the half moon, clear and white, – in the distance, and all colouring so soft. I never saw Windsor in greater beauty, or more lovely and peaceful, in the evening hour, – everything so fresh green, and everything out, or coming out, – the lilacs in full bloom and fragrance. Albert picked me some.[42]

However, outside the Palace and the intimate domestic circle, Albert was not liked. He was seen to be 'cold and distant in manner' and too characteristically German for British tastes.

Victoria, Albert and children

Once safely wed, Victoria needed to produce an heir to the British throne. There was great rejoicing when Queen Victoria and Prince Albert's first child, Victoria (Vicky), was born nine months after the wedding on 21 November 1840. The couple were fecund. Early the following year, the Queen was pregnant again and on 9 November 1841 Albert Edward (Bertie), the Prince of Wales, heir to the throne, was born. Seven others – Alice (1843), Alfred (1844), Helena (1846), Louise (1848), Arthur (1850), Leopold (1853) and Beatrice (1857) – followed. For 18 years between the ages of 20 and 38, Victoria was generally either pregnant or recovering from giving birth. In this sense, the Queen shared the experience of most married women. Over 40 per cent of married women had at least seven babies and a particularly fertile 15 per cent had ten or more. The average wife was either pregnant or breastfeeding for a lot of the time between marriage and the menopause. There was no maternity leave for a monarch and Victoria, as with the rest of her female subjects who were in paid employment, was expected to keep working. Planning a pregnancy was not an option. At the time of her marriage, birth control literature was illegal and the technology of birth control in its infancy: the condom, which, until the vulcanisation of rubber in the 1840s, was made from animal intestines on the sausage-skin principle, was the only contraceptive device available. Condoms, however, were used with prostitutes as a prophylactic against venereal disease; therefore married women like Queen Victoria were not only reluctant to use them themselves but also saw them as encouraging immorality in others. As late as 1877, Annie Besant and Charles Bradlaugh horrified the Queen by publishing a pamphlet on birth control. Of course she may have thought differently if Albert had still been alive.

The Queen, a number of historians claim, hated being pregnant, suffered from post-natal depression, found breastfeeding abhorrent, thought newborn babies unattractive, was a poor mother and left household affairs to Albert. Certainly, it is safe to say that Victoria did not conform to the idealised version of a married woman: happy to be pregnant, happy to breastfeed and happy to be a mother. Indeed, Queen Victoria was despondent when she became pregnant one month after her marriage. Her later letters to her eldest daughter warned her of the lot of a married woman, telling her of the 'enjoyments to give up . . . constant precautions to take' and telling Vicky that she herself had to 'put up' nine times, which tried her sorely.[43] She called pregnancy the 'shadow side' of marriage and disliked the fact that it interrupted her sex life. 'What made me so miserable' she confided 'was to have the two first years of my married life utterly spoilt by this occupation.'[44] When her eldest daughter became pregnant, she told her that 'what you say of the pride of giving life to an immortal soul is very fine, dear, but I own I cannot enter into that; I think much more of our being like a cow or a dog at such moments; when our poor nature becomes so very animal and unecstatic'.[45] In Victoria's opinion, women who were always 'enceinte' were quite disgusting: they were more like rabbits or guinea-pigs than anything else. Children, she believed, should come at a leisurely pace, otherwise life was wretched, as one became so 'worn out and one's nerves so miserable . . . it is very bad for any person to have them very fast'.[46] The belief that Victoria disliked babies was largely because of the letters she wrote – much later – to her eldest daughter. However, in her journals, Victoria described her babies with as much love and admiration as the most doting mother.

In childbirth Victoria suffered similar indignities, pain and exhaustion as the rest of her female subjects. Victoria feared childbirth, a reasonable anxiety, since childbirth was dangerous. Women going into labour faced a one in five chance of survival. Maternal mortality was even high in fit young women who had been well before pregnancy – the previous heir to the throne, the young healthy Princess Charlotte, had died in childbirth after a 50-hour labour, the birth of a stillborn son and severe haemorrhaging – a fact of which Queen Victoria was well aware. Puerperal or childbed fever, an infection of the uterus following childbirth, was the most common cause of death. (Women are prone to infection directly after giving birth because the placenta leaves a large wound in the uterus, which takes about a month to heal.) High standards of hygiene were essential to prevent this occurring but unfortunately precautions were rarely taken. Doctors were often the major sources of puerperal fever because they were carriers of infection. The historian of sexuality, Angus McLaren, noted that the doctor could and did carry to the woman in labour 'laudable pus from his surgical cases, droplets from scarlet fever cases and putrefaction from the corpses he dissected'.[47] The Hungarian obstetrician Semmelweiss blamed doctors for carrying puerperal fever from patient to patient but the rest of the medical profession vilified his ideas. Germs, they believed, were air-borne. When Semmelweiss suggested that doctors scrub their hands with carbolic soap before examining patients, his advice was ridiculed. Sadly, childbirth remained a life-threatening experience for women until the development of blood transfusions after the First World War and penicillin after the Second.

In the nineteenth century, most women gave birth at home where they were cared for by doctors or midwives, family and neighbours. All the Queen's children were born at home and delivered by doctors but, unlike other women, she also had to suffer the indignity of high-ranking courtiers and officials listening to her groans when she was in labour. This was because official witnesses always attended royal births to make sure that the newborn baby was alive, well and not substituted by another. The Queen disagreed with this convention, objected to the number of people generally present to witness a royal birth and only allowed her doctor, a nurse and Albert to be in the room with her. For the birth of her eldest child, Vicky, the cabinet ministers, the Archbishop of Canterbury, the Bishop of London and the Lord Steward of the Household, Lord Erroll[48] all stayed in the next room 'with the door open so that Lord Erroll said he could see the Queen plainly and hear what she said'.[49] Queen Victoria's home may have been palatial with the best doctors looking after her but her experiences mirrored that of her subjects. In addition, Victoria suffered from being so short – she was only 4'11" – and must have experienced more discomfort than taller women. Just before the early hours of the morning of 21 November 1840, the Queen noted that:

> I felt very uncomfortable and with difficulty aroused Albert from his sleep . . . by 4, I got very bad and both the Doctors arrived. . . . After a good many hours suffering, a perfect

little child was born at 2 in the afternoon, but alas! a girl and not a boy, as we both had so hoped and wished for. We were, I am afraid, sadly disappointed.[50]

Fortunately, both mother and baby survived, Doctor Locock was paid £1,000 and the newly washed baby brought out for the inspection of the government.

Victoria suffered in one way or another with seven of her nine childbirths. On 25 April 1843, 'after getting hardly any sleep',[51] her third baby was born. And like most parents, the couple 'discussed what names the new little girl should have, and we nearly settled they should be: Alice, Maud and perhaps Mary'. She pronounced Alice 'an extremely pretty little thing and decidedly larger than the other 2 at that age; she already takes notice and smiles'.[52] As with most mothers, even after 'severe suffering', Victoria's joy at giving birth to her fourth child, Alfred (known as Affie), made her 'forget all I had gone through: It was such a happiness to us both.'[53]

By the time of her eighth child, Leopold, Victoria decided to diminish the pain of childbirth by using chloroform. It was a controversial decision: some religious leaders criticised its use because it interfered with God's natural order. It was believed that pain was a natural consequence of giving birth and should be endured. The Queen did not agree. She employed Dr Snow to administer 'that "blessed Chloroform" and the effect was soothing, quieting and delightful beyond measure'.[54]

Doctors, fearing the Queen's mental as well as physical health, advised Victoria not to have any more children; the Queen too felt sure that if she had another child she would sink under the trauma of it all. Yet, at 2 o'clock on 14 April 1857, Victoria, wearing the same shift she had worn in previous confinements, gave birth to her ninth and last child, again with the help of chloroform, after a 'very long wearisome' labour.[55] She thanked God for granting her 'such a dear, pretty girl, which I so much wished for'. Beatrice Victoria Feodore, as she was called, was a 'pretty, plump, flourishing child' who 'delights everyone, and is the greatest pet, so fond of her dear Papa, and so good with me, so soft and delicious to kiss. . . . She is really a <u>blessed</u> little thing, as her name means!'[56]

Giving birth to a healthy baby ought to result in euphoria but 10–15 women out of 100 suffer from post-natal depression, a recognised illness which makes women feel low, unhappy, exhausted and tearful rather than ecstatic. After the birth of her first son, Albert Edward (Bertie), the Queen felt 'rather weak and depressed'[57] and historians agree that the Queen was probably suffering from post-natal depression. In 1843, a month after the birth of Alice, Victoria was still feeling 'very tired, and feeling stupidly weak. It is too annoying.'[58] She 'felt rather limp and depressed'.[59] At the end of May, Victoria still felt fragile but believed that her 'nerves are daily getting stronger'[60] and continued to read and respond to government memorandums. After the birth of her last child, Beatrice, Victoria noted in her journal that she 'felt better and stronger this time than I have ever done before'.[61]

Victoria did not breastfeed her children. The idea of giving over her body to breastfeeding was anathema to her – her breasts, historians have argued, were sexual rather than maternal and for Albert's pleasure and her own, rather than for supplying food for a baby.[62] This may be a modern interpretation but it is safe to say that Victoria preferred to be a wife rather than a mother. She disliked the thought of her body being held captive to biology, so she employed a wet nurse to feed her babies. By this time the practice of wet nursing by the elite had fallen out of favour but the Queen revived it. Ideally, a wet nurse was a young strong healthy married woman with an upright moral character who lived in the countryside. In practice, the English wet nurse of the period was usually a city dwelling poverty stricken single mother whose own baby had either died or been taken into care. For her first baby, the Queen, by nature of her position, employed 'a fine young woman, wife of a sail maker at Cowes, Isle of Wight'.[63] This was a woman who ticked all the requisite boxes for a wet nurse: married, healthy, young and living in the countryside. The baby thrived. But not all wet nurses suited. Victoria appointed a 'strong healthy Highland woman' as Leopold's wet nurse but 'after weeks of sleeplessness and crying' the wet nurse was changed. Some were even more inappropriate. In June 1854, Bertie's former wet nurse murdered her six children. The news quite haunted the Queen, who saw her as 'a most depraved woman. Morose, ill tempered and stupid she always used to be, when in our house!'[64]

In Christian tradition women were 'churched' after the birth of a child. Feminists in the twentieth century criticised 'churching' as an expression of the Church's misogyny in that women who had just given birth were thought of as impure and needed to be cleansed by a religious rite specified for the purpose. However, this interpretation has been revised. Recently historians have argued that rather than despising the idea of 'churching', it should be seen as a celebration and thanksgiving, a ceremony which acknowledged the difficulties of giving birth and the perils attending it.[65] Victoria was 'churched' after the birth of each of her children, giving thanks for her survival and that of her babies. Indeed, the Queen considered the ceremony as a necessary religious rite, speaking of how she 'was dressed all in white and had my wedding veil on, as a shawl. . . . I look upon it as a holy charm, as it was under *that veil* our union was blessed for ever.'[66]

Naturally, each child was christened. Vicky, the Princess Royal, was dressed in a Honiton lace christening gown specially commissioned by the adoring parents: each successive child would wear the same gown. Generations of royal babies wore it too until the gown became too fragile to use and a replica was made. Today this replica is sometimes on display at Buckingham Palace. At the christening of her third child, Alice,

> Albert had so much to do, as always on occasions of any ceremony and all was bustle and excitement. The ceremony is indeed a holy and most important one, – an 'outward and visible sign of an inward and spiritual grace' and may God bless our dear little Child. . . . Wore my Tiara of Turkish diamonds and Albert's beautiful sapphire brooch, a dress of white watered silk, with my wedding flowers . . . We took up our places, near the altar . . . The Service began with saying of dearest Albert's Chorale, set to English words which was beautiful.[67]

But when the time for the actual baptism came, all was confusion, just as it had been with the coronation. The baby was handed to the Archbishop who was so confused that he was about to baptise her without any name until the Bishop of London intervened and whispered the names to him. The Archbishop, Victoria recalled, was also 'going to forget to sign the cross on the forehead, when the Bishop again reminded him . . . Another clerical misfortune arose, when the leaves of the Prayer Book stuck together, neither the Archbishop or Bishop being able to turn them over, and there was a dead stop! The good little Baby was fast asleep and never moved.'[68] The two older children, Vicky and Bertie, were present. Queen Victoria thought they looked so pretty, all in white. They behaved so

> very well, and we felt quite proud of them. It was a great trial for the poor little things to be stared at such by such a number of people, and they clung to us for support, but did not cry. Albert led them round. Little 'Puss' was very serious, but she has such a gentle little manner, when she is shy, and she was much admired.[69]

Just over a year later, when Alfred (Affie) was christened, the pride that Victoria took in her children was evident:

> How thankful do I feel to be so well, exactly a month after I was confined. . . . I was full of agitation at the approaching ceremony. – at ½ past 5, I began to dress; I wore a white satin dress trimmed with flowers of the wedding lace, in short, just as I wore it on my dear wedding day, now only 4 and ½ years ago, and I reappear in it for the Christening of our 4th Child![70]

Victoria thought her 'dear Chicks' looked very sweet, the two little girls dressed in white satin with lace, and Bertie, 'looking very handsome too in a white "efingle" velvet blouse, with silver braid, white trousers, trimmed with lace and satin shoes'. As a mother, the Queen naturally believed that her children were

> universally admired and we were very proud of them. . . . The Children behaved quite admirably, never once opening their lips the whole time. . . . The Baby looked magnificent, in the same robe and cap worn successively by his sisters and

brother at their Christenings, and more like 3 months old, than 1 month. . . . The 2 eldest remained till ½ past 9, enjoying everything. Bertie asked the Archbishop, pointing to his wig: 'What's that you got on?' and said to me 'You are Queen; got a Crown on.'[71]

Buoyed up by her governess Baroness Lehzen, Victoria was initially the dominant figure in the marriage but gradually, and almost imperceptibly, Albert gained more control, directing the upbringing of their ever-increasing family, acting as her private secretary and even her political advisor. Victoria, at first, held tightly on to her monarchical power. Perhaps fearing marital discord, she refused to allow Albert access to state papers, would not allow him in the room when she was talking to Melbourne and avoided discussing politics with him. Gradually, encouraged by Melbourne, the Queen confided in Albert, he was given the keys to the state boxes, read despatches, attended ministerial meetings and discussed politics. Soon, after Victoria became a mother and especially when Robert Peel became prime minister, Albert's authority and domination expanded.

Notes

1 RA VIC/MAIN/QVJ (W) April 28th 1837.
2 Greville, *Greville Memoirs*, March 11th 1838.
3 Ibid. December 15th 1838.
4 RA VIC/MAIN/QVJ (W) March 20th 1838.
5 Ibid. June 19th 1838.
6 Ibid. January 26th 1838.
7 Ibid. February 5th 1838.
8 Ibid. March 9th 1838.
9 Ibid. April 5th 1838.
10 Ibid. August 8th 1837.
11 Ibid. July 28th 1837.
12 Ibid. November 24th 1837.
13 Ibid. March 7th 1838.
14 Ibid. March 12th 1838.
15 Ibid. January 10th 1839.
16 Ibid. November 9th 1837.
17 *Blackburn Standard*, November 22nd 1837, p. 5.
18 *Caledonian Mercury*, November 23rd, 1837.
19 RA VIC/MAIN/QVJ (W) November 20th 1837.

20 Ibid. April 18th 1839.
21 Victoria to Leopold, April 4th 1838.
22 RA VIC/MAIN/QVJ (W) October 11th 1839.
23 Ibid. October 14th 1839.
24 Ibid. October 15th 1839.
25 Greville, *Greville Memoirs*, November 23rd 1839.
26 J.W. Croker to Lady Hardwicke, November 24th 1839.
27 Greville, *Greville Memoirs*, November 26th 1839.
28 Quoted in Woodham-Smith, *Queen Victoria*, p. 200.
29 *The Morning Post*, February 11th 1840, p. 1.
30 RA VIC/MAIN/QVJ (W) February 10th 1840.
31 See Thompson, *Queen Victoria: Gender and Power*, for an in-depth discussion of this.
32 Eric Hobsbawm and Terence Ranger, *The Invention of Tradition*, Cambridge University Press, 1983.
33 See David Cannadine, 'The British Monarchy, 1820–1977', in Hobsbawm and Ranger, *The Invention of Tradition*, pp. 101–64 for a stimulating discussion on the role of monarchy.
34 William Acton, *The Functions and Disorders of the Reproductive Organs in Childhood, Youth, Adult Age, and Advanced Life*, Churchill, 1862, p. 102.
35 RA VIC/MAIN/QVJ (W) February 10th 1840.
36 Ibid. February 11th 1840.
37 Ibid. February 12th 1840.
38 Ibid. February 13th 1840.
39 This was *Florinda* by F.X. Winterhalter, 1852.
40 RA VIC/MAIN/QVJ (W) June 14th 1841.
41 Ibid. July 25th 1842.
42 Ibid. May 1st 1841.
43 Victoria to the Princess Royal, March 16th 1859, quoted in Fulford, *Dearest Child*, p. 167.
44 Quoted in Arnstein, *Queen Victoria*, p. 58.
45 Victoria to the Princess Royal, June 15th 1858, quoted in Fulford, *Dearest Child*, p. 114.
46 Ibid. p. 196.
47 See Angus McLaren, *A History of Contraception*, Blackwell, 1992 for a full discussion of sexual lives.
48 Lord Erroll married one of the illegitimate daughters of William IV. She became one of Victoria's ladies-in-waiting. David Cameron is a great grandson.
49 Quoted in Woodham-Smith, *Queen Victoria*, p. 216.
50 RA VIC/MAIN/QVJ (W) December 1st 1840.
51 Ibid. April 25th 1843.
52 Ibid. May 12th 1843.
53 Ibid. August 25th 1844.
54 Ibid. April 22nd 1853.
55 Ibid. April 29th 1857.

56 Ibid. October 29th 1857.
57 Ibid. December 2nd 1841.
58 Ibid. May 30th 1843.
59 Ibid. May 28th 1843.
60 Ibid. May 31st 1843.
61 Ibid. April 29th 1857.
62 See Yvonne M. Ward, 'Queen Victoria's Early Motherhood', *Women's History Review*, 8(2), 1999 and Adrienne Munich, 'Queen Victoria, Empire and Excess', *Tulsa Studies in Women's Literature*, Autumn, 1987 for a fuller discussion.
63 RA VIC/MAIN/QVJ (W) December 1st 1840.
64 Ibid. June 13th 1854.
65 Natalie Watson, *Introducing Feminist Ecclesiology*, Continuum, 2002.
66 RA VIC/MAIN/QVJ (W) May 19th 1843.
67 Ibid. June 2nd 1843.
68 Ibid. June 2nd 1843.
69 Ibid. June 2nd 1843.
70 Ibid. September 6th 1844.
71 Ibid. September 6th 1844.

4 Revolutionary times: 1840–1851

On New Year's Day 1840, Victoria felt 'most grateful for all the blessings I have received in the past year. . . . May I only implore Providence to protect me and those who are most dear to me in this and many succeeding years . . . under the guidance of my kind Lord Melbourne. With truth do I say, "From the Tories, good Lord deliver us." '[1] But the Queen's prayers were not answered: by early 1841 Melbourne's government was under threat and he was soon to be defeated on a vote of no confidence. Victoria's next prime minister was to be the Tory Robert Peel, followed by the Whig Lord Russell.

At the end of the 1830s, the United Kingdom seemed blessed: the country was economically secure and politically calm. This equanimity was not to last. By 1850 Victoria, now a budding matron with seven children and increasingly heavy hips, had witnessed an economic collapse, the social catastrophes of the Irish potato famine, contentious reforms such as the repeal of the Corn Laws, and the political unrest of Chartism. In addition, a wave of revolutions broke across Europe affecting the British royal family personally and politically. The period between 1840 and 1850 is sometimes seen as marking a decline in the Queen's power. In each succeeding pregnancy, Victoria relied more and more on her husband to meet with ministers, prepare memos, précis documents and draft replies to her government. In effect, it is argued, Albert became uncrowned king as Britain metamorphosed into a dual monarchy.

The Queen's wish for a tranquil and harmonious period was rudely shattered in summer 1841 when Melbourne and the Whigs were defeated in a general election. They were replaced by Robert Peel and the Tories. Victoria, now four months pregnant, found it 'very upsetting', writing that the 'reality of what has happened, affect and distress me very much. It is so sad to have to part with kind friends and to have to take against my private feelings, people I have not much confidence in.'[2] Nevertheless, the loss of Melbourne was not as painful as it had been two years earlier. The Queen, guided by Albert, had grown up a bit. 'I shall never forget', she wrote, 'what I suffered in '39, though I suffer much now, but it makes all the difference Albert being at my side.'[3] Now, as she admitted in her journal, 'I have my happy home life, and my beloved Husband at my side to share all my difficulties with me.'[4] Moreover any potential difficulties relating to the ladies of the bedchamber had been resolved because Albert's personal secretary, George Anson, 'had seen Peel (which I had no idea of, but which of course Albert must have known) . . . and that the Duchess of Sutherland, Lady Normanby and the Duchess of Bedford, would probably resign'. Peel confided to Albert that he would not allow his party 'to humiliate me; that the best way would be, when the Ladies had resigned, that I should announce it to him, and that he should be quite satisfied'.[5] Both the Queen and Peel agreed to keep the discussion secret.

Sir Robert Peel and domestic policy: 1841–1846

Sir Robert Peel, Victoria's prime minister between August 1841 and June 1846, was a very different character from the light-hearted, worldly and aristocratic Melbourne. Unlike Melbourne he was a reticent man who shunned social life and court gossip. The son of a wealthy cotton manufacturer, he typified the earnest, middle-class, diligent person whose ancestry was new money rather than land-owning aristocracy. Victoria thought Peel difficult until the hard-working, serious-minded Albert, who had found an ally in the equally earnest Peel, gradually convinced his wife of her new prime minister's ability. Victoria later confessed that:

> the more I see of him, the more I am pleased and satisfied. He is a noble minded, very fair, very liberal, straightforward, and very able man. I do not hesitate in saying this, for when

I first took him, I was strongly prejudiced against him, but on getting to know him I have formed quite a different opinion, which entirely coincides with Albert's.[6]

In turn, Albert's authority grew, largely because of Peel's confidence in him: the two men liked each other and were like each other. Meanwhile, the Queen continued to write to Melbourne every day, asking for advice, a correspondence which might have damaged the Queen if the letters had been leaked. But the Queen was incapable of separating friendship and personal feelings from politics, and the letters continued until Melbourne was pressurised to stop writing to his sovereign.

Gradually, spurred on by Victoria's pregnancies, Albert's influence grew. When the two were first married, Victoria deliberately excluded her new husband from affairs of state but soon she needed help, particularly when she was pregnant, about to give birth or recovering from the exhaustion of having a baby. Albert was introduced to the Privy Council, began to accompany Victoria when she met with her ministers, and discussed affairs privately with members of the Cabinet. Victoria began to use 'We' rather than 'I' when she expressed an opinion.

Victoria's second prime minister was appointed during an economic recession: there was large-scale unemployment, weak international trade and a budget deficit of £7.5 million. Peel re-introduced an income tax of between 2 and 5 per cent of income, drawn largely from the middle-class and upper echelons of households, to reduce the government debt. The Queen, now financially secure, very reluctantly agreed to pay the new tax. Earlier, Robert Peel had informed his sovereign that one Radical MP insisted:

that none, not the highest (meaning me) would be exempt from this new Income Tax. This, Sir Robert Peel said, he had no right to do, nor had anyone the right of doing, but that George IV had wished not to be exempt and had paid 10 percent. Sir Robert thought I should also do so (but only 3 per cent, which however, is rather hard) and wished to know whether he might announce this in the House this evening, so that it might appear as a gracious act on my part, without any legislation about it. This of course I at once consented to do. It is very hard for my poor dear Albert, who will have to pay £900.[7]

Peel also steadied the economy by the 1844 Bank Charter Act, which helped stabilise the banking system by restricting the issue of bank notes.

Queen Victoria, who viewed herself as a Whig, nevertheless found Tory governments congenial. When Robert Peel, a Tory with a few Whig sympathies, planned some groundbreaking legislation, the Queen endorsed it. The Mines Act 1842, which prohibited women and children from working in the mines, was one such measure. Queen Victoria approved of the fact that 'all the women have now been removed from the coal pits . . . The Act seems to have done great good.'[8] In 1844 Peel put forward a Factory Bill which restricted the time women and children could work in factories to ten hours a day, only to have it blocked by his own party. Peel discussed the Bill with the Queen, confiding that he was 'much annoyed' at the conduct of his friends 'who had not only voted against him but whose tone had been very offensive'. Peel offered to resign over the issue but the Queen pointed out 'the impossibility (apart from the extreme annoyance it would be to me personally) of his resigning on this question'.[9] The Queen offered her advice, suggesting a limit of 11 hours in order to carry the Bill. Peel refused to compromise. In the end, children between 9 and 13 years of age were limited to working nine hours a day and women for no more than 12 hours. The Ten Hour Bill was passed in 1847, when the Whigs regained power.

In 1830 Britain opened the world's first intercity railway – the Liverpool to Manchester Railway. Further railway expansion followed. Companies built or offered to build thousands of kilometres of railway lines and asked for people to invest. It was seen as a foolproof way of making money and attracted investors who sank all their savings into the railway boom. The Queen, who loved travelling by rail, agreed to accompany the 'great Railway King, Mr Hudson' on a train journey, with the result that investment in railways became even more attractive.[10] The price of railway shares went up, more and more money was invested and the unregulated railway companies promised even further expansion. In 1846 railway mania reached its high point when 272 new railways companies were formed promising to build 15,300 kilometres of track. But the railway companies were built on precarious foundations. In 1847 interest rates were raised and it became apparent to investors that the railway companies could not build the railway tracks they had promised. A financial panic emerged. The collapse of the 'Railway Mania', an example of an early speculative boom, caused misery far beyond that of its investors.

The 'hungry Forties' were tough times for the majority of the British population: food prices were high, wages were low. As ever, diets were inadequate, houses were overcrowded, sanitation was poor and there was a general lack of clean water. The Queen might enjoy cod in oyster sauce, ballotine of duck, roast lamb and a chocolate pudding; the poor made do with bread and potatoes.[11] In 1842 Chadwick published *The Sanitary Conditions of the Labouring Population*, which revealed a direct link between poor living conditions and life expectancy. For example, the average age of death in Manchester was 38 years for 'gentlemen' and professional people but only 17 for the working class.

Not surprisingly, there were protests. In May 1842 a new Chartist petition, signed by over three million people, was submitted – and rejected – by parliament. A wave of strikes, starting in the potteries of Staffordshire and spreading to Cheshire and Lancashire and even up to Scotland, erupted across Britain by workers whose living standards had been eroded by low wages. Queen Victoria, who wanted to hold fast to her monarchical power, had little sympathy for these protesters, commenting in her journal that the 'accounts from Manchester are dreadful, – such disturbances, as also in some other parts, near Sheffield etc.'[12] Peel was worried. Referring to Peterloo, the Reform meeting in 1819, he wrote to his sovereign, 'that something should be done before the 16th, the anniversary of a great mob fight, which took place there in 1819' because 'some great explosion is dreaded for that day'.[13] Victoria feared that what she called 'the evil' had spread into the West Riding of Yorkshire. She heard that 'Huddersfield has been attacked by a mob, and Wakefield threatened. The Yeomanry have been called out. . . . In Warwickshire, also, some disturbances have occurred and in the Pottery districts houses have been burnt and plundered, in open day, with circumstances of aggravated violence.'[14] Meanwhile, the Queen carried on organising her medieval ball, naively insisting that it would give employment to the Spitalfields weavers. When newspapers printed details of the Queen's gem-studded dress, gold-embroidered jacket, ermine-trimmed velvet skirt and red silk shoes studded with diamonds, there was a public outcry at her gross insensitivity and extravagant excess. The monarchy became unpopular: large numbers of British people were hungry and their sovereign did not seem to care very much.

Queen Victoria was overjoyed when the Chartists and their supporters were suppressed. In the dangerous revolutionary world that surrounded her country, the language of democracy was best avoided. Rather than address the cause of the discontent, Victoria approved of straightforward repression, taking delight when the ringleaders of the mob were arrested and the protest was ruthlessly crushed.[15] Victoria was equally pleased when 'the mobs' were

> over awed by the vigour with which the troops acted at Preston and Blackburn, and Bolton, where several prisoners have been taken, and the troops, in self-defence, were compelled to fire, several persons being killed and wounded, among the rioters. . . . Near Newcastle under Lyme, a tumultuous mob, was yesterday charged by a Troop of Dragoons. Some lives were lost and the ringleaders were taken prisoners.[16]

On Thursday 18 August 1842, the Queen was reassured that the rioting was subsiding, a result of strict repression by government forces. Several Chartist leaders were arrested, along with 1,500 followers: about 250 of whom were given prison sentences ranging from 16 months to 21 years; 50 were sentenced to transportation to Australia. The government, keen to know what the Chartists and other rebellious figures might be planning, opened their private correspondence. The Secretary of State, Queen Victoria believed:

> must have the right to open letters in dangerous times. The fact is, in 1842, at the time of the Chartist riots, some great

and alarming assemblages of thousands of people, took place in London and Fergus O'Connor and Mr Duncome were implicated with various of these Meetings, and it is upon this that Sir J Graham kept Mr Duncome's letters for 4 days and had them opened.[17]

In the summer of 1843 the Rebecca riots, a series of protests by agricultural workers against unfair taxation, resurfaced in Wales. On the night of 26 May 1843, a mob of 300 attacked the toll gate of Camarthen and Newcastle Emlyn: soon not a single tollgate remained standing and landlords were sent threatening letters demanding they lower rents. Once more, Victoria had no sympathy for rioters and wrote a letter to the Home Secretary 'urging him strongly to take measures to bring to speedy trial, those abominable people who have led on the Rebecca Riots . . . It is of the utmost importance that the Govt should take severe action.'[18] The government sent in troops.

A few men blamed Queen Victoria personally for their distress and tried to assassinate her. In 1840, just three years after Victoria ascended to the throne, an 18-year-old man fired two pistols at the pregnant Queen while she drove up Constitution Hill in an open carriage. The miscreant was caught, tried and transported to Australia. In 1842, there were two more attempts: one by a 19-year-old unemployed youth, the other by a 4ft tall disabled 17 year old. The courts were less lenient to the former. The Chief Justice pronounced that 'you be drawn on a hurdle to a place of execution, and there be hanged by the neck until you are dead, and that afterwards your head be severed from your body, and your body divided into four quarters'.[19] Fortunately for the would-be assassin, the Queen intervened, sent a royal reprieve and his sentence was commuted to transportation for life. The second youth's attempt was not taken as seriously, so the offender was given 18 months imprisonment. The Queen remained safe for seven years, until an Irish navvy took a pot-shot at her from an unloaded pistol borrowed from his landlady. He received seven years transportation. These first four would-be assassins had several things in common: they were poor, uneducated and powerless individuals. There were altogether eight assassination attempts on her by, respectively, a public house waiter, an unemployed carpenter, a 4ft tall news vendor, a navvy, an army officer, a clerk, an artist and an Irish nationalist.[20]

The Irish question

Ireland dominated British politics throughout the reign of Queen Victoria. In 1801 the Act of Union had united the Kingdom of Ireland and the Kingdom of Britain to become the United Kingdom. Ireland had the right to elect 105 MPs to the House of Commons and select 28 peers to sit in the House of Lords. However, executive power lay in the hands of two British appointed men: the Lord Lieutenant and the Chief Secretary. More importantly, the Irish had little economic power: most land in Ireland was owned by absentee English or Anglo-Irish landlords who paid their workers such low wages that they were the most destitute in Europe.

Predictably, an Independence Movement emerged to free Ireland from English domination and oppression. It was led by Daniel O'Connell who held a series of 'Monster Meetings' across Ireland. Naturally, the Queen disliked any threat to the cohesion of her United Kingdom and was contemptuous of the meetings. She

> read to Albert an account of another immense Repeal Meeting of 60,000 people at which O'Connell presided, wearing a wreath of laurels on his head! Hitherto perfect order has prevailed, but the language used by O'Connell and some of the Roman Catholic Priests is most atrocious, – urging the people to get free, – telling them they were in chains and using altogether most inflammable language. . . . The state of things is very alarming.[21]

The British government reacted by banning further meetings, prosecuting O'Connell and imprisoning him. Eventually, after a huge protest, the House of Lords reduced O'Connell's sentence to three months, a change that the Queen thought was 'too bad!' Nevertheless, Victoria understood the importance of placating the Irish, commenting that 'this way of governing Ireland by Troops, – that is, to keep it quiet by a large force, – is dreadful and cannot last'.[22]

Queen Victoria blamed the Roman Catholic Church for the unrest in Ireland. In her view, the influence of the Catholic Church was near total and often far from benign. Victoria thought the clergy 'were of the worst class – and badly educated', and had an undue authority over their parishioners. Victoria and Albert hoped that an injection of funds and the appointment of better qualified teachers to the Catholic seminary at Maynooth – the main trainer of Catholic priests – might lead in turn to a better educated, and therefore less politically motivated, clergy. The British government, with the Queen's approval, duly increased its funding to the seminary. Regrettably, this led to fierce criticism in England by those who thought it unnecessary and dangerous for a Protestant England to finance an Irish Catholic seminary. The Queen was unsettled by

> the terrible bigotry and uncharitableness, displayed by the Protestant element, which is very much against their honour. I blush for the form of religion we profess, that it should be so devoid of all right feeling, and so wanting in Charity. Are we to drive these 700,000 Roman Catholics, who are badly educated, to desperation and violence. The measures proposed, are to render these people less dangerous, give them a good education and satisfy them! . . . the loss of the Bill would be fatal in Ireland . . . <u>then</u> Ireland can only be governed by the sword, and what an alternative that would be![23]

The Queen's words turned out to be prophetic.

In the summer of 1845 Ireland experienced further calamity when it was hit by a potato blight which turned potatoes into a slimy, decaying black mush. By 1846 the blight had spread across Ireland affecting three-quarters of the harvest; in 1848 it returned in full force. Most of the Irish workforce depended on the potato – it was their main source of food – so the situation soon became critical. The British government did little. Victoria at first seemed unsympathetic, noting in her journal that 'it seems that the former accounts were really exaggerated. At all events it is hoped that it may be found possible to make use of the diseased potatoes by grinding them into meal.'[24] Soon, as reports of skeletal children, 'their features sharpened with hunger and their limbs wasted' reached England, Victoria began to realise the seriousness of the situation. 'We saw Sir Robert Peel . . . and talked of the accounts from Ireland, about the potatoes, which are still bad, and he much fears that by the spring the want will be very great.'[25] During the four years of the potato famine, approximately one million people died from hunger and the associated illnesses of cholera, dysentery, scurvy and typhus, and about two million emigrated. Thousands, who were too impoverished to pay their rent, were evicted from their land by absentee landlords.

The opposition leader, Lord Russell, demanded the repeal of the Corn Laws so that the starving and malnourished Irish people could buy cheaper bread. These Laws, which imposed strict import duties on foreign corn, kept the price of corn high, thus making the price of bread unaffordable for working-class families. At first, Queen Victoria opposed the Repeal. Eventually, encouraged by Prince Albert and Robert Peel, Victoria changed her mind and began to support the Repeal of the Corn Laws and the principle of Free Trade. But the British government remained split over the question. Victoria noted that Peel 'hopes and thinks he will be able to remove the contest entirely from off the dangerous ground upon which it now rests viz; that of a war between the manufacturers, the hungry and the poor on one side, and the Landed Proprietors and Aristocracy, on the other, which can only end in the ruin of the latter'.[26] The government, she now believed, needed to abolish the existing Corn Laws before another national calamity forced it upon the country. In 1846 Peel succeeded in repealing the Corn Laws, at the cost of tearing the Conservative Party apart.

Meanwhile, the damage to the Queen's reputation in Ireland was considerable. Critics in Ireland blamed the callousness of the British government, and by association the Queen, for the distress in Ireland. Victoria was later called the 'Famine Queen'. It is safe to say that Queen Victoria did not look kindly on Ireland. She disapproved of its Catholic religion and its Irish Catholic clergy; she disapproved of Irish nationalism and its veiled threat to separate from the United Kingdom; and she disliked its links to radical movements such as Chartism.[27] Indeed, the Queen blamed individual Irish Chartist leaders such as Fergus O'Connor and James

O'Brien for encouraging dissent and Irish radicals more generally for the popular unrest that brought Britain to the verge of revolution. In the course of a 64-year reign, the Queen only made four visits to Ireland; in contrast, she visited Scotland every year, often for long periods of time. Undoubtedly, the Irish population noted Victoria's Celtic partiality not just in terms of the time she spent in Scotland. She had built a castle at Balmoral, she attended the Highland Games and she created a tartan for herself and Albert.[28] Indeed, Hector Bolitho suggests that if Queen Victoria had perhaps paid as much attention to Ireland as she did to Scotland, the Irish independence movement may have quietly died.[29]

Queen Victoria and foreign policy: 1841–1846

Queen Victoria was more attentive to foreign than domestic policy. She was aware of her own and Britain's status in Europe and the world and sought to maintain, and even increase, it. Moreover, European politics often involved her own family in such a way that Victoria's sympathies and partialities were often tied up with the needs and wishes of her relations.

Victoria's family connections were labyrinthine: she was related to the royalty of France, Portugal, Belgium, Austria-Hungary, Mexico, Spain, Russia and Germany.[30] In the early nineteenth century, German territory was composed of about 39 different kingdoms, duchies, principalities, cities – and Prussia. Most of these places were governed by men who were related to Victoria in some way and they too made links across national boundaries. Her German uncles on her mother's side (all from tiny insignificant German territories) married into well-established powerful European royalty. Her Uncle Leopold married George III's only child, Princess Charlotte, and after her death the eldest daughter of the French king, Louise Philippe; Uncle Ferdinand married the daughter of the Chancellor of Hungary; two other uncles – Alexander and Ernest – married into German nobility. Her British aunts and uncles mostly married into the German aristocracy thus cementing the already strong bonds between the countries.[31]

The upshot of all this inter-marriage was that the royal houses of Europe, and the countries and territories over which they reigned, were bound up in a complex familial network. This, in future, would either help keep world peace or set the scene for destructive internecine conflict. As in most families, tensions often came to the surface. More importantly, Victoria's desire to protect her extended family members sometimes led to conflict with her ministers.

Peel appointed a good friend, Lord Aberdeen, as foreign secretary. Aberdeen adopted a more ameliorative foreign policy than that of his predecessor, Palmerston, preferring traditional diplomacy to strategic sabre-rattling. The shy and reticent Aberdeen enjoyed the trust of the Queen, largely because he listened to her and would change the wording of despatches at her request. Queen Victoria always prized ministers who did what she asked. One of Aberdeen's major achievements was to use diplomacy to resolve conflicts between Britain and the rest of the world. In the 1840s, for example, the relationship between the United Kingdom and the United States was if not hostile, then certainly awkward, particularly over the question of territorial rights. Under Aberdeen's aegis, two important territorial disagreements with the United States were resolved: the 1842 Webster–Ashburton Treaty settled the boundaries between America and the British Canada; and in 1846 the Oregon Treaty settled the US border at the 49th parallel. Victoria, who often saw events in black and white terms, praised the 'admirable manner' in which Lord Aberdeen had conducted the Oregon difficulties while criticising the 'infamous behaviour of the Americans',[32] and the 'late menacing inaugural speech of the President'[33] which spoke of further American expansion. Indeed, the Queen agreed with Peel 'that the United States and their wretched Gvt, in their spirit of aggrandisement, made such a parade of liberty, while retaining all their slaves'.[34]

The Queen was equally delighted when Aberdeen improved Anglo-French relations, and in so doing helped coin the term *entente cordiale* to describe the new relationship. Between 1841 and 1846, Aberdeen and the French prime minister, Guizot, worked hard to revive Anglo-French friendship but it was sometimes a struggle not helped by disputes about the African slave trade, about who controlled Tahiti, and about Greece and Spain. There was, for instance, a distinct wobble in the *entente cordiale* when Britain and France both claimed the right to colonise the island of Tahiti. The Queen worried about 'the awful responsibility that would be incurred by going to war, over such a matter, and bringing on all the miseries it would entail, . . . the idea of <u>my</u> country being at war with that of my dearest relations and friends, would be a terrible grief to me'.[35] Behind the scenes, Aberdeen and Guizot worked hard for a settlement and war was averted.

The situation in India was more challenging. At the time, the East India Company, a private trading company which acted as a managing agent for the British government, governed large parts of India. The Whigs were on good terms with the bankers and the entrepreneurs of the East India Company, and approved of its policies. In contrast, the Tories and the Queen thought that the East India Company was so poorly managed that it would 'end in the Crown having the management of the whole'.[36] One of Peel's first tasks was to select a new governor general to India. He consulted with the Queen who had a penchant for the ultra-Tory Lord Ellenborough. It was a disastrous appointment. Ellenborough was arrogant, opinionated and, more unfortunately, inept. However, Queen Victoria liked him because he communicated directly with her, passing on confidential information that should have been restricted to the Cabinet and the East India Company.[37] In turn, Ellenborough used the Queen as his weapon to fight Whig policy.

When Ellenborough first arrived in India, he had to deal with problems in neighbouring Afghanistan. In December 1841, William Macnaghten, a British civil servant, was murdered by an allegedly friendly ruler (Akbar Khan), decapitated, had his head stuffed with portions of his mutilated body, and was paraded through the capital. The Queen heard directly from Ellenborough

> of the dreadful news – poor William Macnaghten having been killed and all our troops at Cabul having been annihilated . . . he said it was a terrible country to defend, particularly in winter. . . . Akbar Khan had professed to be a friend (but had killed Mcnaghten) in order to prove to his own people, who had accused him of being bought by the English, – that he was not a friend.[38]

Victoria read the 'letter from the assassin himself. . . . He seemed to think it right to do this, as a follower of the Prophet!'[39]

Shortly after the murder of Macnaghten, six thousand British troops were massacred and a large number of women and children taken hostage: 'The unfortunate ladies are in Akbar Khan's hands; the poor troops who were promised safety, after capitulating, were attacked, whilst retiring and nearly annihilated.'⁴⁰ The panic-stricken, and largely incompetent, Lord Ellenborough dithered over what to do. In the end, the army generals took an executive decision, rescued the women and children and retreated from Afghanistan. Ellenborough unjustifiably claimed the credit, and the Queen believed him. She realised that the retreat from Cabul must have been 'one of the most fearful things imaginable'⁴¹ but expressed her delight that 'all the prisoners, including all the Ladies, liberated . . . splendid news, for which we must be deeply thankful'.⁴²

Just after this, Ellenborough peremptorily and without permission became involved in another imperialist fiasco by annexing Sind, today a province of Pakistan. This upset the delicate relationship between the East India Company, the Sind rulers and the British government, and Ellenborough was recalled to Britain. The Queen objected, notified Peel of how much she disapproved of the decision to recall Ellenborough and complained of how ungrateful the East India Company appeared to be for 'Ld Ellenborough's meritorious services'.⁴³ Even though the Queen admitted that Ellenborough was sometimes 'intemperate' and 'provoking', she blamed the East India Company for being 'actuated by mean, unpatriotic pique'.⁴⁴ In fact, the Queen approved of Ellenborough, sharing his dream of imperial expansion. Perhaps more significantly, Ellenborough made her feel important. All too often, the Queen was reminded of the limitations of her royal prerogative whereas Ellenborough made her feel powerful by accentuating the Queen's role as commander-in-chief of the armed forces.

Further annexations of Indian territory, claims Miles Taylor, established the Queen's authority in India, an authority which was independent of the East India Company.⁴⁵ Queen Victoria was indeed living up to her reputation of a 'warrior queen'.⁴⁶ Whenever a territory was annexed, a durbar – a ceremonial gathering – was held at which Indian rulers pledged their allegiance to the Crown. More importantly, the Queen enjoyed direct

informal diplomatic contact with individual Indian rulers such
as the Maharajah of Nepal, the Queen of Oudh and Duleep
Singh. Any behind the scenes negotiation between the Queen and
Indian rulers, of course, might well have undermined the authority of the British government.

Meanwhile, the Tory government was in crisis. On 26 June
1846 Peel tried to get an Irish Coercion Bill passed which would
allow the English to rule Ireland by force during times of unrest.
The Queen thought that disaffected Tories might make 'the state
of politics very uncomfortable. The Irish Bill is to be opposed by
the Whigs (a most senseless move) and by many Protectionists. . . . This is very tiresome.'[47] She was right: on the same day
the Repeal of the Corn Act was passed by the Lords, Peel's
Coercion Bill was defeated by a coalition of Whigs seeking office
and Tory protectionists seeking revenge. Peel duly resigned.

When Peel handed in his seals of office, the Queen wrote that

> on waking up the reality of what is going to happen, or
> rather more what has already happened, broke upon me most
> painfully. . . . He is such a noble character, so thoroughly
> disinterested and with such a high sense of duty. With him
> I felt so safe . . . that he would never recommend any person
> or thing, unless it was for the good of the Country, or for
> our good. Then he never repeated what we said to him. . . . In
> short, I feel the loss (not of an agreeable friend, and com-
> panion in Society, as I did in Ld Melbourne's case) of a
> Minister who was actuated by the highest sense of honour,
> of respect, and of loyalty to his Sovereign.[48]

Nonetheless, this time the Queen did not interfere: she was
now a little more politically astute and a lot more self-aware.
She looked back to 'the year 39' and remembered 'how different
my joy was then to what it is now. Then I had broken off with
the Govt on my own responsibility, without trying to set matters
right, only rejoicing at having my good Ld Melbourne back again;
whereas now, I have behaved with the greatest fairness.'[49] Victoria,
undoubtedly guided by Albert, seemed to recognise that the role
of the British sovereign was to remain politically neutral and to
accept those ministers chosen by her government. The fall of Peel

broke up the Conservative government and split the party: the Conservatives remained out of office for 20 years.[50]

Lord John Russell and domestic affairs: 1846–1852

Queen Victoria invited the leader of the opposition, Lord Russell, a Whig, to take the place of Peel. The Queen, still regarding herself as a Whig, was nevertheless unhappy. 'Poor Ld John' she commented 'looks already so deplorable, so done up, and feeble, that one cannot think that he is the new Prime Minister . . . he speaks so slowly and hesitatingly that one has quite the impression of his being a tired out man.'[51] 'I used formerly always to fancy that Peel was so stiff and cold, but oh! Now, not when one got to know him well.'[52] The Queen expressed concern that Russell would never be able to keep order in the House of Commons because 'everyone seems to be his own master'[53] and MPs would not accept party discipline. In the event, Russell's ministry lasted five years.

Russell's most pressing problem was the Great Famine in Ireland. He immediately allocated £10 million to be spent on public works in order to alleviate the problem of unemployment. It was too little and too late. In 1847 Russell changed tactic, abandoned public works and concentrated on providing direct relief through food distribution. By August over three million people were being fed in soup kitchens but when the harvest appeared good, food distribution was stopped. Large numbers – 200,000 more than normal – entered the dreaded workhouses. Charities sprung up to provide help. The Queen, now deeply troubled by the sufferings of the Irish, pledged £2,000 of her own money and became patron of the British Association for the Relief of Extreme Distress. Charity, of course, could ease but not completely alleviate the terrible calamity that befell Ireland: cholera, dysentery, fever weakened further an undernourished and starving population. Victoria patronised even more charities for the Irish poor and wrote a letter authorising collections in all churches for the destitute in Ireland and Scotland. But the population still starved, too many still entered the workhouse, relied on 'outdoor relief', or else emigrated to England, America or other countries.

The meagre attempts of the British government to deal with the famine led to a resurgence of Irish nationalism. A rebellion, led by William Smith, James O'Brien and James Dillon, had tried – and failed – to gain widespread support. Victoria received 'excellent news from Ireland. . . . The great agitators went to Limerick for a great Meeting, and were so ill received and ill used by the mob, that they had to be protected, and are ready and anxious, to give up political life!'[54] O'Brien was subsequently arrested, tried and transported. In addition, the government decided to suspend the Habeas Corpus Act, an Act which forbade the imprisonment of people without trial. Victoria thought it 'a very wise move. The account continues to be a very alarming and everything seems to be leading to a Rebellion. Every precaution that is possible will be taken to prevent any Irish disturbance in England.'[55] On Saturday 22 July 1848, the Habeas Corpus Suspension Bill was passed. People in Ireland suspected of being rebels could now be imprisoned without trial; this, thought the Queen, was an excellent strategy because it stemmed potential revolution at source. The Queen feared that the revolutions which were sweeping across mainland Europe might spread to Britain and welcomed any plan to thwart rebellion.

In 1849, despite the fear of widespread unrest, Victoria and Albert decided that it was safe to visit Ireland. It had been specifically arranged by Lord Clarendon, the lord lieutenant of Ireland, to demonstrate the royal family's compassion with the destitute and starving. The Queen had never been to Ireland and her advisors were worried that if she did not go, rumours might circulate that she was too afraid to visit. The visit was meticulously organised and choreographed. When the two royals arrived they were greeted with enthusiasm and loyalty by well-orchestrated crowds. 'The waving of hats and handkerchiefs, the bursts of welcome that rent the air, all of which made it a never to be forgotten scene, particularly when one reflects on what state the country was in, quite lately: in open revolt and under martial law.'[56] Victoria thought 'the beauty of the women is very remarkable and struck us very much, such beautiful dark eyes, and hair and such fine teeth'.[57] Even so, the Queen was shocked by the poverty she witnessed. 'The raggedness of the people' she wrote in her journal 'is beyond belief, man and boy, having really hardly any covering.'[58] The trip was seen as a public relations success but Queen Victoria did not really capitalise on it and it had no lasting impact. One royal visit alone could not be expected to undo the economic, social and emotional damage inflicted by the British on Ireland over the centuries.

Life was also tough in England. In 1848, encouraged by continental revolutions, Chartism revived. A mass rally was organised on Kennington Common, London, with the aim of processing to parliament to present a petition. The Queen and her government feared that the Chartist meeting might segue into revolution so

> we should already go out of Town . . . all this and the uncertainty everywhere, as well as for the future of our children, unarmed me and I quite gave way to my grief. Yes, I feel grown 20 years older, and as if I could not any more think of any amusement. I tremble at the thought of what may possibly await us here, though I know how loyal the people at large are.[59]

Albert pacified his wife, encouraged her to be calm and insisted that 'we must keep up and on no account despair. But it is difficult to think and talk of anything else, but what is going on.'[60] Even so, Victoria feared the worst and confided to her prime minister, Lord Russell, that she thought 'of these being very anxious times, and Ld John says that the great danger lies in the ease with which all these Revolutions have been effected. This gives such an alarming example.'[61] The royal family fled to Osborne.

Lord Russell, though theoretically in favour of freedom of speech and universal manhood suffrage, feared riots which, as in some continental countries, might lead to revolution. He placed 8,000 soldiers and 150,000 special constables on duty and banned the Chartists from taking their petition to parliament. In the end, there was no revolution, the Chartist meeting went ahead and its main leader, O'Connor, at the behest of the police, asked the crowds to leave peacefully. The Queen was relieved that the 'meeting dispersed quite quietly, without any disturbances. How wonderful! What a blessing! . . . the determination to put a stop to the proceedings – by force if necessary – have no doubt been the cause of the failure of the Meetings. It is a proud thing for this country, and I trust fervently, will have a beneficial effect in other countries.'[62] England appeared to be safe from revolution.

Palmerston and foreign policy: 1846–1851

In 1846, when the Whig government came to power, Lord Palmerston was appointed foreign secretary. The Queen regretted losing her mild and unassuming foreign minister, Lord Aberdeen, saying that 'his loss is an immense one, to us, the Country, and to all Europe and I tremble for the future and for the consequences it may bring'.[63] At the very beginning, Victoria was comforted by Palmerton's assurance that 'he was ready to do anything I wished'[64] but their initial rapport quickly vanished. Victoria's relationship with Palmerston was very different from that with Aberdeen: unlike Aberdeen, Palmerston was not emollient or deferential and Victoria grew to dislike him, his boastfulness and blustering independence. Over the next few years Victoria's attitude towards her foreign secretary 'hardened into outright hostility'.[65]

Indeed, the Queen and Palmerston struggled continuously over foreign policy, with the Queen testing her royal prerogatives against a foreign secretary who in turn asserted his parliamentary credentials. The Queen, seemingly in a weaker position, complained, threatened and pleaded with him. Infuriatingly, Palmerston always apologised, promised to change – but then continued to do as he and the government, and not the Queen, wished. According to constitutional convention, ministers worked independently of the Crown and the Queen should not have challenged ministerial decisions so vehemently. Theoretically Victoria had the right to be informed and to be heard – but only a modicum of freedom to have her views take precedence over her ministers. Ultimately, it seemed as if she had little real power over foreign affairs. But this did not stop Queen Victoria from interfering.

Palmerston exasperated Victoria: she thought him too impetuous, too rude and too undiplomatic. As foreign secretary, Palmerston failed to keep the Queen informed of current events, failed to show her sufficient courtesy and respect and failed to alter despatches when requested to do so. The Queen was

> extremely annoyed . . . at a letter Ld Palmerston had written . . . before submitting it to us. . . . In this he conveys the substance of what we asked him to do, but in such an improper and disloyal manner as at once to cause a contrary impression. . . . Really the obstinacy of Ld Palmerston is beyond all belief and his behaviour so unkind and improper, as well as impolitic, making himself hated in all countries, and we losing thereby our influence.[66]

At the time, Britain was the most powerful country in the world, making Palmerston by association the most powerful foreign secretary, a reality that perhaps encouraged him to act in the peremptory way he did. Certainly, foreign policy was transformed when Palmerston became foreign secretary since he was more concerned to advance the cause of Britain and of reform than to please the Queen.

The Spanish marriages

One of the first clashes between the Queen and Lord Palmerston occurred over the question of who should marry the teenage Queen of Spain, Isabella. Victoria, who was all too aware that sovereigns wielded influence through marriage alliances as much as by diplomacy, hoped that one of her German cousins, Prince Leopold of Saxe-Coburg, might marry Isabella and thus cement friendship between the three countries. Certainly the British did not want a Spanish queen to marry a French prince in case the King of France exerted his own power in Spain. In order to avoid conflict, the British and French agreed to keep the thrones of Spain, Germany and France separate. Unfortunately, the King of France disregarded the agreement and tried to marry one of his sons to Queen Isabella's younger sister, the Infanta Louisa, in the hope that the Spanish Queen might die childless. The British were furious at France's duplicity. A potential conflict between the two countries was averted when Queen Victoria visited France with the emollient Aberdeen and the two thrashed out an informal agreement with the King of France. The two sovereigns reached an understanding that the King's youngest son, the Duke of Montpensier, *could* marry the Infanta Louisa, as long as the marriage was delayed until Queen Isabella married and had had a child. In return, Victoria promised that her cousin Leopold would abandon his hope of marrying Queen Isabella. As a young girl, Victoria had insisted that she herself marry for love, not diplomacy, rights which she denied to the young Spanish girls in favour of old-fashioned diplomatic marriages.

Unfortunately Palmerston, unbeknown to Victoria, undermined these delicate and private negotiations by continuing to press the suit of Leopold. This had dire results for Anglo-French relationships: the *entente cordiale* wobbled again. The French, annoyed with what they saw as British deceitfulness and without seeking further negotiation, arranged a double wedding between the Spanish Queen and the supposedly impotent Duke of Cadiz and between the Infanta and the Duke of Montpensier. Victoria was outraged: 'the Queen of the French, announcing to me, – just as if it were nothing, – the marriage of Montpensier with the Infanta, . . . This is too bad, for either it is merely a family event, or it is a political step, in violation of all the promises made to us.'[67] And somewhat disingenuously, given that she had formerly been involved in trying to decide the marital fate of the two young women, the Queen commented that 'a feeling of disgust was beginning to be shown, for the shameful manner in which the 2 poor Children at Madrid had been treated, a thing quite unworthy of the times we live in!'[68]

Victoria wrote to the King of France expressing her annoyance

> at this untoward event, which has brought in such a personal element, and forced us to oppose the marriage of a Prince, to whom, as well as to his whole family, I bore a sincere and great friendship. My only hope was, that the dangerous consequences, to which the execution of this marriage would lead, might make them pause.[69]

There were a few tense moments, but the government 'decided not to go to war, – so there remains nothing else for us to do but to keep calm and cold'.[70] In the end, Victoria blamed

Palmerston's interference for the breakdown in relations between Britain and France.

The 1848 revolutions

The year 1848 began ominously. A dark, dense revolutionary cloud overhung all Europe. From the Bay of Biscay to the Black Sea, and from the Bay of Naples to the Baltic, one newspaper later reported 'the very soil appeared to throb convulsively with the suppressed passions of the people. Constitutional sentiments were growing; amongst the governments, reactionary measures were resolved upon. Each understood, hated and dreaded the other'.[71]

In 1848 a series of revolutions brought on by the combined urges of nationalism, longings for political freedom, hunger and the devastating social effects of industrialisation shattered the peace of Europe: nearly all the continental despots were overthrown or compelled to give democratic forms of government to their rebellious peoples. Victoria, now in the later stages of pregnancy with her sixth child, supported the threatened monarchies, particularly the ones to which she was related. In the Queen's view, revolutions were always bad for the country and 'the cause of untold misery to the people. Obedience to the laws and to the Sovereign is obedience to a Higher Power, Divinely instituted for the good of the people, not of the Sovereign who has equally duties and obligations.'[72] In contrast, Palmerston thought that despotic sovereigns deserved to be toppled. In his opinion, gradual change was desirable not only for its own sake but as a safeguard against the more extreme policies favoured by some revolutionaries. Palmerston's blend of principle and pragmatism kept the Queen 'in a constant state of anxiety, as I had no confidence in him and felt uneasy from one day to another as to what might happen, affecting the welfare of this country and the peace of Europe in general'.[73] On more than one occasion, the Queen put pressure on Prime Minister Lord Russell to dismiss Palmerston but he refused to capitulate.

The revolutions began in January 1848 with an uprising in Sicily, forcing its ruler, King Ferdinand II, to grant a constitution. The Queen thought 'the state of Sicily very alarming, the Sicilians being in open revolt and the King obstinate'.[74] In May, Ferdinand regained his confidence, ignored the constitution, bombarded Sicilian cities and treated his rebellious citizens harshly. To the Queen's fury, Palmerston supported the Sicilians against Ferdinand and even allowed arms to be sent to the rebels. She was very angry indeed when she heard

> some startling news – . . . the Sicilians applied to a Merchant to furnish them with guns, who replied that he had none ready, excepting those in the ordnance stores, and asked permission to give them up. This <u>was done</u> and <u>sanctioned</u> by Ld Palmerston!! What does not this point to? This was at the same moment, when we were making professions on neutrality, and Ld Palmerston sanctions such a <u>dishonest</u> proceeding. . . . Affronts and humiliations, keep following closely upon one another, and all <u>all this</u> on account of the unscrupulous behaviour of Ld Palmerston![75]

The French revolution

Soon the political unrest spread to Paris, where serious disturbances on the streets led to revolution. In February, King Louis Philippe was overthrown and a second republic set up; in June, further disturbances shook the newly established Republic; in December, Louis Napoleon was elected president. Queen Victoria was horrified. Of course, she was intimately connected to the French royal family: her favourite uncle, King Leopold, was married to Princess Louise d'Orleans, a daughter of Louis Philippe, and her cousin Victoire was married to one of the King's sons; the French King and Queen had visited her in England and she had made return visits to them in France. Victoria's journal records the escalation of events from the viewpoint of a reigning monarch. She was troubled about the

> good deal of disturbance that took place at Paris yesterday. . . . The troops were out in great force and charged the people, to disperse them, but seeing this had no effect, they attacked with the flat of their swords, and the mob dispersed, but not everywhere, and serious trouble was apprehended for today. It makes one feel very anxious.[76]

She was equally shocked when the King was forced to dismiss his reactionary and unpopular prime minister, Guizot, writing that

> so much, and such extraordinary, incredible things, have been happening these days in France, that I hardly know how and what to write. . . . Guizot has resigned, – the National Guard declared they could answer for nothing if the King did not change his Govt! . . . who yielded! This is a terrible blow for him . . . this forced imposition of a change of Govt had a very bad effect.[77]

And when, on 25 February 1848, Victoria heard that King Louis Philippe had abdicated and left Paris, she thought it

> too incredible, too astounding. We were both horrified and grieved, and full of sorrow and anxiety for the poor dear Family, and our relations. The French are really a very ungrateful nation to forget in one day all the King has done for them these 18 years! . . . the Tuileries and Palais Royal were in the possession of the mob, who were destroying everything, all Paris being in a state of disorder. . . . How dreadful for the poor old King, the Queen . . . To see their nation behave in this harried way, must be too terrible for them.[78]

The French royal family fled to Britain where Victoria heard at first hand how the royal family escaped, of how the King abdicated and was forced to leave the Tuileries 'as fast as he could, with all the family. They had scarcely time to get through the garden, before the mob of blood thirsty ruffians were in the courtyard, and they ran off, just as they were, all on foot through the gardens – the children with them.'[79] Others of the family were not so lucky and 'were dragged away by the crowd and left amongst the horrible shrieking mob, armed with every sort of missile'.[80] Some managed to get away on foot, escaladed the barricades and walked to the railway station to catch the train to Versailles. Eventually, all the royal family escaped, some with their jewels, others with nothing. All were homeless and stateless.

The French royal family arrived in Britain without clothes or money. Victoria was horrified that one of the princesses wore 'rags, her only clothes torn half off, and she very nearly crushed by the mob'.[81] Victoria sent the family 'a number of necessary and all sorts of clothes for the children'[82] and arranged for their expenses to be met from a Secret Intelligence account.[83] She persuaded King Leopold to offer the King and Queen his house at Claremont; the Duke and Duchess of Nemours were given a royal residence at Bushey; and the recently wed Montpensiers were bundled off to Spain. Queen Victoria visited the French family at Claremont, had them to stay with her at Windsor and often commiserated with the fact that they had to live upon the £1,000 sent to them by Prince Ferdinand.[84] Victoria found her cousin 'dear Victoire low and sad. Dear Child, her spirits must give way at times, under such anxiety, such uncertainty, such reversal of fortunes. She is like a crushed rose.'[85] The Queen bought Victoire's jewels when she was forced to sell them, commenting that it showed how 'pinched they must be'.[86]

In June 1848 a second revolution erupted in Paris. Queen Victoria thought that 'we really seemed to have returned to the horrors of the French revolution. The times are too awful. May God preserve this country.'[87] She always believed the worst about the revolutionaries, certain that in Paris 'many assassinations are going on, many, by means of poison, flowers and even cigars are being poisoned'.[88] Palmerston was more sympathetic than his sovereign to the revolutionaries and wanted to establish friendly relations with the new French government. Victoria disagreed. In her view, the lawfully appointed monarch had been overthrown by a bunch of revolutionary upstarts; in Palmerston's opinion, the corrupt autocratic French monarchy deserved to be deposed. The Queen accused Palmerston of

> coquetting with the Republic, as anxious to be on good terms with them, as he was not with the late Govt . . . For us to join with this unrecognised Govt and be the 1st to act in concert with them, in helping revolted subjects to throw off their allegiance, while at the same time we are grappling with Rebellion in Ireland, is to dishonour and disgrace the name of England.[89]

The two battled over what should be the British response to the new Republic, each testing out their own powers. In August

1848, Palmerston forced a reluctant Victoria to recognise the French Republic. However she refused to send an ambassador to Paris or receive a French ambassador in England, thinking it 'unprecedented and unfitting'.[90] In the end, Palmerston insisted and Victoria was obliged to concede.[91]

Revolution in Austria and its empire

Queen Victoria's loathing of revolutions and revolutionaries deepened. In March, spurred on by events in Paris, protestors threatened the Habsburg Austrian Empire: Viennese crowds assembled in the city demanding basic freedoms and a more liberal regime. Serious clashes occurred between the authorities and the Austrian people. The Habsburgs fled Vienna. 'Bad news from Vienna' Victoria commented in her journal 'the emperor has been made to yield to everything – to consent to have only one Chamber, . . . and with the exclusion of any member of the Imperial Family'.[92] Unrest continued and in early October 1848 Victoria heard about a

> horrible new Revolution at Vienna, where the poor Minister of Foreign Affairs, Count Latour, had been murdered and killed in a horrible way with axes and clubs. . . . Vienna is in possession of the mob, this made us all very miserable as we have so many dear ones in Vienna and then <u>what</u> is to be the end of all this – there is to be an end of everything if assassinations are begun.[93]

Foreign Minister Prince von Metternich, who was a hated symbol of reaction and repression, was forced to resign and the Emperor of Austria abdicated in favour of his nephew the Archduke Franz Josef. The Queen, who had feared that Austria might become a republic, thought the Emperor's resignation 'a wise measure and done at the right moment'[94] because it secured the monarchy. The fact that Franz Josef's wife was a Bavarian princess helped. To the Queen's relief the army retook control of Vienna and executed some of the leaders of the revolution.

In 1848 the German-speaking Austrian Empire controlled large parts of modern Europe: parts of Italy, Hungary, Croatia, the Czech Republic, Slovakia and Romania, all filled with different ethnic groups, all with their distinct language and culture. In March 1848 the overriding concern of Austria was unrest in Italy. In 1848 Italy was not a unified country but divided into several separate states, some independent such as Piedmont, some under Austrian rule or with Austrian-dominated rulers. The Pope ruled the Papal States. Revolution broke out in large parts of Italy in opposition to Austrian rule and in support of Italian unity. Victoria was unsympathetic to the cause of Italian independence and unity because – like all good imperialists – she believed that the Italian provinces under Austrian control were the 'lawful possessions' of Austria and should remain so.

On 18 March 1848 the Milanese rebelled against Austrian rule and Radetzky, the Austrian field marshal, was forced to withdraw from the city. Inspired by events in Milan, Charles Albert, king of Sardinia-Piedmont, declared war on Austria. The Queen thought Charles Albert a good for nothing, blamed his 'despicable' actions on Palmerston for giving him 'unfortunate advice'[95] and hoped that the Piedmontese would be beaten. She 'strongly condemned and could not defend' the 'bad news from Italy' when the King of Sardinia 'unjustifiably marched into Austrian territory'.[96] In the Queen's view everything was sacrificed to the 'phantom of Italian independence' and she blamed Palmerston for his misguided advice to the Italians. By his encouragement of Italy, Palmerston was accused of trying to force Austria to give up her lawful possessions. Indeed, Victoria was

> very much troubled again by Ld Palmerston's attitudes towards the Italian question, which he treats with such unfairness and partiality as seriously to alarm me for the honour of England and for the peace of Europe. – all the Italians wish and say is believed, whereas whatever is said in favour of the Austrians is disbelieved and said to be illusions. – It is very bad.[97]

Fortunately for Palmerston, the Queen remained unaware that her foreign secretary had helped arm the leading Italian revolutionary, Garibaldi.

To complicate matters, a violent uprising took place in Rome, the Pope fled and a republic was declared. The new Republic gave away the papal lands to peasants, gave freedom to the press, provided secular education and reformed the prison system. Victoria was unsympathetic believing that 'every day some new horror seems to take place. In Rome there has again been a revolt, the Prime Minister Rossi has been assassinated, the Palace was attacked and one of the Cardinals killed. The Pope was obliged to yield and to dismiss his Swiss Guards, he has been placed under complete constraint. It is really too shocking.'[98] The Pope appealed to the European governments for armed intervention to help him regain his lands: the Queen felt that the matter should be settled by negotiation.[99] In the end, the French restored Rome and the papal states to the Pope.

At first the British and French tried to broker a compromise between the Italians and the Austrians. However, the Austrians rejected mediation, saying they were tired of Palmerston's 'eternal insinuations, his protective and pedagogical tone, both offensive and unwelcome'.[100] The Queen agreed and criticised Palmerston for using 'intemperate and offensive language towards countries like Austria, constantly abusing and intermeddling in their interior policy, and supporting and interceding for Revolutionists and Rebels of every kind and character'.[101] Angry exchanges took place between the Sovereign and her Foreign Minister; the Queen regularly insisting that Palmerston rephrase his letters and Palmerston declining to do so. On one occasion the Queen refused to sign one of Palmerston's letters to the English Ambassador in Austria because she disagreed with Palmerston's accusation that the Austrian army had committed atrocities. Palmerston reluctantly agreed to change his letter but insisted that the reports of the atrocities were correct. He caustically notified the Queen that the leading general, Radetsky, had 'ordered the village to be destroyed, and told the troops employed that he made them a present of the village and its inhabitants to deal with them as they chose'. The Queen angrily replied that 'the cruel part is the war itself and if a government is anxious for the sake of humanity to avoid cruelties, the only real way will be trying to bring about peace'.[102] Queen Victoria was self-deluded: Palmerston would never have sought peace at any price, and certainly not with a regime he considered autocratic and repressive. Even so, the Queen refused to relinquish her beliefs and tried to persuade

Lord Russell to dismiss his foreign secretary and thus reverse government policy. Events favoured Palmerston rather than the Queen: the Liberal government enjoyed popular support, the opposition was weak and ineffective and Palmerston's parliamentary ascendancy inviolable. It would take more than the Queen's cantankerous insistence to be rid of her least favoured minister.

Gradually, as the Austrian domestic revolution quietened, Radetsky and his army regained control. The Queen was overjoyed, noting in her journal that 'the Austrians have (to our great joy and satisfaction) entirely beaten the Italians'.[103] She was less delighted when Palmerston allowed British passports to be given to the 'miscreant Republicans who have been the cause of so much bloodshed, which is too bad, and very false humanity.'[104]

The German revolutions

The March revolution in Austria fuelled the German revolutions. They began in Baden and quickly spread to the German principalities of Hesse-Darmstadt, Bavaria, the Kingdom of Wurttemberg, the Rhineland and even to Prussia. As befitted the time, some middle-class Germans pressed for the classic liberal demands of an elected representative government, freedom of the press and trial by jury. A great many of Victoria's relatives ruled parts of Germany, prompting her personal sympathies to be instinctively on the side of the German princes rather than the revolutionaries. In particular, Albert's brother and her cousin, Ernest, was Duke of Saxe-Coburg and Gotha, and Victoria 'feared that none of the smaller sovereignties can exist (were this to happen to Coburg and Gotha, it would break my heart) and that they might even become a Republic. This would be too dreadful.'[105] Her half-brother Charles, Prince of Leiningen, told her 'such terribly distressing accounts of Germany, . . . there being general disorganisation, no real freedom, or progress – no respect of laws, and all that is ancient and good torn down'.[106]

However, what mattered most was the situation in Prussia, Germany's largest, most economically and militarily powerful state. In Berlin, crowds of people gathered in the city and demanded constitutional change. King Frederick William was forced by the rebels to make concessions, establish a parliament, grant a constitution, abolish press censorship and lead the move towards German unity. His nephew and heir, Prince William, who disagreed with these reforms and tried to suppress the revolution, was forced to flee to England and seek refuge.

The rulers of the various states and principalities, frightened at the prospect of republicanism, agreed to convene a national assembly in Frankfurt to discuss a constitution for a united Germany. Prince Albert sent a draft of a proposed constitution to the meeting but it arrived too late. Surprisingly, Victoria's half-brother, Charles of Leiningen, was elected prime minister of the government formed by the national assembly. Victoria was 'astounded'. It made her

> anxious to see Charles's name figuring in it. It is a great honour, but a great responsibility, of which I trust he will be worthy. Anyway, it shows a reaction in favour of Aristocracy, and that Republicanism is certainly on the decrease. It can only have a good effect on the relations between Germany and this country but it adds to our anxieties to have a near relation in such a responsible position.[107]

Unfortunately, the Assembly could not agree on a constitution and it dissolved. 'Poor Germany', the Queen commented 'how sad and dreadful is her condition – their horrible Republicans should be exterminated.'[108] By autumn 1848 the Prussian aristocrats were once more in control; in December 1848 a new constitution which reasserted the power of the Crown was imposed; the old order was re-established; and in May 1849 the Frankfurt Assembly was dissolved. By the summer of 1849 the German revolution was crushed.

The Hungarian revolution

In Hungary, which at the time was ruled by Austria, the revolution was nationalistic as well as democratic. Under the leadership of Lajos Kossuth, the revolutionaries demanded the usual liberal requirements of a free press, freedom of assembly, civic and religious equality, universal male suffrage, trial by jury and far greater autonomy for the Hungarian government. The leading

Hungarian revolutionary, Petofi Sandor, encapsulates the thirst for violence in his poem:

> The gentry have waxed fat on us
> For long years passed
> But now it's our turn: let our dogs
> On them grow fat.
> So toss them with your pitchforks in
> The dung and mud,
> And there the dogs can make their meal
> Of bones and blood.[109]

On 15 March 1848 the revolution began. A new parliament was appointed and a democratic political system put in place. Hungary, however, consisted of other nationalities such as Serbians, Croatians, Slovaks and Romanians, all of whom wanted similar rights of their own. When the relationship between the Hungarians and Croats turned violent, the Austrians sent Count Franz Lemberg, their commander-in-chief, to negotiate. Instead, he was killed. The Queen was horrified to hear that the unfortunate Lemberg was murdered in horrendous circumstances, 'literally torn to pieces by the mob at Pest. It is too horrid as he was a pleasant man and has left a wife and 8 children.'[110] The Hungarian revolution was short-lived. The Austrians, by exploiting the differences between the various competing national groups, were able to restore order and the main leaders, including the prime minister, were executed. Petofi Sandor was killed in action.

During this period, the Queen became more controlling in her management of foreign policy. Constitutionally, because letters written to foreign governments were sent in Queen Victoria's name, she had the right to review and suggest amendments to diplomatic correspondence. During his period of office as foreign secretary, Lord Aberdeen had mostly accommodated the Queen's suggestions but Palmerston proved less willing to alter despatches, and was 'insufficiently attentive to the monarch's counsel'.[111] This reached crisis point in 1848, the most turbulent year ever experienced by the young Queen. Queen Victoria, now just turned 30, was forced to respond to revolutions often involving her relatives. Not surprisingly she sometimes got it wrong. Queen Victoria pronounced herself a Whig but she did not adhere to Whig principles of democratically elected constitutional government. Not surprisingly, given the fact that she was a queen, Victoria usually favoured the preservation of established authority even when that authority was autocratic. In contrast, Palmerston's commitment to a Liberal philosophy led him to encourage those who favoured representative governments. Palmerston, now identified by his reforming zeal, had positioned himself as a leader of the movement towards constitutional rule. The Queen tried to undermine Palmerston's principles and authority by writing unauthorised letters to other members of the Cabinet and, more cunningly, to other European sovereigns. In turn, Palmerston sent off dispatches without consulting the Queen. The two protagonists clashed over their political differences as well as over the question of who controlled foreign policy. Palmerston may have been regularly subjected to Queen Victoria's injunctions but he had the upper hand. The revolutions of 1848 in particular had made him a prominent and popular figure within the United Kingdom and a commanding figure in parliament, thus rendering it impossible for the prime minister to accede to Victoria's requests to dismiss him. Queen Victoria was forced to accept Palmerston's parliamentary ascendancy and with it the fact that parliament legitimately possessed a greater measure of power than the sovereign, especially when there was a clear-cut majority in parliament and a weak opposition.

Notes

1 RA VIC/MAIN/QVJ (W) January 1st 1840.
2 Ibid. August 28th 1841.
3 Ibid. August 28th 1841.
4 Ibid. May 6th 1841.
5 Ibid. May 9th 1841.
6 Ibid. February 24th 1844.
7 Ibid. March 16th 1842.
8 Ibid. February 23rd 1843. See Angela V. John's *By the Sweat of Their Brow: Women Workers at Victorian Coal Mines*, Routledge, 1980 and *Coalmining Women: Victorian Lives and Campaigns*, Cambridge University Press, 1984 for a discussion of the effects of the 1842 Act on women.
9 RA VIC/MAIN/QVJ (W) March 23rd 1844.

10 Ibid. July 5th 1847.
11 J.F.C. Harrison, *Early Victorian Britain*, 1832–51, Fontana Press, 1989.
12 RA VIC/MAIN/QVJ (W) August 13th 1842.
13 Ibid. August 13th 1842.
14 Ibid. August 16th 1842.
15 Ibid. August 16th 1842.
16 Ibid. August 17th 1842.
17 Ibid. February 23rd 1845.
18 Ibid. June 23rd 1843.
19 Charles, *Kill the Queen!*
20 See ibid.
21 RA VIC/MAIN/QVJ (W) May 29th 1843.
22 Ibid. February 15th 1844.
23 Ibid. April 15th 1845.
24 Ibid. November 9th 1845.
25 Ibid. November 20th 1845.
26 Ibid. December 23rd 1845.
27 See James Loughlin, *Allegiance and Illusion: Queen Victoria's Irish Visit of 1849*, The Historical Association, 2002.
28 Ibid.
29 Hector Bolitho, 'Queen Victoria and Ireland', *The English Review*, May, 1934, p. 534.
30 Leopold's eldest son married Marie Henriette of Austria, daughter of Archduke Joseph of Hungary; his daughter Charlotte married Maximilian I of Mexico, the former Archduke of Austria. One of Prince Ferdinand's sons married the Queen of Portugal; another son and a daughter married into the French royal family of King Louise Philippe. Prince Alexander's son also married into French royalty.
31 Prince William married a German princess, Prince Ernest a German princess, Princes Augustus, Duke of Sussex, married twice, both English ladies; Prince Adolphus, the Duke of Cambridge, married a German princess; Charlotte, Princess Royal, married Prince Frederick of Wurttemberg; Princess Elizabeth to a German prince.
32 RA VIC/MAIN/QVJ (W) March 30th 1845.
33 Ibid. April 5th 1845.
34 Ibid. April 6th 1845.
35 Ibid. September 1st 1844.
36 Ibid. April 14th 1844.
37 Miles Taylor, 'Queen Victoria and India', *Victorian Studies*, Winter, 2004.
38 RA VIC/MAIN/QVJ (W) March 10th 1842.
39 Ibid. March 11th 1842.
40 Ibid. March 10th 1842.
41 Ibid. July 14th 1842.
42 Ibid. November 23rd 1842.
43 Ibid. April 23rd 1844.

44 Ibid. April 24th 1844.
45 Taylor, 'Queen Victoria and India'.
46 Walter Arnstein, 'The Warrior Queen: Reflections on Victoria and Her World', *Albion,* 30(1), Spring 1998.
47 RA VIC/MAIN/QVJ (W) June 10th 1846.
48 Ibid. July 3rd 1846.
49 Ibid. December 20th 1845.
50 Philip Magnus, *Gladstone,* John Murray, 1954, p. 80.
51 RA VIC/MAIN/QVJ (W) June 30th 1846.
52 Ibid. July 3rd 1846.
53 Ibid. Monday July 6th 1846.
54 Ibid. May 2nd 1848.
55 Ibid. Friday July 21st 1848.
56 Ibid. August 6th 1849.
57 Ibid. August 3rd 1849.
58 Ibid. August 6th 1849.
59 Ibid. April 3rd 1848.
60 Ibid. April 3rd 1848.
61 Ibid. April 4th 1848.
62 Ibid. April 10th 1848.
63 Ibid. June 29th 1846.
64 Ibid. July 5th 1846.
65 Brown, *Palmerston,* p. 280.
66 RA VIC/MAIN/QVJ (W) January 27th 1847.
67 Ibid. September 10th 1846.
68 Ibid. September 23rd 1846.
69 Ibid. September 26th 1846.
70 Ibid. September 28th 1846.
71 *The Bradford Observer,* Jan 1st 1852.
72 RA VIC/MAIN/QVJ (W) August 6th 1848.
73 Ibid. September 19th 1848.
74 Ibid. February 2nd 1848.
75 Ibid. January 22nd 1849.
76 Ibid. February 23rd 1848.
77 Ibid. February 24th 1848.
78 Ibid. February 25th 1848.
79 Ibid. February 28th 1848.
80 Ibid. February 27th 1848.
81 Letter to Lady Pembroke, February 28th 1848, *Correspondence of Sarah Spencer, Lady Lyttelton, 1787–1870,* edited by Mrs Hugh Wyndham, John Murray, 1912, p. 320.
82 RA VIC/MAIN/QVJ (W) February 27th 1848.
83 Stanley Weintraub, *Uncrowned King: The Life of Prince Albert,* John Murray, 1997, p. 194.
84 Ferdinand was the father of Princess Victoire who was married to Prince Louis, Duke of Orleans, the son of the deposed French king.

85 RA VIC/MAIN/QVJ (W) May 16th 1848.
86 Ibid. April 2nd 1848.
87 Ibid. June 25th 1848.
88 Ibid. July 1st 1848.
89 Ibid. July 24th 1848.
90 Ibid. August 6th 1848.
91 Ibid. August 11th 1848.
92 Ibid. May 23rd 1848.
93 Ibid. October 13th 1848.
94 Ibid. December 8th 1848.
95 Ibid. August 12th 1848.
96 Ibid. May 21st 1848.
97 Ibid. October 8th 1848.
98 Ibid. November 28th 1848.
99 Ibid. March 9th 1849.
100 Prince Felix zu Szhwarzenberg's Dispatch to Austrian representatives abroad, quoted in Langer, *Political and Social Upheaval, 1832–1852*.
101 RA VIC/MAIN/QVJ (W) December 7th 1849.
102 Letters May 22nd 1848 quoted in Brian Connell, *Regina v Palmerston, The Correspondence between Queen Victoria and Her Foreign and Prime Minister, 1837–1865*, Evans, 1962, p. 74.
103 RA VIC/MAIN/QVJ (W) August 4th 1848.
104 Ibid. July 20th 1849. Since 1794, passports have been issued by the secretary of state.
105 Ibid. April 13th 1848.
106 Ibid. April 13th 1848.
107 Ibid. August 8th 1848.
108 Ibid. October 13th 1848.
109 Lines from 'Dicsöséges nagyurak', March 1848, translated by Frank Szomy 1972, privately printed. I am grateful to Teresz Kleisz for this reference.
110 RA VIC/MAIN/QVJ (W) October 7th 1848.
111 Brown, *Palmerston*, p. 286.

5 Victoria and motherhood: 1842–1861

Queen Victoria has often been characterised as a domestic tyrant, who disliked the heir to the throne, was over-protective of the haemophiliac Leopold, over-indulged the youngest Beatrice and was generally a control freak. Victoria, of course, was no ordinary mother and had to cope with the tensions between her role as parent and her role as monarch. Her position as queen may have interfered with her responsibilities as a mother whereas the regularity of her pregnancies may have undermined her effectiveness as queen. True, Victoria and Albert enjoyed a lot of help. The young couple, in common with many aristocratic families, had a raft of nannies, governesses, nursery maids and other staff to help look after their children. In April 1842 Lady Lyttelton was put in charge of the nursery and remained there until 1850 when she was replaced by other aristocratic ladies. But each night Prince Albert visited the children's nursery to make sure that the locks were secure and that the children were all tucked in safely.

Victoria has even been accused of disliking her children. In December 2012, one BBC documentary, *Queen Victoria's Children*, portrayed her as a needy and domineering mother who resented her children. This is not the case at all. Her first child, 'Baby' as young Vicky was initially called, was adored and Victoria's journals are full of comments about her, and her many sketches of Vicky and her other children are those of a devoted mother. Like all very young first-time mothers, the Queen worried about Vicky and 'never thinks the baby makes progress enough or is good enough. She has her constantly with her, and thinks incessantly about her.'[1] Most mothers boast about their children and Victoria was no exception, writing that 'our dear little Child . . . gets daily prettier, and is so "éveillé" [wide awake] for her age. . . . She has large, bright, dark blue eyes, a nice little nose and mouth, a very good complexion, with a little colour in her cheeks, very unusual for so young a Baby.'[2] The Queen thought that Vicky 'was so dear and merry; she is quite a little toy for us and a great pet; always smiling so sweetly, when we play with her'.[3] By April 1841, she had been nicknamed Pussy. Victoria's journals are full of love for her daughter, speaking of 'our dear little Victoria', who was 'such a darling', proudly commenting that 'she now always sits up, taking such notice of everything and looking about her', or saying she 'looked such a duck, for she has beautiful little arms'. The Queen was delighted when Pussy came down and 'sat on my lap and was very dear and very good', insisting that her daughter 'really gets more intelligent each day'. She liked it when her infant daughter 'came into my room, and was so playful and funny, sitting on the sofa and playing so sweetly with her Papa'. When Victoria returned home after a day out, she 'went up to the Nursery, where we found dear little Victoria, just out of her bath, looking such a duck, and so pretty. We were quite delighted with her.' Victoria, like many a mother, took delight in the progress of her first-born child. She took one of her favourite aunts upstairs 'to see Victoria take her food, which she does so nicely . . . Pussy came down, looking so pretty with blue ribbons, and having to our great delight, cut a 3rd tooth. She says "Papa" and "Mama" to us now, and can stand alone, with a little help.' She clearly enjoyed watching Vicky grow, taking 'such a pleasure to see her improve so, and to watch the developing of the little mind'.[4] When she visited the nursery, she spoke of how 'Ly Lyttelton and I, nearly died of laughter at Pussy's drollness; she laughed and talked, inventing words and laughing at her own funniness. Albert came in as she was running round the bath without any clothes, trying to climb up into the bath.'[5] Sometimes 'Vicky was so absurd, that it made us die of laughter; she makes funny remarks, like a grown up person.'[6]

As with most young mothers, Queen Victoria was most worried when her young daughter fell ill, 'went up several times to see Pussy, who was very languid and wretched. It is such a worry.' When Vicky was teething, she was anxious about her 'ailing state, though not dangerous, fusses and worries me so much'. At times the Queen admitted 'feeling very low about our poor dear little one, who certainly is not well. . . . Till the end of August she was such a magnificent, strong, fat child, that it is a great grief to us to see her so thin, pale and changed.' It made her 'so melancholy to see a poor little thing like that suffering, and unable to express what it feels'.

She saw the infant Princess every day and missed her on the rare occasions she was absent from home, complaining that she was 'deeply grieved at leaving our darling little Pussy' and 'Missed Pussy so.'[7] However, when she later corresponded with Vicky, she spoke of how she had never seen a 'more insubordinate and unequal-tempered child' than her eldest daughter and told her of how she used to stand on one leg, laugh violently, cram food into her mouth and deliberately waddle when walking. 'The Trouble', Victoria wrote her daughter 'you gave us all – was indeed very great.'[8] But it was said with obvious love and affection.

It is often the fate of the second child, and certainly the third, fourth, fifth, sixth, seventh, eighth and ninth, to be overlooked. As Victoria wrote to her eldest daughter, one made more fuss about the first than the rest. 'We used' she said 'constantly to see you and Bertie in bed and bathed – and we only see the younger ones – once in three months perhaps' at bath time and at bedtime.[9] Victoria did not write about her later children with the same intensity but her love for them was evident. Some historians believe that her second child, and heir to the throne, Albert (Bertie), whose title was Prince of Wales, Earl of Chester, Duke of Cornwall and Rothsay, Earl of Carrick, Baron of Renfrew, Great Steward of Scotland and Duke of Saxony (as Albert's son), was less liked. It is thought that Victoria's annoyance at having two babies so soon, one after the other, combined with the difficult labour she had endured, had given him 'a bad start in life'.[10] However, Bertie's eventual inheritance meant that the parental lens was focused more intently on his behaviour, character and upbringing than on the others. Expectations were high as Victoria and her husband wanted the future sovereign of Britain and its empire to be a good king. And so, the heir to throne, perhaps the least able of all the children, carried all the hopes and aspirations of his demanding parents and of Victoria longing for him to be a carbon copy of his father.

At first she was proud of her new 'Baby', writing in her journal how he 'now stands up at a sofa or chair and crawls extremely well and quickly'.[11] 'The Baby also came down, and it was so funny to see my dear Albert dancing the 2 Children, to the time of the organ, one on each knee. The Baby is very fond of his Father.'[12] Her journals are full of the 'dear little Boy', who looked 'so healthy and well, and so rosy and pretty. It was a great pleasure to us.'[13] No mention was made in her journals of Bertie's well-known tantrums and temper, his violent screaming, stamping of feet and habit of throwing things around the room. However, Victoria sometimes wrote about her disappointment with her eldest son. For example, Bertie was the only child who did not perform on one of Victoria's birthdays: Arthur and Alice sang a duet, Louise said a poem, Alice and Affie played the violin, Alice played a complicated piece by Beethoven but 'the only one of all the children, who neither drew, wrote, played or did anything whatever to show his affection . . . was Bertie. Oh! Bertie alas! Alas! That is too sad a subject to enter on.'[14]

The other children, like children in most large families, bundled along as best as they could. Victoria was extremely proud of Alice who was as 'placid and happy as possible, cries very little, and begins to laugh and even crow, which at six weeks old is early'.[15] She spoke with pride when Alice was able to sit up 'since 10 days and is really very pretty, so chubby, and had such nice little features; she is so intelligent, and laughs so dearly, whenever one speaks to her'.[16] Alfred, who was destined to inherit the Coburg kingdom, was thought fearless because he climbed out of windows 30 feet high and balanced on the ledge outside, slid down banisters and jumped over streams before he could swim. Victoria was delighted when her fifth child Helen (Lenchen) appeared 'fat and healthy . . . runs about delightfully by herself'.[17] On her second birthday, Victoria called her 'our good funny little pet'[18] and generally found her to be 'very talkative and very amusing'.[19] 'Little Lenchen', Victoria believed, 'is the drollest most amusing child I have ever seen.'[20] Louise, the sixth child, although at times very naughty, was thought 'a very sweet child, of the most placid and amiable disposition'.[21]

Arthur, the seventh child, was a favourite son. When he was eight years old, Victoria told Albert that 'this Child is dear, dearer than any of the others put together, thus after you he is the dearest and most precious object to me on Earth'.[22] Victoria and Albert's eighth child, 'poor Leopold', suffered from haemophilia and 'still bruises as much as ever, but has not had accidents of late. He is tall, but holds himself worse than ever, and is a very common looking child, very plain in face, clever but an oddity – and not an engaging child though amusing.'[23] Victoria and Albert's last child, Beatrice, was over-indulged and there is no doubting the love that Victoria felt towards her:

> Our precious little Beatrice's first birthday! No words can express what that sweet, pretty, intelligent little creature is to us! . . . The darling little birthday child, looking lovely, in a very pretty frock . . . was in ecstasies, over all her fine toys, and kept clapping her hands, as she always does when she wants anything. She is so engaging, and such a delight to kiss and fondle. If only she could remain, just as she is.[24]

Beatrice remained 'Baby' to her mother well into adult life and remained spoilt in comparison to the other children. Victoria's journals are full of adulatory comments about her latest child. Beatrice 'is too great a duck; when she is in the greatest good humour she says: "dee, dee little Mama, and dee little Papa"'.[25] In November 1859, when the family attended an army parade, the two-year-old Beatrice 'had hold of my hand; at first she did not mind the firing, but towards the end got a little unhappy, and kept saying to herself "good little girlie, good little girlie"'.[26] The proud mother wrote that her youngest was 'extraordinarily sharp and forward for her age, speaking so plainly, reciting little verses and understanding everything. She is quite the pet of the family.'[27] On Victoria's forty-second birthday, when Beatrice was four years old, the Queen was delighted that 'sweet little Baby was there, chatting away, amusing all, by her perpetual funny remarks. She begged to stop for my health being drunk, and Albert made her propose it, which she did standing up on a chair.'[28]

Infant mortality was high in the nineteenth century and naturally the Queen fretted about her own offspring when they fell ill. The children suffered from many childhood complaints, including teething pains. Teething not only caused red, swollen and tender gums but also led to disturbed sleep, loss of appetite, irritability and high temperature. Vicky suffered terribly from troublesome teething attacks and 'poor little Alice had got such a rash, from teething, that she could not appear'.[29] In June 1853 'Bertie has got the measles!' wrote the Queen. This was followed by Alfred, Albert, Vicky, Alice, Helen and Louise. Victoria stayed with those who had caught the measles, sent the two uninfected ones away, and caught the illness herself.

Victoria promoted unpopular and controversial medical practice. In 1842 the young Prince Albert Edward – later known as Bertie – and his parents were vaccinated against smallpox from the arm of the same child. Smallpox epidemics had swept across Europe since the sixteenth century, affecting rich and poor alike: a fresh epidemic between 1837 and 1840 had led to approximately 36,000 deaths, the vast majority among infants and small children. There was no cure for it. Those who survived were often left deaf, blind, brain damaged or crippled. Its marks did not go away and people's faces and bodies were badly disfigured with pock marks. In 1796 Edward Jenner, developing a technique that had first been used by Lady Mary Montagu, started to use the cowpox virus to prevent smallpox – he called it vaccination from the Latin word *vacca* meaning cow – but many people were opposed to it believing that it interfered with God's will; some even thought they might turn into a cow! A young child who was infected with cowpox was brought into the Palace and used to infect each child. When 'poor Princess Alice was vaccinated from a "magnificent" baby', the Queen remarked on the 'duet of shrieks the two kept up'.[30]

Victoria fussed most about her youngest son, Leopold, worried that he was thin, under-weight and cried a lot more than her other children. As an infant, he was diagnosed as suffering from a rare, serious, and in the nineteenth century, mysterious illness: haemophilia, an inherited blood disorder which reduces the blood's ability to clot. Leopold's arms and legs were frequently covered with bruises, his urine was pink, and there were often other signs of internal bleeding. Even natural childhood physical developments such as teething were especially uncomfortable and painful for the little boy and he screamed incessantly. Haemophilia mostly affected boys but it was generally handed on through the genes of a seemingly unaffected female. Queen Victoria, herself a physically healthy woman, passed the genes on to Leopold who was the only victim in her immediate family. Two of her daughters, Alice and Beatrice, conveyed the disease to other European royal families; Alice's daughter Alexandra transmitted haemophilia to the heir of the Russian throne with devastating consequences for the Tsarist autocracy.

Victoria was naturally more concerned about Leopold than the other children, especially after an onset of bleeding. She was sometimes forced to leave him behind at Balmoral or Osborne when she and Albert returned to London but 'felt it almost wrong that we should have to leave him behind . . . but Albert has a great deal to do. . . . should there be any change for the worse, . . . we could at once come down'.[31] The anxious Queen kept in contact by telegram with the doctors about her son and was once 'greatly alarmed by a telegram from Dr Jenner about poor dear Leopold. There had been frequent bad nose bleeding, he was weak and restless and some measle spots had shown themselves on his face . . . However at 11 there came another telegram, which greatly relieved us, saying the dear Boy had had some refreshing sleep, his pulse was good.'[32] On medical advice, Leopold went to the south of France for the winter. But the Queen was not a sentimental mother and wrote about Leopold's physical appearance without sentimentality, writing that 'he walks shockingly – and is dreadfully awkward – holds himself as badly as ever and his manners are despairing, as well as his speech – which is quite dreadful'.[33]

Educating the children

Queen Victoria wanted a 'good, moral, religious, but not bigoted or narrow-minded education' for her children.[34] Victoria and Albert, guided by Baron Stockmar, aimed to tailor the children's education to fit their future situation in life: Bertie to be king of England, Alfred to join the navy and hopefully inherit the Coburg dukedom, Arthur to have a career in the army, Leopold merely to survive and the girls to marry into continental royalty. The younger children of the British aristocracy were generally educated at home by a governess or tutor; in this case Lady Lyttelton acted as first royal governess. When upper-class boys reached 13, they were sometimes bundled off to public schools such as Eton or Harrow, then studied at the universities of Oxford or Cambridge; girls were tutored at home. Victoria sometimes instructed her children in religion, taught history to her eldest daughter and instilled the fact that Albert was the head of the family into all her children. All were brought up to be trilingual and spoke English, German and French fluently, possibly because their parents had an eye on marriages to the various rulers of Europe. The children were severely punished if they were disobedient. The maxim 'spare the rod, and spoil the child', though reprehensible to modern eyes, was a cherished belief of nineteenth-century parents. During this period, children were regularly subjected to harsh discipline, verging on cruelty, at home and at school. Prince Albert in particular, thought physical chastisement should be applied routinely: even his daughters were whipped[35] and had their hands tied together. Poor little Alice, at the age of four, was whipped for telling a lie.

In 1847 Victoria and Albert divided the children into two classes: the first class for the children up to the age of six under the charge of Lady Lyttelton; the second under a new, more intellectually challenging, governess. Victoria and Albert agreed that Bertie should be educated to be a constitutional monarch.[36] In 1849, now aged seven, Bertie embarked on a rigorous educational programme devised by Albert. He was given his own tutor who taught him maths, geography and English while others were engaged to teach him languages, religion, handwriting, drawing and music. Lessons took place between 8am and 6pm seven days a week with a daily progress report sent to his parents. Bertie was also taught riding, gymnastics, dancing, skating, swimming and croquet. Victoria, who believed that her eldest son was a copy of herself, warned Bertie's tutor about his 'nervous and unmanageable temper'. She was therefore pleased when, on a walk with her eldest son, Bertie began to understand his own position in the royal hierarchy:

> He generally lets out to me, when he walks with me, something or other, that is occupying his mind. This time it was how I came to the throne . . . He said he had always believed

Vicky would succeed me, but now he knows that in default of <u>him</u>, Affie, little Arthur and 'another brother, if perhaps we have one' would come before Vicky.[37]

He understood the laws of primogeniture – yet Victoria was still anxious about his academic progress. 'Dear Bertie's 13th birthday, which seems a dream. I wish it were only his 10th as he has so much to learn, and it is rather a difficulty for him.'[38] Bertie wanted an army career; Victoria was concerned. 'Bertie, to whom learning is always a great difficulty, should be told that if he could fit himself to pass the exam: <u>all</u> young Gentlemen, who intend entering the Army <u>must</u> pass, and did it well, he might get a Commission, or at least be allowed to wear the uniform of one of the Regts of the Guards.'[39] In the end, Victoria vetoed an active military career, so Bertie only enjoyed an honorary rank – but with no need to take an exam. In 1859 Bertie spent the summer studying at the University of Edinburgh, then went to Oxford and lastly to Cambridge.

Victoria and Albert's second son, Alfred (Affie), was more academically able and his parents delighted in his desire to learn. Albert thought it better for Alfred, now nearly 12 years old, to be sent away to study with his own tutor and away from what the parents thought as Bertie's bad influence – the two had been caught smoking together. On 3 June 1856 Alfred 'came to take leave, sobbing bitterly and indeed I was much upset at this 1st separation in our family, for it is the 1st child who leaves the paternal roof, and such an amiable, dear child, still, however hard, it is necessary, and for his good.'[40] Alfred's lessons focused on mathematics, geometry, seamanship and navigation in order to prepare him for a sailor's life. When Alfred returned home for his twelfth birthday, the Queen felt 'as if he were no longer <u>quite</u> my own, from having been away from home'.[41] In 1858 Alfred passed his naval entrance exams, and was appointed to join HMS *Euryalus*, a ship in the Mediterranean fleet as a midshipman. He would sleep in a hammock just like the other sailors, and share naval quarters. He was 14 years old.

Victoria missed Alfred's 'dear face which shed sunshine over the whole house'. She wrote to her daughter, comparing him to Bertie 'Dear Child, I feel so proud of the hardship he has endured – the way he has worked and when I think of – ! The very best there is wretched mediocrity. The joy of having Affie in the house is so great and alas! with – it is such a contrary feeling.'[42] 'Affie is going on admirably . . . and oh! When I see him and Arthur and look at – (you know what I mean!) I am in utter despair! The systematic idleness, laziness – disregard of everything is enough to break one's heart and fills me with indignation.'[43]

Victoria's daughters were brought up to marry into European royalty, and in common with the daughters of the upper class, learned how to play the piano, to paint in watercolour and to embroider. They were also expected to do charitable works: Vicky and Alice, for instance, accompanied their mother when she visited army hospitals.

Fun and games

Victoria and Albert's children worked hard but their lives were not confined to endless swotting. Their parents provided fun activities for them. Unlike her own lonely experience, the Queen's children had each other to play with in the nursery and in their parents' room. Children are naturally boisterous and Victoria and Albert's were no exception: 'we had the Children playing in our room, and they were very noisy'.[44] Her journals show a mother who appears more tolerant of high-spirited youngsters than one expects. Victoria regularly spoke of how 'Bertie and Vicky romped about in my room, in the wildest way possible';[45] 'had the Children with us, and the 3 eldest were very wild, running about, and having great fun together'.[46] Affie, she noted 'is beginning to get very determined and fights with Alice in the drollest way, which makes one nearly die of laughter'.[47] Albert often played in the nursery with the children, with the often-pregnant and somewhat incapacitated Victoria looking on and commenting that she 'never saw a kinder father, or one more ready to play with his children, in every way. He had been blowing soap bubbles with them before we went out.'[48] The royal family also had friends over to play with them, leading the Queen to comment wistfully that Bertie had 'play fellows almost every day' unlike herself at that age.

Victoria watched proudly as her children performed in plays and concerts put on at home. When a little French comedy was performed in French by Vicky, Bertie, Alice, Affie and Lenchen, the Queen thought that 'Vicky acted admirably, Alice very nicely, also Bertie. Affie knew his part perfectly . . . dear little Lenchen could hardly be got to say her part, without Mme Rollande prompting her very loud.'[49]

Birthdays, of parents and children, were celebrated extravagantly. The children were all dressed prettily, often given new outfits for the occasion, and each held a small bouquet of flowers to present to the birthday child. All their presents were arranged on a table before the birthday boy or girl came in. Victoria was delighted that 'dear little Alice . . . was very happy with all her toys, and Albert sat down on the floor with her to play with some bricks'.[50] The children had birthday parties, including conjurors, dancing puppets and Hungarian singers. On her second birthday, Beatrice had a party with four other little two-year-old girls who ran around after supper and had 'great fun together. . . . the merriment of dear, innocent little Children is very cheering'.[51] The parents were thoughtfully affectionate with their presents: a dog for Bertie, a sailor suit for Affie, numerous military toys for Arthur and once a pet lamb 'decked out with ribbons' for Alice.[52] Christmas too was celebrated splendidly with Christmas trees, individual tables laid with 'toys of every possible kind', many of which had been chosen by their parents, and with lots of squeals and running around by the excited children. Victoria took delight in her children's happiness and even spoke tolerantly of 'what a great noise the children made when taking down their Christmas tree on Jan 6th!', so one can imagine the din made by nine over-excited youngsters on the day itself.

Victoria wanted her sons and daughters to have the youthful fun she had missed as a child. All the children were taken regularly to the zoo, the pantomime and the circus. As a young girl, Victoria had disliked pantomimes, finding them 'vulgar and noisy',[53] but she unselfishly took her children to see shows such as Aladdin and the Lamp because she thought they would enjoy them. Six of them even visited Madame Tussaud's waxworks and maybe saw the Chamber of Horrors where the grisly victims of the French Revolution were on show. On one occasion, when Victoria and Albert took five of their children to the zoo, the children were largely delighted but 'Lenchen took a strong dislike to anything ugly or with an unpleasant smell, and did not much like the lions and tigers, still less the birds of prey, repeating "I don't like it."[54]

It was clear that Victoria was developing a taste for 'low-brow' entertainments. She delighted in taking her children to see the Red Indian show with its two war chiefs

> wrapped in buffalo hides, with leggings and sleeves of the same and wore various kinds of beads and ornaments and a head dress of feathers . . . their faces are so thickly painted with black and red stripes, that no features are discernible. The men then went out to prepare themselves for dancing . . . When the men returned, the spokesman carried a little drum . . . singing or rather more yelling a very extraordinary kind of song, the others dancing round and screaming, and whenever they stopped, giving a most horrid whoop, which quite startled one.[55]

Despite Victoria's obvious enjoyment of such unsophisticated programmes, she wanted her children to experience high culture too. At one time, Victoria took seven of her children to see the paintings at the Royal Academy. In February 1850 a performance of *Julius Caesar* was held in Windsor Castle for the children to watch. Queen Victoria considered the play

> such a finely written Tragedy, full of beautiful and celebrated speeches. The part of Julius Caesar was very fairly acted by Mr C Fisher . . . the 2 principal characters of Brutus and Marcus Antonius were performed by Macready and C Kean . . . Kean's acting was quite perfection, and he gave the celebrated speech in the Forum, admirably. Poor Macready, I thought not good, ranting too much, and being so affected in manner, – his voice cracking and gulping, and having an unpleasant way of stopping between every word.[56]

The children also listened to classical music and learned to play the piano. Victoria adored Mendelssohn's music and invited him to play at Buckingham Palace; in 1858 Mendelssohn's 'Wedding March' was played at her eldest's wedding.

Victoria, Albert and their children read books by George Sand, Alexander Dumas, Charlotte Brontë and Charles Dickens. She found Harriet Beecher Stowe's *Uncle Tom's Cabin*

> a most interesting book, but too painful, – really terrible. To what can human nature descend! It makes one's blood curdle to think of the inhuman feelings given way to and the treatment practiced on these wretched creatures by the Slave Traders. Many of the slaves are Quadroons, as white as ourselves and the description of wives torn from their husbands and little children, some, infants, from their mothers is too horrid! It quite haunts me![57]

Holiday homes: Osborne House and Balmoral

Aristocratic families often owned a country estate as well as a house in London. The Queen inherited the Brighton Royal Pavilion but both she and Albert disliked its style, its association with her profligate uncle and 'the tiresome people running so after us'.[58] In 1850 it was sold for £50,000 to Brighton town. In 1844 Victoria and Albert bought Osborne House on the Isle of Wight for £26,000, demolished it and built a new large modern house, with plumbing and sanitation, on its site. It was an ideal holiday home, especially for children, and the Queen was delighted with her purchase largely because 'the grounds are so extensive, and the woods would be lovely anywhere, but going down to the edge of the sea, as they do, makes it quite a Paradise'.[59] The two furnished it together, with Albert designing lamps and Victoria choosing Aubusson carpets. Both chose the works of art: statues of naked men and paintings of nude women are plentiful at Osborne. These were not secreted away. A huge fresco of *Neptune Resigning the Empire of the Seas to Britannia*, which depicts a naked Neptune and various other naked people, was placed at the top of the main staircase for all the family and visitors to see. Victorian prudery, with its discreet placing of fig leaves on certain parts of the anatomy, was not in evidence at Osborne House.

Whenever the weather was fine, the royal family would board the big grand yacht, *Victoria and Albert*, or the smaller *Fairy*, and sail around the island. The first time that Bertie went on the yacht he 'was quite delighted with everything, – the salutes, the ships, etc, and ran wildly about the deck'.[60] Or they walked on the seashore, picking up shells, and sometimes bathing in the sea. In July 1845 Victoria 'went into the bathing machines, where I undressed and bathed in the sea (for the 1st time in my life) a very nice bathing woman attending me. I thought it delightful till I put my head under water, when I thought I should be stifled.'[61]

Victoria and Albert's children would always have servants to look after them but their parents wanted them to experience how to make things and how to cook. At Osborne, the children were given their own gardens, their own garden shed and their own tools, in which the children grew vegetables and flowers. In 1853 the foundation stone for a Swiss cottage, a children's house which was a smaller replica of an adult home, was built. All the children, including three-year-old Arthur, laid the first stone, 'each putting on some mortar and striking the stone with a small hammer. . . . Bertie read aloud the inscription of the date, with all the signatures, written at full length on a piece of parchment. This was deposited in a bottle, which was put into a hole in the stone work. The Children were greatly excited and delighted.'[62]

In 1852 the Queen and Prince Albert bought a house in Balmoral, Scotland and again pulled it down to build a larger and more modern country house in its place. Queen Victoria adored Scotland, spending six weeks there every summer when parliament was in recess. Here the family went on pony expeditions, walked in the hills, ate picnics, went deer-stalking, shooting and fishing and collected wild flowers to press into books. In the evenings they sometimes listened to, or danced to, Scottish bagpipes:

> All the Highlanders are so free from anything like bluster, so straightforward, – no flattery, so simple, and honest. They are never vulgar, never take liberties, are so intelligent, modest and well bred. I also like the other gillie, John Brown, very much, a good-looking tall lad of 23, with fair curly hair, so very good humoured and willing, – always ready to do whatever is asked, and always with a smile on his face.[63]

Matrimonial affairs

The eldest, Vicky, was the first to marry. As the Princess Royal, she was expected to make a top rank dynastic marriage. When Vicky was only four, her parents discussed the possibility of a match with the Prussian heir to the throne, Prince Frederick. Both parents wished to secure an Anglo-Prussian alliance which would act as a safeguard against French or Russian ambitions in Europe. Undoubtedly, this was a political match. Vicky's Liberal English upbringing was thought beneficial to Germany and it was hoped that it would influence her new husband. 'It may be God's will, that this dear Child should some day play, if not <u>openly</u>, still <u>really</u> a great part in Germany, which . . . may be a great blessing to both Countries!'[64] The two sets of parents connived for the two to meet. In September 1855, when Vicky was 14, the 24-year-old Prince Frederick was invited to stay, with the intention of securing a marriage alliance. 'The visit', Queen Victoria noted in her journal, 'makes my heart beat as it <u>may</u>, and probably <u>will</u> decide the fate of our dear eldest child.'[65] Prince Frederick (Fritz) duly complied as:

> after breakfast and talking with Fritz, there was a momentary pause, when he said a new life was opening out to him – his great wish to belong to our family. I could only squeeze his hand and say how happy we should be. . . . he thought the Princess Royal so sweet and charming, so clever, and natural. . . . Albert equally expressed our great pleasure, adding with what joy and complete confidence we should give our child to him! . . . (Fritz) begged however that she should know nothing of it at present. . . . to this we agreed . . . The marriage itself should not be till she was 17. The matter was therefore to be kept an entire secret.[66]

The Princess Royal was not party to the discussion. The Queen may have insisted on marrying the man of *her* choice but had no desire to allow her eldest daughter the same rights. The Queen was nonetheless anxious that Vicky might refuse and 'slept very little all night, being so excited and agitated. Of course now we are agitated about what Vicky herself may feel and think, and so anxious she should love Fritz as he deserves, and as I do not doubt she will.'[67]

Parents from the upper classes were expected to provide their daughters with a dowry, usually a large sum of money, when they married. Queen Victoria and Prince Albert thought it was the responsibility of the government to finance it. After much discussion, the government gave a dowry of £40,000 and an annuity of £8,000 per annum to the Princess Royal on marriage. The Queen not only expected the government to provide Vicky's dowry but fiercely defended her family's right to be kept by the British taxpayers. Latterly she had been annoyed when the government refused to increase the Royal grant, more than once complaining that such alleged parsimony by the state 'put me out a good deal for to see all one's economy and care, all that one has done to keep out of debt with such a large family, and such reduced incomes, repaid by the answer that as one <u>had</u> done this, one could <u>go on without</u> any further grant, is very hurtful to one's feelings'.[68] Here the Queen was disingenuous, as it was money saved from the British taxpayer that had bought Osborne House and Balmoral. Before she became queen, Victoria was virtually impoverished. Undoubtedly, Victoria liked money. In 1852 she was astounded and pleased to be told that a man had died without any relations and 'leaving all his personal property amounting to ½ million of money to me!! . . . We were astounded – and of course greatly pleased, for it is a mark of loyalty and confidence, which is very gratifying.'[69] 'I shall have £12,000 a year by it!! This is as much as the Duchy of Lancaster yields.'[70]

Princess Victoria, now aged 17, and Prince Frederick, now aged 27, were married on 25 January 1858 in the same chapel where her parents had married. The wedding nearly eclipsed Victoria and Albert's wedding. European royalty: kings, princes, princesses, royal highnesses from Germany, Italy, Belgium and France all came to see the young couple get wed. Queen Victoria and Albert had arranged the match but the Queen was bereft. Her first letters to her daughter were full of remorse, telling the newly wed Vicky that her 'first thoughts on waking were very sad – and the tears are ever coming to my eyes and ready to flow again'.[71]

Soon Vicky became pregnant. In August 1858 Albert and Victoria went to visit her in Germany having 'given up the idea, of coming over for her confinement (which everyone expected) . . . though I feel it bitterly to have to forego my natural right and duty to be with my dear Child in her hour of trial, as every mother does'.[72] The Queen, naturally, worried about her daughter's pregnancy. She was delighted that she was about to be a grandmother, wished that she could go through the pregnancy for her daughter and save her 'the annoyance'.[73] When news arrived that Vicky had delivered a healthy baby boy, she

> called all the Children in, and ran along to the Rubens Room where Albert was . . . to bring him the blessed news. Such joy! . . . Ran back to send numberless telegrams. . . . Truly grateful and happy, – relieved from a great weight, which we would not acknowledge, but which had pressed upon us both from morning till night. . . . Children in ecstasies at Uncle and Aunt-ship. Arthur shouting out 'I'm an Uncle!'[74]

Later on Victoria learned that she nearly lost both her daughter and her first grandson; and that the young Prince had been born with a permanently damaged left arm. She had a yearning to be with 'our dear Child. It seems so dreadful not to be able, like almost every mother, to go and see her, and our 1st grand-child!'[75] When her eldest daughter came to visit in May 1859, Victoria was delighted that she 'could fold her in my arms! I could not speak for joy.'[76] Victoria, still only 39 years old, was thrilled at being a grandmother, writing to her daughter to 'never fear to tire me in writing about the darling, it gives me the very greatest pleasure and I shall be ready to spoil him as much as all grand-mamas'.[77] Her youngest daughter, Beatrice, was only two years older than her first grandson.

Notes

1 Letter to Caroline Lyttelton, in Wyndham, *Correspondence of Sarah Spencer*, p. 320.
2 RA VIC/MAIN/QVJ (W) December 11th 1840.
3 Ibid. February 24th 1841.
4 Ibid. May 22nd 1842.
5 Ibid. July 10th 1842.
6 Ibid. September 14th 1844.

7 Ibid. January 11th 1842.
8 Victoria to the Princess Royal, July 28th 1858, quoted in Fulford, *Dearest Child*, p. 125.
9 Ibid. May 2nd 1859, p. 192.
10 John Van Der Kiste, *Queen Victoria's Children*, Sutton, 2003.
11 RA VIC/MAIN/QVJ (W) August 11th 1842.
12 Ibid. November 8th 1842.
13 Ibid. October 2nd 1843.
14 Victoria to the Princess Royal, May 26th 1858, quoted in Fulford, *Dearest Child*, p. 108.
15 Letter to Hon Mrs Henry Glynne from Caroline Lyttelton, April 29th 1848, in Wyndham, *Correspondence of Sarah Spencer*, p. 381.
16 RA VIC/MAIN/QVJ (W) August 1st 1843.
17 Ibid. September 22nd 1847.
18 Ibid. May 25th 1848.
19 Ibid. October 5th 1848.
20 Ibid. December 18th 1848.
21 Ibid. March 18th 1851.
22 See Van Der Kiste, *Queen Victoria's Children*, p. 174.
23 Victoria to the Princess Royal, November 24th 1858, quoted in Fulford, *Dearest Child*, p. 146.
24 RA VIC/MAIN/QVJ (W) April 14th 1858.
25 Ibid. October 28th 1859.
26 Ibid. November 9th 1859.
27 Ibid. November 21st 1859.
28 Ibid. May 24th 1861.
29 Ibid. November 9th 1843.
30 Letter to Caroline Spencer, February 1844, in Wyndham, *Correspondence of Sarah Spencer*, p. 339.
31 RA VIC/MAIN/QVJ (W) May 31st 1861.
32 Ibid. June 5th 1861.
33 Van der Kiste, *Queen Victoria's Children*, p. 175.
34 Quoted in Longford, *Victoria*, p. 186.
35 Whipping was a blanket term used to cover a wide range of physical punishments, from a slap through to a cane. The cane was abolished in British state schools in 1987 and in private schools in 1999. Today 'reasonable' physical chastisement of children by parents is still not unlawful in Britain.
36 RA VIC/MAIN/QVJ (W) December 12th 1847.
37 Ibid. February 12th 1852.
38 Ibid. November 9th 1854.
39 Ibid. March 27th 1855.
40 Ibid. June 3rd 1856.
41 Ibid. August 6th 1856.
42 Victoria to the Princess Royal, February 29th 1860, quoted in Fulford, *Dearest Child*, p. 235.
43 Ibid. March 8th 1858, p. 73.

44 RA VIC/MAIN/QVJ (W) February 11th 1846.
45 Ibid. February 21st 1845.
46 Ibid. November 6th 1844.
47 Ibid. November 1st 1846.
48 Ibid. April 21st 1850.
49 Ibid. January 5th 1850.
50 Ibid. April 25th 1846.
51 Ibid. April 14th 1859.
52 Ibid. April 25th 1848.
53 Ibid. January 25th 1836.
54 Ibid. June 11th 1849.
55 Ibid. December 20th 1843.
56 Ibid. February 1st 1850.
57 Ibid. February 27th 1853.
58 Ibid. February 25th 1842.
59 Ibid. March 30th 1845.
60 Ibid. May 10th 1845.
61 Ibid. July 30th 1847.
62 Ibid. May 5th 1853.
63 Ibid. October 3rd 1850.
64 Ibid. June 18th 1856.
65 Ibid. September 14th 1855.
66 Ibid. September 20th 1855.
67 Ibid. September 21st 1855.
68 Ibid. January 6th 1850.
69 Ibid. September 3rd 1852.
70 Ibid. September 4th 1852.
71 Victoria to the Princess Royal, February 4th 1858, quoted in Fulford, *Dearest Child*, p. 30.
72 RA VIC/MAIN/QVJ (W) August 22nd 1858.
73 Victoria to the Princess Royal, June 30th 1858, quoted in Fulford, *Dearest Child*, p. 120.
74 RA VIC/MAIN/QVJ (W) January 27th 1859.
75 Ibid. January 28th 1859.
76 Ibid. May 21st 1859
77 Victoria to the Princess Royal, March 16th 1859, quoted in Fulford, *Dearest Child*, p. 168

Figure 1 Victoria, Duchess of Kent, with Victoria.
Royal Collection Trust © Her Majesty Queen Elizabeth II, 2015/Bridgeman Images

Figure 2 The Queen and Prince Albert at home.
© Museum of London/Heritage Images/Getty Images

EN CHINE
Le gâteau des Rois et... des Empereurs

Figure 3 The royal cake: dividing up the world. The Western empires sharing China between them. From left to right: Queen Victoria, Kaiser Wilhelm II, Tsar Nicholas II, Marianne and Mutsuhito, Emperor of Japan.

Figure 4 The extended family of Queen Victoria.
© Universal History Archive/UIG via Getty Images

Figure 5 Queen Victoria.
© FPG/Getty Images

6   Queen Victoria, Palmerston and political interference: 1850–1860

The Whigs continued to be the most powerful political party in Britain. Lord Russell remained as prime minister until 1852. Queen Victoria appointed three more prime ministers during this ten-year period: the Earl of Derby, a Whig (1852 and 1858–9); Lord Aberdeen, a Tory (1852–5); and Lord Palmerston, a Whig (1855–8 and 1859–65). For much of this period, to the Queen's exasperation, Russell and Palmerston alternated the roles of prime minister and foreign secretary.

In 1850 the Queen reigned over a country in which scientific, technological, engineering and industrial advance was clearly visible. Victoria's journals rarely record Britain's colossal domestic achievements, the one exception being the 1851 Great Exhibition organised by Prince Albert. The Exhibition attracted 13,000 exhibitors from all over the world and six million visitors. The Queen visited the Exhibition the day before its official opening and returned

> quite dead beat and my head really bewildered by the myriads of beautiful and wonderful things, which now quite dazzle one's eyes. . . . We went up into the Gallery and the sight from there into all the Courts, full of all sorts of objects of art, manufacture etc – had quite the effect of fairyland. The noise was tremendous as there was so much going on, of all kinds and sorts, and at least 12 to 20,000 engaged in work of every kind. The collection of raw materials is very fine; the clocks and articles of silver, stuffs, English ribbon, lace etc are beautiful. Indeed it shows off <u>what</u> immense use to

this country this Exhibition is, as it goes to prove that we are capable of doing almost anything.[1]

Victoria maintained that the day of the Exhibition's opening on 1 May was one of the 'greatest and most glorious days of our lives, with which, to my pride and joy the name of my dearly beloved Albert is for ever associated! . . . my beloved Husband the creator of this great "Peace Festival", inviting the industry and art of all nations on earth, all this, was indeed moving, and a day to live forever.'[2] The Great Exhibition, Victoria insisted, 'had taught her so much . . . had brought her into contact with so many clever people . . . and with so many manufacturers'.[3]

The 1851 Exhibition marked the beginning of an economic boom. For some of the 18 million people who lived in Britain, it was an age of improvement: the manufacturers, merchants, managers, business executives, bankers and stockbrokers enjoyed unprecedented prosperity in their suburban mansions. It was the 'golden age' of farming and landowners enriched themselves as the price of corn and other farming produce increased. Others benefited very little: the agricultural labourer, the casual labourer, the sweated worker remained in desperate poverty, subsisting on starvation-level wages, living in overcrowded slums and sharing an outside lavatory sometimes with hundreds of others. Queen Victoria was not indifferent to poverty: between 1837 and 1871 she gave away 15 per cent of her privy purse each year to various charities – in 1852 she donated £100 to Great Ormond Street hospital – and became patron of 150 institutions, ranging from those which provided relief to aged, infirm and distressed printers to homes for Scottish children orphaned by wars. Nonetheless, her journals, her memos and her private letters show little concern for the plight of her unfortunate subjects dislocated by industrialisation.

Queen Victoria did not have to contend with any large-scale domestic political measures in this period. Lord Russell tried hard to bring in franchise reform to allow more men to vote but his Bills either failed or were thwarted by war. Lord Palmerston, in the short time he was home secretary, was responsible for some social reform. He put forward a Factory Act which made it illegal to employ young people between 6pm and 6am; a Truck Act which stopped employers paying their workers in goods rather than cash; a Smoke Abatement Act to control pollution; a Vaccination Act which made the vaccination of children against smallpox compulsory; an Act which outlawed the burying of dead inside churches; and an Act which ended transportation to Tasmania. In 1857 Palmerston personally supervised one of the most important domestic reforms of this period – the Matrimonial Causes Act, often viewed as a watershed in legal history because it established civil divorce for the first time. Previously, if couples wanted to divorce, they had to apply for a costly and lengthy special Act of Parliament. Under the new legislation, men were able to divorce their wives for adultery. It was not so easy for women to sue for divorce as wives could only divorce their husbands for bigamy, rape, sodomy, bestiality, cruelty or long-term desertion. Queen Victoria approved of the Bill but was anxious in case the stories told in the new Divorce Court would be made public. Divorce cases, she wrote to the Lord Chancellor, 'fill now almost daily a large portion of the newspapers, and are of so scandalous a character . . . None of the worst French novels . . . can be as bad as what is daily brought and laid upon the breakfast-table . . . and its effect must be most pernicious to the public morals of the country'.[4] Newspapers, driven by increased sales, reported the salacious details of divorce cases, which later prompted the Queen to ask the Bishop of London to find 'some means . . . to prevent the publication of these horrible proceedings in the Divorce Courts'.[5]

Queen Victoria was not immune from the daily life of her subjects. In the unseasonably hot summer of 1858, the problem of sanitation reached a new level when the Thames overflowed with sewage and the smell overpowered Londoners. It was known as the Great Stink. The population of London had soared from one million to 2.5 million, which meant the pressure on London's 200,000 cesspools increased, with calamitous results. London was filthy and exceedingly malodourous: streets were caked with excrement, rubbish lay uncollected, cemeteries overflowed with only partially buried bodies and the air was polluted with noxious fumes from factories and workshops. When the Queen travelled on her barge to Deptford, she was 'really half poisoned with the fearful smell of the Thames!'[6] Not surprisingly, there were further epidemics of cholera. In the Queen's Speech at the close of the parliamentary session, the government granted £3,000,000 to enable the Metropolitan Board of Works to purify the river. In 1858 a revised Public Health Act was passed which abolished the Central Board of Health and replaced it with local boards responsible for preventative action. The clean-up of England was set to begin: Joseph Bazalgette designed a new sewer system which Londoners, including the present royal family, still use today.

At this time, Victoria had to deal with the religious conflicts which re-emerged between the largely Protestant Britain and its Roman Catholic minority. The Queen was deeply ideologically committed to the low-church version of Protestantism and abhorred any pageantry and ceremony in religious services. She was annoyed when in October 1850 the Pope issued a Bull restoring the Roman Catholic diocesan hierarchy, which had been demolished in the Reformation, to Britain. The Pope without consulting the Queen or her government, divided Britain into archbishoprics and bishoprics, declared that England was again restored to Catholic power and that the religious disgrace of the Reformation had been wiped out. Queen Victoria thought this

> inconceivable and it is in the highest degree wrong of the Pope, to act in such a manner, which is a direct infringement of my prerogative, without <u>one</u> word as to his intentions being communicated to this Govt. It is I fear the result of such a number of our Clergy having at the present time such a leaning towards the Romish Church . . . It will I fear, raise intolerant cries against innocent Roman Catholics.[7]

The Queen's alarm was realised when anti-Catholic processions were held over England, windows of Catholic churches were broken and effigies of an archbishop were burned. In 1851 an Ecclesiastical Titles Act was passed, making it a criminal offence to use any city, town or place in the United Kingdom as an episcopal title. But tensions remained. In 1852 Victoria

> read the accounts of some sad riots, which took place at Stockport . . . between low Irish Roman Catholics and

foolish, equally low rabid Protestants. The dispute began with 1 or 3, ending in a distressing riot, in which I am grieved to say many were wounded, and one was killed. Many Roman Catholics had their houses destroyed and their Chapel was gutted . . . – very lamentable. I cannot bear these sort of things![8]

In June 1850 the Queen was subjected to a fifth assassination attempt, this one by an unemployed man, a mentally disturbed ex-army officer. Victoria recounts how

a young gentleman whom I have often seen in the Park, pale, fair, with a fair moustache, with a small stick in his hand. Before I knew where I was, or what had happened, he stepped forward, and I felt myself violently thrown by a blow to the left of the carriage . . . My bonnet was crushed, and on putting my hand up . . . I felt an immense bruise in the right side. . . . Certainly it is very hard and very horrid that I, a woman, – a defenceless young woman and surrounded by my Children, should be exposed to insults of this kind, and be unable to go out quietly for a drive. . . . This is by far the most disgraceful and cowardly thing that has ever been done; for a man to strike <u>any woman</u> is most brutal and I, as well as everyone else, think this <u>far</u> worse than an attempt to shoot, which, wicked as it is, is at least more comprehensible and courageous.[9]

The would-be assassin was transported to Australia for seven years.

Foreign affairs

Foreign affairs dominated the 1850s. During this decade, Queen Victoria had to deal with governmental instability and two major wars. These were the Crimean War and the Indian Mutiny, both of which could have been avoided. In some ways the Queen was to blame for the Crimean War. Victoria continued to regard the Foreign Office as her private personal province and kept interfering in matters, much to the annoyance of her ministers and sometimes to the detriment of international relations. In addition, Prince Albert took an increasing interest in British foreign policy, thereby adding to the tensions between the monarch, her government and the country.

In many ways, the decade was marked by the continuing disagreements between the Queen and Palmerston over foreign policy, her repeated attempts to get rid of him and the ensuing governmental and national chaos which followed. The Queen's relationship with Palmerston reached what one historian has called 'a point of almost hysterical exacerbation'.[10] Part of the problem lay with the Queen's reluctance to accept that she would have to negotiate with her government rather than impose her will on her foreign secretary, especially one so implacable. The *Morning Chronicle* maintained that Palmerston would never be 'a placid and complying tool, a mere automaton, whose hands are directed by the wily and unseen influences of foreign prompters'.[11] The newspaper was referring to Prince Albert. By this time, it was evident that the Prince was taking more and more of an active role in British politics especially when the Queen was pregnant or recovering from giving birth.

The Don Pacifico incident 1850

In January 1850, the Queen and Palmerston were in conflict over the latter's belligerence, his 'gunboat diplomacy' as it became known. Three years earlier, the home and the stores of a Jewish British merchant, Don Pacifico, were destroyed during riots in Athens, riots which had an anti-Semitic edge. When the Greek government declined to compensate Pacifico, he wrote to the British government for help. Palmerston did indeed help, demanded compensation from the Greeks, threatened to blockade the port of Athens and stated that 'a British subject, in whatever land he may be, shall feel confident that the watchful eye of the strong arm of England will protect him against injustice and wrong'.[12] Queen Victoria was furious. She complained:

> Ld Palmerston has thought fit to desire the Greek Govt to make instant reparation, for losses some English have sustained, and should this demand not be complied with within

24 hours, the Port would be blockaded by the Fleet! Greece has no doubt behaved ill, and the Govt is a bad one, but are these English claims worth the serious measure of blockading a port and of them oppressing a small, weak Power, whose independence we have guaranteed. . . . Really <u>what</u> a name we get abroad![13]

The Queen, probably directed by Prince Albert, asked her prime minister, Lord Russell to write to Palmerston 'a good and strong letter . . . to try an alter his tone, and that if he could not, he must take some other office'.[14] Russell replied that he could not get rid of his foreign secretary. 'This' thought the Queen, 'is too weak and miserable. . . . And thus this mischievous man kept them in constant hot water, and is to remain for the discomfort of the whole world, <u>merely</u> because people are <u>afraid</u> of him.'[15] In the end, the French mediated between Britain and Greece, which Victoria thought 'humiliating enough after all the blustering of Ld Palmerston! But his policy is entirely personal, dictated by pique and spite . . . It is a very hard thing for me to have to lend my name to all these things.'[16] For a second time in this parliamentary session, the Queen attempted to oust Palmerston; he was also censured in the House of Lords. However, in a singularly able and masterly four and a half hour speech, Palmerston defended his actions in the House of Commons and received thunderous cheers. He was now more secure in the Foreign Office than ever, seen as a defender of human rights and a potent symbol of British fortitude. More importantly, Palmerston's defence of Don Pacifico was thought a good omen for the safeguarding of British commercial interests since foreign governments would be inclined to suppress those who threatened British property.

Meanwhile, Palmerston continued to write despatches to foreign ministers which Victoria believed to be 'in so little accordance with the calm dignity she likes to see in all the proceedings of the British Government'.[17] The Queen certainly had a constitutional right to see all despatches before they were sent and often tried to alter Palmerston's drafts. Every time she did so, Palmerston ignored her advice. Queen Victoria made no attempt to hide her annoyance, complaining of Palmerston publicly and not concealing 'my opinion of his being utterly untrustworthy and that

England was lowered and degraded by all he has done and has become detested by other nations'.[18]

The deteriorating relationship between Queen Victoria and Lord Palmerston reached crisis point in August 1850 when the Queen, according to Brian Connell, wrote 'one of the strongest letters ever written by a British sovereign to a Prime Minister' asking him to remove Palmerston.[19] Her memo to Lord Russell stated in precise terms her expected relationship between the Queen and her foreign minister. First, Victoria demanded to be informed in advance of any diplomatic action. Second, she insisted that any memo which she had approved should not be arbitrarily changed after she had signed it. Third, she wanted Palmerston to be dismissed. Lord Russell dutifully tackled Palmerston about these issues 'the outcome of which' the Queen

> grieved to say, is that he remains where he is, a constant thorn in my side, and to the detriment of the whole Country, as well as of Europe. . . . Besides that, Ld Palmerston's conduct towards me, in frequently not answering my letters, and taking no notice of my observations etc was quite unbecoming. . . . It is too unfortunate that every good opportunity for getting rid of Ld Palmerston has invariably failed.[20]

The relationship between the Queen and Palmerston deteriorated to the point at which Prince Albert felt obliged to intervene. The Prince told Palmerston that the Queen wanted him to show 'more respect and attention towards me, – that I expected to be informed of what was going to be done; . . . otherwise I should consider it necessary to use my Constitutional Right of dismissing the Minister'.[21] This was blatant intimidation of a minister but it was an idle threat: the two royals had already tried to pressurise the prime minister to dismiss Palmerston but had not succeeded. Nevertheless, in that highly deferential age, Palmerston was obviously disturbed by the conversation with Albert. Victoria was told that Albert had never seen anyone so cast down as Palmerston 'quite in tears, shaking and saying, that if it was known that he had behaved with disrespect towards me he could never show his face again in society'.[22] However, when it came to policy, Palmerston continued to do what he thought best.

The incident of General Haynau

In September 1850 the Queen and Palmerston quarrelled once more, this time over the treatment of an Austrian general who was visiting England. 'I must not omit' the Queen wrote in her journal in September 1850 'to record a most disgraceful outrage on Gen Haynau which has for the 1st time tarnished our name for hospitality, and that of this land, for safety.' Victoria was referring to the Austrian military commander General Haynau, who was deeply unpopular in Britain for his brutal suppression of the 1848 Hungarian revolutionaries. The General had just visited a brewery in London where he 'was insulted by cries of "Down with the Austrian Butcher", was assailed with dirt and blows, all the brewers starting to belabour and attack him, pulling his clothes nearly off his back, so that he had to run for his life and seek refuge in an Inn . . . which fortunately the infuriated mob, now numbering nearly 500, did not find'.[23] The Queen blamed Hungarian and Polish refugees, insisting that such behaviour 'is so unlike our people here, who never trouble themselves about foreign concerns, and have never touched even many of those wicked French and German Socialists and Revolutionists who are here. I hope the authors of this abominable outrage will be found out and that the ringleaders will be well punished.'[24] It was a blot, the Queen thought, on the fair name of Britain and she complained to the former Whig prime minister, Lord Grey, about the atrocious attack. However, the police refused to press charges or identify any of the 'horrid people. This is a very bad thing', the Queen believed, 'for such behaviour ought not to go unpunished. There has been a shocking meeting of the very worst character of Socialists, eulogising this brutal attack.'[25]

Queen Victoria instructed Palmerston to write a letter to the Austrian government expressing 'the deep regret of this government at the brutal outrage on one of the Emperor's distinguished generals and subjects'. Palmerston not only refused to offer an official apology but also in a draft dispatch added that they should have tossed Haynau in a blanket, rolled him up and sent him away in a cab. The Queen was furious, ordered Palmerston to retract his words and commanded him to write a more emollient letter.[26] This he did. Reluctantly. Nevertheless, the Queen could not completely silence Palmerston's voice, however much she tried to force him into submission. In that sense alone, Palmerston – perhaps inadvertently – became the champion of ministerial independence, constantly challenging the weakening prerogatives of the Queen.

At the beginning of 1851, Palmerston seemed invincible, riding the wave of popular support for both his liberal principles and his strong defence of British interests. Queen Victoria remained immune to the charisma and appeal of her foreign secretary. In March 1851 the Queen reminded Russell of her objections to Palmerston and once more asked that he be dismissed. Russell refused, citing the dangers of the Queen interfering in government appointments. The Queen

> was excessively annoyed, really most upset, by this announcement. . . . Ld John said he was very anxious that it should be he . . . who would bear the responsibility of removing Ld Palmerston from the foreign Office and not me. My refusal (to have Palmerston in Government) could only appear to the general public as a personal objection on my part. . . . I was mortified, vexed and discouraged, to the highest degree at this result of so much trouble and anxiety.[27]

Russell's unwillingness to dismiss his foreign minister had less to do with his disapproval of the Crown trying to exercise control over foreign policy and more about the parliamentary ascendancy of Palmerston. For Russell to have dismissed such a popular foreign minister would have amounted to the governing Whig Party committing parliamentary suicide. Russell was never going to do that.

The affair of Lajos Kossuth

In December 1851 the Queen and Palmerston squabbled yet again. The leader of the Hungarian revolution, Lajos Kossuth, came to Britain seeking asylum and Palmerston wanted to give him an official welcome. Victoria 'tried in vain, to make Ld Palmerston feel, that he ought not to see Kossuth'.[28] When Kossuth arrived she thought it 'quite disgusting to see the absurd fuss that is being

made about him'.[29] Lord Russell, instructed by the Queen, asked
Palmerston not to meet Kossuth but Palmerston refused, sending
a reply, according to Victoria 'of such an impertinence hardly to
be credited or equalled'. Palmerston had told the Queen that he
did not choose to be dictated 'as to whom I may or may not
receive in my own house'.[30] The Queen wrote a terse reply to her
foreign secretary threatening that she 'could not expose myself
to having my orders disobeyed by one of my public Servants.
Therefore should Ld Palmerston persist in his intention, he could
not continue as my minister.'[31] In Victoria's opinion, Kossuth was
a destructive force who had committed every cruelty to undermine
the legitimate government of his country. He was, she maintained,
'a great liar'.[32] Eventually, after Cabinet pressure, Palmerston
agreed not to invite Kossuth to his home but it was a clear case
of constitutional impropriety by the Queen. No sovereign had
the right to stop a minister receiving guests in a private capacity.
Lajos Kossuth remained in Britain for 17 years, with the Queen
longing that he 'could be found doing something illegal' and could
be 'shut up for a time'.[33]

Louis Napoleon and Palmerston's dismissal

In late 1851 the Queen had her revenge on Palmerston. On
2 December the French president, Louis Napoleon, who was due
to step down from government, organised a *coup d'état* so that
he could remain in office. The British government – largely because
of Queen Victoria's insistence – agreed to adopt a position of
neutrality towards the French position. Naturally, the Queen's
loyalty to the French royal family who were still living in Britain
made her think that Louis Napoleon was a usurper. In contrast,
Palmerston, without informing either his colleagues or the Queen,
told the French Ambassador that he, and by inference the government, approved of Louis Napoleon's new role. Inevitably, his
action angered the Queen who commented on 'what an extraordinary and unprincipled man Ld P is and how devoid of every
feeling of honour and consistency'[34] and – yet again – pressurised
Russell to dismiss his foreign secretary. This time, Russell obeyed
and accused Palmerston of 'violations of prudence and decorum'
and asked for his resignation because 'the conduct of foreign

affairs can no longer be left in your hands'.[35] It was a sobering and humiliating moment for Palmerston but the Queen's relief was 'great and we felt quite excited by the news, for our anxiety and worry during the last 5 years and ½ which was indescribable was mainly, if not entirely, caused by him. It is a great and unexpected mercy.'[36]

However, it was to be a pyrrhic victory for the Queen. When Victoria pressed her government to review its foreign policy, her appeals went unheeded in the Cabinet. Moreover, when the news reached the press about Palmerston's resignation, it was met with universal disapproval: some even believed that Russell had forced his most popular, patriotic and able minister to resign because of pressure from the Queen, who was herself under the undue influence of Prince Albert. Indeed, a section of the press insinuated that Lord Palmerston's resignation was due to 'an influence behind the throne'. 'It is quite sufficient', one radical newspaper reported 'for the English people to be ridden rough-shed over by their own native oligarchy, without being subjected to the sinister influence of the "Royal Highness" of one of the paltriest hole-and-corner nooks in Europe . . . the Puddledock Duchy of Saxe-Coburg-Gotha.'[37] In the eyes of the press and the British population, Palmerston was a domestic hero, a defender of the national interest and a campaigner against autocracy; some called for him to replace Russell as prime minister. More worryingly, Palmerston remained a potent political force, no longer constrained by ministerial office.

In February 1852, Palmerston wreaked his revenge by – perhaps inadvertently – bringing down the Russell government. When he put forward an amendment to a minor Militia Bill, it quickly turned into vote of confidence in the government. Palmerston's amendment was carried and Lord Russell and his government were forced to resign. The Conservative Lord Derby became prime minister in what was dubbed the 'Who? Who? Ministry' because the ministers were all considered nonentities. The Queen commented that 'no-one expected it to be able to carry any important measure . . . they were very inexperienced, and many devoid of <u>all</u> talent'.[38] Derby's government only lasted between February and December 1852. It was followed by a coalition of Whigs, Peelites and Irish MPs, led by Lord Aberdeen. Disraeli once remarked that 'Coalitions . . . have always found this, that their triumph has been brief. . . . England does not love coalitions.'

Queen Victoria called the coalition a 'great experiment' and feared that it would be no easy task to bring together MPs who had for so long been opposed to one another. Nevertheless, the Queen approved of Aberdeen as she once again had a prime minister who was a 'personal, truly attached and much esteemed friend'.[39] His 'Ministry of All the Talents', as it was quickly dubbed, consisted of many of the ablest men in government: Russell as foreign secretary, Gladstone as chancellor of the exchequer . . . and Palmerston as home secretary. The Queen, as ever, remained opposed to Palmerston and wrote a long letter detailing her concerns. But the messenger charged with its delivery got drunk and it never reached the Cabinet until after Palmerston's appointment.

The Crimean War: March 1854–February 1856

On New Year's Day 1854, Victoria opened her diary with the comment that 'The year opens gloomily, as regards the affairs of Europe. War seems almost inevitable.'[40] Three months later, on 28 March, Britain declared war on Russia: it was the start of the Crimean War.[41] In a letter to the King of Prussia, Victoria quoted the words of Polonius in Shakespeare's *Hamlet*: 'Beware of entrance to a quarrel; but, being in, bear it that the opposed may beware of thee.'[42]

Britain declared war because she feared that Russia would expand its empire by taking over land controlled by the Ottomans. It was a war which could have been averted if Britain had taken a strong stand at an early stage. In 1853, when Russia had threatened to invade the Ottoman Empire in order to 'protect' the large numbers of Christians who lived there from Islamic harassment, Victoria proposed negotiation and her compliant prime minister, Lord Aberdeen, agreed. The Queen, thought to be swayed by Prince Albert, believed that 'it would never have done for this country to be in the position, of being dragged into a war, by these fanatical half uncivilised Turks'.[43] The fact that members of Victoria and Albert's family had recently married into the Russian

nobility might also have influenced them. However, Palmerston --
who was now home secretary – had argued that more vigorous
measures were needed in order to shock Russia into revoking its
plans. In his view, a strong independent Turkey was necessary for
the economic and commercial prosperity of Britain and the balance of power in Europe. The Queen and Albert were annoyed
with Palmerston's pro-Turkey stance, considering him 'obstinate
and very warlike'. Both objected to Palmerston's hawkish policy
and favoured conciliation and appeasement. Military action, they
believed, should only be taken after due deliberation by the Queen
and the House of Commons, a period of consultation with potential
allies and negotiations with Russia. In the midst of all this,
Palmerston resigned as home secretary – over a Reform Bill rather
than Foreign Policy – but his resignation, the Queen realised,
would be attributed to the Turkish/Russian question largely because
Palmerston had earlier declared that he did not wish 'to remain
with such cowards, who had not the courage to make war'.[44]

Russia, possibly sensing British ambivalence over a prospective
conflict, invaded the Ottoman-ruled Danubian Principalities of
Eastern Europe and destroyed a Turkish fleet in the Black Sea.
The invasion by Russia presented Victoria, the government and
the rest of the European community with a dilemma: do nothing
and Russia would certainly expand its territories and threaten
the peace of the region. Declare war and risk the death of thousands. After much indecisiveness, military intervention seemed
the only course and so the Crimean War began. Britain and the
Ottoman Empire were joined by France and Piedmont in the fight
against Russia. Palmerston was vindicated as the 'outbreak of
war seemed to validate Palmerston's insistence on the need for a
clear brake on Russia'.[45]

In a way, Queen Victoria can be held partly responsible for
the Crimean War by her constant undermining of Palmerston and
her refusals to have him as foreign secretary. Russia might have
been deterred, and a peaceful solution arrived at, if Palmerston
had still been at the Foreign Office because he would have immediately – and forcefully – made it clear that Britain was prepared
to go to war on the issues involved. As a letter to *The Times*
indicated, 'With Lord Palmerston in the Cabinet . . . Englishmen
had no fear . . . the very name of "Palmerston" had grown into

a salutary terror.'[46] *The Times* asked 'Would he have averted it?'[47] with an underlying suggestion that he would have. Certainly, the lack of decisiveness on the part of the British government, and particularly Aberdeen's lack of leadership, was seen as one important factor in bringing the war about.[48]

The Crimean War increased Prince Albert's unpopularity. Queen Victoria's anger and incomprehension grew as the press waged a campaign against her husband. Albert was accused of directing British policy on the Eastern Question because he was 'under the triple influence of his brother the reigning Duke of Saxe-Coburg-Gotha, the King of the Belgians and the Orleans family. . . . Is it not degrading and humiliating to a degree, for the British people to reflect that the Foreign Policy of their country is thus entirely ruled *by foreigners*?'[49] Albert was accused of illegitimate interference in State affairs, of being the prince prime minister, and the chief agent of the 'Austrian-Belgian-Coburg-Orleans clique, the avowed enemies of England, and the subservient tools of Russian ambition.'[50] *Reynolds's Weekly Newspaper* believed that Albert's 'chief end is the preservation of the Coburg principality, and to this, the traditions, interests, honour, and faith of England, as well as the integrity of the Ottoman Empire, are all to be subordinated and sacrificed'.[51] Letters to the press accused the Prince of trespassing on political affairs by attending ministerial briefings and writing directly to British ministers serving in foreign courts. Prince Albert, it was maintained, had no right to send letters of instruction to British embassies abroad: 'When he takes upon himself to perform ministerial acts in opposition to the men appointed by the voice of the nation to advise the sovereign, he directly violates the great principles of the English constitution.'[52] It was alleged that the court, and not the ministers, were giving the impetus and the tone to English foreign policy.[53] *Reynolds's Weekly Newspaper* unhesitatingly and openly ascribed the government's reluctance to help Turkey to 'the predominating influence exercised by foreigners in the councils of the Sovereign. . . . The German influence apparently acts as a narcotic upon the coroneted set of cringing sycophants, by whom the destinies of a great country are so unworthily betrayed.'[54] The paper threatened that 'if the Prince Consort thinks he will carry matters with a high hand, we beg to inform him that England is neither a dirty little German principality, nor will its inhabitants tamely submit to the impertinent meddlings of a person, who, we verily believe, loves us only for what he can get'.[55] Such was the unpopularity of Albert that in January 1854 crowds gathered outside the Tower of London hoping to see Prince Albert and Lord Aberdeen imprisoned for treason. The crowd was disappointed that only effigies of the two figures were burned.

The Queen, unsurprisingly, was indignant about

> the abominable attacks against my beloved Albert, which are going on again and he thinks they come from the over excited state of people's minds upon the Eastern Question and their desire for war. He says that the low, wicked and jealous opponents of the Govt, try out of spite and anger to work upon the minds of the people, by writing these horrors.[56]

She wrote to Stockmar telling him that 'the stupidest trash is babbled to the public, so stupid that (as they say in Coburg) you would not give it to the pigs to litter in'.[57] Palmerston, she believed 'was behind it all!' As a result of her complaints and entreaties, one of her ministers wrote to the press 'to desist from these unwarrantable attacks'.[58] The Queen was furious when at least one editor refused the request because 'it made the Paper sell!'[59]

War was eventually declared on 28 March 1854. At first it seemed to go well. Once hostilities had begun, the Queen and Prince Albert did a U-turn, became fervently martial and backed the war effort – to do otherwise would have been not just imprudent but potentially traitorous. As soon as the Queen cast aside her initial reservations she became 'very enthusiastic about my dear army and navy'. Indeed she regretted 'exceedingly not to be a man and to be able to fight in the war'. As head of the army, the Queen saw the soldiers and sailors as her own men. On 5 May 1854 the Queen, who took an 'anxious interest in everything that goes on', was delighted with reports of Odessa being shelled and its fortifications, batteries and military stores destroyed, 12 war vessels sunk and 13 Russian vessels, laden with munition, taken. She believed that 'her' sailors behaved beautifully and 'ever show themselves so brave and so judicious. There is nothing in the world like our Navy!'[60] When news of the Battle of Alma, usually considered the first battle of the Crimean War, reached Britain, Victoria wrote exultantly that 'never in so short a time has so strong a battery, so well defended, been so bravely and gallantly taken'.[61] Successful battles at Balaklava and Inkerman confirmed her initial optimism, especially since her generals sent her favourable reports.

But soon news reached Britain of the chaotic way the war was being waged. The gross mismanagement of the Crimean campaign, the divisions within the army command, the breakdown of the transport system and the deplorable state of the hospitals soon became public knowledge. Victoria became all too aware of the poor management of the war. Her journals speak of officers with dirty clothes full of vermin, the misery of the men from the wet, the lack of clothes and other covering, the bad roads, and the 'miserable condition of the poor wretched half-starved horses'. She was conscious that the 'poor young recruits die very fast after arriving. All this is heartbreaking.' She studied reports in *The Times* from the Crimea which spoke of trenches full of water 'so that one had to lie up to one's waist in them', of men who slept in their wet clothes, froze and when they pulled off their boots, portions of their feet would come off with them. 'Our troops', she wrote, 'suffered much in their health, from fever and diarrhoea and still <u>worse</u>, from the wearing constant fatigue and night work. . . . the food was much the same, constantly salt pork, with only occasionally fresh meat, no bread, no vegetables, at least rarely, and never any milk'.[62] Certainly the organisation of the war was chaotic: there was a shortage of tents, huts, boots, knapsacks food and medical supplies. More casualties were inflicted by scurvy caused by lack of vitamin C than by the Russians.[63]

Queen Victoria noticed that the French army was well provided and bemoaned 'the sad state of our noble Army in the Crimea, and the total lack of all management and foresight in those who are responsible. For, such great sufferings and privations are quite <u>unnecessary</u> and they really are heartrending.'[64] Victoria, by this time reflecting public sentiment, condemned her generals for the lack of equipment,

> which is quite inconceivable considering all that was sent out . . . the poor men had been without their kits or any of

the necessaries quite essential to a solder. They had therefore
never been able to help themselves or make themselves comfortable, and were in need of everything . . . The things never
came, never were sent for, and when inquired about, no one
knew where they were. Hence all the misery and suffering.
This is really unpardonable.[65]

Cholera raged through the army and the navy and more soldiers
and sailors died of this and related diseases than were killed in
battle: out of a total of 21,097 deaths, 2,755 were killed in action,
2,019 died of wounds and over 16,000 died of disease. Finally,
after much prevarication by the medical establishment and pressure from the government, the Duke of Newcastle informed the
Queen that 'he had settled to send out 30 Nurses for the Hospitals
at Scutari and Varna, under a Miss Nightingale, who is a remarkable person, having studied both Medicine and Surgery and having
practised in Hospitals in Paris and in Germany'.[66] In September
1856 the Queen gave an audience to Florence Nightingale. Victoria noted in her journal:

It is impossible to say how much pleased we were with her.
I had expected a rather cold, stiff, reserved person, instead
of which, she is gentle, pleasing and engaging, most ladylike,
and so clever, clear and comprehensive in her views. . . . But
she is entirely free of absurd enthusiasm, without a grain of
'exaltation' . . . without the slightest display of religion or
particle of humbug.[67]

She met Florence Nightingale several times, often commenting
on her excellence and 'truly Christ-like spirit of true charity', and
envying her 'being able to do so much good'.

In November 1854, Queen Victoria's government was badly
shaken by news of an avoidable catastrophe at Balaclava where
the Light Brigade was virtually annihilated as a result of a mis-
understanding between two quarrelsome British officers. Victoria
was horrified:

Alas! The 2nd Charge of the Light Cavalry was . . . a fatal
mistake. . . . All behaved like heroes, and not one better than

poor Ld Cardigan who led them to the murderous fight. 13 Officers killed, 17 wounded and 160 men killed, besides over 300 horses. I trembled with emotions, as well as pride in reading the recital of the heroism of these devoted men. . . . To hear of their sufferings, their being killed, and on this occasion so unnecessarily, is very harrowing.[68]

The ineptitude of the command and the bravery of the soldiers was encapsulated in Tennyson's poem 'The Charge of the Light Brigade', written in response to a report of the battle in *The Times*. It added fuel to the popular belief of brave soldiers led by incompetent Generals.

> Forward the Light Brigade
> Was there a man dismayed?
> Not tho' the soldier knew
> Someone had blunder'd.
> Theirs not to make reply,
> Theirs not to reason why,
> Theirs but to do and die.
> Into the valley of Death
> Rode the six hundred

Soon after Balaklava, suggestions appeared in the press that Palmerston be appointed minister of war. *The Times* insisted that 'among living British names there is one especially European. Feared at Courts, ever in the mouths of diplomatists, subscribed to many a document . . . the name of Palmerston belongs to the world.'[69] *The Times* asked 'What is Lord Palmerston doing? What does he think of the war? Would he have averted it? Would he have brought it earlier to a crisis?'[70] 'This is incredible', said the Queen about the potential replacement, 'Ld Palmerston would be totally incapable of doing it . . . I could never consent to such a thing.'[71] Lord Palmerston, the Queen believed, was 'totally unfit for the post'[72] and so Palmerston remained as home secretary. But the prime minister, Lord Aberdeen, was an inept leader and showed no willingness to press for victory in the Crimea. In January 1855 a radical MP, John Roebuck, demanded a parliamentary investigation into the Crimean War. Prime Minister Aberdeen viewed it as a 'vote of no confidence' of the coalition government and resigned; Victoria was sad at losing her 'dear kind excellent friend, Lord Aberdeen'.

The return of Palmerston

Lord Palmerston, it was generally felt, 'was the man to whom the country looked at the present moment'.[73] Victoria disagreed. She thought that 'Ld Palmerston was totally unfit for the task, having become very deaf, as well as very blind, being 71'.[74] The Queen was determined to exhaust everything before she sent for Palmerston. First of all she sent for Derby to form a government; then she sent for Russell. When neither man was able to form a government, she reluctantly sent for Palmerston, confirming in a memorandum that it 'would be very objectionable in many respects, and personally not agreeable to me, but I think of nothing but the country . . . my own personal feelings would be sunk if only the efficiency of the government could be obtained'.[75] Victoria wrote to her uncle King Leopold that she had had no alternative: Aberdeen had been discredited as a war leader; Derby's party was unfit to govern and Russell's credibility was too damaged.[76]

Queen Victoria viewed her new prime minister with alarm. However, Palmerston's vigorous prosecution of the Crimean War helped change the Queen's attitude. Within days of taking office, Palmerston outlined his plans for army and naval reforms, including changes of personnel, which would increase the efficiency of the war effort. He remodelled the army's medical department, increased the number of hospital ships, issued instructions for twice-daily health inspections, set down basic clothing provision and re-organised the supply chain. He advised on campaign tactics too, asking that the armed forces focus more narrowly on the blockade of the Russian fleet, on the capture of Sebastopol, on the destruction of the Russian fleet and on the expulsion of Russians from Georgia. After a ten-month bitter siege of a city which had become the symbol of an incompetent war, Sebastopol was captured in September 1855. The Queen's 'delight was great' and she praised God for the splendid news;[77] Palmerston thanked Britain for striking a mortal blow against an enemy who had threatened the world.

At the outbreak of war, Victoria became entirely taken up with military affairs. She soon had an impressive command of the allied positions in the Crimea, signed the commission of every officer, wrote encouraging letters to her generals and personal letters of condolence to the widows of commanders, knitted woollen socks, mittens and scarves for the troops, made regular visits to military hospitals and continued to take a keen interest in the work of Florence Nightingale. The Queen was visibly moved each time she visited the wounded and her journals are full of comments about 'the sight of such fine, powerful frames laid low and prostrate with wounds and sickness on beds of sufferings, or maimed in the prime of life, is indescribably touching to us women, who are born to suffer, and can bear pain more easily, so different to men, and soldiers'.[78] On one occasion, Victoria saw 251 patients, of whom 127 had served in the Crimea:

> there were 15 cases of amputation amongst the wounded. I never saw such a number without legs or arms. . . . We saw 2 totally blind men. Another young man had had a bullet through his nose, entering his nostril and carrying away part of his palate and coming out the back. . . . there were some very severe cases which made one very sad to see.[79]

It fitted Queen Victoria's sense of deep gratitude that there should be a public recognition of the efforts of her army. In 1854 the Queen created her own campaign medal which she conferred on all those who had fought in the Crimea:

> At first I felt so agitated, I could hardly hold the medals as I handed it with its blue and yellow edged ribbon. . . . all touched my hand, the 1st time that a simple Private has touched the hand of his Sovereign, and that, a Queen! I am proud of it, – proud of this tie which links the lowly brave to his Sovereign. . . . I feel as if I could cry while writing these lines, the recollection of it all is so moving.[80]

Eventually the war ended. In March 1856 the Allied Powers and Russia signed the Treaty of Paris, which imposed severe terms and restricted Russia's naval power in the Black Sea. It had cost

Britain £76 million and the lives of 22,700 men. Queen Victoria wrote that 'I own the peace rather sticks in my throat, and so it does in that of the <u>whole</u> nation!'[81] Even so, she realised that

> with the great sickness prevalent in the French Army and the unwillingness of the Emperor and his people to proceed any further with the war, it is better it should be so, for I am sure . . . We could not have hoped to gain any successes. This has reconciled me to the Peace, which, otherwise, I consider, came too suddenly and is not a very favourable one for <u>us</u>.[82]

When the war ended, Queen Victoria welcomed back each and every one of her army regiments as well as the return of a fleet of 240 ships. When she greeted the first of the troops, she commented that she could not describe the emotion Albert and she felt

> as toil worn, very sunburnt men, advanced in splendid order. They all had long beards and were heavily laden with large knapsacks, their cloaks and blankets on top, canteens and full haversacks, and carrying their muskets – quite the picture of <u>real</u> fighting men, such fine tall, strong men, some strikingly handsome.[83]

In the early summer of 1856, the Queen reviewed her troops in a series of military days at Aldershot. She was majestically dressed in a newly designed scarlet jacket with gold braid, brass buttons and a gold and crimson sash tunic and a hat with a white and red feather and golden tassels. She looked the very image of pomp and splendour. On 8 July, the Queen was, for the first time ever, confident to address her troops. She learned her speech by heart:

> I stood up, wonderful to say, no longer nervous as I had been before, dreading I might make mistakes, and said my speech loudly and distinctly, without one moment's hesitation, or a single mistake. On beholding all those gallant, sun

burnt, weather beaten heroes around, I felt courage all at once come over me.[84]

On Friday 26 June 1857 the Queen distributed her first Victoria Crosses, instigated by her to honour acts of valour in the Crimean War. It was the highest military decoration, awarded to members of all ranks 'for gallantry of the highest order'. It held a pension of £10 a year. The event was a royal spectacle as 4,000 troops and about 100,000 people witnessed the now quite plump 38-year-old Queen, dressed in her full army uniform of red scarlet tunic and black skirt, bend down from her horse and pin the cross on the breast of 47 men. She was 'full of agitation for the coming great event', but thought it a 'beautiful sight and everything admirably arranged . . . it was indeed a most proud, gratifying day'.[85] She personally donated £1,000 to set up a Patriotic Fund for the widows and orphans of soldiers who died during the war.

This expensive and, it is generally held, futile war confirmed Palmerston as the saviour of the nation. By the end of the Crimean War, even Victoria considered Lord Palmerston to be the 'one who gives the least trouble, and is most amenable to reason, and most ready to adopt suggestions. The great danger and great difficulty with him however, is foreign affairs.'[86] Vindicated by events and emboldened by his successful prosecution of the war, Palmerston remained 'the same and his Despatches are written precisely as they used to be' but the Queen confessed that it did not bother her so much.[87] Queen Victoria never held grudges. She bestowed the Order of the Garter on Palmerston, the most senior British Order of Chivalry for those who have held public office. It is a mark of royal favour; only 24 men could hold this honour at any one time.

Relationships between Queen Victoria and Palmerston improved further – for a time – when trouble arose in China. The Chinese Emperor refused to allow foreign merchants into Canton, and seized a British ship. Palmerston wanted liberty and security for British trade and in true 'gunboat diplomacy' style he ordered the bombardment of Canton. His policy was defeated in the House of Commons, a general election took place and Palmerston was returned with an increased majority; Queen Victoria, who had just given birth to her last child, Beatrice, congratulated him.

The Indian Mutiny 1857

No sooner had Palmerston returned to office than the Queen and her government were faced with a mutiny in India. A large proportion of the army in India were native troops (Sepoys) because the British government disliked spending too much money on a large standing peacetime army staffed by British troops. Indeed, there were 151,000 men in the Bengal army compared to 23,000 British troops based in India. The Sepoys were subjected to a range of educational, army and civil service reforms brought in by the governor-generals, and resented it. Many other Indians agreed with the Sepoys, believed that the British had over-Westernised India and feared that they would ultimately suppress both Hindu and Muslim religions. In addition, the British seized the lands of a number of Indian rulers on the spurious pretext that they misgoverned their subjects.

The spark for the mutiny occurred when a new rifle was introduced to the Indian army. Soldiers, who had to bite the ends off the cartridges before inserting them into the rifle, found that the cartridges were greased with animal fat: anti-British protesters told Hindus that the fat came from the cow, while Muslims were told that the fat came from the pig. This had a cruel significance when, in the early summer 1857, an Indian Mutiny – known more in India as a war of independence – began near Calcutta and spread rapidly when soldiers refused to load their rifles. Victoria heard 'such sad accounts from India, – the mutiny amongst the native troops spreading, sad murders of Europeans at Meerut, and still worse, at Delhi'.[88] The restoration of the Islamic Mogul Empire was proclaimed.

Victoria was haunted by the 'dreadful' reports from India, of the 'horrid' murders of British women and children which had taken place at Cawnpore.[89] In July 1857, 120 women and children were hacked to death, dismembered with meat cleavers and the remains thrown into a well by Indian forces who had captured them. Victoria read the 'dreadful details in the papers of the horrors committed in India on poor ladies and children, who were murdered with revolting barbarity'.[90] She thought the 'details of horrors committed on women, ladies and children too appalling! If they had only been shot down, it would not be so ghastly, but everything that can outrage feelings, – every torture that can be conceived, has been perpetrated!! I cannot bear to think of it! . . . One's blood runs cold, and one's heart bleeds.'[91] She later reflected on the 'horrors of shame and every outrage which women must most dread, as well as of exposure, surpass all belief, and it was a great mercy <u>all</u> were <u>killed!</u> It should never have been made known, now that no good can be done any more and it can only distract for life, the unhappy relations.'[92] At Lucknow too, soldiers as well as civilians including women and children, were forced to retreat to the Governor's residency where they were besieged for months, suffering from semi-starvation, lack of water and the incessant Indian heat as well as bombardment. On Wednesday 23 December 1857, Victoria received the 'blessed news' that Lucknow had been relieved and that the 'Ladies, women, children and sick' had left.

This time, Queen Victoria had no relatives to placate, and nor did she have any personal agenda which would conflict with the needs of her country. She was anxious to squash the rebellion and claim India as her own. Palmerston was written to regularly and exhorted to use vigorous measures and re-inforcements to quell the mutiny. Victoria spoke 'most strongly' to Palmerston about 'the necessity of recruiting the whole army, – of taking energetic measures at once, and not miserable half measures'.[93] She was anxious to impress upon Palmerston 'the necessity of taking a comprehensive view of our military position . . . instead of going on without a plan, living from hand to mouth and taking small isolated measures without reference to each other'.[94] Palmerston, who was concerned about the damage to trade, agreed with his sovereign and sent out more troops to suppress the mutiny.

Affairs in India improved for Victoria and her British Empire: Delhi was recaptured and Lucknow relieved. Reprisals were cruel as the British victors wreaked a pitiless revenge, firing mutineers from cannon, hacking them to pieces and hanging them in their hundreds. In Lahore, two mutineers were lashed across the muzzles of guns, the two guns fired simultaneously and 'shreds of cloth, bone and bloody hunks of flesh were spewed onto the parade ground' in front of the assembled sepoys.[95] It was a gruesome deterrent: viciousness, it was believed, should be attacked with viciousness. Victoria, who preferred reconciliation to retribution, 'spoke strongly' to Palmerston about the 'bad vindictive spirit, exhibited by many people here . . . and of the absolute necessity for showing our desire to be kind to the peaceable inhabitants'.[96] In her view the death penalty should not be used indiscriminately on all those involved in the mutiny, for she felt there was a wide difference between those who committed murders and atrocities and those who had just run away. She told Lady Canning, wife of the Governor-General of India, that the greatest care should be taken not to interfere with Indian religions 'as once a cry of that kind is raised among a fanatical people – very strictly attached to their religion – there is no knowing what it may lead to and where it may end'.[97] The Queen asked that Indian princes and troops who had remained loyal be rewarded, advice which showed a wisdom and integrity that would do credit to experienced politicians.

The long-term problem of the governance of India remained. Palmerston announced his decision that the 'Government of India by the East India Company must be terminated.'[98] The Judge Advocate, the legal advisor of the armed forces, told the Queen that the British people felt that India should belong to the Queen and not to the East India Company. Moreover, he believed that Indians would feel differently 'to what they do now, wounded and hurt, by the vulgarity and lack of breeding and proper feeling which has been so conspicuous in the E. I. Co.'.[99] In 1858 the government passed a Government of India Act which abolished the East India Company and put India firmly under the control of the British government. The pace of educational and civil reforms slowed down. At the same time more British troops were sent out.

Continental politics

On the evening of 14 January 1858, an assassin tried to kill Louis Napoleon, the French emperor, and his wife on their way to the Paris opera. An Italian revolutionary, Felice Orsini, was charged with the crime. The British were implicated: Orsini had taken political refuge in England and had allegedly bought his bombs in Birmingham. The French foreign minister, Walewski, complained to Palmerston about the British tradition of offering sanctuary to potential political assassins. Palmerston ignored the letter. The Queen, however, agreed with Walewski. In her opinion, if similar assassins were 'tolerated in France and came over to attempt to do something against us here, the whole British nation would demand instant reparation'.[100] In the end, Palmerston introduced a Conspiracy to Murder Bill aimed to combat terrorism. However, this was defeated when news reached the House of Commons about Walewski's letter: parliament was outraged at what it saw as interference in Britain's domestic policies and disapproved of Palmerston's undue compliance. Queen Victoria, 'much vexed and thunderstruck' by these events accepted Palmerston's resignation.

The Queen's next government under the leadership of Lord Derby was weak and limped on for 15 months before it conceded defeat. 'So', wrote the Queen 'we are in for a crisis!'[101] In June 1859, after a failed attempt to appoint Lord Granville as prime minister, Victoria invited Palmerston once again to lead the House of Commons even though she feared 'the bad effect Ld Palmerston's name would have in Europe'.[102] Predictably, Palmerston's next premiership opened amid European conflict and the rapport between Queen Victoria and Lord Palmerston which had built up during the Crimean War soon disintegrated. Once more, the two disagreed over Italy. As usual, the Queen tended to protect her family's interests whereas Palmerston's sole purpose was to protect Britain's. In 1859 friction between Piedmont, a region in north-west Italy and Austria flared up into a second Italian war of independence. The Queen, who had a number of relatives in the Austrian court and army, disagreed with her government's policy over Italy: she thought Palmerston's commitment to a free and independent Italy a 'dangerous doctrine' and resisted any dilution of Austrian control. Victoria feared Palmerston's sympathy towards Italian unity and his visceral dislike of Austria. At one time the Queen stubbornly refused to sign letters supporting Italian independence, even threatening to abdicate and emigrate to Australia. In the Queen's opinion, Palmerston had put forward an 'unfortunate policy and still more, imprudent private language, showing their wish to persecute Austria and trying to deprive her of all influence in the Italian Confederation. . . . Lamentable!'[103] She 'felt quite in despair and overwhelmed at the dangers we are being dragged into, step by step. . . . It seems dreadful!'[104]

France, which hoped to gain land from the conflict between Austria and the Italian rebels, went to war against Austria, defeated them and liberated most of northern Italy. In July 1859 Austria and France signed a secret treaty – the Treaty of Villafranca – which ceded parts of Italy to France and restored some of the deposed rulers. In October 1859 the British approved the annexation of central Italian states by Piedmont and pressurised Austria to accept. Queen Victoria was 'greatly alarmed, and thought it a very immoral act' and worried that war might come as a result: 'I said, I could never be a party to this.' She 'lamented bitterly over the utter folly and recklessness of Ld Palmerston and Ld Russell and the inconceivable attitude they had taken up with regard to Italy. All might have been settled . . . had they only not encouraged the revolutionary party.'[105] Queen Victoria thought that her government, by which she meant Palmerston, 'are really a misfortune'.[106] In her opinion, Palmerston would only see the Italian question 'in <u>one</u> light',[107] leading to wrong and misguided policy. Britain, the Queen insisted, had forfeited and undermined her position in Europe by the injudiciousness and folly of Palmerston who had encouraged the Italians in their ambitions, instead of advising them to be moderate and reasonable. Queen Victoria had approved of German unity but always perceived Italian unification as a threat.

This latest disagreement between Queen Victoria and Lord Palmerston was typical of the conflicts between the two. Palmerston clashed with the Queen not only over his progressive liberalism and encouragement of struggles against absolute monarchy but also over his playing of a continuous diplomatic game of 'checks and balances' – in particular when he tried to contain the ambitions of Russia against a weakening Ottoman Empire. In many ways, the 1850s can be regarded as a battle between Queen Victoria and Palmerston over the direction of British foreign policy. The Queen won a few of the skirmishes and even managed to get rid of Palmerston at one point. In the end, parliament triumphed and the Queen was forced to bow to the will of the people, particularly over the Crimean War. When war was seen to be inevitable, Queen Victoria, who saw herself as a soldier's daughter, took on her role as head of the armed forces with dogged and unwavering resolution. Consequently, the war brought unexpected unity between Queen Victoria and Lord Palmerston. Palmerston's focus on the living and working conditions of her army, his transformation of the army medical services and supply chain and his determination to ensure sufficient munition supplies meant that the Queen eventually warmed to her prime minister. For perhaps the first time, the two protagonists saw themselves as fighting the same battle, on the same side. Unfortunately, the truce between Victoria and Palmerston did not last as animosities re-emerged over European policy.

Notes

1 RA VIC/MAIN/QVJ (W) April 29th 1851.
2 Ibid. May 1st 1851.
3 Ibid. August 9th 1851.
4 Queen Victoria to the Lord Chancellor, December 20th 1859.
5 RA VIC/MAIN/QVJ (W) March 19th 1865.
6 Ibid. June 28th 1858.
7 Ibid. October 29th 1850.
8 Ibid. July 1st 1852.
9 Ibid. June 27th 1850.
10 Connell, *Regina v Palmerston*, p. 95.
11 *Morning Chronicle*, June 26th 1850, p. 2.
12 Palmerston, *Hansard*, June 1850.
13 RA VIC/MAIN/QVJ (W) February 4th 1850.
14 Ibid. January 30th 1850.
15 Ibid. January 30th 1850.
16 Ibid. February 14th 1850.
17 Connell, *Regina v Palmerston*, p. 102.
18 RA VIC/MAIN/QVJ (W) February 24th 1850.
19 Connell, *Regina v Palmerston*, p. 74.
20 RA VIC/MAIN/QVJ (W) August 7th 1850.
21 Ibid. August 15th 1850.
22 Ibid. August 15th 1850.
23 Ibid. September 9th 1850.
24 Ibid. September 9th 1850.
25 Ibid. September 14th 1850.

26 Ibid. October 11th 1850.
27 Ibid. March 3rd 1851.
28 Ibid. October 14th 1851.
29 Ibid. October 24th 1851.
30 Ibid. October 31st 1851.
31 Ibid. October 31st 1851.
32 Ibid. November 13th 1851.
33 Ibid. March 6th 1853.
34 Ibid. December 11th 1851.
35 Russell to Palmerston, December 17th 1851.
36 RA VIC/MAIN/QVJ (W) December 20th 1851.
37 *Reynolds's Weekly Newspaper*, February 1st 1852, p. 1.
38 RA VIC/MAIN/QVJ (W) December 17th 1852.
39 Ibid. December 19th 1852.
40 RA VIC/MAIN/QVJ (W) January 1st 1854.
41 See Hugh Small, *The Crimean War*, Tempus Publishing, 2007 for a provocative discussion on the Crimean War.
42 Queen Victoria to the King of Prussia, March 17th 1854.
43 RA VIC/MAIN/QVJ (W) October 23rd 1853.
44 Ibid. December 15th 1853.
45 Brown, *Palmerston,* p. 367.
46 *The Times*, January 24th, 1854, p. 8.
47 Ibid. November 2nd, 1854, p. 6.
48 Norman McCord, 'Lord Aberdeen' in Blake, *The Prime Ministers*, p. 64.
49 *Reynolds's Weekly Newspaper*, December 25th 1853.
50 See Rhodes James, *Albert, Prince Consort*, p. 222.
51 *Reynolds's Weekly Newspaper*, December 8th 1853.
52 *Lloyd's Weekly Newspaper*, January 8th 1854.
53 *Freeman's Journal and Daily Commercial Advertiser*, December 24th 1853.
54 *Reynolds's Weekly Newspaper*, December 25th 1853.
55 Ibid. January 8th 1854.
56 RA VIC/MAIN/QVJ (W) January 4th 1854.
57 Quoted in Rhodes James, *Albert, Prince Consort*, p. 222.
58 RA VIC/MAIN/QVJ (W) January 26th 1854.
59 Ibid. January 26th 1854.
60 Ibid. May 10th 1854.
61 Ibid. October 9th 1854.
62 Ibid. November 30th 1854.
63 Magnus, *Gladstone*, p. 118.
64 RA VIC/MAIN/QVJ (W) December 26th 1854.
65 Ibid. January 17th 1855.
66 Ibid. October 18th 1854.
67 Ibid. September 21st 1856.
68 Ibid. November 12th 1854.

69 *The Times,* November 2nd 1854, p. 6.
70 Ibid. November 2nd 1854, p. 6.
71 RA VIC/MAIN/QVJ (W) November 25th 1854.
72 Ibid. November 26th 1854.
73 John Heathcot Amory quoted in *The Times,* February 13th 1855, p. 8.
74 RA VIC/MAIN/QVJ (W) January 31st 1855.
75 Quoted in Brown, *Palmerston,* p. 377.
76 Victoria to Leopold, February 6th 1855.
77 RA VIC/MAIN/QVJ (W) September 10th 1855.
78 Ibid. March 3rd 1855.
79 Ibid. November 28th 1855.
80 Ibid. May 18th 1855.
81 Ibid. March 11th 1856.
82 Ibid. March 30th 1856.
83 Ibid. March 13th 1856.
84 Ibid. July 8th 1856.
85 Ibid. June 26th, 1857.
86 Ibid. August 21st 1856.
87 Ibid. February 25th 1856.
88 Ibid. July 1st 1857.
89 Ibid. August 1st 1857.
90 Ibid. August 3rd 1857.
91 Ibid. August 31st 1857.
92 Ibid. December 14th 1857.
93 Ibid. July 16th 1857.
94 Victoria to Palmerston July 19th 1857, quoted in Connell, *Regina v Palmerston,* p. 220.
95 Byron Farwell, *Queen Victoria's Little Wars,* Victorian Book Club, 1973, p. 97.
96 RA VIC/MAIN/QVJ (W) November 1st 1857.
97 Quoted in Hibbert, *Queen Victoria,* p. 250.
98 Quoted in Brown, *Palmerston,* p. 407.
99 RA VIC/MAIN/QVJ (W) November 23rd 1857.
100 Ibid. January 28th 1858.
101 Ibid. June 11th 1859.
102 Ibid. June 11th 1859.
103 Ibid. August 5th 1859.
104 Ibid. September 7th 1859.
105 Ibid. November 23rd 1859.
106 Ibid. January 5th 1860.
107 Ibid. January 13th 1860.

7 Life after Albert: 1861–1868

On 16 March 1861 Victoria lamented 'the dreaded calamity' which had befallen her 'which seems like an awful dream, from which I cannot recover. My precious darling Mother has been taken from us. . . . She breathed her last, my hand holding hers to the last moment.'[1] The Duchess of Kent had died and the Queen was distraught. She confided to Albert that she now regretted the sorrow and distress that her 'beloved Mama had often undergone and the misunderstandings, so often caused by others'.[2] Victoria was experiencing the natural grief of a daughter, tortured by the memory of her teenage behaviour when she had been unable to assess her mother's strengths clearly.

Victoria's mother's death was the prelude to a much bigger, much less expected death. Later that year, on 14 December 1861, Albert died from what was diagnosed by his doctors as typhoid: he was 42 years old, the same age as Victoria. The shock of Albert's early death was too much for the Queen, who suffered from all the normal stages of grief, vacillating between denial, depression and anger. She wrote to her eldest daughter crying, 'How am I, who leant on him for all and everything – without whom I did nothing, moved not a finger, arranged not a print or photograph, didn't put on a gown or bonnet – to live?'[3] The Queen arranged for Albert's clothes to be laid out each evening, and hot water and a clean towel placed for him to shave, a ritual which was still being observed more than twenty years later. Each night she slept with Albert's coat over her, his dressing gown near her and his night gown close to her face. If she could smell him, then he remained alive. She went on 'a kind of pilgrimage' to the places that Albert had been: to his home in Germany, even to the place he shot his last stag.

Victoria's mourning permeated the Palace but her royal status prevented anyone comforting her since 'in a court grounded in formality and protocol, they could hardly give her a hug or hold her hand'.[4] The Queen wailed in her all-consuming grief that 'there is noone to call me Victoria now'. With Albert and her mother both dead, Victoria had no adult to put her as first in their lives: her eldest daughter Vicky was 21 and married, her youngest only four. Vicky was told that four-year-old Beatrice was the

> only thing I feel keeps me alive, for she alone wants me really . . . the wretched, broken-hearted mother . . . is now daily learning to feel that she is only No 3 or 4 in the real tender love of others. And dear child, all this is right and natural, but to me most agonizing . . . the belonging to no one, any more.[5]

At the moment of her greatest need, the Queen was left with no adult in whom she could confide, no one to share her thoughts, no one to turn to for sympathy or guidance – and no one with the authority to curb her unaccountable caprices and idiosyncratic behaviour. In time it became apparent that the Queen had no wish to be relieved of her excruciating unbearable pain, and preferred to wallow in her anguish, to the detriment of her sanity, the needs of her children, the demands of the government and, perhaps more importantly, her popularity with the British people.

During the first few weeks after Albert's death, the Queen depended on her 18-year-old daughter Alice for emotional support. This young woman, who herself was grief-stricken over the loss of her beloved father, was forced to submerge her own feelings to look after her selfishly obsessed disconsolate mother. Alice was on duty all day, every day, even sleeping in her mother's room. Eventually, in July 1862, she was able to escape by marrying Louis of Hesse, another impoverished prince from an obscure German province. The wedding was predictably low key; the Queen wore black, her ladies wore the half-mourning colours of lilac or grey, and only Alice and her bridesmaids were permitted to wear white. Victoria remarked to her daughter Vicky that the ceremony had been more like a funeral than a wedding.[6]

With the death of both her mother and her husband, a heavy weight of grief threatened to crush Victoria. She lost weight. Over the years, the Queen's figure had spread so much that many thought she resembled a barrel; a few kilos less of the Queen would be welcome. More significantly, for over 20 years, Victoria relied on her husband for support and guidance yet now she felt rudderless, a single mother of 42 with nine children. Death rituals in the nineteenth century were elaborate but Victoria took her mourning to a new level. Her bereavement lasted her lifetime: she always wrote on black-edged writing paper and dressed in widow's weeds.

And Victoria did what so many people do who have lost loved ones: she got angry and blamed others. The target of Victoria's wrath was her eldest son, Bertie. Albert had died, Victoria claimed, as a result of that 'dreadful business' and the intolerable pain of it all. Bertie had been caught in a sexual relationship with an Irish actress, Nellie Clifden, and the already sickly Albert went to Cambridge to discuss the affair with his son. Shortly after, Albert died – killed, Victoria wilfully decided, by the wickedness of the world that was 'too much for him to bear'.[7] She told her eldest daughter that she could never look at Bertie again 'without a shudder'.[8] And so poor Bertie, who was also grieving for his father, had to shoulder the responsibility for his death. In fact, Bertie had always been a disappointment to his mother. The Queen often complained that her eldest son was so utterly different from Albert, always uneasy that Bertie had adopted the Hanoverian vices of sexual incontinence and hedonism. Victoria, who had hoped to establish a new pure and virtuous dynasty, was appalled by Bertie's lifestyle and decided to have him married as soon as possible. She was keen not to support a marriage alliance that might be construed as anti-German and only reluctantly agreed to Bertie marrying Princess Alexandra from the impecunious royal house of Denmark. She disliked the end of the 'German Connection' whereby British heirs to the throne wed a German relative.[9]

Many hoped that the wedding on 10 March 1863 of the heir to the throne would be marked by a grand ceremonial affair at

Westminster Abbey. In her grief, Queen Victoria missed a chance to reverse her diminishing popularity by a royal pageant, instead insisting on a small private ceremony in St George's Chapel at Windsor. The Queen supervised all the arrangements for Bertie's wedding, even deciding on the dress code. The bride was permitted to wear traditional white and the groom was allowed to wear the colourful scarlet and gold uniform of his regiment. The rest of Victoria's children were required to wear grey or lilac. Victoria, who watched the wedding ceremony from a balcony, wore her customary black. As soon as she had signed the wedding register, she left the Chapel and went down to the mausoleum to see Albert's grave. Victoria lamented 'Oh! What I suffered in the Chapel. . . . I felt as if I should faint. Only by a violent effort, could I succeed in masking my emotion! . . . Sat down feeling strange and bewildered.'[10] She complained about Bertie, saying 'Oh! What will become of the poor country when I die! I foresee, if B succeeds, nothing but misery – for he never reflects or listens for a moment and he would . . . spend his life in one whirl of amusements.'[11]

When Prince Albert died, Victoria seemed to shut down politically. For the first few months, her ministers and the country forgave her absence, fully aware that the distraught widow might easily be overwhelmed by even the simplest official function. Yet, when the heir to the throne offered to help his mother with her despatch boxes, Victoria rejected his support. The last thing she wanted, Jane Ridley argues, was for Bertie 'to communicate directly with ministers, undermining her'.[12] However, Britain needed a figurehead and the responsibilities and obligations of a sovereign were expected to take precedence over a widow's feelings. As a bereaved woman, a plain Mrs Wettin,[13] she was expected to mourn deeply and privately, wear black and avoid public events; as a queen, the country felt she should abandon these traditions, appear on display, dress like royalty – and behave with commensurate confidence and authority. When the raw pain of grief diminished, Victoria's mourning entered a deeper level and she grew depressed. She found sleeping difficult, she lacked energy and she felt exhausted and apathetic. For the next decade or so the Queen's self-indulgent retirement was dubbed the 'luxury of woe'. She was regarded as a 'royal malingerer', squeezing every inch of sympathy from a now dried-up country.

'The mass of people', wrote a leading politician, 'expect a King or Queen to look and play the part. They want to see a Crown and a Sceptre and all that sort of thing. They want the gilding for their money. It is not wise to let them think . . . that they could do without a sovereign.'[14] Even Bertie warned his mother that if the sovereign was 'not more seen in London, the loyalty and attachment to the Crown will decrease'.[15] However, the Queen, as egocentric as ever, took no notice and decided to spend five months of the year at Balmoral, an estate 600 miles and a 24-hour train journey away from London.

Unlike elected representatives, Victoria felt entitled to cherry pick the parts of her job she wished to do. Certainly, she seemed more concerned with her rights than her responsibilities. On the one hand, she avoided her responsibility for engaging in public ceremonials such as the opening of parliament or entertaining visiting royalty; on the other hand, she exerted her rights particularly in foreign affairs, and most especially when matters concerned her extended family. If presidents or prime ministers chose to ignore vital elements of their job, then they would be forced to resign, or be voted out by the electorate. But the British people had no such recourse – except to get rid of the monarchy.

In March 1864, a notice was placed on Buckingham Palace's railings. It stated that 'these premises to be let or sold in consequence of the late occupant's declining business'. At the time, the Queen declined to appear in public; she refused to open parliament and refused to wear the monarch's official regalia, preferring to dress in black. The Queen, seemingly oblivious to the fact that her seclusion might damage the monarchy, gave in to her inherent shyness, her heartache and her obstinacy, and stayed at home grieving over the death of Prince Albert. Some feared she was deranged, subject to the same mental illness that had affected her grandfather, King George III. This phase of political seclusion – the Queen only opened parliament seven times in this period – meant that a popular republican movement grew apace. Some believed that Victoria sacrificed her duty to Britain to a 'morbid indulgence in the sorrows of her personal bereavement'.[16] The Queen, it was felt, should either abdicate or return to ruling the country. Even the usual pro-monarchy *Times* had a leader article commenting that 'it is impossible for a recluse to occupy the British Throne without a gradual weakening of that authority. . . . For the sake of the CROWN . . . we beseech HER MAJESTY to return to the personal exercise of her exalted functions.'[17] Victoria complained that the article was vulgar and heartless.

Victoria's mourning was soon viewed as pathological, selfish and exceedingly inconsiderate. Time and time again, the Queen used arguments that reflected a conventional femininity rather than a monarchical authority. She wrote to her ministers grumbling that she 'was <u>always</u> terribly nervous on <u>all</u> public occasions, but <u>especially</u> at the opening of Parliament. . . . Her nerves are <u>so</u> shattered that <u>any</u> emotion, <u>any</u> discussion, <u>any</u> exertion causes much disturbance and suffering to her whole frame'.[18]

Undoubtedly, Victoria's double identity of Queen and woman conflicted, and her notions of femininity soon came to hinder her position as a monarch. Her private role as grieving widow became more and more antithetical to her public role as Queen, especially when she refused to participate in state ceremonials. Years after Albert's death, when she was asked to delay her departure to Balmoral to prorogue parliament, she wrote that 'she had seen from long experience that the more she yielded to pressure and alarm . . . it only encourages further demands . . . It is abominable that a woman and a Queen laden with care and with public and domestic anxieties which are daily increasing should not be able to make people understand that there is a limit to her powers.'[19] She even resorted to emotional blackmail by threatening that too much work would kill her, as it had Albert. However, many of the British public disapproved of the widening gap between Victoria's femininity and her role as sovereign; they wanted their queen to be visible and began to object to a weak, vainglorious and feeble woman who would not fulfil her ordained role. Ministers and the country were initially sympathetic to the Queen's loss but as the Queen's seclusion set in, many British people lost their patience and anti-monarchical feeling grew.

The Queen's popularity was not helped when John Brown, a tall, handsome, strongly built Scot, was brought down to Windsor in order that the Queen could continue to ride and thereby help draw her out of her continuing melancholy. By February 1865 he had become a permanent fixture at court with a new title 'The Queen's Highland Servant' and a new role as the Queen's personal servant, taking orders only from the Queen and with an ever-increasing salary. Queen Victoria, seemingly attracted by his untamed manliness and uncultured directness, appeared to idolise him and would tolerate no criticism of her beloved servant. To the consternation of the court, the usually protocol-conscious Queen allowed Brown to call her 'wumman' and gave him access to her apartments. Indeed, the two slept in adjoining rooms and shared a dram or two of whisky together, all of which suggests a marital-like familiarity rather than a relationship between sovereign and subject. Soon rumours spread that the Queen had married Brown. Jokes were made about Mrs John Brown and the satirical journal *Punch* printed scurrilously written articles about the alleged relationship. The Queen's decision to spend even more time at Balmoral – with her beloved John Brown – seemed to confirm the rumours.

Even today, people remain fascinated by the relationship and want to know whether or not the Queen had an affair with, or even married, John Brown. Some believe that Queen Victoria's large sexual appetite was assuaged by Brown who became her morganatic husband. This theory was apparently confirmed by the rumoured deathbed confession of Rev McLeod, Dean of the Royal Chapel and trusted friend of Queen Victoria, who claimed that he had married the couple in Scotland. These are, of course, speculations. Indeed, there is strong evidence to suggest otherwise: the Queen may once have enjoyed physical intimacy with Albert but after the birth of nine children, a prolapsed womb, and possibly suffering from early stages of the menopause, her sexual desires may have diminished. More likely still, it is common among the aristocracy to have a favoured servant, someone who enjoys a familiarity with their employer and who is allowed liberties denied others. In many ways, Brown played the part of the traditional fool, a well-loved character and symbol of common sense and honesty, who enjoyed a privileged status within the court. Fools had the leeway to criticise their boss, ridicule pomposity and deliver a few home truths, saying things that no other character in their social bracket could possibly say.

Certainly, the evidence that Queen Victoria and John Brown were lovers is ambiguous at best. On the one hand, Queen Victoria spoke of Brown as a servant. When he died, in March

1883, the Queen wrote in her journal that her son Leopold 'broke the dreadful news to me, that my good, faithful Brown had passed away early this morning. Am terribly upset by this loss, which removes one, who was so devoted and attached to my service and who did so much for my personal comfort. It is the loss not only of a servant, but of a good friend.'[20] In her will, Victoria stated that she hoped to 'meet those who have so faithfully and so devotedly served me especially good John Brown and good Annie Macdonald'. However, when Brown died, the Queen preserved his room as he left it, had a fresh flower put on his pillow each day, commissioned statues and busts of him and was only thwarted from publishing a book about Brown's life when her family objected. When she died, Victoria was buried not only with mementoes of Albert and her children but also with a lock of John Brown's hair, a photograph of Brown in her left hand and his mother's wedding ring on the third finger of her right hand – the wedding ring finger of German women – all of which suggests that the relationship had developed beyond that of mere servant.

Today, many remain curious about the relationship between Queen Victoria and John Brown, but is it historically important? Dorothy Thompson suggests that the Brown controversy remains significant because it illustrates the double standards required of men and women in this period and throws a light on Victorian hypocrisy. It was accepted that kings – William IV, George IV – might have extra-marital affairs, but not queens and especially not the previously morally righteous Queen Victoria. In Thompson's view 'if it could have been shown that the queen . . . had indulged in a sexual liaison . . . a great many cherished taboos and judgements would have been challenged'.[21] Women, even those as high and mighty as Queen Victoria, would perhaps be viewed as lustful creatures rather than the domestic, passive and unsullied characters of popular belief.

We will never know for certain if Queen Victoria married John Brown but we do know that the growing friendship between the two helped the Queen to accept Albert's death. On 10 February 1865, the day which would have been Victoria's silver wedding day, she wrote 'oh! To think of what it would have been and what it is! The contrast is too fearful. Still in the midst of my crushing sorrow and longing for the past, I do feel that it is

better to have loved and lost, than never to have loved at all!'[22]
It was soon clear that the Queen was 'getting over', or at least
beginning to accept the death of Albert. Her diaries contain less
of 'woe is me' and more about the events she was now enjoying,
like the gillie's ball, children's birthday parties, watching her
children play charades, playing the piano and singing and listening to music.

Lord Palmerston: 1861–1865

The death of Prince Albert was a turning point for the Queen,
politically as well as personally. Between 1837 and 1841 Lord
Melbourne had influenced the Queen; between 1841 and 1861,
Prince Albert. Now Victoria reigned alone. As Frank Hardie
observes, only after Albert's death can Victoria 'be seen acting
as a constitutional monarch entirely on her own responsibility'.[23]
The Whigs, now referred to as Liberals, remained in the ascen-
dant. Lord Palmerston continued as Queen Victoria's prime minister until his death in 1865 and was followed by Lord Russell
(1865–6). The period ended with two conservative prime ministers: Lord Derby (1866–8) and Disraeli (1868).

After Albert's death, Queen Victoria began to adopt the mantle
of Great Matriarch of Europe as more and more of her family
married into the ruling royal families. She took a lively interest
in the marriages, births, illnesses and deaths of her increasingly
extended family, trying to patch up family quarrels or taking
sides in them. Unfortunately, sometimes Victoria's subjective family preferences conflicted with the objectivity increasingly expected
of a British monarch. The Queen and her prime minister clashed
for the last time over Victoria's expressed partiality for Germany
and Palmerston's sympathies for Denmark.

Foreign policy: Schleswig-Holstein 1863–1864

Queen Victoria remained especially interested in those aspects of
foreign affairs closely related to her family. At times her personal
involvement was so intense that she could not summon up the
detachment which was more and more expected of a constitutional
monarch – the growing notion that British monarchs should be

above politics was not one she seemed to share. Jane Ridley observes that 'the fact that the monarch was supposed not to pursue a foreign policy of her own but support her government's policy worried her not at all'.[24] The Schleswig-Holstein question in particular tormented the Queen, and it was here that she made her first political intervention since the death of Albert. At the time, Schleswig-Holstein was an independent Duchy, linked to Denmark. However, because it consisted mainly of German speakers, Prussia aspired to annex it. In November 1863, when the Danish King died and a new one ascended the throne, the Prussians demanded self-determination for the German speakers living in Schleswig-Holstein.[25]

For Queen Victoria, the Schleswig-Holstein question was as much a family question as a political one. At such times, Queen Victoria's morbid passivity in some areas of royal activity contrasted sharply with the determined energy she exhibited when her personal interests were concerned. She made no attempt to remain neutral when her two eldest children took opposing sides in the Prussian–Danish conflict. Her eldest daughter, Vicky, was married to the Prussian heir to the throne and took Prussia's side, while Bertie was married to Alexandra, the King of Denmark's daughter, and favoured Denmark. At the time, Alexandra was expecting her first baby and living nearby at Frogmore, a house set in the grounds of Windsor Castle. Victoria recognised her daughter-in-law's anxiety but was unsympathetic to the Danish point of view. She lamented that 'Oh! If Bertie's wife was only a good German and not a Dane! . . . It is terrible to have the poor boy on the wrong side, and aggravates my sufferings greatly.'[26] She reminded Bertie that his whole family were German, that he was half-German and that he must never be a Danish partisan 'or you put yourself against your whole family and against your Mother and Sovereign – who has been as impartial as anyone ever was'.[27] Queen Victoria's 'impartiality', of course was self-delusion as the Queen was wholly on the German side, writing to her eldest daughter that her 'heart and sympathies are all German'.[28] The Queen's opinion was not the voice of the experienced constitutional monarch expressing balanced and carefully considered opinions – it was the opinion of a 'violent partisan inspired by emotion rather than reason'.[29]

In 1852 the London Protocol, signed by Austria, France, Prussia, Russia and Britain, had guaranteed the independence of Schleswig-Holstein. Any invasion of its territory was breaking the terms of the contract. Palmerston, who feared Prussian expansion, wanted to help Denmark and even discussed sending troops to defend the beleaguered nation. He believed that if Prussia thought that the British government was committed to the integrity of Denmark, peace might be preserved. In contrast, the Queen insisted that Britain must not help Denmark because she could not inflict 'upon her subjects all the horrors of war'. She impressed upon her government her 'aversion to being dragged step by step into a war . . . for Germany was as good a friend to us as Denmark'.[30] This highly moralising approach to the Schleswig-Holstein question serves merely to demonstrate how the Queen's concern for her subjects was just a convenient argument to bolster her pro-Prussian views. Moreover, she persistently tried to alter the course of events by trying to influence the opinions of individual Cabinet members by secretly corresponding with them, actions which the Queen knew was exceeding the bounds of constitutional propriety.

Unfortunately, Queen Victoria did not recognise that Germany was changing. She held on to Albert's dream of a liberal Germany, united by Prussia, which would be ruled by her son-in-law Fritz when King Wilhelm I died. In reality, Minister President Otto von Bismarck, a conservative statesman who dominated Prussia, wanted to unite at least northern Germany by 'blood and iron' and create a new royal state. In many ways the Queen unwittingly helped Bismarck by obstructing her government's attempts to help Denmark. This isolated the small country, making it feasible for Bismarck to invade Denmark without fear of reprisal from Britain and take another step towards German unity.

Palmerston recognised only too well the danger the monarchy faced if the Queen was thought to favour Prussia over Denmark. In January 1864 he wrote to the Queen in his capacity as prime minister, reminding her that 'he is sure that your Majesty will never forget that you are Sovereign of Great Britain, and that the honour of your Majesty's Crown and the interests of your Majesty's dominions will always be the guide of your Majesty's conduct'.[31] He told her bluntly to stop the gossip in her household that the Queen favoured Prussia. A few days later, in a long, well-reasoned, politically informed and erudite letter, Palmerston advised his sovereign that Prussia seemed 'bent upon wantonly inflicting those horrors upon the unoffending and peaceful Danish population. The Germans are acting like a strong man who thinks he has got a weak man in a corner, and that he can bully and beat him to his heart's content.'[32] He warned the Queen that 'if Denmark was to be dismembered, all Treaties might be thrown into the fire as waste paper, or used to wrap up cartridges'.[33] Palmerston's political acumen, his immense knowledge of foreign affairs and his understanding of diplomatic complexities made the Queen feel out of her depth. At times like this, when the Queen found herself outclassed by the political sophistication of Palmerston, her political uneasiness was sometimes expressed petulantly: on one occasion she asked her private secretary to reply to one of Palmerston's long, detailed and logically argued missives by saying that the 'Queen has been unwell all day . . . and has directed me to acknowledge the receipt of your letter'.[34]

In February 1864 Prussian and Austrian forces invaded Schleswig-Holstein. Prussia occupied Schleswig and claimed it as its own, while Austria took control of Holstein. The British government was not prepared to respond to Prussian and Austrian aggression with anything more than diplomatic platitudes and accordingly remained outside the conflict. Denmark, in the face of an overwhelming military force, surrendered Schleswig-Holstein. It was a humiliating defeat for Denmark but for the Prussians it marked the first formal annexation of territory in the move towards a united Germany. Palmerston wrote to the King of the Belgians, Victoria's Uncle Leopold, that the annexation of a small state was a shameful abuse of power by Prussia and Austria. The events of the war, Palmerston maintained, did not form a 'page in German history which any honourable or generous German hereafter will look back upon without a blush'.[35] In 1866, Schleswig-Holstein was incorporated into Prussia. The Germans began their successful climb to national unity, with Germany emerging as the most powerfully military state in Europe – an outcome which would eventually threaten European peace.

It appeared as if the monarchy was out of step with a large section of the British population who supported the besieged

Denmark. Many people objected to the fact that a great power had violated the sovereignty of a small state unable to defend itself against the might of the Prussian army. There were hostile comments in the press about the Queen's pro-German sympathies. The *London Review* protested that the policy of the government was inspired by deference 'to the personal wishes of the Sovereign in a matter in which the Constitution makes her despotic'.[36] Queen Victoria was even reproached in the House of Lords. On 26 May 1864, the Conservative Lord Ellenborough who had once enjoyed a friendly relationship with Queen Victoria complained that 'in all public questions relating to Germany, her Majesty's Ministers have much difficulty in carrying out a purely English policy'.[37]

Queen Victoria's partisanship, and the negative public reaction to it, alarmed Palmerston. He even sent the Queen a newspaper which maintained

> that an impression is beginning to be created that your Majesty has expressed personal opinions on the affairs of Denmark and Germany which have embarrassed the course of the Government. . . . It would be a great evil if public opinion were to divest your Majesty of that proper and essential protection which the Constitution secures for the Sovereign by making the responsible Ministers answerable for all that is done or not done; and if your Majesty's personal opinions and views were to become the objects of criticism or attack.[38]

The Queen, rarely willing to acknowledge even just criticism, tersely replied that she 'exercised her functions for the good of the country alone' and must disregard unjust remarks in obscure papers.[39] It was evident that the relationship between Queen Victoria and Lord Palmerston had reached an all-time low.

When it became publicly known that Queen Victoria had, without the knowledge of her ministers, written letters of support to the Prussians, she was accused of behaving unconstitutionally. Some blamed the Queen for the war because her obvious pro-German stance had encouraged Prussia to be aggressive. Of course, it is hard to measure the precise impact of the Queen's intervention in the Danish question. Even so the Queen's well-known German sympathies might have played a part in the calculations of the Prussian government as to whether or not they should invade Denmark. Just as importantly, Queen Victoria's persistent attempts to undermine the policies of her government represented not just a disagreeable state of affairs but also a potential despotic threat to the developing British constitution.

The Queen, however, dismissed the concerns of her critics, believing that 'people are so foolishly mad and excited . . . for they run away with an idea of the great oppressing the weak, and talk a heap of nonsense'.[40] Indeed, Victoria rejected all criticism, often pleading womanly weakness. She complained when one Lord insinuated

> indirectly that I . . . had prevented the Govt from doing what it ought to have done and wished. What a cruel accusation, against a poor unprotected widow, who is no longer sheltered by the love and wisdom of her beloved Husband, when I only live on to work and toil for the good of my country and am half torn to pieces with anxiety, sorry and responsibility, seeing this Country lower itself and get more and more into difficulties, – and above all, have always sought to be so impartial! Such monstrous calumnies have made me feel quite ill.[41]

Here, as elsewhere, Queen Victoria shows herself to be a good advocate, willing to use any stratagem to get her own way.

Familial and European politics became even more complicated when Victoria decided that her third daughter, the 24-year-old Helena, should marry the penniless 35-year-old Prince Christian of Schleswig-Holstein-Sonderburg-Augustenberg. In 1848, Christian's family had sided with Prussia when it threatened Danish autonomy. Bertie, concerned about the feelings of his Danish wife when yet another German prince was added to his relatives, protested about the marriage. Victoria took no notice as she was more concerned about her own welfare. She wanted Helena to marry someone who would make their home in Britain, insisting that she 'must have Lenchen with me for the greater part of the year when she is married'.[42] Prince Christian, who was impoverished, had no choice but to agree. On 5 July 1866 Queen Victoria 'led Lenchen, who walked between Bertie and me, and I gave her away'[43] ostensibly because she felt that she 'was the only one to do it. I never could let one of my sons take their father's place while I live.'[44] In fact, Bertie threatened to boycott the wedding altogether. He had objected to the match and only attended the marriage ceremony after a lot of pressure.

Queen Victoria gave more support to Palmerston's government when family interests were not at stake. Indeed, the Queen is credited with helping to heal the broken relationship between the United States and the United Kingdom. During the American Civil War, Palmerston's government had allowed two war ships to be built in British shipyards for the Southern Confederates; one ship, the *Alabama*, was used to attack the Unionists in the North. The Unionists held Britain responsible for the damage that the *Alabama* inflicted on northern forces and compensation was called for – the Americans were later awarded reparations of 15.5 million dollars by an international tribunal. But bad feeling remained between the two countries, overcome largely through the intervention of Queen Victoria who worked behind the scenes to ameliorate the dispute. On 26 April 1865, Victoria received 'dreadful news'[45] from America, that Abraham Lincoln had been assassinated. The Queen was asked to write a personal letter to Lincoln's widow as 'a very good effect would be produced in conciliating the feelings of the United States'.[46] Victoria complied. In her letter the Queen told the widowed Mrs Lincoln:

> that these many sad and striking events had convinced me more and more of the utter nothingness of this world, of the terrible uncertainty of all earthly happiness and of the utter vanity of all earthly greatness. . . . sorrow levelled all distinctions. I would as soon clasp the poorest widow in the land to my heart, if she had truly loved her husband and felt for me, as I would a Queen.[47]

The letter was warmly received by the American government and was felt to help improve relationships between the two countries.

Lord Russell: 1865–1866

On 18 October 1865, two days before his eighty-first birthday, Lord Palmerston died. Victoria commented that it was 'strange and solemn to think of that strong, determined man, with so much worldly ambition, – gone! He had often worried and distressed us.'[48] She wrote to her Uncle Leopold that she 'never liked him, or could ever the least respect him'.[49] Palmerston's death forced the Queen to return to London to appoint a new prime minister: Lord Russell. Against expectation, on Tuesday 6 February 1866 the Queen opened parliament for the first time since she became a widow. She dreaded it, saying 'it was a fearful moment for me . . . I had great difficulty repressing my tears. . . . When I entered the House, which was very full, I felt as if I should faint! All was silent and all eyes fixed on me, and there I sat <u>alone</u>.'[50] Cynics remarked that the Queen needed annuities for two of her children: Prince Alfred, her fourth child, was soon to come of age and Princess Helena, her fifth, needed a dowry to marry her penniless German prince. Victoria disappointed those who came to watch a royal spectacle. She made it difficult for everyone concerned, changed the date of the ceremony to suit her travel plans, refused to travel to parliament in the state coach and dressed in a black dress and black cap rather than the expected ermine robes and a jewelled crown. As soon as the Queen had opened parliament she escaped to Osborne.

Before the event, Queen Victoria instructed her private secretary to write to Russell cautioning him that it was 'difficult perhaps to estimate the sacrifice that the Queen has made in consenting to open Parliament in person; it was always a ceremony which, even in her happier days, she dreaded more than anything else, and now it will be a very severe trial to her, and she will probably suffer from it two or three days before and after.'[51] Victoria complained directly to Russell that she could only compare opening parliament to that of an execution and thought that the wish for her to open it was

> so <u>unreasonable</u> and unfeeling a nature, as to <u>long</u> to <u>witness</u> the spectacle of a poor, broken-hearted widow, nervous and shrinking, dragged in <u>deep mourning</u>, ALONE in STATE as

a <u>Show</u> . . . to be gazed at, without delicacy of feeling, is a thing <u>she cannot</u> understand. . . . she owns she hardly knows how she will go through it . . . and she will suffer much for some time after.[52]

Once more, the Queen's perception of this aspect of her role – if her emotional outburst was genuinely felt – was hopelessly myopic.

Yet, Queen Victoria was physically fit and emotionally collected enough to take part in other public events. In 1866 the Queen held courts at Buckingham Palace, visited the Highland Gathering, opened waterworks at Aberdeen, visited a number of hospitals and prisons and unveiled a statue of Albert in Wolverhampton. She was also strong enough to resume her military reviews. At one such review, the march of soldiers past the Queen occupied more than three hours, during which the rain descended in torrents. The Queen was in an open carriage, 'but, true soldier's daughter as she was, she paid no heed to the weather . . . She did not leave the Park until the last man had passed. By this time the carriage was full of water, and pools of it . . . dropped from the dresses of herself and her ladies.'[53] And here lay another contradiction. On the one hand, the Queen asked to be left alone with her widow's grief when it meant taking part in events she disliked. On the other, the Queen willingly took part in military reviews and clearly enjoyed her philanthropic visits to hospitals and prisons. Nonetheless Victoria could not abrogate her responsibilities as Queen. It was essential to show the British people, not just her army and a favoured few, that she was their sovereign. But the Queen remained stubborn and obstreperous. Sometimes she would behave autocratically in a manner more suited to a despot; at other times she would assume conventional nineteenth-century notions of femininity and plead physical frailty.

Austro-Prussian war: March–May 1866

Meanwhile, Victoria continued to deal with the emotionally charged politics of Prussia and continued to try to placate her increasingly fractious family. Prussia declared its intention to annex all the German states, including Hanover and Hesse-Darmstadt to create a united Germany. Austria, who feared a Prussian-dominated Germany, challenged this. Most of the states, Hanover and Hesse-Darmstadt among them, were equally concerned about a Prussian take-over and sided with Austria. Victoria, however, felt passionately that a 'strong, united, liberal Germany would be a most useful ally to England'[54] and as ever she expressed her opinions vociferously.[55]

By March 1866 news reached Britain that Prussia was about to provoke a war with Austria. Victoria endeavoured 'with tears, prayers and pen to avert a conflict in which her children would be fighting on different sides'.[56] Her daughter Vicky was married to the Prussian heir, while her daughter Alice was married to a prince of Hesse-Darmstadt. In April 1866 she wrote to Vicky's father-in-law, the Prussian King, pleading for him to avert

> the Calamities of a war, the results of which are too fearful to be ever thought of and in which thousands of innocent lives will be lost, and brother will be arrayed against brother. . . . do pause before you permit so fearful a wrong to be committed as the commencement of a war, the respon-sibility of which will rest on <u>you alone</u>.[57]

The plea, hidden in a private letter, was despatched by a servant to be delivered personally to the Prussian King. As ever, the Queen's views were influenced by dynastic interests and 'her methods of diplomacy also were first and foremost dynastic'.[58] Queen Victoria had not consulted her ministers. After despatching her letter, the Queen sent a copy to her prime minister who fortunately approved of his sovereign's initiative. As a result, a potential constitutional quarrel over diplomatic niceties was averted.

The Queen's intervention in Prussia was not limited to family letters. Victoria took an active interest in the official policy of her government and freely expressed her opinions.[59] These views were not shared by her government. When the Queen wanted Britain to intervene in the German question, Lord Clarendon, the foreign secretary, declined to do so, privately declaring that 'the idea of our spending one shilling or one drop of blood in the banditti quarrel which is now going on in Germany is simply absurd'.[60] On one occasion, when Clarendon had irritated 'the Queen a good deal by the contemptuous tone in which he spoke of Germany; she gave it him pretty sharply, telling him he forgot the stock she came of, and he should not speak that way to her'.[61] On other occasions, the Queen would refuse to sanction policy she considered objectionable, protests which could have caused a constitutional crisis had it not been for Clarendon's tact and diplomacy and the Queen's willingness – in the end, and after much blustering – to defer to her ministers.

Queen Victoria's entreaties to her Prussian family failed and, provoked by Bismarck, Austria declared war against Prussia and the German states in June 1866. The war, which lasted for seven weeks, resulted in an overwhelming victory for Prussia and marked another step towards German unity as Prussia promptly annexed the German states which had sided with Austria. The North German Confederation came into being, representing the beginning of German unification. Lord Stanley, a leading Conservative, expressed the view that the Queen was 'indifferent to business, except where pressed on by relations'. He claimed that she 'interferes little, and only where Germany is concerned, or Belgium'.[62]

Domestic events came to a head when a national political crisis threatened to derail the monarchy. On 13 June 1866 Russell tried to extend the franchise to the respectable skilled male working class, a Bill which was defeated by 11 votes. The government had no choice but to resign. The Queen, alarmed at the prospect of a parliamentary election and reluctant to leave Balmoral, insisted that it was 'the bounden duty' of Russell and her government 'to set aside all personal considerations, and to continue at their posts. . . . the Queen could not accept their resignations'.[63] Letters between the Queen and Russell were exchanged: the Queen reiterating her desire for the government to continue; Russell reiterating its resignation. The Queen was constitutionally obliged to return to London to accept Russell's seals of office but, in what Rappaport calls 'old-style absolutism', refused until she was ready to do so. Again, in any other occupation, the Queen would have been sacked for not doing her job. Eventually, the Queen conceded and returned to London to accept her government's resignation. She called for the Conservative leader, Lord Derby, to form a government.

A Tory interlude: 1866–1868

In June 1866 Lord Derby became prime minister of a minority Conservative government. He appointed Benjamin Disraeli to be both chancellor of the exchequer and leader of the House of Commons. In the short period it enjoyed power, the government took a 'leap in the dark' towards greater democracy when it passed the Second Reform Act.[64] There was a popular appetite for an expansion of the electorate: meetings attracting enormous numbers of people had been held in London, Birmingham, Dublin, Glasgow, Leeds and Manchester. Disraeli brought in a new measure to give the vote to a wider body of men, a measure that was even more radical than the previous Liberal government's. Disraeli was given the unenviable task of constructing the Bill and of steering it through a fractious House of Commons. He had the support of Gladstone and the Liberals but drew criticism from his own party, many of whom disliked any extension of the franchise.

By this time, Queen Victoria had come round to supporting an extension of the franchise and urged 'an early settlement of the question'. She had been persuaded that the new voters would be reliable and loyal. Moreover she feared political unrest, anxious lest the government fell and 'their supporters, would become very angry and dissatisfied, so that much mischief might be done'.[65] Indeed, at the time there was significant public discontent and Republicanism reached new heights of popularity. The Queen was hissed and booed in public, with the press increasingly hostile towards the monarchy. The Conservative Lord Salisbury claimed that 'the monarchy was practically dead'. Fortunately, Queen Victoria showed greater political acumen than usual. When Derby asked the Queen to open parliament in person that year because of the 'present state of political affairs', she agreed to do so. And so for the second year in succession, Victoria opened parliament but she insisted that she did so 'under the peculiar circumstances of the time, the Queen must have it clearly understood that she is not to be expected to do it as a matter of course, year after year'.[66] Normally, the Queen remained stubbornly impervious to requests that she take a more visible role in public life and continued in her self-obsessed way to behave as she pleased.

Parliamentary reform featured in the Queen's speech to parliament. Privately, Queen Victoria was willing to facilitate the reform, offering to Derby that she would smooth the way for an 'amicable understanding' with the Liberal Party. Derby thanked the Queen, saying how grateful he would be for 'any influence which your Majesty may be pleased to exercise'.[67] In this instance, irresolvable differences emerged within the Tory Cabinet rather than between the parties. In February 1867 Disraeli informed the Queen about the difficulties, and that General Peel, a senior Tory minister and brother of the late Robert Peel, had threatened to resign over the Bill. The Queen 'asked if I could do nothing to shake this and Mr Disraeli said yes . . . if I wrote to Gen Peel simply calling on him not to desert the Govt at such a moment of vital importance for the country, – he might yield'.[68] Victoria duly wrote to General Peel, and a few days later received a letter 'very handsomely consenting to stay, in consequence of what I wrote'.[69] However, Peel did not keep his word, changed his mind and resigned anyway. He was joined by other senior figures. The situation was tense: Disraeli asked the Queen to 'interfere' once more but this time she declined to write to the dissidents. Fortunately for the Queen and the government, the Liberal Opposition gave its support. After considerable re-drafting and amending, Victoria 'was much relieved at hearing that the 2nd reading of the Reform Bill last night, had passed without a division, Mr Disraeli's speech having been much cheered. This is a great thing.'[70] The Queen wrote to Disraeli thanking him for his efforts.

Electoral reform impacted on the inter-relationships between the Crown, the House of Lords and the House of Commons. First, the 1867 Act enhanced the supremacy of the House of Commons. It brought in voters from previously unfranchised income brackets, thus increasing the electorate by well over a million voters – about one in three adult men could now vote. In one city alone – Birmingham – the electorate rose from 8,000 to 43,000. The House of Commons now represented a larger slice of the British population. Second, the House of Lords remained an unelected assembly, packed with supporters of the

Conservative Party. In future, this upper chamber would find it awkward to challenge a Liberal-dominated government elected by a large section of the population. Finally, the 1867 Act meant that the Queen was even more obliged to recognise the ever-growing ascendancy of parliament and with it the diminution of her monarchical authority. Even so, only a small proportion of the British people could vote – Britain was still far from being fully democratic – allowing the Queen to claim that she embodied the nation, not just the small section of the voting population.

The Queen was consistently unsympathetic to rebels within her own country, even when the discontent was fuelled by genuine suffering. In 1867, three members of the Irish Republican Brotherhood, William Allen, Michael Larkin and Michael O'Brien, attacked a police van carrying two leaders of the Brotherhood, released the prisoners and killed a policeman. Victoria talked with Disraeli about 'the Fenian prisoners and the necessity . . . of an example being made and of no irresolution being shown, for the safety of others, and the country at large'.[71] The Queen was gratified when she heard that the Cabinet had 'unanimously decided that the 3 Fenians, Allen, Larkin and Gould should be executed, while those, who were all probably as culpable as the rest, but had not actually been present when Brett the Policeman was killed, were to have the death sentences commuted to penal service for life'.[72] On the day of the execution, Victoria prayed for the 'poor men'.

Benjamin Disraeli: February–November 1868

In February 1868, Benjamin Disraeli replaced the 75-year-old Lord Derby as prime minister. The Queen approved even though she had taken a long time to warm to Disraeli. In 1844 she had referred to 'obnoxious Mr Disraeli',[73] accusing him of being 'very troublesome' and with a 'bad character'.[74] Two years later, in 1846, her opinion was the same, calling him 'that detestable Mr Disraeli' and considering him pushy and unprincipled. By 1849 she was changing her mind, saying that he had 'made a most brilliant speech'.[75] In April 1852 Disraeli was invited to Buckingham Palace. The Queen found him 'thoroughly Jewish looking, a livid complexion, dark eyes and eyebrows and black ringlets. The expression is disagreeable, but I do not find him so to talk to. He has a very bland manner and his language is very flowery.'[76]

For his own part, Disraeli never forgot that the Queen was a woman as well a monarch and behaved towards her in the manner of an enamoured suitor rather than a premier advising his sovereign. Queen Victoria was lonely; Disraeli befriended her. Dorothy Thompson suggests that Disraeli's gift of diplomacy and his chivalrous attitude towards women persuaded the Queen to agree with his government policy.[77] Disraeli soon established a 'complete ascendancy over the Queen's mind'[78] by treating her with the charm and courtesy that he thought befitted her sex. In many ways, Disraeli can be seen as the man who saved the monarchy from itself – indeed one can witness the Queen's metamorphosis from a melancholic recluse to a more active and politically engaged sovereign under Disraeli's guiding hand. He wrote to the Queen that it would be 'his delight and duty, to render the transaction of affairs as easy to your Majesty, as possible'.[79] He kept his word and wrote his report of proceedings in the House of Commons in a fresh, gossipy storybook style, which endeared him to the Queen, who enjoyed reading the simple, dramatic – and flattering prose. Queen Victoria thought 'his curious notes were just like his novels, highly coloured'. For example, the Queen enjoyed Disraeli's account of putting forward Ward Hunt as chancellor of the exchequer. Disraeli told his sovereign that 'Mr Ward Hunt's appearance is rather remarkable . . . He is more than six feet four inches in stature, but does not look so tall from his proportionate breadth; like St Peter's, no one is at first aware of his dimensions. But he has the sagacity of an elephant, as well as the form.'[80] Unfortunately, when Ward Hunt reached parliament to present his first and only Budget, he forgot to bring the 'Red Box' with him. Since that day each time British chancellors leave Downing Street on Budget Day, they hold the box aloft for the crowd to see.

Disraeli's minority government staggered on for ten months until November 1868 when he was forced to call an election over the question of the Church in Ireland. The issue centred upon the fact that the Protestant Church of Ireland was maintained by taxes levied on the Irish while the Roman Catholic Church, to which five-sixths of the country belonged, had to rely on voluntary Sunday collections to keep going. In March 1868, William Gladstone put forward a motion in parliament that the Church of Ireland should be disestablished, that is, separated from the British state. The Queen was appalled. Mr Gladstone, she wrote in her journal, 'imprudently, declared for the downfall of the Established church in Ireland! This is so abrupt, that it will call forth a burst of indignation and fury against the Roman Catholics on the part of the ultra-Protestants.'[81] She expressed a 'great fear, that this Irish Bill would do great harm.'[82] However, Gladstone's proposal was popular in the House of Commons. On 3 April Gladstone won a majority of 56 votes in a motion in favour of Disestablishment and subsequent resolutions were carried with ever increasing majorities. By November, Disraeli was compelled to call an election: the government was defeated. When the ministers gave back their seals of office, the Queen remarked that she was sorry because 'they had never been in better hands'.[83] As usual, the Queen rejected the notion that she should be above politics.

Notes

1 RA VIC/MAIN/QVJ (W) March 16th 1861.
2 Ibid. March 24th 1861.
3 Victoria to Vicky, December 18th 1861.
4 Rappaport, *Magnificent Obsession*, p. 152.
5 Victoria to Vicky, April 18th 1862.
6 RA VIC/MAIN/QVJ (W) July 1st 1862.
7 Victoria to Vicky, December 27th 1861.
8 Ibid. December 27th 1861.
9 See Richard Mullen, 'The Last Marriage of a Prince of Wales, 1863', *History Today*, June 1981, for a full discussion of the marriage.
10 RA VIC/MAIN/QVJ (W) March 10th 1863.
11 Victoria to Vicky, June 27th 1863.
12 Jane Ridley, *Bertie, a Life of Edward VI*, Vintage Books, 2013, p. 86.
13 Albert had adopted Wettin as his surname.
14 Lord Halifax to Ponsonby, August 28th 1871 quoted in Ponsonby, *Henry Ponsonby*, p. 72.
15 Bertie to Victoria, September 18th 1871.
16 Sir Theodore Martin, *Queen Victoria as I Knew Her*, Blackwood and Son, 1908, p. 284.
17 *The Times*, December 15th 1864, p. 8.

18 Victoria to Russell, December 8th 1864.
19 Memo by Ponsonby on Queen, quoted in Ponsonby, *Henry Ponsonby*, p. 73.
20 RA VIC/MAIN/QVJ (W) March 29th 1883.
21 Thompson, *Queen Victoria, Gender and Power*.
22 RA VIC/MAIN/QVJ (W) February 10th 1865.
23 Hardie, *The Political Influence of Queen Victoria*, p. 20.
24 Ridley, *Bertie, a Life of Edward VI*, p. 83.
25 For a thorough assessment of Queen Victoria's role, see W. E. Mosse 'Queen Victoria and her Ministers in the Schleswig-Holstein Crisis, 1863–1864', *The English Historical Review*, 78, April 1963, pp. 263–83.
26 Victoria to Vicky, February 24th 1864.
27 Quoted in Ridley, *Bertie, a Life of Edward VI*, p. 86.
28 Victoria to Vicky, January 27th 1864.
29 Mosse 'Queen Victoria and her Ministers', p. 282.
30 RA VIC/MAIN/QVJ (W) January 6th 1864.
31 Palmerston to Victoria, January 4th 1864.
32 Ibid. January 8th 1864.
33 Ibid. to Victoria, February 22nd 1864. Palmerston was referring to the London Protocol.
34 Phipps to Palmerston, February 22nd 1864.
35 August 28th 1864, quoted in Brown, *Palmerston*, p. 458.
36 *London Review*, May 7th 1864, quoted in Mosse 'Queen Victoria and her Ministers', pp. 277–8.
37 Quoted in Mosse 'Queen Victoria and her Ministers', p. 278.
38 Palmerston to Victoria, May 10th 1864.
39 Victoria to Palmerston, May 11th 1864.
40 Victoria to Vicky, May 10th 1864.
41 RA VIC/MAIN/QVJ (W) May 27th 1864.
42 Victoria to Vicky, July 1st 1863.
43 RA VIC/MAIN/QVJ (W) July 5th 1866.
44 Quoted in Christopher Hibbert, *Victoria: A Personal History*, HarperCollins, 2000, p. 393.
45 RA VIC/MAIN/QVJ (W) April 26th 1865.
46 Russell to Victoria, April 27th 1865.
47 RA VIC/MAIN/QVJ (W) April 29th 1865.
48 Ibid. October 18th 1865.
49 Victoria to Leopold, October 20th 1865.
50 RA VIC/MAIN/QVJ (W) February 6th 1866.
51 Sir Charles Phipps to Earl Russell, December 10th 1865.
52 Victoria to Russell, January 22nd 1866.
53 Martin, *Queen Victoria as I Knew Her*, quoted in Arnstein, 'The Warrior Queen: Reflections on Victoria and Her World', pp. 1–28.
54 Victoria to Derby, August 8th 1866.
55 For a stimulating article on this conflict, see W. E. Mosse, 'The Crown and Foreign Policy. Queen Victoria and the Austro-Prussian

Conflict, March-May 1866', *Cambridge Historical Journal*, 10, 1951, pp. 205–23.
56 Longford, *Victoria*, p. 380.
57 RA VIC/MAIN/QVJ (W) April 9th 1866.
58 Mosse, 'The Crown and Foreign Policy', p. 222.
59 Ibid.
60 Ibid. p. 213.
61 Grey to Wood, undated, quoted in ibid., p. 213.
62 Quoted in Weintraub, *Victoria: Biography of a Queen*, p. 350.
63 Victoria to Russell, June 19th 1866.
64 The 1867 Reform Act granted the vote to all male householders in the boroughs as well as lodgers who paid rent of at least £10 per annum and reduced the property threshold in the counties. It was to double the electorate in England and Wales from one million men to two million.
65 RA VIC/MAIN/QVJ (W) January 3rd 1867.
66 Victoria to Derby, January 12th 1867.
67 Derby to Victoria, January 10th 1867.
68 RA VIC/MAIN/QVJ (W) January 17th 1867.
69 Ibid. February 20th 1867.
70 Ibid. March 27th 1867.
71 Ibid. November 11th 1867.
72 Ibid. November 20th 1867.
73 Ibid. June 17th 1844.
74 Ibid. June 18th 1844.
75 Ibid. February 2nd 1849.
76 Longford, *Victoria*, p. 248.
77 Thompson, *Queen Victoria*, p. 122.
78 Hardie, *The Political Influence of Queen Victoria*, p. 40.
79 Disraeli to Victoria, February 26th 1868, quoted in ibid., p. 36.
80 Disraeli to Victoria, February 26th 1868.
81 RA VIC/MAIN/QVJ (W) March 17th 1868.
82 Ibid. March 24th 1869.
83 Quoted in Weintraub, *Victoria, Biography of a Queen*, p. 350.

8   Victoria, Gladstone and Disraeli: 1868–1880

On Wednesday 9 December 1868, William Gladstone became Queen Victoria's eighth prime minister. He was a clever man who had followed what is today a familiar political route, gaining a double first at Oxford, serving as president of the Oxford Union, training as a barrister, entering parliament at a young age and swiftly rising up the ranks. Gladstone served as prime minister four times: 1868–74, 1880–5, 1886 and 1892–4. He was advised to treat the Queen as a woman, that is, as a conventional nineteenth-century gentleman was expected to treat a lady, and told that he could 'not show too much regard, gentleness, I might even say tenderness towards her'.[1] But the prime minister ignored this advice and decided to speak to her as an intellectual equal. It did not occur to Gladstone to use different language with his sovereign from that which he was normally accustomed to use.[2] Gladstone's behaviour to the Queen was as to a monarch and head of a great empire, not as an empty-headed female, with the result that Victoria was as much out of her depth as she had been with Palmerston, 'lost in the fog of the long and far from lucid sentences of her Minister'.[3]

It is claimed that the evolution of the relationship between Queen Victoria and William Gladstone 'decisively affected the future course of constitutional monarchy in Britain'.[4] Gladstone was a convinced monarchist whose fervent religious belief made him regard Queen Victoria's rule as sacred. Nevertheless, Gladstone was a realist, fully aware that the Crown was dependent on public opinion for its continuation. He was the first prime minister to focus on the need for a ceremonial monarchy, doing his best to persuade Victoria that her job as sovereign was to be seen. In his opinion, ritual was an essential part of being queen and he took pains to explain how essential it was for Victoria to be present on ceremonial and state occasions if the monarchy was to survive. It was clear to Gladstone that ceremonies were a visible representation of the power of the sovereign, reminding the population of the long history of an independent and self-governing Britain. Naturally, such events should be carried out in style: in 1815 the future George IV, the Prince Regent, had ridden in a coach with a cavalry escort to parliament, arriving to a cannon salute. But Queen Victoria, with striking disdain, now preferred to avoid all such display.

The first significant breach between the Queen and Gladstone occurred in 1869 when the Queen declined to open parliament in person, claiming that she was too weak. She had agreed, under duress, to open parliament the previous two years but had warned her previous governments that they could not expect her do so regularly. Lord Grey wrote to Gladstone saying that neither 'health nor strength was wanting, were inclination what it should be. It is simply the long, unchecked habit of self-indulgence that now makes it impossible for her . . . to give up, even for ten minutes, the gratification of a single inclination, or even <u>whim</u>'.⁵ The Queen, encouraged by Disraeli's past defence of her seclusion, refused to compromise. Moreover, Victoria only reluctantly, and only under protest, would entertain foreign dignitaries at her palaces. This too was considered an essential part of her monarchical role. She complained that 'as a lady, <u>without a husband</u>' and at 'her <u>own expense</u>' she would not invite 'foreign Potentates to her house'.⁶ Once again, the Queen used her femininity as an excuse not to do her job.

In 1871, when Gladstone asked the Queen to delay her departure to Balmoral until she had prorogued parliament, the two clashed once more. Victoria refused, pleaded illness and threatened to abdicate if too much pressure was brought to bear on her. Gladstone, all too aware of growing Republicanism, wrote to her private secretary that the Queen's refusal was 'the most sickening . . . I have had during near forty years of public life. <u>Worse</u> things may easily be imagined: but small and meaner causes for the decay of Thrones cannot be conceived.'⁷ For once, the Queen was not malingering: her throat was so sore that she could not eat, an abscess developed under her arm and she rapidly lost weight. Victoria had not been this ill since her bout of typhoid in 1835. When Gladstone went to Balmoral the following month, the Queen pleaded her illness as an excuse not to see him for several days and when she did he commented that 'the repellent power which she so well knows how to use has been put in action towards me'.[8]

A universal feeling of discontent at the Queen's seclusion found voice in all the leading newspapers and journals. Between 1871 and 1874 alone, 84 republican clubs were founded in Birmingham, Cardiff, London, Aberdeen and other big cities, calling for the Queen to abdicate or be deposed. In November 1871, the radical politician Charles Dilke delivered a widely reported speech at Newcastle inciting people to overthrow the Queen and set up a republic. In addition, Queen Victoria was accused of appropriating large amounts of money from the Civil List – supposed to be used for public ceremonials – and using it to increase her family's personal wealth. In 1871, the Radical MP Charles Trevelyan published a very popular pamphlet which asked 'What does she do with it?' Trevelyan criticised the Queen's well-known parsimony and wanted to know how money paid by the government for regal displays, court banquets, entertaining visiting royalty, public appearances and other expenses was spent. Trevelyan alleged that the Queen squirreled away £200,000 a year and was thus able to amass a private royal fortune which he considered 'unconstitutional and most objectionable'. In reality, the Queen had saved £500,000 from the Civil List since the beginning of her reign, a fact that Gladstone refused to let his government make public in case there would be further public criticism of the Crown.

The Queen, and the monarchy, was saved by three brief episodes: a wedding, a brush with death and an assassination attempt. First, the Queen enjoyed a brief surge in popularity when, in 1871, her daughter Princess Louise married the Marquess of Lorne. The wedding marked a significant break with the royal tradition of marrying foreigners and it was the first time since the sixteenth century that a princess had married someone below their rank. The Queen's recently appointed private secretary, the Liberal grandee Sir Henry Ponsonby,[9] no doubt shared the view of most of the population when he commented that he was thankful that there was no 'talking now of this or that Seidlitz-Stinkinger'[10] joining the royal family. Certainly, another marriage to a German might have further undermined the monarchy. Then Bertie, the Queen's eldest son, became ill and his illness helped stem the rising tide of Republicanism. In December 1871 he contracted typhoid – the same illness thought to have killed his father – and it was feared that he might die. After a long struggle, Bertie pulled through and there was considerable public rejoicing. Gladstone took this opportunity to stage a carefully orchestrated parade of thanksgiving, persuading a reluctant queen to take part in it. On 27 February 1872, the Queen and Bertie drove in semi-state to St Paul's Cathedral to give thanks for the survival of the heir to the throne. The British public, desiring a much-needed fix of royal pomp and ceremony, came out in their thousands to witness the royal procession. The Queen, pleasantly surprised by the emotional outburst of her people, spoke of the 'millions out, the beautiful decorations, the wonderful enthusiasm and astounding affectionate loyalty shown. The deafening cheers never ceased the whole way. . . . It was a most affecting day, and many a time I repressed my tears.'[11] Queen Victoria may have been moved by the loyalty of her subjects but the British public would have to wait another 15 years for a similar celebration. Nevertheless, the illness of the Prince of Wales, his recovery and the subsequent thanksgiving ceremony marked a turning point in the reign of Queen Victoria. From now on, she would not have to face the threat of Republicanism.

Two days after the thanksgiving service a sixth assassination attempt on the Queen drew her people even closer to her. It was difficult for her to describe, as it 'was all over in a minute . . . suddenly someone appeared at my side . . . Then I perceived that it was someone unknown, peering above the carriage door, with an uplifted hand and a strange voice . . . in a terrible fright I threw myself over Jane C calling out "save me", and heard a scuffle and voices!'[12] John Brown, the Queen's gillie, rescued his monarch and held the would-be assassin tightly. When the Queen saw the pistol lying on the ground, she was filled with horror. Her companions 'were as white as sheets. . . . It is to good Brown and to his wonderful presence of mind, that I greatly owe my safety.'[13] A 17-year-old boy had climbed over the railings of Buckingham Palace, accosted the Queen in her carriage as she returned home and thrust a pistol in her face. The teenager was Arthur O'Connor, the grand-nephew of Chartist leader Feargus O'Connor, who had wanted the Queen to sign an order freeing Irish political prisoners incarcerated in England. These three episodes helped to mitigate the growing criticism of the Queen.

Domestic affairs: 1868–1874

Historians believe that Gladstone's first ministry was the greatest reforming ministry of the nineteenth century.[14] In August 1869, in order to effect a smooth passage of his proposed Bills, he asked the Queen to create 10 new peers and 14 baronets. The Queen objected. She knew it was

> essential to make the Hse of Lds a little more liberal, and to bring it more in harmony with the Hse of C. I see the force of this argument, but the object cannot be attained by the creation of a few Peers, even if there were to be 20, and it is a measure that is sure to damage the Govt.[15]

One of Gladstone's hopes was that Lionel Rothschild should be made an English peer, the first Jewish man to be so honoured. The Queen, however, was 'strongly against' the idea, claiming that she would 'have to refuse on the score of his religion, as much as on that of his wealth, being in fact derived solely from money contracts'.[16] The Rothschilds had to wait until 1885 before Nathanial Rothschild, eldest son of Lionel, was given a seat in the House of Lords, possibly as a reward for his father's loan to the government when it was negotiating to buy shares in the Suez Canal.

Gladstone's government introduced reforms which affected education, the army, alcoholic licensing, ballots, trade unions and Ireland. The 1870 Education Act laid the foundation for the British elementary school system and marked the first major step of the state's intervention into education by establishing Board schools for poor children. This was followed in 1871 by the University Entrance Act, which abolished the need for students to be Anglicans and allowed Methodists, Catholics and Jews to study at Oxford and Cambridge. In the same year the Bank Holidays Act established the first Bank Holidays in the United Kingdom, a Trade Union Act permitted trade unions to be formed, though the Criminal Law Amendment Act took away much of its power by making picketing punishable by three months imprisonment with hard labour. In 1872 a Licensing Act restricted the number of public houses, introduced closing times, regulated the content of beer and created an offence for being drunk in public or of riding a horse, driving a steam engine or carrying a loaded fire-arm when inebriated. In addition, the Secret Ballot Act stopped employers and landowners intimidating their workers and tenants by the introduction of secret ballots at government and local elections. Victoria was convinced that the ballot would lead 'to grave mistakes, from the secrecy, enabling people to promise one way, and vote another!',[17] a view shared by a number of politicians of both parties. In her view, Gladstone wanted radical change in too many areas.

The Queen raised objections to at least three domestic issues: one was about taxation, one concerned women and one the army. Gladstone wanted to minimise public expenditure and attempted to meet the government's deficit by taxing matches: a halfpenny on plain wooden matches and a penny on waxed matches. Thousands of match-makers, mainly from the Bryant and May factory in the East End, marched to parliament demanding its withdrawal. The Queen sympathised and wrote 'strongly' to Gladstone that the tax would

> make no difference in the consumption by the rich; but the poorer *classes* will be *constantly* irritated by this increased expense . . . it seems certain that the tax will seriously affect the manufacture and sale of matches, which is said to be the sole means of support of a vast number of the very poorest people and little children.[18]

The tax was withdrawn, in response to the Queen's remonstrances as much as to the match-girls opposition. At the time, no one appeared concerned about the health of the workers whose jaw bones abscessed, glowed a greenish-white colour in the dark and later rotted away, all caused from working with phospho-rous. Many years later, in 1888, the match-girls rebelled against their poor working conditions by refusing to work.

In 1868 the National Union for Women's Suffrage was formed to campaign for votes for women. For once, Queen Victoria and her prime minister found themselves on the same side of the argument. In 1870 Victoria wrote to Albert's biographer, Sir Theodore Martin, that she was 'most anxious to enlist every-one who can speak or write to join in checking this mad, wicked folly of "Woman's Rights", with all its attendant horrors, on which her poor feeble sex is bent, forgetting every sense of wom-anly feeling and propriety. Lady *** ought to get a good *whip-ping*.'[19] It is a subject, the Queen insisted, that made her so furious that she could not contain herself. God, she insisted, had created men and women different and each should remain in their own position. She wrote to Gladstone to call attention 'to the mad and utterly demoralising movement of the present day to place women in the same position as to professions – as *men*. . . . Woman would become the most hateful, heartless, and disgusting of human beings were she allowed to unsex herself.'[20] Gladstone, who believed that women's place was within the home not the House of Commons, similarly disliked the idea of women's suf-frage and let it be known that he, and any governments he formed, would resist any amendment to enfranchise women. He later defended his view saying that 'the fear I have is, we should invite her unwittingly to trespass upon the delicacy, the purity, the refinement, the elevation of her own nature'.[21] The fact that the Queen – herself a member of the delicate sex – was head of the most powerful country in the world did not appear to strike either of them as ironic.

The main domestic conflict between Gladstone and Victoria concerned army reform. Queen Victoria was constitutionally head of the armed services and was keen to be involved in any changes affecting them. In 1868 she was caught up in a conflict between her cousin the Duke of Cambridge, commander-in-chief of the army, and Edward Cardwell, secretary of state for war. As cousin as well as commander in chief, the Duke of Cambridge kept the Queen informed fully and frequently on all army matters, 'whether the subject was the design of the gold lace worn by field marshals and generals or the preservation of flogging as a form of army discipline'.[22] However, the government believed that the army was inefficient, unprofessional and badly led by old and often imbecilic officers who had purchased their commissions rather than received them on merit. The Crimean War had all too clearly revealed the failures of the British army and the ineffectiveness of the officers who led it.

In 1870 Cardwell began to re-organise the War Office and placed the commander-in-chief of the army under War Office control. In effect, the government wanted the commander-in-chief to lose his independence and become subordinate to the war secretary. Victoria, who feared that any diminution in the authority of the commander-in-chief would be highly injurious to the Crown, met with Cardwell several times and tried to prevent some of the reforms from taking place. For example, the Queen objected to the suggestion that the commander-in-chief held office for only five years, not for life.[23] She met with Lord Grey, the elder son of the former prime minister and leading Liberal politician, and 'talked to him very strongly on the subject, begging him to tell Mr Gladstone and Mr Cardwell, that unless George was entirely satisfied and his position remained unimpaired, I could not consent to the proposals'.[24] In the end, her private secretary had to remind his sovereign that she was a constitutional monarch who needed to support the government of the day. Queen Victoria had chosen to forget that she was only titular head of the army and could do little to alter reforms put forward by parliament.

The Irish question

Throughout Ireland people continued to live in wretched poverty exacerbated by the high rents demanded by English landlords and by the taxes which they were required to pay to the Anglican Church. Not surprisingly, dissent was widespread yet no one could agree on what action to be taken, or how to heal the divisions which had unsettled the island for centuries. Certainly, Queen Victoria and Gladstone disagreed over what to do about it all. When he became prime minister, Gladstone said 'My mission is to pacify Ireland.' He thought that there were three main areas to reform – the Church, land and education – before peace would come to Ireland. Queen Victoria opposed Gladstone's first proposal, the Disestablishment of the Church of Ireland.[25] Her bishops had advised her that 'what the Irish peasantry wanted, was the settlement of their land and <u>not this</u> measure'.[26] Moreover, the Queen's 'principal concern was to safeguard the rights of the crown'.[27] As head of the Anglican Church, she wanted to keep her church firmly united to the state.

On 31 May 1869 the Disestablishment Bill passed its third reading with a comfortable majority in the House of Commons. However, the Bill was opposed by the Conservative-dominated House of Lords: in the nineteenth century, the Lords had the right to veto any Bill put forward by the Commons. Victoria thought 'the danger of a collision with the House of Commons is very serious especially at a moment when many of the highest Peers are ruined by gambling and betting and their prestige stands very low. – Wrote to Lord Derby very earnestly, asking him to desist from this mad course.'[28] The Queen feared the potential conflict between the two Houses more than she did Disestablishment, particularly when the Liberals threatened to take away some of the powers of the Lords if they blocked legislation put forward by the House of Commons. Fortunately for the House of Lords, this did not happen. The Queen acted as mediator in the dispute, and after a lot of behind-the-scenes negotiations, the Bill was eventually passed. In 1869 the Irish Church was disestablished, its bishops lost their seats in the House of Lords and the Church lost its state funding. 'How thankful I feel!' commented the Queen. 'I warned strongly against any imprudence for the future, or doing anything respecting land, in Ireland, or affairs in general, which might lead to a belief that more things were to be disestablished.'[29] For the moment, the House of Lords was safe, partly because of the Queen's negotiating skills.

In an attempt to pacify the Irish still further, Gladstone tried to link the royal family more positively to Ireland. He recommended that the Queen buy a royal residence in Ireland and to visit it occasionally instead of going to Balmoral. Queen Victoria refused on the grounds of health. Then Gladstone tried to establish a viceroy for Ireland and appoint the Prince of Wales to it. He advised the Queen that a princely viceroy would improve relations between Monarchy and Nation, thinking perhaps that it might quell unrest if the royal family were seen there. Queen Victoria refused his requests because she wanted her son to remain in England. Consequently, an opportunity to meld Ireland more tightly to the rest of the UK through a visible royal presence was scuppered. Ireland felt ignored and unwanted and Gladstone was forced to try other means to pacify the country. It has even been argued that as a result of her neglect of Ireland, Queen Victoria lost the country for Britain.[30]

In 1870 Gladstone put forward his Irish Land Act to give Irish tenants greater rights. This Act had three main areas: first, tenants could not be evicted if they paid their rent; second, tenants could be re-imbursed for any improvements they had made; and third, tenants would be helped to buy the land they rented. The Queen thought Gladstone had brought in the Irish Land Act very successfully and had made a 'fine speech' in its support.[31] Unfortunately for Anglo-Irish relationships, the Land Act was bound to fail: landlords found it easy to circumvent the Act by putting up rents so high that tenants could not afford them.

In March 1873 Gladstone tried to re-organise higher education in Ireland. His Irish University Bill aimed to annex a number of colleges to Dublin University and transform it into a secular national university. The Bill was defeated by three votes because of a religious controversy over the syllabus. Gladstone graciously submitted his resignation but Victoria, persuaded by Disraeli to exercise her constitutional prerogative, refused to accept it. Gladstone, whose government could legitimately run on for another two years, agreed to continue in office.

Foreign affairs: the Franco-Prussian War, July 1870–May 1871

Meanwhile, on 19 July 1870 war broke out between France and Prussia, sparked off by French fears of further Prussian expansionism. During the Franco-Prussian conflict, Victoria reminded her government of the need for 'for great prudence and for not departing from our neutral position'.[32] However, unofficially, the Queen's sympathies remained with Prussia. France, who had expected to win the war, was swiftly beaten by the better equipped and disciplined German army with its up-to-date, efficient technology. Privately, Victoria was jubilant: while she 'was dressing for dinner came the astounding overwhelming news, of a great battle fought and victory gained today . . . Fritz [son-in-law] commanding in person. . . . What wonderful news! I am so thankful he is safe! . . . Everyone was full of and discussing the news, being greatly struck at the unexpected failure and defeat of the French.'[33] Victoria took pleasure in the French loss, commenting 'What a tremendous defeat! 4,000 French prisoners, 30 guns, 6 of the supposed invincible and murderous Mitrailleuses and 2 Eagles taken! A great panic at Paris.'[34] Fritz thanked his mother-in-law for 'the warm good wishes you have always shown for Germany, and for our Army'.[35] His father, now the German emperor, wrote saying 'Dear Sister, The lively sympathy with the unexpected and glorious successes of the war, which you have several times expressed through Fritz, has been a source of much gratification to me.'[36]

The drama continued throughout the autumn until the spring of 1871. On 2 September 1870, Napoleon III surrendered to Otto von Bismarck, the German chancellor. In the Queen's opinion, 'the cause of the complete failure and total defeat of the French army was the great lack of discipline . . . the ruin and disorganisation of France were so complete'.[37] The limitations of the French army were evident but it was the superior strength of the well-trained Prussian army that was the decisive factor. Nonetheless, the capture of Napoleon did not stop the war. The next day – 3 September – angry crowds flooded the Parisian streets, a Third Republic was declared and the French continued to resist the Prussians. The Queen heard news 'that the mob at Paris had rushed into the Senate and proclaimed a Republic!! This was received with acclamation, and the proclamation was made from the Hotel de Ville. Not one voice was raised in favour of the unfortunate Emperor! How ungrateful!'[38] In January 1871, after a long siege during which the starving citizens were forced to eat the local zoo's animals and later even rats, an armistice was signed with the Germans. The German Emperor ignored Queen Victoria's appeal 'for the sake of our old friendship, to allow me to express the hope he would make the terms of peace such as could be accepted by his vanquished enemies'.[39]

On 18 January 1871 at the Palace of Versailles, leaders of the German states proclaimed their union: along with the recently conquered Schleswig-Holstein and Alsace-Lorraine, they now formed part of the German Reich under the Prussian king, Wilhelm I. Bismarck's dream of a united Germany was realised, a dream which had serious repercussions for the balance of power in Europe. Gladstone, who feared a strong Germany, begged Bismarck not to annex Alsace-Lorraine; his pleas were ignored. In a long memorandum to her government, the Queen reassured them that 'a powerful Germany can never be dangerous to England, but the very reverse'.[40] In this instance, Queen Victoria was proved wrong. The German invasion of France and the imposed treaty not only poisoned Franco-German relationships but some attribute French determination to regain its lost territory as a cause of the First World War. In 1919, France regained Alsace-Lorraine when Germany was forced to sign its own humiliating treaty in the same Palace: the Treaty of Versailles.

War is often the midwife of revolution. In the wake of Napoleon III's defeat, a left-wing revolt broke out in Paris. It was sparked off by the French provisional government's decision to disarm the National Guard and spurred on by a fear that the Orleans dynasty might be re-instated. A few days later, on 26 March 1871, the revolutionaries won the municipal elections and formed the 'Commune'. The Paris Commune was an idealistic venture: its leaders wanted a secular state, increased democracy, the right of employees to take over businesses – and the abolition of night work in the Paris bakeries. Feminist leaders advocated gender equality, the right of divorce for women and the elimination of prostitution. When the news of the Paris uprising reached Victoria, she thought it 'very bad news from Paris. . . . The Red Republicans had refused to give up the guns . . . Great alarm.'[41] In her view, the Paris Communards 'go on quite as in the days of the old Revolution in the last century, though they have not yet proceeded to commit all the same horrors. They have however thrown Priests into prison etc. They have burnt the guillotine and shoot people instead.'[42] Each day, Victoria lamented the 'very bad news from Paris. The Arch Bishop and many priests put in prison and the Churches shamefully sacked! Atheism openly avowed!'[43] In her view nothing could 'exceed its state of Moral and physical degradation'[44] of the Paris Commune. She believed that the women were the 'most ferocious',[45] and dreaded the accounts from Paris 'of the bloodshed and cruelty, endless people being shot and I fear many innocent ones. The savageness of the prisoners, especially that of the women is too dreadful, and fills one with horror.'[46] At the end of May 1871 the Paris Commune was brutally crushed by the French army.

The deposed emperor, Napoleon III and his wife, escaped to Britain where, like many ousted foreign rulers, they were welcomed by Victoria: the Queen may have supported Germany in the war against France but she loathed emperors being toppled even more. When Queen Victoria saw the Empress, she contrasted it to her last visit here where it 'was all state and pomp, wild excitement and enthusiasm, and now?? How strange that I should have seen these 2 Revolutions in 48, and in 70!'[47] Queen Victoria liked Napoleon, going to the door to meet him and embracing him '*comme de rigeur*'. It was a moving moment for Victoria who remembered

> the last time he came here in 55, in perfect triumph, dearest Albert bringing him from Dover, the whole country mad to receive him, – and now! He seemed much depressed and had tears in his eyes . . . He is grown very stout and grey and his moustaches are no longer curled or waxed as formerly, but otherwise there was the same pleasing, gentle and gracious manner.[48]

In a poignant twist of fate, the French royal family who had been given asylum in England for 23 years departed for France. Louis d'Orleans, the son of the deposed King Louis-Philippe and the Queen's cousin by marriage, and his family came to visit the Queen, and bid goodbye. They had been allowed to return to France from exile.

At the beginning of 1874 Gladstone, who was temporarily depressed, unexpectedly asked the Queen to dissolve parliament and call for a general election.[49] The Queen relished Gladstone's resignation. She had earlier told her private secretary, Ponsonby, that she felt that 'Mr Gladstone would have liked to <u>govern</u> HER as Bismarck governs the Emperor . . . she always felt in his manner an overbearing obstinacy and imperiousness.'[50] The Queen, although still professing to be a Liberal, disliked Gladstone's politics, disapproved of his democratic leanings and his support for radical change. Moreover, Queen Victoria disliked Gladstone personally for not being able to explain politics simply. The Queen may have been glad to get rid of Gladstone but she was not happy about the timing, commenting on the inconvenience of doing so when she was about to receive her son Alfred and his new wife, Princess Marie, the Emperor of Russia's only daughter. 'People are apt', she told Gladstone 'to forget that the Queen is a <u>woman</u>, who has far more on her hands, and far more to try mind and body, than is good <u>for any one</u> of her sex and age'.[51] This time the Queen's pleas were ignored and new elections were called. The Liberals were defeated.

The return of the Tories: Benjamin Disraeli, 1874–1880

In February 1874 Disraeli became prime minister once more with a majority of 50 over the other parties. The Queen thought it 'a triumph'.[52] And she was especially delighted when Disraeli fell to his knees to kiss her hand and 'repeatedly said <u>whatever I wished SHOULD be done</u>'. It is widely believed that whereas Gladstone rather carelessly lost the favour of the Queen, Disraeli, with care, style and attention, actively cultivated it. The Queen

> was struck by his [Gladstone's] want of foresight, and a strange lack of knowledge of men and human nature . . . which does not give me the idea of his having any great <u>grasp</u> of mind. . . . I think that Mr Disraeli's is the larger mind. He is not such an earnest man, nor has he such strong conviction as Mr Gladstone but he seems to me, almost more unselfish.[53]

Disraeli's position was strengthened by his 'unscrupulous encouragement of the Queen's partisan tendencies which were very feminine but quite unconstitutional'.[54] Gladstone called him the 'artful dodger.'[55]

The 54-year-old Queen grew to like the 69-year-old Disraeli more and more. Victoria once again had a prime minister with whom she could work amicably, who made her feel good and flattered her intellectual accomplishments. Disraeli wore his learning lightly and brought, as Melbourne had once done, a sense of fun to politics. No longer would Victoria be lectured and hectored. The Queen enjoyed Disraeli's relaxed, charming and courteous manner and responded well to his more personal approach. She loved his extravagant style and may have even been amused by Disraeli's theatricality and his over-the-top flowery compliments. Certainly, ministerial visits became a pleasure again. Disraeli reached beyond Victoria's role as monarch. In effect, he wooed her. For the first time since the death of Albert, a man 'made her feel desirable, ready for a little gentle flirtation'.[56] And he definitely enhanced her self-esteem. Each Valentine's Day the two exchanged small gifts: Victoria told Lord Rosebery how touched she had been when Disraeli sent her a small trinket box with a heart on one side and the word *Fideliter* on the other. In return she sent him primroses to which he 'gratefully thanks your Majesty for your Majesty's delightful present. He likes the primroses so much better for their being wild: they seem an offering from the fauns and dryads of the woods of Osborne; and camellias, blooming in the natural air, become your Majesty's Faery Isle.'[57] He called the now seriously overweight, frumpy Victoria his Faery Queen. Disraeli did not treat Queen Victoria as an intellectual equal, preferring to pander to her whims and preferences and treating her like an empty-headed female while at the same time giving Queen Victoria an inflated sense of her role as head of state.

Disraeli further endeared himself to the Queen by supporting the idea of a memorial statue of Albert. This, he told the Queen, should 'represent the character of the Prince himself in the harmony of its proportions, in the beauty of its ornament, and in its enduring nature. . . . a testimony of a sublime life and a transcendent career'. Many would have thought this eulogy a little too melodramatic; Victoria was flattered. In reply, she sent a copy of Albert's speeches bound in white leather and wrote a letter expressing her 'deep gratification' at the tribute he paid to her adored, beloved and great husband. Victoria also congratulated Disraeli on his novel *Coningsby*. In her journal she confessed that she thought it a 'very remarkable, strange book. There are some beautiful sentiments in it, and some very striking opinions, – a sort of democratic conservatism, but the same large, patriotic views, he holds now. The story is strange, and the language too stilted and unnatural.'[58] Victoria's fondness of Disraeli was unbounded. In 1876, she made him Earl of Beaconsfield and allowed him to wear the 'Windsor uniform', the name of a special dark-blue uniform worn by men of the royal family and a few very senior courtiers at Windsor castle.[59] Only a few non-royals such as Melbourne and Wellington were ever given permission to wear it.

Disraeli's wife had died in 1872 and both he and the Queen regularly talked about how they missed their respective spouses. More importantly, Disraeli encouraged Victoria to become less self-pitying and to recover some of her natural vitality. Soon the Queen discovered a renewed sense of purpose: she began to take more of an interest in public affairs. She enjoyed reading Disraeli's letters – unlike those Gladstone's which had been so long that she requested a summary of them. Victoria regarded Disraeli as a servant of the Crown rather than of the people, a belief that Disraeli encouraged. Some thought it an unnaturally close working relationship especially when the two spent hours together in discussion and wrote directly to each other rather than go through their private secretaries. And as with Melbourne, Victoria's relationship with Disraeli made her dislike anyone who questioned or opposed policies put forward by her friend. Albert's insistence on the sovereign taking a neutral position had long faded. As a result, the Queen left herself open to the same fluctuations in popularity as that suffered by politicians more generally. Undoubtedly the Queen became increasingly Conservative during Disraeli's time of office. Certainly she shared Disraeli's visions of imperial grandeur underpinned by a spirited foreign policy and even more than he was, she was captivated by tales of the romance and fascination of India. Disraeli, a consummate politician, was thus able to harness 'the monarchy for the uses of popular, revivified Conservatism'.[60]

The Queen's social conscience was never particularly strong and she rarely took any interest in the lives of the British people,[61] showing as little interest in the social reform agenda of the Disraeli ministry as she had been to the previous Whig reforms.

In 1875 Disraeli's government passed the Artisans Dwelling Act, a Public Health Act, a Sale of Food and Drugs Act, a Factory Act, the Climbing Boys Act, a Merchant Shipping Act and a Trade Union Act. Queen Victoria instructed her private secretary to write to Disraeli expressing her satisfaction of the regulation of Labour Laws and of the Artisans Dwelling Act but did not comment specifically on the other reforms.

In contrast, Queen Victoria took her role as head of the Church of England very seriously. Nevertheless, the monarch preferred Presbyterian simplicity to high Anglican splendour and was the first sovereign to take communion in the Scottish Kirk. Before her accession to the throne, Victoria attended short and plain religious services but on becoming Queen she was forced to switch to the more grandiose rituals of royal Anglican Communion. Victoria disliked lavish worship and particularly viewed the ostentatiousness of cathedral services with distaste. Not surprisingly, the Queen wanted the Anglican Church to remain uncontaminated by what she saw as Romanish influences. The Oxford Movement, a group of High Church members based at the University of Oxford, had successfully urged the Church to reinstate some of the older pre-Reformation forms of Christian worship, namely the use of incense, Eucharistic vestments, candles and the idolisation of the Virgin Mary. In the Queen's opinion, the Church of England had misguidedly returned to these older traditions, leading to schisms in the Christian Anglican faith. She was concerned that 'the progress of these alarming Romanising tendencies has become so serious of late, the young clergy seem so tainted with these totally anti-protestant doctrines, and are so self-willed and defiant, that the Queen thinks it absolutely necessary to point out the importance of avoiding any important appointments and preferments in the Church which have ANY leaning that way'.[62] Her point of view was certainly a valid one as leading churchmen and other clergy had converted to Roman Catholicism while others had turned to Anglo-Catholicism.

The Queen required her Anglican clergy to be firmly Protestant and her church to return to the low-church rituals she preferred. She urged Disraeli to check the most 'dangerous and objectionable' Romanish forms of worship that had been appropriated by some Anglican clergy. Early in 1874, the Queen persuaded

Archbishop Tait, the archbishop of Canterbury, to introduce a Public Worship Regulation Act in order to curtail the growing Roman Catholic influences on the Church of England. Disraeli shepherded what he called 'the Queen's Bill' through parliament and cemented the undying gratitude of Victoria who believed that her personal wishes had been carried out.[63] In fact, the Bill undermined the Queen's impartiality: constitutional monarchs were supposed to be above politics and many believed it dangerous for the Queen to advance such a politically controversial measure. Moreover, it alienated high churchmen in the Anglican Church and at the same time heightened anti-Roman Catholic prejudice.

Foreign policy

As ever, the Queen was more interested in foreign policy than domestic affairs. And once again, her family relationships made her partisan. Victoria had disapproved of Gladstone's approach which, she believed, had Britain playing a submissive role in international affairs. Gladstone had wanted to get rid of land ruled by England; Disraeli, however, sought to enhance English power. During Disraeli's ministry, the words *jingoism* and *jingoists* began to be used, terms which had first been used in a popular music hall song:

> We don't want to fight but by jingo if we do
> We've got the ships, we've got the men
> We've got the money too[64]

In 1875 Victoria was overjoyed when Disraeli secretly bought shares in the Suez Canal which were being sold by the impoverished ruler of Egypt. The Suez Canal, which was built by the French, was a strategic waterway between the Mediterranean and the Red Sea, and with it the route to India. In 1869, 44 per cent of the Suez Canal, jointly owned by Egypt and France, was put up for sale by the Egyptians. Without consulting his Cabinet, Disraeli borrowed £4 million from the Rothschild bank and bought the shares on behalf of the British government. 'It is just settled, you have it, Madam,' he wrote to Victoria. The Queen believed that the purchase 'gives us complete security for India and altogether places us in a very safe position! An immense thing. It is entirely Mr Disraeli's doing. Only 3 or 4 days ago I heard of the offer and at once supported and encouraged him, when at that moment it seemed doubtful, and then today all has been satisfactorily settled.'[65] In the Queen's view it was a 'source of great satisfaction and pride to every British heart!'

It got better. Queen Victoria had long been fascinated by India and was ecstatic when, on 1 May 1876, the Royal Titles Bill was passed and Disraeli presented Queen Victoria with the title Empress of India. However, the Royal Titles Bill did not have a smooth passage through parliament. A number of Liberal MPs objected because they felt that it was a title associated with continental despots rather than constitutional monarchs. Gladstone thought it theatrical bombast and folly. Even some in the House of Lords objected. The Queen heard 'that the Duke of Somerset's language had been most ungentlemanlike and unusual in the Hse of Lords, disrespectful to me and very offensive to Mr Disraeli, insinuating that it was all a trick to get my children a higher position at the German Courts! Really too bad and too ridiculous, as it is an absolute falsehood.'[66] However, the Duke of Somerset had a point. The Queen was definitely annoyed by continental royals regarding the children of tsars, emperors and kaisers as more important than her own children. More significantly, she had long been aggrieved that every other major European monarchy – Austria, Germany, France and Russia – had an emperor. In 1871, when the German Empire was inaugurated, the new German Emperor thought himself superior to Victoria who was merely a queen. Certainly, the Queen delighted in adding the title of 'Ind Imp' on new coins and signing herself Victoria RI (Regina and Imperatrix) on her correspondence.

The Eastern Question: 1875–1878

Between July 1875 and July 1878, the Queen and Disraeli were absorbed in the 'Eastern Question', trying to reconcile the opposing parties of the Ottoman and the Russian Empires. The once powerful Turkish Empire had grown steadily weaker and both the Queen and Disraeli noticed that the rest of Europe looked on in anticipation of new territorial acquisitions should the empire fall. Britain and Russia competed to dominate the Mediterranean: the Russians were keen to gain Turkish territory; the British were determined that the Russians should not.

In July 1875 the first threat to the Turkish Empire emerged when the people of Bosnia-Herzegovina rose in rebellion against the Turkish occupation of their country. A Bulgarian uprising followed shortly afterwards. Disraeli and the Queen, who both feared that a weakened Turkey would upset the balance of power in the region, supported Turkish claims to these territories. During the summer of 1876, the brutal atrocities committed by Turkish mercenaries against the Bulgarian nationalists dominated British politics. The Bashi Bazouks, as the mercenaries were called, massacred approximately 15,000 people, at one time burning down a church where a thousand women and children had taken refuge. At first Queen Victoria dismissed the atrocities as fictional scare-mongering but was eventually forced to recognise that 'the Bashi Bazouks were horribly cruel, killing by torturing in a dreadful way, mutilating before killing. They were horrid looking people, wild peasants with narrow faces, and pointed beards, dressed in no uniform, but the national dress, with many knives stuck about in their belts.'[67]

In September, Gladstone, now leader of the Opposition, published *Bulgarian Horror and the Question of the East*, calling upon Britain to withdraw its support for Turkey and proposing independence for the afflicted occupied countries. In the pamphlet, Gladstone declared that 'no refinement of torture had been spared'; that 'women and children had been violated, roasted and impaled'; and urged Europe to 'let the Turks now carry away their abuses in the only possible manner, by carrying off themselves'.[68] The Queen thought that Gladstone had 'most unadvisedly written a violent pamphlet on the "Bulgarian Atrocities", adding fuel to the flame, really too bad'.[69] She was 'greatly annoyed at the violent language at the so called "Atrocity" meetings, held by Mr Gladstone. . . . It is so unpatriotic to make use of this troublesome question for party ends.'[70] Soon the Queen was forced to accept the truth of the atrocities perpetrated by the Bashi Bazouks on the Bulgarians. Even so, she felt that 'the violence and excitement of people here and against the Govt is most unreasoning'.[71] Not for the first time, Victoria misread the mood of the country. There was a public outcry when news of the Bulgarian atrocities was published: Gladstone's pamphlet sold 200,000 copies in the first month of its publication.

The British called on Turkey to introduce reforms and demobilise its Bashi Bazouks. When Victoria heard that 'the Turks will hear of no concessions and nothing can be done, only privately!',[72] she met the Sultan unofficially and urged him to agree to the British suggestions for reform.[73] The next day the Sultan sent a message 'that he himself saw no fatal objection to our terms, but that he could not manage his ministers and was afraid of being dethroned' unless the terms were modified.[74] Queen Victoria may have enjoyed this brief exercise of her power but it came to nothing.

On 24 April 1877, in the hope of regaining territories lost in the Crimean War, Russia declared war on the Turkish Empire. Queen Victoria was furious and wrote to one of the critics of Turkey, the Duke of Argyll: 'I wish therefore to state <u>solemnly</u>, that I know that this war . . . <u>would</u> have been <u>prevented</u>, had Russia not been <u>encouraged</u> in the strongest manner by the extraordinary, and, to me, incomprehensible, agitation carried on by some Members.'[75] She was referring to Gladstone and others who criticised the Ottoman Empire. In May 1877 the Queen told Disraeli that she 'had secret communication from a source I could not divulge, that the Russians were determined to have Constantinople . . . – therefore we ought to keep ourselves in readiness'.[76] She insisted that the Russian Emperor 'should be told distinctly though confidentially that we will <u>not allow</u> him to go to Constantinople'[77] and instructed her ministers to make it clear that any occupation of Turkish territory would be viewed as a belligerent action.[78] And with a Palmerstonian flourish, the Queen directed her ministers to write to Russia stating that if Russia seized Constantinople, then Britain would declare war. She also persuaded Disraeli's government to strengthen the British Army and to send the British fleet to Constantinople. Here the Queen was merely iterating government policy anyway. Nonetheless, many disliked this truculent reaction, fearing that there would be another Crimean War, with similarly disastrous consequences.

At the beginning of August 1877, the Russian advance was halted. The Queen, guided by Disraeli, once more intervened – and this time without the knowledge of Foreign Secretary Lord Derby. A top-secret private message was sent to the Tsar warning him that British neutrality would come to an end if the Russians continued with their campaign. The military attaché in Russia, Colonel Wellesley, was asked to deliver the message. Wellesley 'felt great difficulty and delicacy about this secret mission, of which Ld Derby (the foreign secretary at the time) was to know nothing'.[79] Colonel Wellesley not only dreaded being put in an embarrassing position if he was questioned by the Emperor but feared that one of the Emperor's staff would inform Derby.[80] Queen Victoria overrode his objections and gave Wellesley

> his formal, official answer to deliver, after which he would say, as from himself, that he had several confidential conversations with me, as well as the Prime Minister, and then he was to state what had been agreed on, that this was perhaps his last chance of stopping the war and above all of preventing our being forced into taking part in it, by showing how determined we were.[81]

Even in this age of secret diplomacy, this was an extraordinary action for both the Queen and Disraeli to take, and most definitely unconstitutional: to negotiate secretly with a foreign government without the knowledge of the foreign secretary and the Cabinet was little short of sedition, an offence seen to undermine the authority of the state. If the foreign secretary, the Cabinet and parliament, let alone the British population, had found out about these secret communications, it would have shaken confidence both in the monarchy and in the prime minister.

During the crisis, Victoria wrote to Disraeli every day and telegraphed him every hour, exhorting him to strong action. The Queen grew more and more belligerent as the crisis developed. She told Disraeli 'Oh, if the Queen were a man she would like to go and give those Russians . . . a beating.'[82] Queen Victoria was displeased by Derby's conduct of foreign policy, believing him to be the 'most difficult and unsatisfactory Minister' she had ever suffered.[83] She put enormous pressure on her foreign secretary, made him aware of her views and 'very strong feelings' and insisted that British interests be 'defended by force if necessary'.[84]

Indeed, the Queen told him that she expected 'her Government' to give her 'an assurance that we shall not again hear of difficulties, and impossibilities, and neutrality . . . we must see our <u>rights</u> <u>secured</u> as well as those of our former faithful ally, Turkey, whom we have by our forced neutrality cruelly abandoned to a most unscrupulous, aggressive, and cruel, foe'.[85] She later wrote to Disraeli insisting that 'Lord Derby <u>must</u> go'. Disraeli did not contest the Queen's wish since he suffered from a fractured relationship with his foreign secretary. Derby resigned. In effect, Disraeli was allowing Queen Victoria to get away with running parts of the Foreign Office: she was now at the height of her political powers and probably at her manipulative worst.

On 31 January 1878, after bitter conflict and acrimonious negotiation with the Turks, the Russians agreed to accept an armistice offered by the enemy. But almost immediately the Russians broke the truce and continued to advance on Constantinople. In March 1878 the Turks were forced to make a peace treaty with the Russians, the Treaty of San Stefano. In the treaty Bosnia and Herzegovina were given independence, a huge autonomous Bulgaria was created and Turkey was forced to concede territory to Serbia and Russia. Disraeli objected to the humiliating treaty imposed on the Turks and threatened war: the fleet, as Queen Victoria had recommended, was sent to Constantinople and arrangements were made to move troops to the Mediterranean. In July 1878 the Great Powers – Britain, Austria, France, Germany, Italy, Russia and Turkey – signed the Treaty of Berlin. It was agreed to re-draw the map of the Balkans: Bulgaria was divided into three, Austria took Bosnia-Herzegovina and Britain gained Cyprus. It was considered a triumph of British diplomacy; Disraeli returned home claiming he brought 'peace with honour'. The Queen was more than delighted, sending Disraeli a huge bouquet of flowers and offering him the Garter and a Dukedom. Disraeli declined the Dukedom but accepted the Garter.

The Zulu wars

Meanwhile, British imperialists were keen to control South Africa: they wanted to manage the trade route to India that passed around the Cape and they wanted to exploit the huge diamond deposits recently discovered there. In short they wanted to annex the area before other European countries had the same idea. But the native population, the Zulus, did not want Britain on their land. In January 1879, when the governor of the Cape Colony, Sir Bartle Frere, tried to extend British power in South Africa, further fighting broke out between the British and the Zulus. Disraeli had urged Bartle Frere to avoid war, thus he was exceedingly annoyed when he heard that his orders had been disobeyed. He was even more vexed when the army was defeated and Britain had to send in extra forces to defeat the Zulus. Queen Victoria, unusually, disagreed with Disraeli. She sympathised with Bartle Frere, for she, like him, espoused an expansionist foreign policy. When the Commander of the victorious British forces returned to England, the Queen wanted him given a hero's welcome; Disraeli refused to meet him.

On 24 March 1880 the Queen set off on her spring vacation. She began by visiting her daughter Alice in Darmstadt to see her two granddaughters confirmed, before travelling to Baden-Baden for a relaxing holiday. In the meantime a general election was taking place in Britain. Two weeks after Victoria had arrived in Germany she heard 'news regarding the elections, increasingly bad, which depresses me, as I grieve at the thought of parting with friends, especially Ld Beaconsfield'.[86] Her fears were confirmed when the Whigs, now commonly referred to as the Liberal Party, swept to power, winning 349 seats to Disraeli's 243 Conservatives and 60 Irish MPs. The Queen was devastated that her beloved Disraeli, Lord Beaconsfield, was no longer prime minister and blamed the 1872 Secret Ballot Act for it. The ballot, she insisted, 'had led to people's breaking their word very much, which was a very bad thing'.[87]

On 15 April the Queen left Baden-Baden. Victoria, now in her sixties, was 'obstinate, opinionated and entirely dependent on her own judgement'.[88] A year earlier, she had said 'I could never take Mr Gladstone . . . as my minister again, for I never COULD have the slightest particle of confidence in Mr Gladstone after his violent, mischievous, and dangerous conduct for the last three years'.[89] When she returned to Britain, she tried to prevent Gladstone from becoming prime minister, insisting that her private secretary impress on the Liberal Party 'that Mr Gladstone she could have nothing to do with, for she considers his whole conduct since '76 to have been one series of violent, passionate invective against and abuse of Lord Beaconsfield'.[90] She swore that 'she will sooner <u>abdicate</u> than send for or have any <u>communication</u> with that <u>half mad firebrand</u> who would soon ruin everything and be a <u>Dictator</u>. Others but herself <u>may submit</u> to his democratic rule but <u>not the Queen</u>.'

Disraeli was asked for advice. Her former prime minister may have lost the election but he still wielded power with the Queen and recommended that Hartington, now leader of the Liberal House of Commons, be asked to form a government. Queen Victoria was more than willing to take her former prime minister's advice and summoned Lord Hartington rather than Gladstone to lead the country. He wisely declined and advised the Queen that a new government could not be formed without Gladstone. The Queen replied 'I could not give Mr Gladstone my confidence. His violence and bitterness had been such . . . that he had . . . rendered my task and that of the Govt so difficult . . . I instanced the violence of his language . . . the violence against my Government.'[91] And still the Queen would not give up. She commanded Hartington to visit Gladstone to determine whether or not he would serve with Hartington. Hartington did his duty, Gladstone refused to commit himself and Hartington returned to his sovereign to tell her the bad news. Eventually the Queen was forced to accept Gladstone but insisted that 'there must be no democratic leaning, no attempt to change the Foreign Policy, no change in India, no hasty retreat from Afghanistan and <u>no</u> cutting down of [army] estimates.'[92] Queen Victoria, cossetted and indulged by Disraeli, had forgotten an important lesson: she was expected to reign. She was neither expected nor required to rule.

Notes

1 Wellesley to Gladstone, quoted in Magnus, *Gladstone*, p. 159.
2 See Ponsonby, *Henry Ponsonby*, p. 177.
3 Martin, *Queen Victoria as I Knew Her*, p. 51.
4 William Kuhn, *Democratic Royalism, The Transformation of the British Monarchy, 1861–1914*, Macmillan, 1996, p. 33.
5 Lord Grey to Gladstone, June 9th 1869 quoted in Magnus, *Gladstone*, p. 200.

6 Victoria to Gladstone, May 31st 1869.
7 Gladstone to Ponsonby, August 16th 1871, quoted in Hardie, *The Political Influence of Queen Victoria*, p. 60.
8 Gladstone to Granville, October 1st 1871.
9 Victoria had a number of different private secretaries: Prince Albert (from 1840 acted in an unofficial capacity); Sir Charles Phipps (1861–6); Hon. Charles Grey (1861–70), Sir Henry Ponsonby (1870–95) and Sir Arthur Bigge (1895–1901).
10 Quoted in Hibbert, *Victoria: A Personal History*, p. 394.
11 RA VIC/MAIN/QVJ February (W) 27th 1872.
12 Ibid. February 29th 1872.
13 Ibid. February 29th 1872.
14 For example, E.J. Feuchtwanger, 'W E Gladstone' in Blake, *The Prime Ministers*.
15 RA VIC/MAIN/QVJ (W) August 23rd 1869.
16 Ibid. October 31st 1869.
17 Ibid. April 7th 1880.
18 Victoria to Gladstone, April 23rd 1871.
19 Martin, *Queen Victoria as I Knew Her*.
20 Victoria to Gladstone, quoted in Roy Jenkins, *Gladstone*, Macmillan, 1995, p. 341.
21 Quoted in Constance Rover, *Women's Suffrage and Party Politics in Britain, 1866–1914*, Routledge and Kegan Paul, 1967, p. 120.
22 Arnstein, 'The Warrior Queen', pp. 14–15.
23 RA VIC/MAIN/QVJ (W) January 22nd 1871.
24 Ibid. January 27th 1871.
25 Victoria to Gladstone, quoted in Jenkins, *Gladstone*, p. 341.
26 RA VIC/MAIN/QVJ (W) February 11th 1869.
27 See J.C. Beckett, 'Gladstone, Queen Victoria, and the Disestablishment of the Irish Church, 1868–9', *Irish Historical Studies*, 13(49), March 1962, p. 40.
28 RA VIC/MAIN/QVJ (W) June 6th 1869.
29 Ibid. July 25th 1869.
30 Hardie, *The Political Influence of Queen Victoria*, p. 177.
31 RA VIC/MAIN/QVJ (W) February 16th 1870.
32 Ibid. February 8th 1871.
33 Ibid. August 6th 1870.
34 Ibid. August 7th 1870.
35 Fritz to Victoria, January 3rd 1871.
36 Ibid. January 14th 1871.
37 RA VIC/MAIN/QVJ (W) February 18th 1871.
38 Ibid. September 5th 1870.
39 Ibid. September 18th 1870.
40 Memorandum by Victoria, September 9th 1870.
41 RA VIC/MAIN/QVJ (W) March 19th 1871.
42 Ibid. April 8th 1871.
43 Ibid. April 16th 1871.

44 Ibid. April 24th 1871.
45 Ibid. May 28th 1871.
46 Ibid. May 31st 1871.
47 Ibid. December 5th 1870.
48 Ibid. March 27th 1871.
49 Magnus, *Gladstone*, p. 226.
50 Victoria to Ponsonby, November 18th 1874 quoted in Magnus, *Gladstone*, p. 218.
51 Victoria to Gladstone, February 14th 1874.
52 Victoria to Theodore Martin, February 10th 1874.
53 RA VIC/MAIN/QVJ (W) December 13th 1868.
54 Magnus, *Gladstone*, p. 219.
55 Quoted in Theo Aronson, *Victoria and Disraeli. The Making of a Romantic Partnership*, Macmillan, 1977, p. 133.
56 Van der Kiste, *Sons, Servants and Statesmen*, p. 80.
57 Disraeli to Victoria, April 21st 1875.
58 RA VIC/MAIN/QVJ (W) October 31st 1878.
59 Court uniform was worn by those holding particular offices attending the royal court. There were different uniforms for different grades of officials: the one Disraeli was allowed to wear was the highest.
60 Wilson, *Victoria: A Life*, p. 167.
61 Aronson, *Victoria and Disraeli*, p. 138.
62 Victoria to Gladstone, January 20th 1874.
63 Aronson, *Victoria and Disraeli*, p. 133.
64 It was written in 1878 in response to the surrender of Plevna to the Russians in the Russo-Turkish war.
65 RA VIC/MAIN/QVJ (W) November 24th 1875.
66 Ibid. April 2nd 1876.
67 Ibid. August 8th 1877.
68 Quoted in Magnus, *Gladstone*, p. 242.
69 RA VIC/MAIN/QVJ (W) September 8th 1876.
70 Ibid. September 20th 1876.
71 Ibid. August 30th 1876.
72 Ibid. January 8th 1877.
73 Ibid. January 15th 1877.
74 Ibid. January 16th 1877.
75 Victoria to the Duke of Argyll, June 4th 1877.
76 RA VIC/MAIN/QVJ (W) May 14th 1877.
77 Victoria to Disraeli, August 9th 1877.
78 Victoria to Salisbury, November 18th 1876.
79 RA VIC/MAIN/QVJ (W) August 14th 1877.
80 Ibid. August 14th 1877.
81 Ibid. August 16th 1877.
82 Moneypenny and Buckle, quoted in Arnstein, *Queen Victoria*, p. 23.
83 Victoria to Granville, May 1880, quoted in Hardie, *The Political Influence of Queen Victoria*, p. 128.

84 Victoria to Derby, February 10th 1878.
85 Ibid.
86 RA VIC/MAIN/QVJ (W) April 5th 1880.
87 Ibid. April 20th 1880.
88 Hardie, *The Political Influence of Queen Victoria*, p. 71.
89 Victoria to Marchioness of Ely, September 21st 1879.
90 Victoria to Ponsonby, April 8th 1880.
91 RA VIC/MAIN/QVJ (W) April 22nd 1880.
92 Victoria to Ponsonby, April 8th 1880.

9 Trading places – Victoria, Gladstone and Salisbury: 1880–1892

On Christmas Day 1880, Queen Victoria wrote to W. E. Forster, chief secretary of Ireland, insisting that she 'cannot and will not be the Queen of a democratic monarchy; and those who have spoken and agitated . . . in a very radical sense must look for another monarch'.[1] Victoria never carried out her threat of abdication even though the years between 1880 and 1892 were difficult ones for the sovereign. This period was marked by bitter conflicts at home and overseas, largely sparked off by the continuing crisis of Ireland, franchise reform, problems in the Middle East and the collapse of the Liberal Party. At key moments such as these, Queen Victoria was prepared to use all the means available to achieve her goals, even when it meant breaking more constitutional conventions. Theoretically the Queen continued to regard herself as a firm supporter of the Liberals, whereas in reality she preferred the acquiescence and protection of the Tory Party. During this period, Queen Victoria appointed two prime ministers, both of whom held office twice: William Gladstone from 23 April 1880 to 9 June 1885; Lord Salisbury from 23 June 1885 to 28 January 1886; Gladstone from 1 February 1886 to 20 July 1886; and Salisbury from 25 July 1886 to 11 August 1892. Victoria thought democracy a fine thing when it got rid of Gladstone; a defect in the constitution when the Conservatives were voted out of office.

It became even more evident, particularly after the 1884 Reform Act, that the Queen's duty as a constitutional monarch was to remain politically neutral and act on the advice of her prime ministers. She was expected to fulfil the role of head of state, to be the symbolic head of Britain, to summon and prorogue parliament and to act as a buttress against politicians seeking too much power. The Queen was not expected to govern the country. Yet it was difficult to avoid the impression that the Queen remained a commanding political force. It might even be argued that Queen Victoria posed the greatest threat to constitutional monarchy as she set about undermining governments of which she disapproved, attempted to destabilise the Liberal Party or tried to manipulate domestic and foreign policy.

It was during this period that the Queen's last two children married. On 27 April 1882 the haemophiliac Prince Leopold married Princess Helena of Waldeck and Pyrmont, a sovereign principality in the German Empire. Victoria wrote that 'my anxiety was naturally great, as to how Leopold would get through the ceremony. . . . contrary to my expectation, dear Leopold walked the whole way up the Nave. He was supported on either side by Bertie and Louis. . . . It was very trying to see the dear Boy, on this important day of his life, still lame and shaky.'[2] Three years and three months later, on 23 July 1885, Victoria's last child, Beatrice, married the Germanic Prince Henry of Battenburg. At first, the Queen refused to allow Beatrice to marry, believing like many mothers that her youngest daughter should remain single, stay at home and take care of her mother. When Victoria heard that Beatrice wished to marry Henry, her mother wrote: 'what despair it caused me and what a fearful shock it was . . . it made me quite ill'. These anxieties indicate an unappealing, selfish element in the Queen's character, more concerned about her own happiness than that of her younger daughter. After several months of refusing to speak to her daughter, Victoria agreed to the marriage – but only on condition that Henry give up his German commitments and make his home with the Queen. When the couple married, Victoria thought Tennyson's poem written for her maiden daughter's marriage with the lines 'the mother weeps at that white funeral of the single life' all too appropriate. Gladstone was not invited, a mean-spirited action on the part of the Queen and a personal insult to Gladstone as other political leaders had been asked.

Queen Victoria, now in her sixties, continued to cope with the deaths of friends and family. In March 1881, Queen Victoria was distraught when Disraeli died. She was 'most terribly shocked and grieved for dear Ld Beaconsfield was one of my best, most devoted, and kindest of friends, as well as wisest of counsellors. His loss is irreparable, to me and the country. To lose such a pillar of strength, at such a moment, is dreadful!'[3] The Queen had written regularly to Disraeli after he lost his premiership, often secretly asking him for political advice. When he died, Victoria mourned that there was no one left to halt the pace of Liberal reform. Three years later, 'another awful blow' fell upon the Queen when her son Leopold, who had travelled to Cannes to escape the British winter, slipped and fell injuring his head. He died in the early hours of 28 March from a cerebral haemorrhage. Her 'beloved Leopold, that bright, clever son, who had so many times recovered from such fearful illness . . . has been taken from us . . . I am a poor desolate old woman, and my cup of sorrow overflows!'[4]

In March 1888, the German Emperor, William I, died and the throne passed to his son, Frederick III, husband of Vicky, Victoria's eldest daughter. Unfortunately, Frederick had throat cancer. Three months later, on 15 June, he too died. His place was taken by Queen Victoria's eldest grandson, who was crowned William II. Victoria, aware of the brittle relationship between her grandson and his mother, wrote to William immediately expressing her anxiety about his mother's position and asking him to do his utmost for her.[5] The new Emperor had great respect for his grandmother but took little notice of her entreaties. Victoria thought her grandson high-handed, vulgar and absurd. He was mocked in the family as 'William the Great'.[6] Neither Victoria nor anyone else in British politics at the time could see how these complex and often thorny family networks would eventually pose a threat to Europe. But Victoria was particularly astute about the Emperor's character.

Three years later, on 14 January 1891, Prince Albert Victor (Eddy), Bertie's eldest son and heir, died unexpectedly from pneumonia. He was due to be married to his cousin, Princess May of Teck, a few weeks later. The Queen found that 'words are far too poor to express one's feelings of grief, horror and distress! Poor, poor parents; poor May to have her whole bright future to be merely a dream! Poor me, in my old age, to see this young promising life cut short!'⁷ His younger brother, Prince George, became second-in-line to the throne. In March 1892 her son-in-law, Louis, husband of Princess Alice, died. Victoria could hardly write about it. 'Too, too terrible! Darling Louis, whom I loved so dearly, who was devoted to me and I to him for more than 30 years, it is too dreadful to have to lose him too! . . . I was so upset I could not go to church, but read prayers in my room.'⁸

Gladstone's second ministry: 23 April 1880–9 June 1885

Queen Victoria's dislike of the 71-year-old Gladstone turned to unequivocal hostility during his second ministry when the Queen objected to 4 out of 14 members of his proposed Cabinet. Victoria seemed determined to be as difficult as possible. She was 'astonished, and somewhat put out, at hearing from Mr Gladstone, submitting the name of Mr Chamberlain, one of the most advanced Radicals, for a place in the Cabinet, and of Sir Charles Dilke, as Under Secretary for Foreign Affairs! Wrote to Mr Gladstone, expressing my regret and surprise.'⁹ Queen Victoria was determined not to accept Sir Charles Dilke as a minister because 'it is well known that he is a democrat – a disguised republican. . . . He has been personally most offensive . . . to place him in the Gvt . . . would be a sign to the whole world that England was sliding down into democracy and a republic.'¹⁰ Objections continued when Gladstone 'submitted "more unexpected names". Mr Mundella (one of the most violent Radicals) for President of the Board of Agriculture, the equally violent, blind, Mr Fawcett as Post Master General'.¹¹ The Queen's private secretary remarked 'I do not envy the coming Ministry.'¹²

Gladstone continued to find his sovereign obstinate and obstructive during his second term of office. He even judged that the Queen's partisanship might bring the Crown into disrepute, making notes in his Cabinet meetings which contained 'frequent references to the Queen's intolerable and ill-judged attempts at interference'.¹³ Undoubtedly, Gladstone would have been even more troubled had he discovered that his sovereign was also in contact with the opposition. When he was alive, Victoria had confided to Disraeli that she always tried to avoid dealing with

Gladstone and never wrote to him 'except on formal official matters . . . I always look to you for ultimate help'.[14] Part of the problem lay with the fact that Gladstone remained impervious to the Queen's feminine guile and 'never gave in to her ways . . . certainly did not comply with her wishes as they have been complied with in the last 6 years'.[15] In addition, Gladstone's second premiership was dogged by controversy: the Bradlaugh affair, the extension of the franchise, the Irish question and problems in Afghanistan, Egypt and the Sudan. The Queen disagreed with Gladstone's approach to every one of these matters.

On 29 April 1880 the new parliament met for the first time. Each MP swears a religious oath of allegiance to the Queen before taking his seat in the House of Commons but Charles Bradlaugh, well known for his Republicanism and radical ideas, wanted to affirm rather than take the oath. He was not allowed to do so. Victoria was happy at this outcome since she thought that Bradlaugh was a 'horrible, immoral Atheist'.[16] Bradlaugh was duly ousted from his seat in the House of Commons and a by-election took place in his constituency. His Northampton electorate were annoyed at the removal of their elected representative and returned Bradlaugh as its MP – in June 1880, July 1881, August 1881, February 1882 and also in 1884. Each time Bradlaugh refused to take the oath, each time he was forbidden to take his seat and each time he was re-elected. There were frequent skirmishes between Bradlaugh and the police officers who tried to prevent him from taking his seat. The Queen, who disliked radicals, and disliked none more so than Charles Bradlaugh, spoke of how 'there was a most frightful scene this evening, in the Hse of C on Mr Bradlaugh trying to force his way in, and being ejected. Much violence was displayed, and Mr Bradlaugh got his clothes torn!'[17] On one occasion Bradlaugh was forced to spend the night in a prison cell under Big Ben. In 1886, after the reports of two select committees and four re-elections, Bradlaugh was eventually allowed into parliament to represent his constituency. Democracy, after a four-year battle, had won the day but Queen Victoria predictably was not amused.

At this time Gladstone dominated the House of Commons and his government put forward a number of reforms. The 1882 Married Women's Property Act consolidated and amended the

English, Welsh and Irish law relating to the property of married women by allowing married women to have the same rights over their property as single women. The Queen, who by the virtue of her position had sole control over her property, made no comment. In 1883 the Corrupt and Illegal Practices Act aimed to eliminate corruption in elections by making it a criminal offence to bribe voters. Once more, the Queen expressed little interest. However, encouraged by her eldest son, Bertie, she voiced her disquiet at the deplorable condition of housing in the towns. The Queen asked Gladstone to mitigate 'this great and growing evil which threatens the prosperity of this country'. She wanted 'to learn whether the Government contemplated the introduction of any measures . . . to the true state of affairs in these overcrowded, unhealthy and squalid abodes'.[18] In March 1884 a Royal Commission on the Housing of the Working Class was set up: and Bertie was on the commission. It was a hard-working commission which met 51 times, toured the slums and interviewed a range of public officials. It was left up to the next prime minister, Lord Salisbury – on 24 July 1885 – to introduce a Bill into parliament which granted local authorities the power to shut down substandard houses.

Third Reform Act: 1884

Gladstone and his Liberal government were keen to increase democracy further by extending the vote to men in rural areas. The Queen was against the idea because she disliked the increased power that a wider electorate would give the House of Commons. Not only did she complain that the present House of Commons was 'allowed to dictate and arrogate to itself the power of the executive, disregarding both the House of Lords and the Crown'[19] but – once again – she threatened to abdicate. The Conservatives, who feared an increase in Liberal votes if the franchise was extended, agreed with the Queen.

On 29 February 1884, Gladstone introduced a Franchise Reform Bill to extend the household suffrage enjoyed by town dwellers to those living in the country. It would add about six million to the number of men who could vote. The Bill, however, did not run smoothly. 'The Franchise Bill', Victoria noted in her journal, 'which I consider a misfortune, drags on in the House of Commons.'[20] Eventually, in June, the Bill was passed. Not surprisingly, the Bill caused a renewal of difficulties between the Queen, the House of Lords and the House of Commons. In Victoria's view, the Commons was gaining too much power at the expense of the House of Lords and the Crown; in Gladstone's view, the Lords was undermining democracy. The Lords, which had been encouraged by both the Queen's disapproval and the Conservative opposition in the Commons, refused to pass the Reform Bill unless one condition was met: the introduction at the same time of a Redistribution Bill. This was perhaps a fair request as the new Reform Act would make it necessary to redraw boundaries to make electoral districts more equal. Gladstone and his government agreed that a Redistribution Bill was needed but had no wish to be bullied by the Lords into this and refused. A political impasse ensued: many viewed it as the 'Peers against the People'.

The Queen's sympathies lay with the Upper House. In her view, the House of Commons was only one out of three elements in the Constitution and should not send up Bills to the House of Lords to which the Lords could not agree. In response, Gladstone – who now nicknamed his sovereign 'Her Infallibility' – insisted that the House of Lords had been a 'habitually formidable opponent to Liberal policy'.[21] He later threatened the Queen with curtailing, and perhaps even abolishing, the House of Lords, telling her that the House of Lords was 'purely Tory and out of harmony with the prevailing sense of the nation, and ought to be reformed'.[22] Indeed, the more radical politicians spoke so strongly against the tendency of House of Lords to block Liberal reform that the Queen complained to 'Mr Gladstone, that hardly a day passed, without some violent and contemptuous language against the Hse of Lords. . . . Mr Gladstone appeared to think there ought to be a Radical Hse of Lords . . . so that any Radical measure should pass. The monarchy would be utterly untenable, with no restraining balancing power left.'[23]

It was a tense situation. Her eldest son, Bertie, considered the crisis so serious that any remedy would be justifiable to avert a conflict which would be 'dangerous to both Party and Constitution'.[24] Gladstone once again told the Queen that the House of Lords had, 'especially during the last 30 years, been a formidable opponent of the Liberal policy and its tendency to separate from the People was becoming more marked' and 'only by great discretion and moderation in the use of wholly irresponsible power, could the Hse of Lords continue in possession of it.'[25] Victoria was angered by Gladstone's threats and wrote a draft letter to him insisting that 'to threaten the House of Lords . . . is in fact to threaten the Monarchy itself. . . . she will not be the Sovereign of a Democratic Monarchy'.[26] The letter was amended by her private secretary with this provocative paragraph removed.

Finally, after protracted discussions and in order to avert a constitutional crisis, the Queen was persuaded to end the deadlock between the government, the opposition and the House of Lords. She wrote to both Gladstone and Salisbury suggesting that the leaders of the two parties meet together personally and privately to discuss the Reform issue.[27] A secret meeting duly took place behind closed doors in the Carlton Club, not in parliament where the debate should properly have taken place.[28] An agreement was reached: the Conservatives in the Lords would pass the Reform Bill if the Liberals promised to put forward a Redistribution Bill after it was passed. Gladstone graciously wrote to the Queen thanking her 'for that wise, gracious and steady exercise of influence . . . which has so powerfully contributed to bring about this accommodation and to avert a serious crisis of affairs'.[29] The Queen relished the compliment, but was more pleased when another leading Liberal told her (more simply) that she should be 'proud of the influence I had exercised in the settlement of this burning question'.[30] Nonetheless, it is reasonable to assume that the crisis could have been averted if the Queen had only withheld her views on parliamentary reform.

Ireland: 1880–1885

Once more, Ireland represented a blot on the political landscape. Queen Victoria faced the biggest threat to the composition of the United Kingdom whenever Gladstone became prime minister because he grew increasingly sympathetic to Home Rule. Naturally, Victoria disapproved of any disintegration of her country. However, in the eyes of the Irish, England was to blame for

Ireland's suffering. In the early 1880s Irish farmers faced a series of poor harvests, which, combined with a significant dip in agricultural prices, resulted in destitution and starvation for many. Large numbers of tenant farmers were unable to pay their rent: between 1879 and 1883, 14,600 tenant farmers were evicted from their property. Ireland was set to be the main political problem facing the Queen until the mid-1890s.

In 1879 the Irish Land League was formed to protect tenants from eviction and to obtain rent reductions. Led by Charles Stewart Parnell, an Irish MP and Home Ruler, the League channelled the anger of the poor and dispossessed into rent strikes, boycotts and violence against English property owners. The League hoped to make Ireland ungovernable and thus force England to grant Irish independence. In the Queen's opinion, the Irish Land League had caused mischief and was to blame for 'the crime, distress, murders &c' and the refusal to pay rent.[31] She resisted any attempt to separate Ireland from the rest of the United Kingdom.

Tensions escalated further when Parnell proposed that land-agents who took over farms where someone had been evicted should be ostracised. One particular land-agent, Captain Boycott, who had evicted tenants for non-payment of rents, subsequently found himself without domestic servants or farm labourers. Shops refused to serve him. This system of 'boycotting' as it became known spread throughout Ireland. And violence continued. Victoria criticised the government in 'allowing a state of affairs like the present in Ireland to GO ON. The law is openly defied, disobeyed, and such an example may spread to England. It MUST be put down.'[32] The Queen was so agitated by Irish unrest that on Christmas Day she wrote to Forster, chief secretary for Ireland, insisting on the immediate suspension of habeas corpus in Ireland before any attempt at land reform took place.[33]

The Liberal government was split as to what to do. Some wanted the rebels imprisoned whereas others felt the need to redress the agricultural injustices which prompted the rebellions. Queen Victoria thought it was more important to repress than redress and she 'tried to impress upon Mr Gladstone very strongly, the necessity of not bringing land measures forward, until, a strong one was brought in to put down this dreadful state of affairs'.[34] Forster, however, believed in a combination of repression and emancipation and brought in two Bills to address the problem: a Compensation for Disturbance Bill which reimbursed tenants who had been evicted and a Coercion Bill to enable the government to arrest people without trial who were 'reasonably suspected' of crimes. For the rest of his term in office, Gladstone was caught in a vortex of Irish violence which he tried to curb by a mixture of repression and reform. Queen Victoria, on the other hand, favoured crackdown.

The Irish Compensation Bill was rejected by the House of Lords; the Coercion Act was passed. This Act suspended *habeas corpus,* thus enabling the authorities to arrest and imprison anyone it considered a threat. Shortly after, in April 1881, Gladstone attempted to remove the underlying injustices which led to rebellion by putting forward an Irish Land Act based on the three Fs: fair rents, fair sales and fixity of tenure. This Act provided Irish tenant farmers with greater security and fairer rents. Victoria approved of the principles of fairness but warned that it should not be done at the expense of the 'innocent Landlord' who needed the security of an adequate rental income. The Act did not quell unrest in Ireland and the Queen wrote to Gladstone 'that greater efforts may be made to arrest the agitators . . . and to punish those who are intimidating and alarming the well affected inhabitants'.[35]

The government's solution to the continuing disturbances was to imprison the Land League's leaders and outlaw the organisation. Charles Parnell and 13 of his followers were arrested and duly imprisoned in Dublin's gaol. The Queen thought it a 'very good thing'.[36] However, rather than diminishing, the unrest escalated even more: secret societies terrorised Ireland, burning farms, destroying cattle and murdering land-agents. Victoria was told 'the state of affairs is as bad as possible, and the insecurity of everything, dreadful. . . . In many parts, the people behave really like savages.'[37] In the Queen's opinion the need for strong measures was essential. She had not visited Ireland since 1861 and had no intention of visiting in the near future. This was a pity as the Queen, a symbol of constitutional order, might have quelled the unrest if only she had shown the slightest bit of affection for this part of her country.

In the end the government decided to release Parnell. Queen Victoria 'very reluctantly'[38] agreed: she could not do otherwise, as her consent was merely a formality. The Queen feared that Parnell's release would be a 'triumph to Home Rule' and was anxious that it might undermine the 'maintenance of authority and respect of law and order'.[39] At the same time the government eased the operation of the Coercion Act and helped tenants in arrears with their rents. In return for his release, Parnell promised to curb the violence against landowners and work with the Liberals to promote Home Rule constitutionally.

Parnell's assurances were futile. In May 1882 the new chief secretary, Mr Burke, and Lord Cavendish were murdered in Phoenix Park, Dublin. Naturally, the Queen thought it 'too terrible. . . . Everyone was horror struck. . . . How could Mr Gladstone and his violent radical advisors proceed with such a policy, which inevitably has led to all this?'[40] The Queen held those who recommended the release of Parnell responsible and called on the government to 'take such strong measures as may give her and the country security . . . that valuable lives will not be brutally murdered'.[41] Gladstone was advised to 'make no concessions to those whose actions, speeches and writings have produced the present state of affairs in Ireland'. Queen Victoria told him how much she regretted the 'sudden and hurried release' of the Irish prisoners and Gladstone was instructed to 'protect her subjects from murder and outrage'.[42] The Queen would never admit that the Irish rebels had legitimate grievances. In 1883 the murderers were caught, five were hanged and three sent to prison.

A new, and even more repressive, Coercion Act was put forward on 11 May 1882, the same day as Lord Cavendish's funeral. This authorised special judges, rather than juries, to hear serious crimes. It also gave increased powers to the police force. When the Queen heard of these measures, she told Gladstone that 'she rejoices to hear that a vigorous measure' was to be brought in.[43] Not surprisingly, the Irish MPs opposed the Bill. The Queen stood firm, telling her government to 'resist any attempt to give way'[44] while complaining to her private secretary about Gladstone's 'strangely indulgent' attitude towards the Home Rulers.[45] In July 1882 she was pleased when 18 Irish MPs were suspended because of their conduct in parliament when the Coercion Bill became law.[46] Bloodshed in Ireland continued.

In 1883 a wave of violence perpetrated by Irish protesters swept across Britain: in January a gas works was blown up in Glasgow and attempts were made to blow up an aqueduct in March. The Queen was 'horrified to hear of an explosion'[47] in Whitehall. There was an endeavour to blow up *The Times* offices; in April a nitro-glycerine factory was discovered in Birmingham; in October two explosions took place in the London Underground. The Queen was thankful when on 9 April an emergency and stringent Explosives Bill was passed regarding the 'dreadful explosions'.[48] But the violence continued. In February there were explosions at Victoria Station and attempts were made at Paddington, Charing Cross and Ludgate Hill but failed; in May considerable damage was done to Scotland Yard and St James's Square; in December an arch of London Bridge was damaged. There was a fear that Queen Victoria might be a target, therefore when she returned to London from Balmoral 'the stations were kept quite clear, for prudence sake'.[49]

Violence was endemic throughout Europe. In February 1881 Victoria had been shocked by the assassination of Tsar Alexander II. The Queen heard of how the Tsar 'was killed on the spot, from concussion of the brain, having been blown high up into the air, and everything destroyed and pulverised . . . he can never have felt anything, or breathed, after the explosion'.[50] She later received reports of how the Tsar 'was carried up in a carpet and the marks of blood were all over the staircase. The mattress, on the small camp bed which he drew his last breath, was absolutely saturated with blood!'[51] Alexander III became the new tsar; his wife Maria was the Danish sister of Alexandra, Bertie's wife, thus forging another link in the royal chain. Even so, Queen Victoria later confessed her 'dislike of the fat Czar. I think him a Paul-like violent Asiatic full of hate, passion and tyranny.'[52]

Foreign policy

In 1883, the American journal *Harper's Weekly* reported that the 4ft 11ins 64-year-old Queen weighed two hundred pounds (14st 4lbs; 90 kilograms) and was getting comfortably fatter every day.[53] Her increasing girth mirrored her belief in the enlargement of empire. Queen Victoria wanted to expand the British Empire whereas Gladstone wanted it slimmed down. Not surprisingly, serious disagreement occurred between the Queen and Gladstone over foreign policy. The Queen continued to believe that foreign policy was the peculiar preserve of the sovereign, whereas Gladstone was convinced that the Queen's partisanship could only bring the throne into disrepute. By now Victoria was a Conservative imperialist and acutely conscious of Britain's status and reputation in the world. She wanted to rule over as much of the world as possible and saw Gladstone as seeking to undermine that ambition. Indeed, Gladstone was a Liberal anti-imperialist who believed that Britain should never be seen to support a cause that was morally wrong. His government had been elected on an anti-imperialist platform and the prime minister did his best to keep to this promise. For her part, the Queen missed Disraeli's flamboyant imperialistic foreign policy and made little effort to hide her hostility to Gladstone. Moreover Disraeli used to explain policy in simple language whereas Gladstone continued to make little effort to render politics palatable or attractive to the Queen.

Victoria's first outburst occurred over the Queen's Speech. This was a speech that, even at the time, was considered the speech of the ministers rather than the speech of the monarch. It was written by the government and formally read out by a representative of the Queen when she or her spokesperson opened parliament. The speech outlined, and still does, the government's proposed legislative programme for the year ahead. One of the first flash points concerned the proposed withdrawal of British troops from Afghanistan, based there to protect the Emir Abdul Rahman against insurrectionist forces. The Queen refused to sign the speech unless the sentence about withdrawal was removed: she was wholly opposed to the removal of British troops. Eventually, after much discussion, the speech was approved. The Queen told her private secretary that she had 'never before been treated with such want of respect and consideration in the forty three and a half years she had worn her thorny crown'.[54] In the course of the year, the British forces withdrew from Afghanistan.

The Arabi rebellion

Victoria and Gladstone differed over Egyptian foreign policy too. Gladstone had disapproved of Disraeli's purchase of shares in the

Suez Canal, thinking it an unnecessary extravagance. Nevertheless Gladstone recognised that Egypt was an important trading partner: 44 per cent of Egyptian imports were British and 80 per cent of Egyptian exports were sent to Britain.[55] In addition, Britain relied on the Suez Canal as a route to India. Gladstone also recognised the need for a stable Egypt to facilitate trade – but there were problems. Egypt had borrowed heavily and could not repay its loans. As a result, the two leading creditors, France and Britain, installed an Anglo-French Commission in the country to sort out the Egyptian debt. This Commission increased taxes and cut government expenditure even though the country was already hard pressed.

In response, Colonel Arabi, a nationalist leader who deplored the Egyptian ruler's submissiveness to Britain, seized power in Egypt. He declared 'Egypt for the Egyptians' and did everything possible to obstruct the work of the English and French Commission. On 11 June 1882, encouraged by Arabi, there was a riot and massacre of foreigners in the port of Alexandria. Victoria urged Gladstone to stand firm. Gladstone, who was appalled by both Arabi's desire to establish a dictatorship and his refutation of Egypt's financial obligations, needed little encouragement. He ordered the bombardment of Alexandria and sent the British Army to reverse the coup and re-install the previous ruler. The Queen had earlier told her private secretary that Egypt was vital to Britain and 'we must take it'[56] rather than allow Egypt to be independent.

On 13 September 1882, the British army defeated Arabi at Tel el-Kabir, promptly occupied Cairo, arrested Arabi and crushed the rebellion. The Queen commented, 'What an immense satisfaction this is!'[57] The war was popular in Britain and for a while the Queen was at one with her government and her subjects. Victoria was personally as well as politically involved as one of her sons, Prince Arthur, went out to fight. When she first heard that 'her darling, precious Arthur' was to go to Egypt she thought 'it seemed like a dreadful dream' and 'went with a heavy heart to bed'.[58] Nonetheless, like many other army mothers, she did not want her precious son to 'shirk his duty'. General Wolseley, the general in charge, gave Arthur command of a brigade. At the battle of Tel el-Kabir, Arthur exhibited obvious courage. Victoria was proud of the way in which he had fought and was delighted when General Charles Beresford was 'full of praise of dear Arthur, how much pluck he had shown and what care he had taken of his men. . . . That I could be well proud of my son, which I said I was.'[59] On 21 November 1882 the Queen honoured her son with a medal for gallantry.

In the Queen's opinion, Arabi and the other rebels should be 'severely punished', as if not, revolution and rebellion would be greatly encouraged.[60] Arabi was handed over to the Egyptian authorities to be tried but to the Queen's intense irritation, he insisted that a British lawyer defend him. Gladstone's government granted Arabi's request. Victoria was furious that her government agreed to 'let Arabi have an English Counsel, a thing contrary to Egyptian law! After sending out and sacrificing numbers of our brave men, in order to put down this man, everything is to be done now to save him! It is inconceivable! One step forward, two steps backwards!'[61] The Queen protested to Gladstone that she was

> distressed and alarmed at the great facilities given to that arch rebel and traitor, Arabi . . . appearing to <u>protect</u> the very man we sent out our best troops and spent much treasure to <u>defeat</u>. . . . And <u>why</u> in the world should Englishmen defend this wicked man, who is the cause of thousands of innocent lives being lost and many poor people maimed for life?[62]

Gladstone duly noted the Queen's opinion but continued to do as he pleased.

Eventually it was agreed with the Egyptian ruler – the Khedive – that Arabi be exiled to Ceylon. The Queen again complained to Gladstone. He ignored her protests and instead asked his sovereign to send a personal message to the Khedive congratulating him on his magnanimity to Arabi. The Queen refused as she '<u>highly disapproves</u> of the weakness which actuated it. It is for the British Government, who are solely responsible for this act . . . to send him this message.'[63] Queen Victoria was reluctant to relinquish her authority but the threefold increase in the electorate had irretrievably shifted the balance of power to parliament. As more and more men were included in the political process, the Queen's authority diminished.

The British government promised to control Egypt for only five years and then leave. The Queen thought it foolish to fix a date and told her ministers 'that I could not agree to their binding this country to evacuate Egypt in a given time, 5 years. That I felt most strongly, it would be a fatal step.'[64] She complained to Ponsonby that:

> the conduct of the Government in this Egyptian business is <u>perfectly miserable</u>; it is universally condemned; and this weakness and vacillation have made us despised everywhere. . . . the Queen feels <u>much</u> aggrieved and annoyed. She was never listened to, or her advice followed, and <u>all</u> she foretold <u>invariably</u> happened and what she <u>urged</u> was <u>done</u> when <u>too late</u>! It is dreadful for her to see how we are going downhill, and to be unable to prevent the humiliation of this country.[65]

Ponsonby, using much more ameliorative language, communicated the Queen's anxieties to Gladstone, writing that 'the Queen maintains emphatically that it would be unjust to this country and to future Governments to make a promise now which it may be out of their power to keep . . . another Ministry would find themselves hampered'.[66] In fact, the British did not leave Egypt, the country remained a British protectorate until 1914 and the British had a military presence there until 1956.

Crisis in the Sudan

The revolt in Egypt sparked a crisis in the Sudan. At the time, the Sudan was ruled by Egypt but sensing a weakness in Egyptian rule, Muhammad Ahmad, who considered himself the Mahdi or redeemer of Islam, rebelled against the Egyptian forces. Victoria and Gladstone once more differed over what the British should do. Gladstone thought that the expense of keeping the troops in the Sudan was prohibitively expensive, proposed to withdraw them and appointed General Gordon to do it; Queen Victoria wanted to crush the revolt and tried to pressurise Gladstone to remain in the Sudan because it 'would be fatal to our reputation and honour if we were to <u>abandon</u> active operations and still more to withdraw from the Soudan'.[67] The government remained unyielding. The Queen told the leading Liberal Lord Hartington that her 'heart bleeds to see such short-sighted humiliating policy pursued, which lowers her country before the whole world'.[68]

On 18 January 1884, General Gordon left London for Khartoum in order to evacuate the soldiers and civilians and to leave the country with them. But when Gordon arrived in Khartoum, he disobeyed orders and rather than evacuate the troops began organising a defence of Khartoum and asking for more troops to defend the city. Soon the city of Khartoum was under siege by the rebel Ahmad's army, and was to remain so for 320 days. Victoria believed that any withdrawal would be 'utterly ruinous'.[69] And she was at her fiercest when the crisis was at its height, directing Gladstone to send a force to rescue Gordon saying that she 'trembles for General Gordon's safety'.[70] She threatened to 'hold the Government responsible for any sort of misfortune which will happen. Parliament should be told the truth and how Gordon has again and again told them what to do, and that they have refused.'[71] When her advice was ignored, the Queen pleaded with Gladstone: 'if only for humanity's sake, for the honour of the Government and the nation', Gordon must not be abandoned.[72] But the Queen was not able to influence the incorruptible and principle-driven Gladstone in the way she had Disraeli.

At first Gladstone refused to send a relief mission and only reluctantly agreed to do so when it was too little and too late. Britain's most eminent general, Wolseley, was given command of the Sudan expeditionary force. At one time, the Queen wrote secretly to General Wolseley asking him to 'resist and strongly oppose all idea of retreat' and confided that she thought some of her Government were unpatriotic. She asked Wolseley to destroy the letter as 'it is so very confidential . . . or perhaps lock it up and destroy it later, but if he fears it might get into wrong hands, pray destroy it at once'.[73] This was seriously illegitimate behaviour by a sovereign. By this time, the Queen recognised that she was only titular head of the armed forces and her insistence on secrecy shows that she was well aware that she had no right to instruct her generals.

By the time Wolseley arrived, Gordon and his entire 7,000 army garrison had been killed and rebel troops were in charge of the city. On 5 February 1885 news of Gordon's death reached Britain. Victoria heard the 'dreadful news, after breakfast. Khartoum, fallen . . . All greatly distressed. . . . It is too fearful. The Govt is alone to blame, by refusing to send the expedition, till it was too late.'[74] She confided to Ponsonby that:

> Gladstone should remember what SHE suffers when the British name is humiliated . . . and he can go away and resign but she MUST REMAIN and she has suffered so cruelly from humiliation and annoyance from the present Govt since the unlucky day when Mr Gladstone came in. . . . Mr G never minds loss of life etc and wraps himself up in his own incomprehensible delusions and illusions.[75]

The Queen believed that 'Mr Gladstone and the Government have – the Queen feels it dreadfully – Gordon's innocent, noble, heroic blood on their consciences.'[76] Nonetheless, Gladstone refused to reverse his foreign policy and continued to withdraw from the Sudan. This led to the Queen complaining to Ponsonby that she could not 'express her indignation at Mr Gladstone's behaviour. No Minister has ever yet set her positive orders at such utter defiance. How she prays he may give up – for he is insufferable arguing and never listening to anything said.'[77] Queen Victoria had forgotten – or chose to forget – that the sovereign was not expected to give orders to her ministers.

Queen Victoria's anger led her to disregard state protocol. Telegrams between the Queen and her ministers were always sent in code. Just after Gordon's death, Victoria sent Gladstone an uncoded telegram, copied to the war minister and the foreign secretary. In it, the Queen formally rebuked the prime minister saying 'to think that all this might have been prevented and many precious lives saved by earlier actions is too frightful'.[78] Naturally, the content of these telegrams soon became public knowledge, which in turn fuelled the already vociferous public outcry at what was seen as Gladstonian bungling. Indeed, Gladstone's affectionate nickname of GOM – Grand Old Man – was now replaced by MOG – Murderer of Gordon. Not surprisingly Gladstone was furious that the Queen should have sent a confidential telegram in this manner, and more so when she refused to express regret for it. Relationships between the Queen and the prime minister deteriorated further when the Queen was discovered passing confidential documents to the leader of the Conservative Party.

Victoria was well aware of the damages of war – she visited military hospitals on a regular basis. She had seen

> some dreadful wounds. Two in the Cavalry had had their heads nearly cut off, by double handed swords, and axes, and there was a large piece taken out, frightful to look at. . . . Two had lost their legs. . . . a man, whose face was scarred with sabre cuts . . . saw Captain Dalrymple . . . suffering much, as splinters, and bits of bone keep coming away.[79]

Nonetheless, in her opinion, the continuation of British rule in the Sudan was worth the suffering which went with it.

The Gordon calamity weakened the government and on 9 June 1885 it was unexpectedly defeated over a proposal to increase duties on beer and spirits. The Irish Nationalists voted with the Tories and many Liberals abstained. As the government stumbled to defeat, Gladstone, now aged 75, sent a telegram handing in his resignation. A ministerial crisis ensued: for nearly a fortnight the United Kingdom was without a government because the Queen was at Balmoral and refused to return to London to appoint one. She summoned her former prime minister to Scotland to hand in the keys to his office. Gladstone, as obstinate as his sovereign, refused replying that he had not much more to say and wished to avoid travelling because he had to pack up 10 Downing Street. He advised his sovereign to return to London to appoint a new prime minister. Queen Victoria ignored his advice and summoned the Conservative peer Lord Salisbury to Scotland.

Robert Gascoyne-Cecil, Lord Salisbury: 23 June 1885–28 January 1886

Lord Salisbury was in a difficult position. His Conservative Party was in a minority in the House of Commons; a general election would have to be called. Unfortunately, no election could take place until the new electoral registers required by the 1884 Reform

Act were ready but nonetheless the country needed a government. Salisbury was initially reluctant to take on the job and only the Queen's tearful pleas made him agree. On 24 June 1885, Salisbury became prime minister of a minority government. Victoria liked his relaxed, down-to-earth, non-intellectual manner – Salisbury only managed to gain a fourth-class degree from Oxford – and she considered him a welcome relief from the cause-obsessed, too-clever-by-half Gladstone. In fact, Salisbury was a very clever man but, unlike Gladstone, he wore his learning lightly. Salisbury's daughter-in-law Violet claimed that it was 'easy to see that she is very fond of him, indeed I never saw two people get on better, their polished manners and deference to and esteem for each other were a delightful sight and one not readily to be forgotten'.[80] Salisbury may have lacked the sparkle of Melbourne or Disraeli but his nonchalant approach to politics appealed to Victoria who often spoke with admiration 'as of one in whom she had great confidence'.[81] Moreover, the Queen was able to coerce Salisbury more than she ever could Gladstone. For example, when Salisbury was forming his government and suggested one Colonel Stanley be appointed to the War Office, the Queen insisted that he 'ought not to go to the War Office, as he had done even more harm there . . . Ld Salisbury was vexed at this, but I urged it very strongly.'[82] Salisbury conceded. Salisbury was appointed prime minister three times, each time leading the Conservatives from the House of Lords. He was the last prime minister to do so.

Salisbury's Conservative government would inevitably be short-lived. The creation of a new electorate in 1884 meant that new elections would take place – and the increase in the franchise would undoubtedly favour the Liberal Party. The general election held in November and December 1885 resulted in 334 seats for the Liberals, 250 for the Conservatives 250 and 86 for the Irish Nationalists. The effect of the new franchise was greater in Ireland than in the rest of the British Isles, as it increased the Irish electorate by 230 per cent and doubled the number of Parnell's supporters. The Conservatives, though in a minority, again returned to office because the Irish MPs supported them.

However, events moved swiftly. In December 1885 Gladstone announced his conversion to Home Rule and the Irish MPs switched sides. They liked the prospect of Home Rule because it would mean a separate Irish parliament based in Dublin which would control all Irish affairs, except defence and foreign affairs. In early January 1886 Salisbury was defeated in the House of Commons when Irish MPs voted with the Liberals to overthrow him. During this crisis the Queen refused to leave Osborne. Bertie, the Prince of Wales, asked Ponsonby to persuade the Queen to come to Windsor as 'the inconvenience to ingoing and outgoing Ministers is obvious. People are much astonished that she has not come up at once, and most unfavourable criticisms are made on the subject.' Ponsonby replied that the suggestion had already been made, however, he had been told by the Queen's doctor, that 'I had made H.M. quite ill with such a proposal, and that I must not do so, as her health would suffer.'[83] Typically, Queen Victoria would do as she pleased, backed up by her very compliant physician.

As a result, the Queen remained comfortably settled at Osborne and wrote to Salisbury that she would not accept his resignation until she had seen him. At the same time, acting with her familiar style of constitutional impropriety, she once more tried to avoid appointing Gladstone as prime minister, writing furious and indiscreet letters to Goshen, a leading Liberal, appealing to him

> and to all moderate, loyal and <u>really patriotic</u> men . . . to rise above party. . . . You must convince Lord Hartington of what is at last his duty and of what he owes to his Queen and his country, which really goes before allegiance to Mr Gladstone. . . . You <u>must </u>act, or the country will be ruined. No-one knows of this letter.[84]

She complained that the resignation of her government had come like a 'thunderbolt. . . . to change the Government will be very disastrous. I hope and think Mr Gladstone could not form a Government. . . . He will ruin the country if he can, and how much mischief has he not done already!'[85] Even when it was obvious that Gladstone was the only candidate to become prime minister, the Queen tried to stop it. The Queen 'does not the least care but rather wishes it should be known that she has the greatest possible disinclination to take this half crazy and really in many ways ridiculous old man. . . . She will not throw herself blindfold into incompetent hands.'[86] Victoria, peeved by the prospect of another term of Gladstone, made the 'unprecedented announcement in the *Court Circular* that she had accepted Salisbury's resignation "with much regret"'.[87] The Queen still did not accept that democracy had moved on since 1837, 1867 and 1884; she still wanted to influence decisions about the appointment of ministers and prime ministers as she had tried to do in the past.

Gladstone's third ministry: 1 February 1886–20 July 1886

The Queen once again 'abominated the idea of sending for Gladstone' and made it difficult for him to form a government.[88] She insisted that she would refuse objectionable people such as Sir Charles Dilke, 'on account of his dreadful private character. . . . What a dreadful thing to lose such a man as Lord Salisbury for the country, the world, and *me*!'[89] She pressed for the Earl of Rosebery to be foreign secretary and for Sir Henry Campbell-Bannerman to be secretary of state for war. Gladstone was preoccupied with the Irish question and therefore reluctantly complied with his sovereign's choice. At moments like this, when the prime minister was absorbed in other pressing issues or when the governing party was divided, Queen Victoria was able to coerce leaders to agree to her proposals, sometimes with distressingly unanticipated consequences.

Behind the scenes, Victoria tried to split the Liberal Party and put pressure on George Goschen, a leading Liberal and party organiser, to create a new coalition party. She was aware that several leading Liberals such as Lord Hartington and Joseph Chamberlain disagreed with Gladstone's policy on Ireland and she set out to use these differences to engineer a split in the party. Goschen was asked to 'work strongly and earnestly to gather and unite all who wish to maintain the constitution and the Empire, so that a split between these theoretical radicals headed by a wild fanatical old man of 76 – and the moderate constitutional Liberals . . . may take place when Parliament meets'.[90] The Queen bombarded Goschen with letters asking him to 'keep Lord Hartington up to the mark and not let him slide back into following Mr Gladstone and trying to keep the party together'.[91] This was risky constitutional territory. By this time, the sovereign was definitely expected to be above politics and Queen Victoria's duplicitous action in attempting to undermine a party in government bears the mark of a monarch scheming to retain her power rather than accept her role as a constitutional monarch.

First Home Rule Bill: 1886

Gladstone returned to government committed to Irish Home Rule; and the old arguments surrounding the Irish question were reignited and reinvigorated. In the Queen's opinion, Gladstone was 'in the hands of Mr Parnell without his knowing it'.[92] Victoria was 'dead against' Home Rule and shared her feelings on the matter with the opposition leader, Lord Salisbury. On 1 February 1886 the Queen had an audience with Gladstone where they discussed policy – a private and confidential discussion – but the Queen wrote an abbreviated account of this conversation to Salisbury and included copies of the relevant correspondence between Gladstone and herself. Once more, the Queen was open to charges of partisanship when she should have been exhibiting royal impartiality.

The situation in Ireland was becoming increasingly dangerous. On 8 April 1886, Gladstone introduced his First Home Rule Bill designed to establish a separate parliament in Dublin and end the representation of Ireland at Westminster. The Queen warned Gladstone that she disapproved of Home Rule for Ireland and could only see danger in the course Gladstone was pursuing.[93] Queen Victoria had no need to worry. Home Rule was not only unpopular in England but the proposed constitutional changes in Ireland required a large majority in parliament, something which Gladstone did not have. On 18 June 1886, after several weeks of debate, the Home Rule Bill was defeated. 'When I got up, a telegram was brought in to me, which gave the news that the Govt had been defeated by a majority of 30! Cannot help feeling relieved.'[94] The government was defeated because 93 Liberals – that is nearly a third of Liberal MPs – voted against their party. Lord Hartington, Joseph Chamberlain and other Liberals had formed a political alliance with the Conservatives in opposition to Home Rule. As a result, the Liberal Party divided into Gladstonian Liberals and Liberal Unionists (i.e. anti-Home Rule Liberals). The Queen took pleasure in the fact that the old Liberal Party was no more. A telegram from Mr Gladstone tendering his government's resignation brought her even greater satisfaction.[95]

With the government defeated, new elections were held, and in the second general election held that year, the Unionists enjoyed a resounding victory with a joint 394 seats: Salisbury and his Conservatives won 316 seats, the Liberal Unionists won 74, all at the expense of the Liberals who won a humiliating 191. The Liberal Party, assisted as much by the Queen's unconstitutional behind-the-scenes behaviour as much as Gladstone's personal commitment to Home Rule, was destroyed, leaving the Conservative Party to enjoy nearly two decades of political supremacy. When Gladstone trekked to Osborne from London to give up his seals of office, the Queen ungraciously declined to offer him lunch.

Lord Salisbury: 25 July 1886–11 August 1892

In August 1886, Queen Victoria welcomed Salisbury back. At the same time she wrote to Gladstone demanding that he cease campaigning for Home Rule,[96] and instructed the leading Liberal Unionists 'to support Lord Salisbury's Government'.[97] Here, Victoria was clearly undermining the political process: opposition is one of the most fundamental components of democracy, a constant reminder to the population that there is a viable alternative to the status quo. Victoria, however, only approved of opposition if and when she disagreed with the policies put forward by a government she disliked.

The Irish problem continued under Salisbury. In 1887 a new Criminal Law Bill – which suspended the right of trial to those boycotting landlords – was put forward in order to pacify Ireland. It was strongly opposed by Gladstone, the Gladstonian Liberals and the Irish Nationalists, all of whom wanted Home Rule rather than repression. In another example of monarchical irregularity, the Queen instructed her private secretary to write to Lord Selborne, a leading Liberal, to put pressure on Gladstone to cease campaigning for Home Rule. Selborne was told that 'her Majesty commands me to ask whether it would be possible for you to call his attention to the harm he [Gladstone] is doing to his own name and to the country by his apparent support of those who defy all law and order'.[98] Queen Victoria's observance of constitutional conventions seemed limited to those conventions with which she agreed.

Meanwhile clashes took place between the British government and the Irish Nationalists. The Irish National League intensified its opposition to tenant evictions; in response, the government outlawed the League as a dangerous organisation and issued a warrant for the arrest of its leader, William O'Brien. The behaviour of the Irish, the Queen believed, was simply dreadful as 'the Irish hope to force Home Rule, by making themselves as disagreeable as possible'.[99]

The Irish Home Rulers reacted. In September 1887, at Mitchelstown in County Cork, several thousand took part in a demonstration. The police fired a volley which resulted in two people being killed and several injured. The Queen was unsympathetic. She spoke of

> a riot at a meeting of Home Rulers, at which that horrid Labouchere, Mr O'Brien and others were to speak and agitate. They would not let a Govt Reporter in, fought, and the Police were driven back and went to the Barracks, where they were attacked. A man was killed, and another very badly wounded. And now they want to call it murder![100]

She cannot have been pleased when Labouchere suggested that Buckingham Palace be converted into a home for fallen women.[101]

But the repression in Ireland evoked sympathy, if not from the Queen, then from among a small section of the left wing. In November 1887 a demonstration was organised jointly by the Social Democratic Federation and the Irish National League against unemployment in England and coercion in Ireland. The leaders included William Morris and Annie Besant; George Bernard Shaw was also present. Despite the celebrity presence the demonstration led to violence as police tried to stop the 30,000 or so demonstrators from entering Trafalgar Square. Clashes took place between the police and demonstrators. Once again, the Queen was unsympathetic, noting in her journal that 'the mob wanted to force their way into Trafalgar Square . . . Two squadrons of Cavalry and 400 Foot Guards were called out, and kept Trafalgar Square, where it had been announced the people would no longer be allowed to meet'.[102] Over 200 people were hospitalised; three were killed; 400 were arrested.

Fortunately for Queen Victoria, the Irish Nationalist cause was all but destroyed by the publication of Charles Parnell's adultery with Kitty O'Shea. In 1890 Kitty O'Shea's husband sued for divorce, citing Parnell as co-respondent. The Queen thought it 'a scandalous trial and divorce case in which Parnell did not attempt to defend himself, but is shown up as not only a man of very bad character, but as a liar, and devoid of all sense of honour or of any sort of principle'.[103] The resulting scandal and the squalid revelations in court destroyed Parnell and split the Nationalist Party, whose members began to attack each other rather than the British government. In October 1891 Parnell died a broken and embittered man; and the Irish Nationalist Party fell into even greater disarray.

The Golden Jubilee: June 1887

On Monday 20 June 1887, the Queen celebrated her fiftieth year on the throne. It was the high spot of Salisbury's premiership and a turning point in the Queen's popularity: the British population had not witnessed such a celebration for decades. The Queen hosted a royal banquet at Buckingham Palace for 50 foreign kings and princes and the governing heads of the British colonies. She dined in the Supper Room 'which looked splendid with the Buffet covered with the gold plate. . . . The King of Denmark took me in, and Willy of Greece sat on my other side. The Princes were all in uniform and the Princesses were all beautifully dressed. . . . At length, feeling very tired, I slipped away.'[104]

On 21 June a thanksgiving service was held in Westminster Abbey. Undoubtedly, the splendour and majestic finery of the procession, along with the visibility of a long-absent Queen, heightened the appeal of monarchy. The Queen processed with her entire surviving family: her four sons and five daughters, nine grandsons and granddaughters, and their wives and husbands. Other royals from European dynasties – such as the King of Denmark and the Queen of the Belgians – and rulers such as the Queen of Hawaii, the Japanese, Siamese, Persian and Indian princes joined the Queen in her celebrations. As ever, Queen Victoria disliked pageantry and would neither wear her crown nor any of the other ceremonial trappings of monarchy. Instead, the queen, by now very overweight and as round as a pumpkin, wore black with her traditional widow's bonnet and sat in an ordinary coach rather than the elaborately gilded state one. *The Times* compared the procession to a 'river of gold flowing between banks of extraordinary richness and colour'.[105] The Indian princes 'were attired in the many-coloured, gem-decked turbans . . . the Maharaja Holkar, whose shoulder were covered with bullion woven into his tunic . . . the greatest amount of wonder was the turban of his Highness the Rao of Kutch, which, when the sun flashed upon it, really blazed with the scintillating lights of diamonds, rubies and emeralds.'[106]

Royal ceremonies can appear inclusive and representative, thus binding subjects closer to the sovereign. The effect of the Jubilee on the population supported this. From the earliest moment of dawn until long after night had fallen, the British people celebrated the Jubilee. It was after all a festival holiday with the added enchantment of oodles of glamour attached. A national pageant 'proceeded amidst circumstances of unrivalled splendour, the voice of a mighty people has been heard rejoicing with no uncertain sound'.[107] At night London was turned into a 'fairy city. . . . In all the principal thoroughfares . . . beautiful devices in crystal glittered with light, fairy lamps shed their soft glow.'[108] It was a day, *The Times* declared, which testified 'to the loyalty, gratitude, and affection inspired by fifty years of unswerving devotion and undeviating regard for her people's well-being'.[109] All over Britain, in towns and villages, innumerable Jubilee parties took place where the dull and boring routine of everyday life could be forgotten. In Coventry, Warwickshire a colourful Lady Godiva pageant took place; in Aberdeen 200 paupers were given a meal of beef steak pie, potatoes and plum pudding;[110] Jubilee mugs and packets of tea were given out in Christleton, Cheshire,[111] and in Truro,

Cornwall, the vicar gave thanks for the purity of the Queen.[112] In the empire too, the Jubilee was celebrated and the legitimacy of British rule re-affirmed. In India a national holiday was declared, certain classes of military offenders were pardoned and the Order of the British India awarded to a number of dignitaries. Fifty guns were fired at daybreak at Simla and a statue of the Queen was unveiled in Madras.[113]

Constitutional historians have long recognised that the British monarchy depends on public approval, not merely for its success but also for its very survival. The fiftieth celebration of Queen Victoria's accession to the throne was seen as a pivotal moment in the history of her monarchy. And the Queen paid for most of it: the government's outlay was £16,089; the Queen's over £50,000. It resulted in an 'orgy of national self-congratulation' that increased the country's regard of the Queen.[114] Victoria was touched by the loyalty of her people. She cherished the fact that

> the crowds from the Palace gates up to the Abbey were enormous, and there was such an extraordinary outburst of enthusiasm as I have hardly ever seen in London before, all the people seemed to be in such good humour. . . . The decorations along Piccadilly were quite beautiful. . . . Seats and platforms were arranged up to the tops of the houses – such waving of hands.[115]

There were great volleys of cheers, hats were thrown up into the air, handkerchiefs were waved in welcome and 'everybody vied with his neighbour in active demonstrations of loyalty and delight'.[116] Victoria wrote to Salisbury saying how '<u>deeply, immensely</u> touched and gratified' she was 'by the wonderful and so universal enthusiasm displayed by my people. . . . It is very gratifying and very encouraging for the future, and it shows that fifty years' <u>hard</u> work, anxiety and care have been appreciated.'[117] In a rare letter to her subjects, the Queen thanked them for their loyalty and kindness. It had shown her 'that the labour and anxiety of fifty long years, twenty-two of which were in unclouded happiness . . . while an equal number were full of sorrow and trials . . . have been appreciated by my people'.[118]

There were dissident voices: *Reynolds's Weekly Newspaper*, that old scurrilous radical paper, questioned the value of Queen Victoria and 'her inexhaustible brood of pauper relations' to Britain. Search the records of the reign with a microscope, the paper maintained, and 'you will not be able to discover a single royal act of real benefit to the nation'.[119] It accused Queen Victoria of 'jobbing' all her relatives into the highest public positions, of wringing between 80 and 90 million pounds sterling from the British public, of ranking all of her German cousins more highly than statesmen and scholars and of delighting to 'show her power in the meanest and cruellest manner' by hastening away to Osborne or Balmoral whenever there was a parliamentary crisis. How is it, the paper asked, that an 'ugly, parsimonious German frau is today the Well Beloved of a great nation?' and questioned how so many could worship a 'fat old lady of sullen visage'. Monarchy, in their view, was an expensive luxury. *Reynolds's Weekly Newspaper* was a minority voice. *The Times* probably captured the feelings of the majority when it reported that 'no monarch in history has ever more deeply touched the heart of a nation'.[120] Monarchy, rather than Republicanism, seemed to have triumphed.

The Munshi and his influence

On 18 June 1887 two servants arrived at Windsor Castle to wait on the Queen during her Golden Jubilee celebrations.[121] They had been given as a 'gift from India'. One of them, a handsome 24-year-old Indian Muslim called Abdul Karim, soon became a favourite of the 68-year-old Queen. Karim taught the Queen Urdu, a language associated with the Muslims of Hindustan, and cooked the Queen her first curry. Before long Abdul Karim was as treasured as the deceased John Brown: Queen Victoria liked strong men. However, Abdul Karim felt that his job as a servant was too menial for his status and persuaded the Queen to give him the title of Munshi, an Urdu word meaning teacher. Victoria thought it 'was a mistake to bring him over as a servant. . . . I particularly wish to retain his services, as he helps me in studying Hindustani, which interests me very much, and he is very intelligent and useful.'[122]

Queen Victoria disregarded court protocol when it suited her. She insisted that Abdul Karim be treated as an equal, allowed him to sit among the royal household at private entertainments and at the Scottish Games. At Balmoral, Karim was given John Brown's old room. In September 1889 she and Karim stayed at Glassalt Shiel, a remote house on the Balmoral estate which Victoria had often visited with John Brown. Karim accompanied the Queen on her trips to the French Riviera and participated in the Christmas tableaux vivants held at Osborne House. He was even presented to the King of Italy. In 1889, in her eightieth birthday honours list, the Queen appointed Karim a Commander of the Order of the Royal Victorian Order (CVO). The Queen's letters were signed 'your loving mother', your 'closest friend' and on some occasions her letters were signed with kisses. A portrait was commissioned of Abdul Karim. When in early 1890 Karim fell ill with a boil on his neck, the Queen sent for her doctor, Reid, to look after him; she herself visited Karim twice daily, examining his neck and smoothing down his pillows.

The Queen's indiscreet affection for her new servant and Karim's rise in the royal household created jealousy and friction. The British aristocracy, who on the rare occasions they mixed with Indians only met princes, thought that Karim was a parvenu and an imposter. Historians have noted that Karim's rapid advancement would have inevitably led to problems but the fact of his race complicated matters further. Racism was endemic in Imperialist Britain – the belief that the white race had a genetic right to rule over those with a darker skin colour was held to be self-evident. Victoria did not share this belief and accused her household of 'nasty racial feeling'.[123] The hierarchies, rivalries and racial prejudices of the court could not prevail against the Queen's love for her new Indian friend.

More importantly, the Queen listened to the Munshi's views about British rule in India.[124] She took a special interest in Manipur, a sovereign state in northeast India. Tensions erupted when its leader was driven out by a rebel – Tikendrajit Singh – who then threatened British interests. Events moved swiftly: on 21 February 1891 the Viceroy of India, Lord Landsdowne, ordered the arrest of Tikendrajit Singh; on 22 March 400 soldiers arrived and asked Singh to surrender; two days later British troops attacked Singh's residence, killing many women and children. Not surprisingly, Singh's army took revenge and executed five British officers.[125] Once again, women and children suffered. Queen Victoria was told by one of the ladies who had escaped from Manipur that:

> she was nine days on the horrible March, and almost all the time followed and pursued. . . . She had no clothes but those she was wearing. Once she saw herself being aimed at, and the man close behind her, who was already wounded, was killed, knocking her over and covering her with blood. In this condition she had to go on her way.[126]

The British army eventually defeated Tikendrajit and his rebel force. Queen Victoria knew that the disaster at Manipur was dreadful but maintained that British 'dealings in India should be dictated by straightforwardness, kindness, and firmness, or we cannot succeed'. She thought that hanging Tikendrajit 'would never do; it would create very bad feeling in Manipur and in all India. But shut him up for life in some distant part.'[127] Queen Victoria, who was keen to suppress unrest in Ireland by brute force, believed that the 'principle of governing India by fear and by crushing them, instead of by firmness and conciliation, is one which never will answer in the end'.[128] A special court was formed to put the rebels on trial: Tikendrajit Singh was found guilty and publicly hanged.

In August 1892 new elections took place. The Liberal Party regained some of its key constituencies and won 273 seats, the Conservatives won 269, the Liberal Unionists won 46 and the Home Rulers won 81 seats. Gladstone was returned to power for the fourth time, once again reliant on the Irish MPs for support. The Queen was sad to part with Salisbury. It seemed to her 'a defect in our much famed Constitution, to have to part with an admirable Govt like Ld Salisbury's, for no question of any importance, or any particular reason, merely on account of the number of votes'.[129] Queen Victoria's idiosyncratic views on democracy illuminate much of her political behaviour. Once again, they demonstrate how very far her partisan spirit, coupled with her desire always to have her own way, prompted her to think and act more in the manner of a despot in an autocracy than as a constitutional monarch in a democracy.

Notes

1 Victoria to W. E. Forster, December 25th 1880.
2 RA VIC/MAIN/QVJ (W) April 27th 1882.
3 Ibid. April 19th 1881.
4 Ibid. March 28th 1884.
5 Ibid. June 28th 1888.
6 See Helen Rappaport, *Queen Victoria: A Biographical Companion*, ABC-CLIO, 2003, p. 413.
7 RA VIC/MAIN/QVJ (W) January 14th 1892.
8 Ibid. March 13th 1892.
9 Ibid. April 27th 1880.
10 Victoria to Ponsonby, March 12th 1880.
11 RA VIC/MAIN/QVJ (W) April 28th 1880.
12 Ponsonby, *Henry Ponsonby*, April 5th 1880.
13 Magnus, *Gladstone*, p. 308.
14 Queen Victoria to Disraeli, September 20th 1880, quoted in Magnus, *Gladstone*, p. 279.
15 Ponsonby, *Henry Ponsonby*, April 12th 1880.
16 RA VIC/MAIN/QVJ (W) June 25th 1880.
17 Ibid. August 3rd 1881.
18 Victoria to Gladstone, October 30th 1883.
19 Queen to Granville, September 4th 1880, quoted in Hardie, *The Political Influence of Queen Victoria*, p. 79.
20 RA VIC/MAIN/QVJ (W) May 28th 1884.
21 Gladstone to Victoria, July 14th 1884.
22 RA VIC/MAIN/QVJ (W) July 23rd 1884.
23 Ibid. July 25th 1884.
24 Ibid. July 16th 1884.
25 Ibid. July 16th 1884.
26 Queen's instructions to Granville, August 1884 quoted in Hardie, *The Political Influence of Queen Victoria*, p. 80.
27 Victoria to Salisbury, October 31st 1884; Victoria to Gladstone, October 31st 1884.
28 The Carlton Club was founded in 1832 as a club for members of the Conservative Party.
29 Gladstone to Victoria, quoted in Magnus, *Gladstone*, p. 319.
30 RA VIC/MAIN/QVJ (W) November 18th 1884.
31 Ibid. November 7th 1880.
32 Victoria to Hartington, December 12th 1880.
33 Victoria to Forster, December 25th 1880.

34 RA VIC/MAIN/QVJ (W) November 27th 1880.
35 Quoted in Arnstein, *Queen Victoria*, p. 158.
36 RA VIC/MAIN/QVJ (W) October 13th 1881.
37 Ibid. January 8th 1882.
38 Ibid. May 2nd 1882.
39 Victoria to Gladstone, May 3rd 1882.
40 RA VIC/MAIN/QVJ (W) May 6th 1882.
41 Victoria to Granville, May 7th 1882.
42 Victoria to Gladstone, May 9th 1882.
43 Ibid. May 11th 1882.
44 Victoria to Granville, May 21st 1882.
45 Victoria to Private Secretary, July 1st 1882.
46 RA VIC/MAIN/QVJ (W) July 1st 1882.
47 Ibid. March 15th 1883.
48 Ibid. April 9th 1883.
49 Ibid. November 20th 1883.
50 Ibid. April 8th 1881.
51 Ibid. April 5th 1881.
52 Victoria to Vicky, September 3rd 1886.
53 *Harper's Weekly*, June 8th 1889, quoted in Walter L. Arnstein, 'The Americanisation of Queen Victoria', *The Historian*, 2010, p. 836.
54 Victoria to Ponsonby, January 5th 1881.
55 Wilson, *Victoria: A Life*.
56 Victoria to Ponsonby, May 30th 1882.
57 RA VIC/MAIN/QVJ (W) September 15th 1882.
58 Ibid. July 20th 1882.
59 Ibid. September 29th 1882.
60 Victoria to Gladstone, September 21st 1882.
61 RA VIC/MAIN/QVJ (W) October 17th 1882.
62 Victoria to Gladstone, October 14th 1882.
63 Victoria to Earl Granville, December 12th 1882.
64 RA VIC/MAIN/QVJ (W) May 17th 1884.
65 Victoria to Ponsonby, May 17th 1884.
66 Ponsonby to Gladstone, May 17th 1884.
67 Victoria to Gladstone, April 15th 1885.
68 Victoria to Hartington, May 17th 1885.
69 RA VIC/MAIN/QVJ (W) April 20th 1885.
70 Victoria to Gladstone, February 12th 1884.
71 Victoria to Ponsonby, March 14th 1884.
72 Victoria to Gladstone, March 27th 1884.
73 Victoria to Wolseley, March 31st 1885.
74 RA VIC/MAIN/QVJ (W) February 5th 1885.
75 Victoria to Ponsonby, February 7th 1885.
76 Ibid. February 17th 1885.
77 Ibid. April (undated) 1885.
78 Victoria to Hartington, February 5th 1885.

79 RA VIC/MAIN/QVJ (W) May 16th 1885.
80 Quoted in Van der Kiste, *Sons, Servants and Statesmen*, p. 108.
81 Chaplain to the Queen, quoted in ibid. p. 109.
82 RA VIC/MAIN/QVJ (W) June 12th 1885.
83 Quoted in George Buckle, *The Letters of Queen Victoria*, Third Series, Vol. 1, 1886–1890, John Murray, 1930, p. 39.
84 Victoria to Goschen, December 20th 1885.
85 Ibid. January 27th, 1886.
86 Victoria to Ponsonby, January 29thth 1886.
87 Robert Rhodes James, *The British Revolution: British Politics 1880–1939*, Hamish Hamilton, 1976, p. 136.
88 Ponsonby, *Henry Ponsonby*, p. 208.
89 Memorandum by Victoria, January 28th 1886.
90 Victoria to Goschen, December 19th 1885.
91 Victoria to Goschen, quoted in Ian Cawood, *The Liberal Unionist Party: A History*, I.B. Tauris, 2012, p. 16.
92 Victoria to Goschen, January 31st 1886.
93 Victoria to Gladstone, May 6th 1886.
94 RA VIC/MAIN/QVJ (W) June 8th 1886.
95 Ibid. July 20th 1886.
96 Victoria to Gladstone, July 31st 1886.
97 Victoria to Hartington, August 6th 1886.
98 Ponsonby to Selborne, October 27th 1887.
99 RA VIC/MAIN/QVJ (W) March 4th 1887.
100 Ibid. September 13th 1887.
101 Longford, *Victoria*, p. 619.
102 RA VIC/MAIN/QVJ (W) November 13th 1887.
103 Ibid. November 26th 1890.
104 Ibid. June 20th 1887.
105 *The Times*, June 22nd 1887, p. 5.
106 Ibid.
107 Ibid.
108 Ibid.
109 Ibid. June 21st 1887, p. 8.
110 *Aberdeen Weekly Journal*, June 22nd 1887, p. 5.
111 *Cheshire Observer*, June 25th 1887.
112 *The Royal Cornwall Gazette*, June 24th 1887, p. 5.
113 *Daily News*, June 21st, 1887, p. 5.
114 William M. Kuhn, 'Victoria's Civil List', *Historical Journal*, September 1993.
115 RA VIC/MAIN/QVJ (W) June 21st 1887.
116 *The Times*, June 22nd 1887, p. 5.
117 Victoria to Salisbury, July 21st 1887.
118 Quoted in the *York Herald*, July 2nd, 1887.
119 *Reynolds's Weekly Newspaper*, June 19th, 1887, p. 1.
120 *The Times*, June 21st 1887, p. 5.

121 See Basu, *Victoria and Abdul.*
122 RA VIC/MAIN/QVJ (W) August 11th 1888.
123 Victoria to Reid, April 1898, quoted in Basu, *Victoria and Abdul,* p. 220.
124 Basu, *Victoria and Abdul.*
125 RA VIC/MAIN/QVJ (W) May 2nd 1891.
126 Ibid. July 1st 1891.
127 Victoria to Viscount Cross, June 16th 1891.
128 Ibid. August 11th 1891.
129 RA VIC/MAIN/QVJ (W) August 18th 1892.

10 The last years: 1892–1901

It was a very fine and hot day on 15 August 1892. Victoria breakfasted in her tent at Osborne House and sat outside enjoying the sunshine until it was time for her lunch. At 4pm she went to meet her new prime minister, Gladstone. The septuagenarian Queen found her new prime minister greatly altered and changed, his face shrunk, deadly pale, 'with a weird look in his eyes, a feeble expression about the mouth and the voice altered'.[1] She complained that it was rather trying to have an 82½ year old as prime minister 'who really seems no longer quite fitted to be at the Head of a Govt, whose views and principles are somewhat dangerous'.[2] Gladstone later compared their meeting to that which 'took place between Marie Antoinette and her executioner'.[3]

Gladstone's fourth ministry:
15 August 1892–2 March 1894

Two days before their meeting, Queen Victoria, 'rather contrary to my feelings', had written to Gladstone asking him to form a government.[4] Her note was almost discourteous. It read: 'Lord Salisbury having placed his resignation in the Queen's hands, which she has accepted with much regret, she now desires to ask Mr Gladstone'. Her advisors were again made aware that the Queen 'utterly loathes his very dangerous politics' and could neither respect nor trust him.[5] A couple of months earlier she had told Ponsonby that the idea of a deluded man 'trying to govern England and her vast Empire with the miserable democrats under him is quite ludicrous. It is like a bad joke!'[6] Queen Victoria continued to see herself as a ruling sovereign with the right to influence politics, and once again tried to avoid appointing 'that dangerous old fanatic'[7] as prime minister. The Queen tried – but failed – to find an alternative to Gladstone. She would never admit that she had little power to influence politics when one party had a clear majority. Eventually she was forced to accept the inevitable and to hand over the seals of office to the person who still dominated the House of Commons.

This time the Queen avowed that she had no desire to 'interfere in the formation of this iniquitous Government'.[8] At first, she strove hard not to voice her opinion. Gladstone was thus able to appoint John Morley as chief secretary for Ireland, Sir William Harcourt as chancellor of the exchequer and Herbert Asquith as home secretary without difficulty. However, the Queen could not help being meddlesome and tried to manipulate at least three major appointments, that of a Cabinet minister, a foreign secretary and the viceroy of India.

The Queen disclosed to Gladstone that she was 'very anxious' about Henry Labouchere's appointment as a Cabinet minister because his immoral and dissolute lifestyle (he lived with an actress) brought the Crown and government into disrepute. Gladstone objected but did as his sovereign wished, largely because he too disapproved of Labouchere. It was to be the last time a British monarch vetoed a ministerial appointment. In contrast, the Queen facilitated the appointment of Lord Rosebery as foreign secretary. When Lord Rosebery initially declined the post, Bertie wrote him a secret letter confiding that the Queen 'very much' wished him to be foreign secretary.[9] As a result, Rosebery changed his mind, begging that the communication between himself and the Prince of Wales remain strictly private and personal. Gladstone, as prime minister, knew nothing of these – unconstitutional – intrigues. The last appointment that Victoria tried to influence was that of viceroy of India. Gladstone wanted Lord Elgin to replace Lord Lansdowne as viceroy but the Queen disapproved. In her view, Elgin was too 'shy and most painfully silent, has no presence, no experience whatever in administration. He would not command respect.'[10] Queen Victoria had the constitutional right to advise, and recommended Lord Carrington; Gladstone, who had an equal right to ignore the advice of his sovereign, stuck to his first choice of Lord Elgin.

Ireland: the second Home Rule Bill 1893

Gladstone continued to be caught up in the complexities of the Irish question. In February 1893, despite his majority of only 40 MPs in the House of Commons and virtually no support at all in the House of Lords, Gladstone tried once more to force a second Home Rule Bill through parliament. Victoria noted that 'the parties are so split up and divided, that they don't know how to sit!'[11] After the first reading, the Queen commented in her journal 'it is sad to think it will be read a second time! . . . I am much disturbed about this and other measures I cannot approve of.'[12] The Queen voiced her concern to Gladstone, revealing that she 'cannot conceal from him her feelings of anxiety and apprehension with reference to the provisions of this measure, which tend towards the disruption of her Empire and the establishment of an impracticable form of Government'.[13] Gladstone replied by return of post. He notified the Queen that too great a 'prolongation of the Irish controversy may beget mischief in Ireland by provoking a revival of the far more formidable demand for the Repeal of the Union'.[14] Great Britain, he threatened, would be no more. The Queen remained unconvinced and was most pleased when the House of Commons opposed every clause of the Home Rule Bill.[15]

Once again, Queen Victoria tried to manipulate events surreptitiously. She put pressure on Rosebery to give up Home Rule, insisting that it 'was like rolling a stone uphill'.[16] She urged the Liberal grandee, the Duke of Argyll, to talk to leading figures from both parties to discover 'the future course of action, after the House of Lords have thrown out what I consider a foolish and terrible Bill'.[17] The Queen even proposed dissolving parliament over the Home Rule Bill,[18] and was only dissuaded – confidentially and secretly – by the Conservative politician Lord Salisbury from pursuing this policy. Lord Salisbury persuaded Victoria to see that a Dissolution recommended by the Queen against the advice of her ministers would damage the reputation of the monarchy. It would, he informed his sovereign, involve the resignation of the government with the result that 'their party could hardly help going to the country as the opponents of the royal authority . . . No one can foresee what the upshot of such a state of things would be!'[19] Edward Hamilton, private secretary to Gladstone, thought the Queen was 'thoroughly second-class. She was a bully and had by no means a first-class intelligence.'[20]

On 1 September 1893 Gladstone's second Home Rule Bill passed its second reading in the House of Commons by 43 votes. It had a stormy passage. The Queen was exasperated that 'the House of Commons seems to be going from bad to worse, nothing but wrangling and quarrelling'[21] but decided – correctly as it turned out – that it was because the government was half-hearted about Home Rule.[22] Nevertheless, the Bill duly went to the Upper House to be debated. After only four days' deliberation the Lords – with its built-in Conservative majority – rejected it by 419 votes to 41. The Queen noted approvingly in her journal that it had been 'a crushing majority indeed; and what is most remarkable, the crowd outside cheered very much'.[23] When Gladstone wanted to dissolve parliament and fight the election on the Irish question, his Cabinet refused to allow it and he continued in office. And so his campaign for Home Rule ended, and the British Isles remained united – for the time being.

In March 1894, now aged 84, Gladstone resigned after a political career of nearly 62 years. The Queen thought 'his decision is not to be wondered at because he was growing blind and is already deaf'.[24] When she met Gladstone to accept his resignation, the Queen thought that he 'was looking very old and was very deaf. I made him sit down.'[25] But she did not thank her aged prime minister for all his devoted service to her country. It would also have been courteous, and constitutionally proper, for the Queen to ask Gladstone's advice over who should take his place as prime minister. The Queen did not. Rhodes James maintains that this was 'a heartless, brutal snub which Gladstone felt keenly. It did not reflect well on the Queen.'[26] Moreover, the Queen made no effort to disguise her unutterable relief at her former prime minister's departure. Her loathing of Gladstone and his government's policies had led her to make repeated attempts to destabilise the Liberal Party and its policies. Clearly such behaviour was detrimental to the idea of constitutional monarchy that had been evolving over the century. Gladstone did not leave lightly. In his final speech as prime minister – on 2 March 1894 – he criticised the tendency of House of Lords to reject Bills put forward by the House of Commons. The conflict between the two Houses, he threatened, was a problem which needed to be resolved. In the early twentieth century, further clashes between the Liberal government and the House of Lords convinced the Liberals that reform was vital. In 1911 the Parliament Act removed the ability of the House of Lords to veto money bills and gave the House of Commons the powers to overrule the House of Lords after three parliamentary sessions. In 1999 the Labour Party removed most of the hereditary peers from the House of Lords.

When Gladstone died in May 1898, the Queen confided to Vicky, her eldest daughter, that Gladstone was not a 'great Englishman' as some thought. She complained that 'he never tried to keep up the honour and prestige of Great Britain. He gave away the Transvaal, he abandoned Gordon, he destroyed the Irish church and tried to separate England from Ireland and to set class against class. The harm he did cannot easily be undone.'[27] Queen Victoria's ungraciousness was altogether unwarranted. In effect, Gladstone saved the Crown by trying to distance the Crown from politics while at the same time enhancing its moral and emotional appeal.[28] In particular, in staging the thanksgiving for Bertie's recovery, he had helped boost the popularity of the monarchy.

Archibald Philip Primrose, Earl of Rosebery: March 1894–June 1895

In March 1894 the Queen, neither seeking advice from her ministers nor conferring with Gladstone, sent for Archibald Philip Primrose, fifth Earl of Rosebery, to offer him the premiership. She thought it important for her health that the 'present political crisis should be over in time to allow her to start for Italy on 13th March'.[29] Rosebery, a lifelong Liberal, was the youngest of her prime ministers, making it easy for the Queen to treat him like an 'opinionated schoolboy'.[30] It did not help that he inherited a divided party, a quarrelsome Cabinet and a government with no real policy. His short-lived tenure as prime minister was beset with difficulties: the House of Lords had just rejected the third Home Rule Bill and the Liberals only held office with the support of the Irish MPs. For the next 15 months, Rosebery led a Cabinet constantly under threat of collapse both because of its fractious and unruly members and because a newly confident House of Lords rejected or emasculated any Bill proposed by his Liberal government.

Initially the Queen welcomed Rosebery, especially when he declared that Home Rule would have to wait until the English electorate as a whole gave it its support. As one historian has noted, 'the Gladstonian Liberal party had endured years of strife, division and unpopularity because of its principled adherence to Home Rule'[31] and Rosebery had jettisoned it all in a sentence or two. The Liberal Party and the Irish MPs were horrified; the Queen, however, was overjoyed. Rosebery was a strong Radical and political reformer and he was bound, sooner or later, to clash with his sovereign. The Queen continued to call herself a Liberal but essentially she was a reactionary Tory who would do her utmost to undermine any Liberal government if she disapproved of its policies. Furthermore, she appeared to reject utterly the changes in her constitutional role brought about by increasing democracy. By resisting the evolution of the British Constitution, she remained in a state of perpetual denial, sticking to the same view of monarchy and monarchical rights which had prevailed in her youth.

Queen Victoria's initial joy about the resignation of Gladstone and the appointment of someone more congenial quickly disappeared. Soon, differences of opinion between the monarch and her prime minister began to surface. On 15 February 1894 a French anarchist tried to bomb the Royal Observatory at Greenwich. A few days later the Queen heard about 'a shocking anarchist Club in London, almost entirely composed of foreigners'[32] and wrote to Rosebery protesting about 'allowing these monstrous anarchists and assassins to live here and hatch their horrible plots in our country'.[33] She wanted to expel them. At the time, Britain had a tradition of giving asylum to political refugees, thus the Queen was told that 'it is too soon to exchange our present system for one which would be a departure from our ancient position as regards asylum'.[34] For the moment, political refugees were safe; until 1906 no asylum seeker was expelled from Britain.

One of the early clashes between the monarch and Rosebery occurred over the Liberals' electoral promise to Disestablish, that is, to sever the links between the Scottish and Welsh Churches and the state. The Queen was 'horrified' that her role as Defender of the Faith was being undermined, and urged that it be taken out of the government programme. Her physician told Rosebery that he had 'never seen Her Majesty more upset than she is tonight. I have just left her very much agitated indeed and I feel sorry for her as I am concerned about her.'[35] But Rosebery stood firm and threatened to resign rather than change the government plans. In the end, the Queen, realising that she could not risk losing her government a mere couple of weeks after appointing it, agreed to a compromise: instead of 'Bills for disestablishment' which would have meant some action, the speech said, there would be 'measures for dealing with ecclesiastical disestablishment', which was more of a vague promise. The Church of Wales was eventually disestablished in 1920; the Church of Scotland in 1929.

In addition, Queen Victoria objected when Rosebery brought in a budget which established death duties – these are taxes levied on an estate when the owner dies. Rosebery was told that it was 'wrong in principle and will have such disastrous effects. Can it still be modified? The Queen is much alarmed and distressed about it.'[36] However, Rosebery was adamant, informing his sovereign that it would be impossible to make any change in the Bill's provisions, even though he 'recognised that it would have a negative effect on the class to which he himself belongs. But believed it was logically just.'[37] The Act was passed in August 1894. Cleary the Constitution was being modified by the practical power struggle between monarch and government.

The biggest disagreement between Queen Victoria and Rosebery occurred over the fundamental question of who led the country: the elected House of Commons or the hereditary House of Lords. The failure of Home Rule and other Liberal measures in the House of Lords convinced Liberals that reform of the Upper House was essential if the government of the day was to represent the electorate. Victoria's relationship with her prime minister deteriorated when Rosebery referred to the House of Lords as a permanent barrier against the Liberal Party and pronounced that the next election would be fought on the 'great national danger' of the House of Lords. Queen Victoria advised her prime minister to curb his radicalism:

> The House of Lords might possibly be improved, but it is part and parcel of the much vaunted and admired British Constitution and CANNOT be abolished. It is the ONLY REALLY independent House, for it is not bound as the House of Commons is . . . by their constituents. . . . The House of Lords is not merely there to do all the House of Commons wishes, but to act as a check (and the only one that is) to measures of the House of Commons which of late, go far to upset many safeguards of the Constitution.[38]

Queen Victoria may also have realised that if the Lords were abolished, then the other hereditary element in the constitution, the monarchy, might be next.

Rosebery was not as easily intimidated as the Queen hoped. He reminded his sovereign that the House of Commons was a more representative chamber than the House of Lords – it was elected by six million voters – yet it was controlled by an unelected, unrepresentative and hereditary chamber. When the Conservative Party was in power, Rosebery claimed, the House of Lords was redundant as it simply passed 'whatever the Conservative Government brings it from the House of Commons without question or dispute; but the moment a Liberal Government is formed, this harmless body assumes an active life, and its activity is entirely exercised in opposition to the Government'.[39] Naturally the Queen did not agree. In her view the House of Lords represented the opinion of those who had the greatest stake in the country, namely land, commerce, employers, church men and an 'independent opinion which the House of Commons alas! does not represent!'[40] Queen Victoria disliked MPs being swayed by the electorate.

In October 1894 Rosebery decided to inhibit the right of the Lords to 'summarily mutilate and reject' Bills put forward by the Commons. He notified the Queen that 'the cry' in the Liberal Party, vexed by constant blocking of its Bills, was for the abolition of the House of Lords. The Queen was warned that her prime minister would put the reform of the House of Lords before the country. Immediately the Queen wrote back voicing her concern that if the reform became law, the House of Lords would be 'compelled to accept whatever passes through the Commons . . . This is tampering with our Constitution and where will it stop?'[41]

On the same day, the Queen telegraphed the opposition leader, Lord Salisbury, urging him to help, stating that she 'cannot let the Cabinet make such a proposal without ascertaining first whether the country would be in favour of it'.[42] She also wrote to her son the Prince of Wales asking him to intervene – he sensibly declined. Queen Victoria was on dangerous constitutional grounds for it represented a serious breach of her political impartiality. It was the duty of the Queen to take advice from her ministers, not to consult others without the approval of her prime minister. The Queen seemed fully aware of the impropriety of her behaviour because she insisted that her discussions remain absolutely confidential.

Lord Rosebery went ahead with his plans for reforming the House of Lords. He made a series of speeches to the electorate, telling his audiences that the next election would be fought on the question of the House of Lords. The Queen was furious. She criticised Rosebery's speeches and demanded that he 'gain her approval before speaking'.[43] Rosebery remained unruffled and reminded the Queen that she had no right to sanction his political debates: it was unnecessary, he told her, for a minister to receive the approval of the sovereign before putting policy before a popular audience.[44] He repeated his complaint that the House of Lords, rather than being an independent body, was a party organisation dominated by the Conservatives and that the 'constitution cannot long stand the strain of a permanent control exercised by a Conservative branch of the legislature on all Liberal governments'.[45] The Queen, 'bothered and troubled beyond measure by this House of Lords question'[46] thought this disloyal. Fortunately for the Queen there seemed to be little public appetite for Lords reform, thus a serious constitutional crisis was averted. However, House of Lords reform continued to be a really vexatious issue for the British sovereign and the Liberal Party. Later, both Edward

VIII and George V were reluctant to accept a diminution in the power of the Lords and it took two successive general elections before it was accepted that their Lordships' powers should be watered down.

Queen Victoria and Lord Rosebery worked better together over the question of army reform. The government wished to remove the Queen's cousin the 76-year-old George, Duke of Cambridge, from his post as commander-in-chief of the British Army. Unfortunately, the aged George was reluctant to resign. He had been in the post for 39 years. He complained to Victoria that he was anxious to 'do what is best for the Crown and to maintain the Office of Commander in Chief, so that it should never become Parliamentary. . . . What he wishes is not to be kicked out by these violent radicals, who have made such attacks on him'.[47] Victoria acted as intermediary between the government and her cousin. The three – the Queen, her cousin and her prime minister – agreed that the Duke should leave in November 1895. However, the Duke grew obdurate and reneged on his commitment until threatened with dismissal. Even when he accepted the inevitable, he tried to delay his departure and demanded a pension of £2,000. His delaying tactics tested the patience of an already impatient Queen. The Cabinet refused to grant the pension and the mortified Duke retired to be replaced by General Wolseley. According to the Queen, Wolseley was not a success: Victoria had wanted her son Arthur to be given the post as commander-in-chief and was disappointed when he was turned down.

Rhodes James argues that Rosebery's 'government drifted dismally towards inevitable disaster, its councils acrimonious, its leaders divided, its supporters dispirited or violently disillusioned, its stature at home and abroad visibly disintegrating'.[48] On 21 June 1895 the Rosebery administration ended abruptly and unexpectedly over a debate on ammunition supplies. During the debate, the Conservative opposition criticised the Secretary of State for War for failing to ensure there were sufficient supplies of arms and demanded a reduction in his salary of £100. The opposition won by seven votes. The next day Rosebery travelled to Windsor to hand in his resignation. The Queen, who had warmed again to Rosebery, said she was very sorry to lose him. Rosebery replied that 'to him personally it would be an immense relief . . . as the scenes in the Cabinet had been quite dreadful. His only regret was to leave me.'[49] In Rosebery's view there were 'two pleasures in life. One is ideal, the other real. The ideal is when a man receives the seals of office from his Sovereign. The real pleasure is when he hands them back.'[50]

A Conservative revival – Lord Salisbury: June 1895–1902

In June 1895, the Queen sent for Salisbury again. He was to be Queen Victoria's last prime minister, remaining in office after her death. As soon as Salisbury came into power he quickly dissolved parliament. In the July general election, the Conservatives won 350 seats and enjoyed a crushing majority of 152 seats over the Liberals' 177 (Irish Nationalists won 82; Liberal Unionists 71). The less than impartial Queen was delighted. She agreed that it was an 'important sign of the good sense of the country, which did not wish for violent changes, like Home Rule, and the violent attacks on the House of Lords'.[51] When she met with Salisbury, they talked 'on many subjects, including the wonderful majority'.[52] In 1895 the parties re-aligned when the Liberal Unionists, led by Joseph Chamberlain, joined with the Conservative Party. The Queen was satisfied with this outcome because she had worked covertly behind the scenes for this political repositioning to happen. Victory in the general election marked the beginning of a long period of Conservative Unionist rule.

Salisbury's record of domestic reform was not impressive. There were modifications in the administration of the Poor Law; a London Government Act (1899) which established 28 London boroughs; these were legal reforms concerning infant life protection, running of the prisons and money-lending; amendments to the Factory Acts; Bills to improve the working conditions of miners, cotton workers and shop assistants; and laws destined to improve working-class housing. The Queen hoped that something would be done 'rendering education more practical for the working classes, who were being taught useless things'. She had earlier 'pointed out the great danger of over education and the necessity for making the people feel and realise that to be labourers and house servants was as good and necessary, as being Clerks'.[53]

The Diamond Jubilee

On Sunday 20 June 1897 Queen Victoria, now aged 78, prepared to celebrate her sixtieth year on the throne: her Diamond Jubilee. Hers had been the longest reign in British history. As ever, there was a substantial number of foreign royal representatives including the Grand Dukes and Duchesses from Mecklenburg-Strelitz, Hesse and Russia, the Prince and Princes of Bulgaria, Prince and Princess Charles of Denmark, the Crown Prince of Siam, the Hereditary Grand Duke of Luxemburg and the Prince of Persia.[54] Nevertheless, this time there were no other sovereigns to witness the ceremony – the Queen refused to invite them because the exertion and expense of entertaining them would be too much for her. When Joseph Chamberlain suggested that representatives of the colonies should be invited instead, the Queen acquiesced, pleased that they would be cheaper to entertain and considerably less troublesome than kings, queens and emperors. As a consequence, the Jubilee became an extravagant celebration of Britain's imperial triumphs and marked the zenith of national enthusiasm for empire.[55] Certainly, there was a strong imperial tinge to the event as representatives – prime ministers, presidents, governors – from every colonised country came to attend this very special occasion. Most of the country was swept up in a patriotic fervour: the British seemed to love an excuse to party. Once again, flags, flowers, bunting and other decorations were put up on buildings to celebrate Queen Victoria's reign. The Mansion House, the official residence of the Lord Mayor of London, was decorated sumptuously: the royal crown, flanked on each side by the letters V.R., took centre stage, a central pillar was adorned with a large royal standard surrounded by 25 national banners and wreaths; a shield of London was displayed; windows were swathed with crimson curtains and gold ornaments; and a banner with 'God Bless our Queen' written on it was prominently displayed.[56] People were in a mood to celebrate: a public holiday was declared. Tons of fireworks – 3,000,000 coloured stars, 100,000 rockets, 100,000 Roman candles, 500 V.R.s, and 100 firework portraits of Queen Victoria – were ordered from one pyrotechnic firm alone.[57] A few days before the ceremony the branches of trees just outside Buckingham Palace were lopped off and 'cartloads of leafy limbs' carried away so that people could see the Queen in her carriage. The trees were encircled with barbed wire to prevent people climbing them to get a better view.[58]

Queen Victoria, who hated public events like these, 'felt rather nervous about the coming days, and that all should go off well'.[59] On 21 June she left Windsor for Buckingham Palace, and was thrilled by 'a most enthusiastic reception. It was like a triumphal entry . . . The streets were beautifully decorated, also the balconies of the houses, with flowers, flags and draperies. . . . The streets, the windows, the roofs of the houses, were one mass of beaming faces and the cheers never ceased.'[60] That night, Monday 21st, she hosted a dinner for visiting royalty: the first to be presented was Archduke Franz Ferdinand of Austria, the heir to the Austrian throne who was later murdered at Sarajevo. Victoria dressed for the occasion in her familiar black but the front of her dress was embroidered in gold, diamonds sparkled in her widow's cap, and she wore a diamond necklace.[61]

On Tuesday 22nd the Queen drove in state from Buckingham Palace to St Paul's Cathedral. Just before the Queen left the Palace, she felt a 'good deal agitated for fear anything might be forgotten or go wrong'.[62] There was no need to worry. The Diamond Jubilee, unlike previous celebrations, was meticulously planned by a committee chaired by the Prince of Wales. Even minutiae as to whether the Queen's horses might defecate or urinate during the most solemn moments of the religious ceremony were discussed. At 11:15am the Queen set off in an open state carriage drawn by eight cream horses. Vicky, her eldest daughter, was in the next carriage. Sixteen royal carriages, containing other royal princesses, the odd duke, and top civil servants joined the procession. Her eldest son, Bertie, and her cousin, the Duke of Cambridge, commander-in-chief of the army, rode on each side of her carriage while her son Arthur rode a little at the rear. Just before she left the Palace, the Queen touched an electric button which started a message telegraphed throughout the whole empire saying 'From my heart I thank my beloved people. May God bless them.'[63]

By now the Queen was too frail and elderly to walk up the steps of St Paul's Cathedral so she stayed in her carriage while a short service was held in the open air. Later she wrote that 'in front of the Cathedral the scene was most impressive. All the

Colonial troops, on foot, were drawn up round the Square. My carriage, surrounded by all the Royal Princes, was drawn up close to the steps, where the Clergy were assembled, the Bishops in rich copes, with their croziers.'[64] After this, the Queen processed over London Bridge and along the Borough Road in order that the 'very poor population' could witness the event. The Jubilee Committee shared the belief that the appearance of the Queen in working-class districts might quell any remaining vestiges of Republicanism and bind her subjects more closely to the monarchy. Queen Victoria thought it a 'never-to-be-forgotten day. No one, ever I believe, has met with such an ovation as was given to me, passing through those 6 miles of streets. . . . The crowds were quite indescribable, and their enthusiasm truly marvellous and deeply touching. The cheering was quite deafening, and every face seemed to be filled with real joy.'[65]

All over Britain, as with the 1887 Jubilee, the population celebrated. In Liverpool, children who lived in institutions – from the Orphan Asylum, the Bluecoat Hospital, the Deaf and Dumb school – were taken to see the marine display;[66] a Jubilee parade of about 1,000 cyclists was held in Battersea Park;[67] a Jubilee Regatta took place on the Clyde; at Hartlepool public houses stayed open an hour later; in Ireland 55 carcases of Australian mutton was given to the Catholic poor; in Paisley, Scotland, 13,000 children were treated to an afternoon of games and biscuits, cakes and sweets; a whole ox was roasted on a beach in Norfolk; and Alfred Austin, as poet laureate, wrote a curious commemorative poem, judged inexplicably by The Times as 'graceful and appropriate'. One verse speaks of 'And, panoplied alike for War or Peace/Victoria's England furroweth still the foam/To harvest Empire, wiser than was Greece/Wider than Rome!'[68] Nottingham, Bradford and Kingston-Upon-Hull were all given city status. Somewhere else, a painter was killed falling off a ladder when putting up Jubilee decorations, and a Mancunian woman who was fined half-a-crown for being drunk a few days earlier pleaded that she was only celebrating the Jubilee holiday early.[69]

Not all shared the Jubilee enthusiasm. In Ireland, the leading Republican James Connelly presided over an anti-Jubilee meeting in Dublin where a black flag was flown. It had the inscription 'The Record Reign, '39–'97. Starved to death, 1,225,000. Evicted,

3,658,000. Forced to emigrate, 4,168,000.'[70] One speaker proclaimed that Ireland might well curse the day that Victoria ruled the empire, as the first 60 years of her reign had brought more ruin, misery and death in their land than any previous period.[71] In England too there were criticisms. *Reynolds's Weekly Newspaper* predictably complained that:

> never has a Civil servant, whose establishment costs the nation about a million a year, been so shy of facing her employers . . . We are told by way of excuse that – She is an old woman. Then let her retire if she cannot fulfil the meagre duties of constitutional monarchies. . . . For 36 years since the death of the Prince Consort the royal family have drawn £36,000,000 out of the taxation of this country. . . . And now we are celebrating her Diamond Jubilee . . . for more than half the time she has failed to discharge her principal business, that is making a show of herself. It is a big sum to pay for half a reign, in which the sovereign has played so contemptible a part. We have no sympathy with those who say the monarch is not to be criticised because she is old, or because she is a woman. She is a servant of the State.[72]

Foreign affairs

Queen Victoria shared Salisbury's approach to foreign affairs, and consequently his premiership marked a peak period of imperial expansion. For most of his time in office, Salisbury was more interested in foreign affairs than domestic policy. He led the British partition of Africa: the Queen was delighted when Kenya, Uganda, Nigeria and Rhodesia submitted to her imperial rule. Salisbury was a prime minister who would listen to her and, more importantly, take her advice. Even so he complained when more and more colonies were acquired, sure that they would be a burden rather than a benefit.

Crises in the Ottoman Empire

In August 1895 Queen Victoria and Prime Minister Salisbury were faced with renewed tension in the Balkans, an area still controlled by the Sultan of the Ottoman Empire. The Queen and her government, ever fearful of Russian expansion, always took care to support the Ottomans but an outbreak of Turkish atrocities against the Armenians shocked them both. The Armenian population who lived under Turkish rule wanted their freedom; the Ottomans responded to their demands with brutal repression. Thousands of Armenians lost their lives. 'The state of Turkey', the Queen noted 'is dreadful. The shameful, savage massacres of the unfortunate Armenians, men, women and children and the misrule in Constantinople is too dreadful. The Ambassadors are at their wit's end.'[73]

The Queen begged the Sultan 'for the cause of humanity and in obedience to God's law; for the sake of your Imperial Majesty's throne, and for the safety of the Ottoman Empire, I earnestly entreat your Imperial Majesty to exercise your great power to restore peace'.[74] Salisbury was 'not hopeful' about the Queen's appeal to the Sultan, believing that 'he cares about two things only – 1. Himself 2. Islam. He has not what we call "human" feeling.'[75] Salisbury's apprehensions were valid: in August 1896 there were further massacres in Constantinople in full view of foreign ambassadors. The Ottomans ruthlessly suppressed the uprising, killing between 80,000 and 300,000 Armenians.

In April 1897, just as the Armenian crisis was ending, war broke out between the Ottoman Empire and Greece over the status of the island of Crete. At the time, the Ottoman Empire controlled Crete but the largely Christian islanders wanted to be part of Christian Greece, not Islamic Turkey. Greece landed with an army on the island to support the Cretans. By now, Victoria was decidedly unsympathetic to the Ottoman Empire. Her instinctive sympathy towards countries which held members of her family was deeply ingrained in her emotional self. And some of her family ruled Greece: her granddaughter, Sophie (daughter of her eldest daughter Vicky and sister of Kaiser Wilhelm) was married to the Crown Prince of Greece. Grandmother and granddaughter were very close: Sophie had often stayed with her grandmother whom she adored. Greece was eventually defeated by the Turks but the Great Powers – Britain, France, Italy and Russia – decided that Turkey was unable to govern Crete adequately. In December 1898 they appointed Prince George of

Greece and Denmark – husband of Princess Bonaparte, cousin of Tsar Nicolas and a relation by marriage to Queen Victoria – as governor-general of an independent Crete. Queen Elizabeth II's husband, the Duke of Edinburgh, is his direct descendant.

Queen Victoria's mounting hostility towards the Ottoman Empire may have also been influenced by her developing affection towards Russia and its rulers. In April 1894, another of the Queen's much-loved granddaughters, Alexandra, the fourth daughter of Princess Alice, became engaged to Nicholas, the heir to the Russian throne. The Queen, who had disapproved of the match and had worked ceaselessly to prevent it, was 'thunder-struck'.[76] She confided to one granddaughter that the state of Russia was 'so bad, so rotten that at any moment something dreadful might happen'.[77] Later she confessed that the more 'I think of sweet Alicky's marriage the more unhappy I am. Not as to the personality, for I like him very much but on account of the Country, the policy and differences with us and the awful insecurity to what that sweet Child will be exposed . . . my whole nature rises up against it'.[78] In October that year, Nicholas succeeded to the Russian throne; in November, Nicholas and Alexandra married. The Queen's thoughts were constantly with 'dear Alicky, whose wedding takes place today. . . . I felt so sad I could not be with her. . . . I thought of Darling Alicky and how impossible it seemed that that gentle little simple Alicky should be the great Empress of Russia!'[79] Once Alexandra was married to Nicolas, Queen Victoria's feelings towards Russia softened and she began to view the country more favourably.

Less than two years later, Nicolas and Alexandra were crowned on 26 May 1896. It was a disastrous event: Victoria was told of a most

> horrible and ghastly catastrophe . . . has cast quite a gloom over all the rejoicings. There was to be a great National Fete and unfortunately and inconceivably, no Police or troops were on the ground, where the people began to congregate in thousands. They got impatient to get to the booths where food was distributed, and special mugs given from the Emperor. In the stampede as many 1000s are reported to have been knocked down and killed.[80]

Victoria's Ambassador in St Petersburg told her of scenes and incidents 'too terrible and harrowing for the Queen's ears'.[81] The next day Victoria received more sad accounts of the 'awful tragedy at Moscow. . . . The papers say that the people of Moscow are showing signs of anger and exasperation at the frightful misman-agement of the authorities. It makes me anxious.'[82] Certainly, the mayhem at the Russian coronation and the later reported death of 3,000 people as a result was an inauspicious start to a new regime. Tsar Nicholas and Tsarina Alexandra were the last Romanovs to rule Russia: in 1917 they were forced to abdicate and were later murdered by the Bolsheviks. Their cousin King George V and the British government had refused them asylum.

Eastern and African affairs

The Queen continued to take a personal interest in Indian affairs. In 1898 a new viceroy of India, George Curzon, was appointed. Victoria, possibly influenced by Abdul Karim, told her prime minister that the future viceroy must be free from his 'red-tapist, narrow minded Council and entourage. He must be more inde-pendent, must hear for himself what the feelings of the Natives really are, and do what he thinks right, and not be guided by the snobbish and vulgar overbearing and offensive behaviour of many of our Civil and Political Agents.'[83] In the Queen's opinion, the British should avoid trampling on its foreign subjects and stop making them feel that they were a conquered people. They must feel 'that we are masters' she advised, but it should be done 'kindly and not offensively'.[84] For all that these sympathetic senti-ments reflect those of a politically astute sovereign, Queen Victoria rarely thought to apply them to anywhere else but India.

By the 1890s, the whole continent of Africa, apart from Liberia and Ethiopia, was under European control. The work of the explorers such as David Livingstone, who charted the rivers, provided maps and indicated the wealth that existed, convinced Europeans that Africa could yield high profits. Salisbury, a com-mitted imperialist, issued Charters to British companies to exploit the Continent, in what is sometimes called 'settler sub-imperialism'. They built harbours, roads and railways, cleared forests and jungles – and extracted gold from the mines. Not surprisingly, there was resistance from the indigenous people. In December 1895 the British declared war on the Ashanti Empire, a sovereign state located in what is now modern Ghana, because the Ashanti population had turned down an offer to become a British protectorate. To the Queen's 'astonishment and concern' her son-in-law Prince Henry of Battenburg (Liko) told her that he wished to go on the Ashanti expedition. Victoria 'told him it would never do'.[85] Beatrice, Henry's wife, persuaded Victoria to change her mind by telling her mother that Henry had 'set his heart on going. He smarted under his enforced inactivity, and this was about the only occasion which presented no difficulties. . . . He felt he was a soldier, brought up as such.'[86] Queen Victoria, who always had a soft spot for the army, relented, but her worst fears were confirmed when Henry died of malaria contracted while on duty. There was, the Queen recorded in her diary, 'such grief in the house. Dear Liko was so much beloved. Went over to Beatrice's room and sat a little while with her, she is so gentle, so piteous in her misery. . . . My heart aches for my darling child.'[87] The war was brief and ended in February 1896 with Britain victorious.

In April 1896, Salisbury informed the Queen that he wanted to recapture the Sudan.[88] Victoria relished this turn of events since she shared Salisbury's view of British imperialism. Gordon had lost the Sudan in 1884; Salisbury authorised the British army, under the command of Lord Kitchener, to re-conquer it. In April 1898 the army occupied Omdurman and then had taken Khartoum. Some 35,000 Dervishes attacked British troops with 'great boldness and determination. . . . After one hour's fighting the Dervishes were driven off with great loss . . . completely defeated. . . . the whole Dervish army has been practically destroyed.'[89] The Dervish loss was 11,000; the British lost 23 men. It was an unsurprising victory: the Dervishes fought with rifles, bayonets and spears; Kitchener's army fought with machine guns. A memorial service was held to the memory of Gordon 'on the spot where he was killed! Surely he is avenged.'[90] The Queen telegraphed Kitchener congratulating him 'warmly on the brilliant victory so splendidly won'.[91] The Sudan had been defeated but its leader, the Khalifa, remained at large until November 1899 when the Queen received 'great and satisfactory' news that the

Khalifa was killed.[92] She 'rejoiced at the success . . . which gives us entire possession of the valley of the Nile'.[93]

South Africa – the Boer War: 1899–1902

The situation in South Africa had long been a pressing concern for Victoria and her government. The Dutch Boers (Boer was the Dutch word for farmer) and the British disagreed over who would control the South African Republic, known as the Transvaal, and the Orange Free State. In 1877 the British had annexed the Transvaal, hoping to bring it under British control. This led to the first open conflict in 1880–1, British defeat and Gladstone conceding self-government to the Transvaal.

Britain was keen to re-establish its authority over the Transvaal; the Boers were intent on breaking away from Britain completely. In 1886, when gold was discovered in the Dutch-controlled Transvaal, hordes of developers, prospectors and carpet-baggers flooded in from British South Africa. They were known as Uitlanders, or outsiders, and the Dutch settlers did not like them. The president of the Transvaal, Paul Kruger, refused to grant Uitlanders equal civil rights, including the right to vote. Uitlanders were also taxed more heavily than the Boers, who were inclined to treat them as aliens.

In 1894 Cecil Rhodes, multi-millionaire owner of the diamond mines at Kimberley and ruler of the British Cape Colony, visited the Queen and told her 'that the Transvaal, which we ought never to have given up, would ultimately come back to England'.[94] In December 1895 Rhodes and the Uitlander leaders organised a rebellion in the Transvaal against Boer injustices. A 'motley band of adventurers' of between 400 and 500 men, under the command of Dr Jameson, the administrator of the British South Africa Company, was sent in to 'protect' British interests and help the Uitlanders. But the plot misfired. Jameson was soon forced to surrender and two days later Rhodes resigned his premiership of the Cape. Many British were outraged at Jameson's unauthorised coup, believing it to be 'a reckless, hopeless fiasco characterised by incompetence, amateurism and wishful thinking'.[95]

However, the country's mood changed when it heard that the German Kaiser, Queen Victoria's grandson, had sent a telegram congratulating Kruger, the Boer president, on his success. Victoria gave William 'a piece of my mind'.[96] She told him that 'as your Grandmother to whom you have always shown so much affection' she could not refrain from expressing her deep regret at the telegram sent to President Kruger as it was considered 'very unfriendly towards this country'.[97] The Kaiser sent an ameliorative reply, insisting that he had meant no harm to British interests. The Queen privately thought her grandson's reply 'lame and illogical',[98] yet for the sake of diplomatic peace wrote accepting his explanation. Chastened by his grandmother's reprimand, William later took Britain's side. Indeed, Victoria was given credit for keeping Germany friendly because of her rapport with her grandson; it was old-style family-based politicking that the Queen enjoyed.

In 1899 tensions between the Boers and the Uitlanders reached breaking point. In March, a giant petition containing 21,684 signatures was sent to Queen Victoria, appealing to her and the British government for help in ending Boer injustices. The petition spoke of how there was no liberty of the press; of how British subjects could be expelled at the will of the President; of how they were overtaxed and had practically no say in government; that the police were entirely composed of Boers and behaved in an arbitrary manner; of how they were not allowed to meet together or present petitions. In response, the British government called up the Reserves, mobilised its army and landed in South Africa; on 9 October the Boers declared war.

People in Britain generally supported the war because it was thought it would be an easy one to win. The Boers were farmers and had no regular army and few guns, while the British army was well trained and supplied with plentiful equipment. The 80-year-old Queen took a great interest in the war and was pleased to be told that the British army trounced the Boers and had 'captured a Boer camp comprising tents, waggons, horses and 2 guns. Boer losses very considerable.'[99] The first few weeks augured well. However, to the Queen's despair, the British were put on the defensive when the Boers attacked 'with considerable vigour'.[100] The next day she heard 'some very sad news . . . to the effect that the column sent out to guard the left flanks, had met with a disaster. It had been surrounded in the hills and after heavy loss, had to surrender.'[101] At first the Boers had the definite advantage: they knew the country; they outnumbered British soldiers; their guns were superior; they were used to the climate; and they wore no uniform making it difficult to distinguish them from civilians.

Queen Victoria felt 'very low and anxious about the war'[102] especially when the first two years brought a series of military disgraces. The Boers besieged the British garrisons at Ladysmith, at Mafeking and at Kimberley, effectively immobilising the soldiers stationed there. The week between 10 December and 17 December 1899 was perhaps the most humiliating – in the space of seven days the British lost three separate battles. They soon learned that a guerrilla force, living among its supporters, cannot easily be defeated. After the first few defeats the Queen wrote to Sir Redvers Buller, commander-in-chief of the forces, that she was 'naturally terribly anxious, and the sad events of the last days grieved us very much. . . . But the Queen Empress has great confidence in Sir R Buller, and she feels sure that he will retrieve the sad failures of brave men.'[103] Buller wanted to 'let Ladysmith go'; the Queen insisted that it was 'impossible to abandon' it'.[104] Queen Victoria was so anxious about events in South Africa that she cancelled her annual Christmas holiday at Osborne and remained at Windsor to be in touch with the news. The siege of Ladysmith was to last several months.

Meanwhile, as it became obvious that Buller was incapable of leading the army against the Boers, the government replaced him with Lord Roberts and Lord Kitchener. On 10 January 1900 the two landed at Capetown: Buller was instructed to stay put until they joined him. However, Buller ignored the directive and attempted one last battle – Spion Kop – in which 200 soldiers died and 300 were injured. It was one of the worst defeats of the war.

As casualties and costs escalated, criticism of the conduct of the war mounted. There were demands for an inquiry. The Queen tried to impress upon Salisbury 'the importance of having no official inquiry into the conduct of the war until it is over. It would only be repeated back to the Boers and to Foreign Countries and would do us a great deal of harm.'[105] She urged 'strongly the necessity of resisting these unpatriotic and unjust criticisms of our Generals and of the conduct of the war'.[106]

Victoria realised that the War Office was at fault but still felt it was important for her government to show a 'firm front' and 'not let it be for a moment supposed that we vacillate'.[107]

In April 1900 the dispatches between Lord Roberts and Lord Shaftesbury were published, criticising the errors of judgement of Buller. The Queen was horrified when these appeared in the press and expressed her distaste and dissatisfaction that these had been broadcast while the war was actually going on. In her view, it was

> to officially brand as incompetent those whom the men have, like all good soldiers, because they <u>are</u> their Generals, hitherto believed in and followed. The Queen is not so much concerned for the Generals as for the whole discipline and <u>esprit de corps</u> of the Army, which must suffer dangerously by this unprecedented exposure to subordinates of the faults of their superiors.[108]

No one, the Queen believed, benefited by the publication of the despatches, 'not the soldiers, whose confidence in their leaders is shaken; not the public, whose trust in the Generals is impaired; not the Generals and superior officers of the Army, who must for the future be prepared for their mistakes to be made the subjects of public censure'.[109] Here, the Queen's political perspicacity was evident but it was a problem that all governments face – that of balancing freedom of information with national security.

Throughout the war, Queen Victoria retained a unique personal interest in her army, and was indefatigable in encouraging her troops and generals by sending them telegrams and letters, in 'bidding God-speed to regiments on departure, visiting wounded in hospital; . . . and in providing comforts for her solders to eat and wear, working for them herself among her ladies'.[110] Certainly, the Queen was gripped by the Boer War. She wrote to the widows and mothers of those killed in action, began an album in which she placed a photograph of every officer killed with the reason for his death, made comforters and caps for the troops and had her staff send a box of chocolates with a picture of herself on the lid to every soldier fighting in South Africa. At her request, 5,818 feather pillows were sent to the hospitals in the Cape. And sitting in a wheelchair, the 82-year-old Queen visited the wounded in Woolwich hospital where she was wheeled up to the 'bed of each man, speaking to them, and giving them flowers. They seemed so touched, and many had tears in their eyes.'[111]

Meanwhile, with the arrival of Roberts and Kitchener, the Boer successes were halted. Kitchener employed draconian measures to subdue all the Boers, whether fighters, women or children. He adopted a scorched earth policy destroying farms, burning crops and killing livestock. Millions of horses, cattle and sheep were shot. He rounded up Boer women and children and interned them in concentration camps – the first use of the term – where conditions were abominable. Many of the women and children were already malnourished from the war and were weakened still further in the camps by being deprived of clothes, bedding, cooking utensils, clean water and medicine. Between 20,000 and 25,000 of the 117,000 incarcerated in the camps died from malnutrition, dysentery, typhoid and related diseases. Most of these were children.

By early 1900 the British seemed to be winning. On 16 February 1900 the Queen received a telegram 'with the most welcome and almost unexpected news of the relief of Kimberley';[112] on 28 February Ladysmith was relieved after a siege of four months; on 17 March Mafeking. Once again, Queen Victoria experienced personal grief when her grandson Prince Christian of Schleswig-Holstein died of malaria contracted from fighting in the Boer War. The Queen could not believe it as 'it seemed too dreadful and heart breaking. . . . Again and again the terrible thought of this fresh blow and irreparable loss, brought tears to my eyes.'[113] A few months earlier, in July, Victoria's son 'Affie', aged 55 years old, died of throat cancer. 'A terrible day! . . . it is hard at 81. . . . I was greatly upset – one sorrow, one trial, one anxiety, following on another. It is a horrible year. Nothing but sadness and horrors of one kind and another. . . . Felt terribly shaken and broken.'[114]

The last days of the Queen

By now, Queen Victoria had lost her husband, both her parents, a few aunts and uncles, three of her children – Alice, Leopold and Alfred – and nine grandchildren, some in infancy.[115] Queen Victoria's health, despite frequent complaints to the contrary, was usually robust. On 23 September 1896 she had reigned for 63 years 7 months, longer than any previous British sovereign. During the last five or six years of her life, however, she became frail. In the mid-1890s she suffered from rheumatism, which made walking difficult, and by the end of the 1890s cataracts greatly diminished her sight. She was barely able to read and was usually wheeled around in a wheelchair. A loss of weight and general sleeplessness pointed to further physical decay. In addition, her once acute memory began to fail. By now, the Queen was feeling 'very poorly and wretched. . . . My appetite is completely gone and I have difficulty in eating anything.'[116] On Sunday 13 January 1901 the Queen wrote in her journal that she had 'had a fair night, but was a little wakeful. Got up earlier and had some milk. Lenchen came and read some papers.'[117] It was the last entry in the Queen's journal.

Notes

1 RA VIC/MAIN/QVJ (W) August 15th 1892.
2 Ibid. August 15th 1892.
3 Rhodes James, *The British Revolution*, p. 136.
4 RA VIC/MAIN/QVJ (W) August 13th 1892.
5 Victoria to Ponsonby, July 26th 1892.
6 Ibid. June 4th 1892.
7 Ibid. July 13th 1892.
8 Victoria to Bertie, August 13th 1892.
9 Bertie to Lord Rosebery, August 14th 1892.
10 Victoria to Gladstone, August 12th 1893.
11 RA VIC/MAIN/QVJ (W) January 30th 1893.
12 Ibid. February 19th 1893.
13 Victoria to Gladstone, February 20th 1893.
14 Gladstone to Victoria, February 20th 1898.
15 RA VIC/MAIN/QVJ (W) June 3rd 1893.
16 Ibid. June 22nd 1893.
17 Ibid. July 11th 1893.
18 Ibid. July 11th 1893.
19 Memorandum by Salisbury to the Queen, August 8th 1893.
20 Edward Hamilton, September 5th 1905, quoted in Leo McKinstry, *Rosebery, Statesman in Turmoil*, John Murray, 2005, p. 330.
21 RA VIC/MAIN/QVJ (W) July 8th 1893.
22 Ibid. September 6th 1893.

290   The last years: 1892–1901

23 Ibid. September 9th 1893.
24 Ibid. September 9th 1893.
25 Ibid. February 28th 1894.
26 Rhodes James, *The British Revolution*, p. 143.
27 Quoted in Van der Kiste, *Sons, Servants and Statesmen*, p. 108.
28 Magnus, *Gladstone*.
29 Reid to Rosebery, March 2nd, 1894 quoted in Leo McKinstry, *Rosebery, Statesman in Turmoil*, p. 292.
30 Algernon Cecil, *Queen Victoria and her Prime Ministers*, Eyre and Spottiswoode, 1953, p. 282.
31 McKinstry, *Rosebery, Statesman in Turmoil*, p. 308.
32 RA VIC/MAIN/QVJ (W) February 17th 1894.
33 Victoria to Rosebery, July 13th 1894.
34 Rosebery to Victoria, July 13th 1894.
35 Reid to Rosebery, March 9th, 1894 quoted in Leo McKinstry, *Rosebery, Statesman in Turmoil*, p. 305.
36 Victoria to Rosebery, July 13th 1894.
37 Rosebery to Victoria, July 13th 1894.
38 Victoria to Rosebery, March 17th 1894.
39 Memorandum by Rosebery, March–April 1894.
40 Victoria to Rosebery, April 9th 1894.
41 Ibid. October 25th 1894.
42 Victoria to Salisbury, October 25th 1894.
43 Victoria to Rosebery, October 30th 1894.
44 Rosebery to Victoria, November 1st 1894.
45 Ibid. November 1st 1894.
46 RA VIC/MAIN/QVJ (W), November 6th 1894.
47 Ibid. May 7th 1895.
48 Quoted in Robert Rhodes James, 'Earl of Rosebery', in Blake, *The Prime Ministers*, p. 159.
49 RA VIC/MAIN/QVJ (W) June 22nd 1895.
50 Rhodes James, 'Earl of Rosebery', p. 147.
51 RA VIC/MAIN/QVJ (W) July 28th 1895.
52 Ibid. August 5th 1895.
53 Ibid. March 10th 1894.
54 I am grateful to the Royal Archives for this information.
55 See Hobsbawm and Ranger, *The Invention of Tradition*, especially David Cannadine's chapter for a discussion of this.
56 *Glasgow Herald*, June 17th 1897, p. 4.
57 RA VIC/MAIN/QVJ (W) June 20th 1897.
58 *The Belfast News-Letter*, June 17th 1897, p. 4.
59 RA VIC/MAIN/QVJ (W) June 20th 1897.
60 Ibid. June 21st 1897.
61 Ibid. June 21st 1897.
62 Ibid. June 22nd 1897.
63 Ibid. June 22nd 1897.
64 Ibid. June 22nd 1897.

65 Ibid. June 22nd, 1897.
66 *Liverpool Mercury*, June 17th 1897, p. 5.
67 *Lloyd's Weekly Newspaper*, June 20th 1897, p. 1.
68 *The North-Eastern Daily Gazette*, June 21st 1897.
69 *Lloyd's Weekly Newspaper*, June 20th 1897, p. 4.
70 *Freeman's Journal and Daily Commercial Advertiser*, June 22nd 1897, p. 6.
71 *Freeman's Journal and Daily Commercial Advertiser*, June 22nd 1897, p. 6.
72 *Reynolds's Weekly Newspaper*, June 20th 1897, p. 1.
73 RA VIC/MAIN/QVJ (W) December 4th 1895.
74 Victoria to Sultan of Turkey, December 28th 1895.
75 Salisbury to Bigge, December 29th 1895.
76 RA VIC/MAIN/QVJ (W) April 20th 1894.
77 Victoria to Princess Victoria, December 29th 1890.
78 Ibid. May 25th 1894.
79 RA VIC/MAIN/QVJ (W) November 26th 1894.
80 Ibid. June 2nd 1896.
81 O'Connor to Victoria, May 31st 1896.
82 RA VIC/MAIN/QVJ (W) June 3rd 1896.
83 Victoria to Salisbury, May 29th 1898.
84 Ibid. May 29th 1898.
85 RA VIC/MAIN/QVJ (W) November 17th 1895.
86 Ibid. November 18th 1895.
87 Ibid. January 22nd 1896.
88 Salisbury to Victoria, April 8th 1896.
89 RA VIC/MAIN/QVJ (W) September 3rd 1898.
90 Ibid. September 5th 1898.
91 Victoria to Kitchener, April 9th 1898.
92 RA VIC/MAIN/QVJ (W) November 25th 1899.
93 Ibid. March 26th 1899.
94 Ibid. December 4th 1894.
95 McKinstry, *Rosebery, Statesman in Turmoil*, p. 399.
96 RA VIC/MAIN/QVJ (W) January 5th 1896.
97 Victoria to William, January 5th 1896.
98 RA VIC/MAIN/QVJ (W) January 10th 1896.
99 Ibid. October 22nd 1899.
100 Ibid. October 30th 1899.
101 Ibid. October 31st 1899.
102 Ibid. December 14th 1899.
103 Victoria to Buller, December 15th 1899.
104 RA VIC/MAIN/QVJ (W) December 16th 1899.
105 Ibid. January 11th 1900.
106 Victoria to Balfour, February 4th 1900.
107 Ibid, February 4th 1900.
108 Bigge to Wolseley, April 22nd 1900.
109 Ibid, April 22nd 1900.

110 Buckle, *The Letters of Queen Victoria*, Vol. 3, 1896–1901.
111 RA VIC/MAIN/QVJ (W) March 22nd 1900.
112 Ibid. February 16th 1900.
113 Ibid. October 29th 1900.
114 Ibid. July 31st 1900.
115 Sigismund, Waldemar, Albert Victor Christian, Alexander, Frederick, Mary, Alfred, Christian Victor, Frederick Harold.
116 RA VIC/MAIN/QVJ (W) November 5th 1900.
117 Ibid. January 13th 1901.

Conclusion

At 6:30pm, Tuesday 22 January 1901, Queen Victoria died in her bedroom at Osborne House on the Isle of Wight. She had reigned for 63 years 7 months. On her death she was surrounded by her immediate family; the only one absent was her eldest daughter, Vicky, who was herself dying of cancer. Long before her death, Victoria had written instructions as to how her funeral was to be organised. She wanted a number of mementoes inside her coffin: Albert's dressing gown, his cloak and a caste of his hand; a lock of John Brown's hair, a photo of him and the wedding ring of John Brown's mother. Victoria, who had always seen herself as a soldier's daughter and as leader of the United Kingdom's armed forces, wanted a military funeral. And, after wearing black since 1861, she wanted her funeral to be in white.

On Friday 1 February 1901, the Queen's coffin, draped in a white and gold cloth and pulled by eight white horses, left Osborne and was placed on the ship *Alberta*. At sea, 18 battleships and 12 cruisers lined her route to Portsmouth. The next day, which was bitterly cold, the coffin made its way to Paddington where it was placed on a train and taken to Windsor. The funeral was held in St George's Chapel; on 4 February her body was taken to Frogmore Mausoleum to rest beside Albert. Tens of thousands of soldiers and sailors conveyed the queen's coffin – more troops than those who took part in the original British Expeditionary Force in 1914[1] to its final resting place. The new King, Edward VII, and the German Emperor, both dressed as admirals of the British navy, were joined by a great number of foreign nobles, nearly all of whom were related to the late Queen.

The Queen certainly 'rescued the royal line . . . Victoria was their strong Princess who replenished not only the nurseries of Windsor but also the thrones of Europe'.[2] Not surprisingly, Victoria was widely acknowledged as the Grandmother of Europe. Her nine children, 36 grandchildren and 37 great grandchildren occupied most of the European thrones. All her children, with the exception of Princess Louise, married into European royalty with the result that nearly every European monarch or consort was related to Queen Victoria in some way or another: the Emperor of Germany was a grandson; the Empress of Russia a granddaughter. Other relatives included King George of Greece, King Christian of Denmark, King Carlos of Portugal, Crown Prince Ferdinand of Bulgaria, Prince Ferdinand of Romania, the King of Norway, the Queen of Spain and the King of France. Victoria, by dint of her personality and her relationship with them, had often prevented the heads of these countries from quarrelling with each other. Unfortunately for Europe, the Queen's death weakened these familial bonds – the First World War was a war between three cousins, all related to Queen Victoria: Tsar Nicholas II of Russia, Kaiser Wilhelm of Germany and George V of Britain.

When Victoria was born, the House of Hanover was undoubtedly at a low ebb, both physically and morally. King George III's sons had produced no legitimate heir and the sexual incontinence of Victoria's 'wicked uncles' had undermined respect for the monarchy. By the end of her reign, Queen Victoria had secured the dynasty and had established a new moral probity in the royal palaces: she banned divorced women from the court and forbade loose talk while she was present. Her early impish personality, when she had enjoyed scurrilous gossip with Melbourne, had faded away while she transformed herself into a symbol of morality. But she was no prude. She had an astonishingly high sexual libido and liked to give nude paintings and mild erotica to Albert on his birthday. And she very much liked to have fun in bed.

As she grew older, Queen Victoria became obese and increasingly frumpy. In her later years photographs often depict her sideways, perhaps to disguise her increasing bulk. Yet this little old lady dressed in black with a white bonnet on her head managed to stamp her identity on the nineteenth century. This was partly because Victoria lived longer, reigned longer and was the head of a larger part of the world than any previous monarch. With a reign of 63 years, 7 months and 2 days, she was Queen for nearly two-thirds of the nineteenth century. She appointed ten prime ministers, fifteen foreign secretaries, eleven lord chancellors, six army commanders, and five archbishops of Canterbury and witnessed the inauguration of eighteen US presidents.[3] The sheer length of Queen Victoria's reign provided a measure of continuity – and stability – in stark contrast to the dramatic changes that took place elsewhere.

The transformation of Britain during Victoria's reign

Queen Victoria is associated with the metamorphosis of the United Kingdom into a world power but perhaps her greatest achievement is the fact that the nineteenth century is called the Victorian age. Yet the Queen did not define the age, rather she was defined by it. In many ways her reign marked the change from old Britain to new Britain, associated as it is with unprecedented transformations in so many areas. Victoria witnessed the development of her realm into an industrialised country, noticed its technological and scientific revolutions, its progress in transport, its political and social advances and its transformation into a world power. On 16 August 1858 the Queen sent one of the first telegraph messages across the transatlantic cable to the American president. Indeed, the Queen saw more technological innovation than any of her forbears: the railway and the steamship; the telephone and the telegraph; gas and electric light; the sewing machine and the typewriter; the bicycle and the glider aeroplane; the machine gun and dynamite; anaesthetics and antiseptics. And the newly invented camera recorded it all. Victoria might also have seen, and given her sweet tooth perhaps even ate, the first Easter egg and the first jelly-baby.

Queen Victoria observed the biggest population boom that Britain had ever experienced. At the time of her birth, the population of Britain was approximately 13 million; by the time of her death it had risen to about 42 million. She of course contributed to the population growth by giving birth to nine babies, all of whom reached adulthood, married and produced lots of children themselves. By the time of Victoria's death, most of the population lived in towns rather than the countryside. New cities had sprung up and older cities had increased in size dramatically: in 1800 the population of Manchester was 90,000 but by 1900 it had increased to 543,900; Sheffield jumped from 31,000 to 409,100. The water and sewage systems were unable to cope with this vast increase in the population and health problems soon followed. No one, not even the aristocracy and the royal family, was immune. Both the Queen and her son survived typhoid, a bacterial disease spread by poor hygiene and sanitation. Prince Albert is said to have died from it.

By 1901 the standard of living had risen, life expectancy had increased, there was better health care, improved sanitation, higher pay and fewer hours of work. It is well known that Victoria popularised the use of chloroform, thus making childbirth a less painful experience, even though she played little part in other improvements. At the time of the Queen's birth, schools were virtually non-existent for the children of the poor but by the time she died, education was compulsory and free. In 1819 a poacher, a picket-pocket and someone out at night with a blackened face could be sentenced to death by hanging; by 1901 the death penalty had been abolished for over 200 types of crime. Britain was becoming civilised. Nonetheless, the poor were helped more by charity than the state. The Poor Law Amendment Act 1834 had consolidated the notorious workhouse system to the detriment of the unemployed, whether they were children, adults or the very old. Charities stepped in to ameliorate the distress. The Victorian era was one of intense philanthropy and many of our modern charitable institutions – the Salvation Army, the Children's Society and the RSPCA – were founded in this period. The Queen was a patron of about 150 of them, often donating money. In 1882 she gave £12,535 to 230 different charities; she also gave one-off donations for the victims of fires, famines and colliery disasters.

In 1837, when Victoria came to the throne, taxes were levied on 1,200 items. Beer was taxed at 200 per cent, sugar, tea and coffee were taxed, bread was taxed, newspapers and even light was taxed. Even today one can still see older houses with windows blocked up, a reminder of the days when the window tax made it worth the owner's while to shut out the daylight. In 1842 Peel reduced the number of indirect taxes and re-introduced a tax on incomes above £150 a year. Most of the population was exempt because few earned so much. Queen Victoria was not obliged to pay income tax but Peel persuaded her to do so by assuring the Queen that it would be a temporary measure. Income tax remained: Disraeli and Gladstone promised to abolish it because, as Disraeli put it, it was 'unjust, unequal and inquisitorial'. Yet still income tax continued. Between 1886 and 1896 Queen Victoria grudgingly paid an average of £6,673 a year income tax; when she died the standard rate of income tax was levied at 2 per cent. Great differences in wealth remained throughout the century as the gap between the rich and the poor widened: a quarter of the entire population lived in poverty; 40 per cent of the country's wealth remained in the ownership of 5 per cent of the population.

Queen Victoria made the royal family rich. When she inherited the throne, the monarchy was in debt yet by the end of her life the Queen was the richest person in Britain. Throughout her reign, Queen Victoria had used her Civil List money, a fixed annual payment awarded by the government to support the royal household in performing its public duties, to build up her private fortune. The purchase and renovations of Osborne House and Balmoral, costing an estimated £400,000, had been funded by savings from the Civil List.[4] There is no doubt that the Queen was economical – newspaper squares were used instead of toilet paper in the lavatories at Windsor castle – but such parsimony cannot account for the vast wealth which Victoria amassed during her reign. She left her fortune to her younger children: her heir to the throne only inherited Balmoral and Osborne House. Bertie found the upkeep of the latter too expensive and was happy to donate Osborne House to the State.

Queen Victoria held firm to the belief that a woman's place was in the home not in the workplace, seemingly oblivious that staying at home was an unattainable luxury for the majority of her female subjects. The Queen professed to be envious of Florence Nightingale's work in the Crimea, yet made few comments about the work of other middle-class women. When Victoria married Albert, she enjoyed a superior status to her new husband – no other British wife could by law claim such a privilege. By the time of her death, the nature of the marriage contract had changed considerably. Legal reforms ensured that women were no longer considered the goods and chattels of their husbands, could no longer be locked up and beaten, were able to own property and goods and could keep their earnings from their work. Victoria made no comment about these changes, yet her attitude was consistent: she was pleased that women remained disenfranchised. She may have been the most important woman in the world but in spite of that she preferred to appear as the domestic ideal of a passive female whose interests centred on her family. Queen Victoria had no desire to be a role model for women's equality.

In truth, Queen Victoria reinforced gender roles. During her reign, monarchy is said to have become feminised. Just as a pretty, jewel-bedecked nineteenth-century wife was used by her husband to demonstrate his own wealth and power, so the Queen was expected to showcase the strength of the British Empire by dressing up for ceremonial events. Indeed, Bagehot's principles of monarchy – the right to be consulted, the right to encourage and the right to warn – are seen more as the rights of a wife than those of a sovereign. William Kuhn even argues that Bagehot helped 'secure the monarchy's future by describing the constitution as a perfectly-adapted marriage between masculine efficiency and feminine dignity'.[5] In one sense, Queen Victoria liked to bolster this image by presenting herself as the epitome of the middle-class female, the quintessential faithful wife and devoted mother living a life of domestic bliss. Yet, once widowed, she had no desire whatsoever to act as the glamour arm of the British Empire and face the gaze of unknown multitudes. The Queen considered ceremonial displays vulgar and in bad taste and for much of her reign steadfastly refused to take part in them.

To be seen and not heard: towards a ceremonial monarchy

When Victoria ascended the throne, many of the principles of constitutional monarchy were either fluid or untested so that both the Queen and politicians sometimes found it difficult to apply them. Nevertheless, political commentators try to impose neat theoretical frameworks on the rather messy Victorian era. In 1867, at a time when activists were campaigning for further parliamentary reform, Bagehot's book *The English Constitution* was published. He divided the British constitution into two parts: the dignified part, that is, the crown (solely a figurehead); and the efficient centres of power, that is, parliament and the courts (where decisions were taken). Following on from this, the twentieth-century historian Vernon Bogdanor suggests that even in the emerging constitutional democratic monarchy of Victorian Britain there were two offices: a head of state – the monarch – and a head of government – the prime minister.[6] Under this system, the monarch had three main functions. There were the constitutional functions such as appointing ministers; there were ceremonial functions such as the opening of parliament; and there was a symbolic function whereby the monarch represented and symbolised not just the state but the nation. However, real life – even historical life – is much too varied to fit into such neat categorisations. Indeed, the triangular relationship between Victoria, her government and her subjects was never constant: it shifted according to the changing status and expansion of the electorate, the governing political party and the foibles, caprices and innate obstinacy of the Queen herself.

Queen Victoria disliked the ceremonial part of her role and tried to avoid it. Clearly, this undermined her effectiveness as a symbolic head. During the last 39 years of her reign, she opened parliament only seven times;[7] she did not prorogue parliament after 1854; and during the last 15 years of her reign she did not appear within the Palace of Westminster at all. Victoria's disdain for the tradition of monarchs opening and closing parliament, of the ceremonial and theatrical aspects of monarchy did much to weaken her hold on government and her subjects. Very often, even at moments of ministerial crisis, Victoria was away from London. In effect the Queen's non-appearance in parliament and her tendency to travel to Osborne, Balmoral or to mainland Europe seriously diminished her influence. Victoria's travels were personal: if one added up her trips to Balmoral, she spent about seven years there – time that many of her subjects thought should be spent on government affairs.

Not surprisingly, the Queen became unpopular and a wave of Republicanism threatened to topple the monarchy. Her people wanted their Queen to be seen: if she was not seen, then she was not reigning. Most of her subjects would not, and could not, ever see a monarch in person but newspapers would have published Queen Victoria's activities . . . if there were any. The seclusion of the Queen occurred at about the same time as revolution was breaking out in France and these two circumstances encouraged the growth of Republicanism in Britain. The early 1870s marked the high point of an organised republican movement as mass meetings were held in Birmingham and Nottingham, Republican Clubs were set up in over 50 towns and cities and Liberal MPs such as Charles Bradlaugh, Charles Dilke and Henry Fawcett questioned the benefits of funding a monarchy which was expensive to maintain and which did little for the country. Indeed, in some radical circles there was a feeling that monarchy was incompatible with democracy. In 1870 Bradlaugh wrote in his paper, *The National Reformer*, that 'the experience of the last nine or ten years proved that the country can do quite well without a monarch, and may therefore save the extra expense of monarchy'.[8]

The monarchy was saved in late 1871 when the Prince of Wales became desperately ill and for many weeks it was feared that he would die. There was a 'universal feeling of sympathy' for the Prince 'expressed in the press throughout the country'.[9] On 2 December 1871 alarming reports that the Prince had 'passed a very bad night, and that for a certain time the gravest apprehensions were entertained' evoked widespread compassion.[10] The daily sympathetic accounts of Bertie's illness which appeared in the press helped to restore the popularity of the Queen and with it the Crown. Gladstone consolidated this trend by organising a National Thanksgiving on 27 February 1872. Newspapers saw this as a 'great event' which was celebrated 'throughout the country' and 'marked with every manifestation of loyalty and rejoicing'.[11] It also, claimed one paper, led to Republicans renouncing their programme because the 'manifested national loyalty of the last few months' demonstrated without doubt that 'loyalty has been evoked and displayed in a manner and to an extent which clearly shows that the throne of these realms is firmly based on the intelligence and affections of the great mass of the people'.[12] William Gladstone's meticulous organisation of the event, the public appearance of Queen Victoria and the Prince of Wales, and the subsequent reverential reporting in newspapers consolidated the trend towards a decline in Republicanism and the beginning of a new kind of royal performance.

Later ceremonial events, particularly the Golden and Diamond Jubilees, further enhanced the status of the monarchy. These were carefully stage managed and methodically organised theatrical affairs which aimed to consolidate the emblematic role of the Queen. The ceremonies, it is argued, 'helped transform the monarchy from an institution with dwindling political power into a tremendously attractive centrepiece'.[13] Equally important was the establishment of Queen Victoria as a new-style monarch: a symbol of the nation, of imperialism, of British world-wide dominance and of continuity, stability and tradition in a world of constant change. In addition, Queen Victoria's gradual emergence from seclusion undercut republican arguments that the monarchy contributed little to national life.

To be heard and not seen: Victoria and constitutional change

Politicians may have wanted their sovereign to represent Bagehot's dignified part of the constitution but after widowhood she did not want to be seen: Queen Victoria wanted to be heard. The monarch of Great Britain merely cocooned herself from public events, not from politics, engaging fully in debates that interested her. Her fundamental purpose was to keep the monarchy intact and her constitutional prerogatives unchanged. In some ways, Queen Victoria was blinkered, refusing to acknowledge the many changes taking place in the relationship between crown and country. When Victoria was born, Britain was ruled by the elite. The electoral reforms of 1832, 1867 and 1884, and the accompanying growth of modern parties and political machines, challenged the very basis of monarchical power by making it virtually impossible for the Queen to control her ministers let alone have her own way with parliament.

In the eighteenth century, monarchs felt more able to appoint prime ministers of their own choosing, confident that their choice would be able to control the House of Commons. Gradually, and spurred on by electoral reform, the Crown lost influence as the House of Commons became more and more powerful. It became increasingly difficult for Victoria to exercise what she thought were her monarchical rights in an age of expanding democracy. Queen Victoria never really adapted to this new situation and her political meddling would sometimes threaten to damage the monarchy. Theoretically the Crown enjoyed – and still enjoys – the prerogative to appoint the prime minister, but in practice the sovereign has to choose someone who can command a majority in the House of Commons. In 1839 Queen Victoria was able to keep Melbourne in power and Robert Peel out of office largely because neither the Whigs nor the Tories enjoyed electoral majorities, nor were there strong party organisations to support them. The 'bedchamber crisis' may have been thought a victory for the Crown, yet the incident eroded Victoria's popularity and brought her image as a constitutional monarch into disrepute. Nevertheless, Queen Victoria continued to test her monarchical limits, often fighting hard to preserve her powers rather than submit willingly to their reduction. At key moments, the Queen was prepared to use all means available to achieve her goals: sometimes she drew on her femininity; at others she threatened. Most of the time, and especially when political parties enjoyed healthy majorities, the Queen lost the battle. Characteristically, she never quit struggling, as witnessed by her opposition to Gladstone and other ministers she found unacceptable. And these struggles helped establish new constitutional parameters.

Moreover, Queen Victoria often tried, sometimes successfully, to prevent Cabinet ministers being appointed: in 1880 she prevented Gladstone from appointing Charles Dilke; in 1885 she stopped Salisbury appointing Colonel Stanley. She influenced, or tried to influence, the choice of colonial governors – she was successful in the appointment of Ellenborough in 1842 but failed to persuade Gladstone to appoint Carrington in 1892. On occasions foreign diplomats were unable to take up their posts because of the Queen's disapproval: in 1848, for example, the Queen refused to receive the French Ambassador.

Ideally, the monarch was supposed to represent the nation, the whole of the nation, and not just one particular party, group or sectional interest. Queen Victoria may have shared this belief, but she still blatantly and without embarrassment voiced her opinions. In her speech, the Queen professed Whig sympathies; in practice she much preferred the Conservatives and Conservative policies. Indeed, the Queen detested Gladstone's political inclinations and tried regularly to thwart his reforms. For example, the messy circumstances of the 1884 Reform Bill could have been avoided if the Queen had not made her opposition to it well known. When Queen Victoria took sides or tried to influence political events, any notion of her as an impartial sovereign who identifies with the nation as a whole was seriously challenged.

Gradually throughout her reign, Queen Victoria lost her authority as the advance of democracy, electoral majorities and a stronger party system led to the dominance of the House of Commons. No longer were there shifting alliances between groups of MPs centred on their allegiances to individuals – a fluid system in which the monarch's influence and patronage could be decisive – but political parties with (more or less) clear-cut agendas. However, when parties were disunited internally, Queen Victoria was able to influence events. In 1886, encouraged by the behind-the-scenes scheming of Queen Victoria, the Liberal Unionists broke away from the Liberals thus allowing the Conservatives to enjoy decades in power.

Queen Victoria never considered herself merely a figurehead. She wanted to rule, not just reign, and often acted like a despot, fighting hard against the control of the politicians who sought to curb her authority. The Queen had very fixed ideas, pressurised her ministers to accept them and frequently endeavoured to engineer their dismissal if they disagreed. When governments held a strong majority and particularly when a prime minister and his Cabinet were united, Queen Victoria's opinions were disregarded. Yet she never stopped trying. For example, she made several attempts to dismiss Lord Palmerston because she disapproved of his progressive Liberalism and his advocacy of revolutionaries who wanted to overthrow autocratic monarchs. At first, Queen Victoria was unable to oust her foreign minister because he was too powerful in the Cabinet and in the country. In 1851 she eventually succeeded when Palmerston pronounced his support for Louis Napoleon's *coup d'état* without clearing it in Cabinet.

Queen Victoria seized this opportunity to pressurise Lord Russell to get rid of his foreign secretary. She was not, and never would be, a model of constitutional propriety. On the contrary, Queen Victoria was determined to dam the crashing waves of reform which brought the flotsam and jetsam of democracy in its back-wash, a tidal surge that threatened to drown the monarchy.

Victoria was all the more engaged when her family interests were at stake, in which case ministers found they had to deal with a very strong-minded woman. Victoria's Germanic back-ground and German relations, for example, shaped her attitudes towards foreign policy, most notably over the Schleswig-Holstein affair in the 1860s. Here the Queen's views diverged from her government when she backed Prussian claims to the Danish-held territory. In retrospect it is impossible to estimate how much Queen Victoria was responsible for British neutrality but the behind-the-scenes pressure she exerted on her ministers to main-tain peace meant that Denmark was left isolated.

Moreover, the authority of the Queen was omnipresent and it was felt in a number of ways. In the highly deferential age of the nineteenth century, Victoria was treated with a respect that was not bestowed upon people outside the royal family; her views were listened to and acted upon. She was, after all, a Queen. The tricky situation over the 1884 Reform Act was both hindered and helped by the various, and somewhat contradictory, interven-tions of the Crown. The longer the Queen lived and reigned, and in spite of an increase in democracy, the more pervasive her personal influence became. She was at the centre of political life and over time her accumulated knowledge of affairs gave her opportunities to influence policy – especially when the Conserva-tives enjoyed power. Benjamin Disraeli, under considerable pres-sure from the Queen, conferred the title Victoria Empress of India on his sovereign and shepherded the Public Worship Bill through parliament at the Queen's insistence. Certainly, Queen Victoria's bellicose missives to Disraeli during the 1876–8 Eastern crisis went beyond Bagehot's constitutional advice of 'the right to warn' and 'the right to encourage'.

By the time she reached old age, Victoria had become the revered symbol of Victorian respectability, diligence and success. Her popu-larity was buttressed by a fortuitous set of circumstances: the expansion of the British Empire. Each year, from 1837 to 1901, the British army was engaged in constant battles to conquer other lands or consolidate its position in the world. Continual warfare, somewhere in the world, resulted in the British Empire becoming the largest empire the world has ever known, so big that it was said that the sun never set on it. It was an A–Z of empire spanning an alphabet of countries known today as Australia, Bangladesh, Bhutan, Botswana, Burundi, Canada, Caribbean islands (such as Bermuda, Jamaica and Trinidad), Cyprus, the Falkland Islands, the Gambia, Ghana, Gibraltar, Hong Kong, India, Kenya, Lesotho, Malawi, Malaysia, Myanmar, Nepal, New Zealand, Nigeria, Pakistan, Papua New Guinea, Somalia, South Africa, Sri Lanka, Sudan, Swaziland, Uganda, Zambia and Zimbabwe. Queen Victoria was the living symbol of imperial unity. She played a crucial part in its expansion, and there is no doubt that she was deeply committed to maintaining and expanding the British Empire, to make Great Britain, and its reputation, Great. In 1876 she reached the summit of her aspirations when she was crowned Empress of India. In the last few years of Victoria's reign, the British Empire was at the height of its power, ruling over 450 million people, one-quarter of the world's population and one-quarter of the entire world.

The modern monarchy

In 2015, Queen Elizabeth II, as head of state, continues to have the right to reign: in reality, the Queen takes little part in government. Unlike Queen Victoria, Elizabeth governs in accordance with accepted constitutional practice rather than according to her own will. Every week she has a private and unrecorded meeting with her prime minister alone at which, in confidence, she discusses the political issues of the day. The Queen remains, and is expected to remain, politically neutral. Even when the Scottish population was discussing the possibility of Scotland becoming an independent country, Buckingham Palace made it clear that the Queen had no wish to influence the Scottish referendum, saying it was 'a matter for the people of Scotland'.[14] Queen Elizabeth's role as a constitutional monarch is limited to non-partisan functions, functions which she takes very seriously.

The sovereign, according to the royal website, 'acts as a focus of national identity, unity and pride' and 'provides stability, continuity and a national focus, as the Head of State remains the same even as governments change'. Royal advisors, if not Queen Elizabeth herself, have read their Bagehot.

Elizabeth II appears more comfortable than her great-great-grandmother in the ceremonial aspect of her role. Each year, as one of her royal prerogatives, the Queen attends the State Opening of Parliament. Since her coronation in 1951, the Queen has opened every parliamentary session except in 1959 and 1963, when she was pregnant first with Andrew and then Edward. The State Opening of Parliament is ritualistically and symbolically significant and the ceremonial role of the Queen governs the way in which the event is organised. Queen Elizabeth arrives at the Palace of Westminster in a horse-drawn gilded coach; she wears full evening dress, full regalia of diamonds and a crown very visibly displayed. Once inside, the Queen puts on the Parliament Robe of State, consisting of an ermine cape and a long crimson velvet train decorated with gold lace, and the Imperial State Crown, consisting of 2,868 diamonds, 273 pearls, 17 sapphires, 11 emeralds and 5 rubies. She then proceeds to the House of Lords to read the Queen's speech in which she outlines the government's agenda for the coming session. The government, not the sovereign, writes the speech and the Queen ensures that this is understood by continuing to repeat 'My Government' when reading the text, always in a neutral and formal tone.

Queen Elizabeth retains other royal prerogatives: she has the power to appoint ministers, to declare war, to negotiate treaties and international agreements and to issue passports. She remains commander-in-chief of the armed forces, accredits British ambassadors and receives diplomats from foreign countries. The legal system in Britain takes its authority directly from the monarch. Criminal prosecutions are brought on the sovereign's behalf and all courts derive their authority from the Queen not from the government. Moreover, the Queen has the 'prerogative of mercy' whereby she can pardon convicted criminals. In addition, the Queen creates all peerages, knighthoods and other honours. This long list of royal prerogatives is held in theory; in practice, the Queen acts on the advice of her ministers. She takes her role to be consulted, to advise and to warn very seriously indeed; there is no evidence to suggest that she interferes in the way Queen Victoria tried to do.

Queen Elizabeth represents Britain all over the world. In 2014 she was sovereign of 15 former British colonies and head of the Commonwealth, a voluntary body of 54 independent countries, created after the dissolution of the British Empire. The Queen receives foreign ambassadors and high commissioners, entertains visiting heads of state and currently makes one or two overseas state visits each year to other countries in order to strengthen diplomatic bonds and to promote British interests.

Above all, unlike Queen Victoria, Elizabeth recognises the need to be visible. In 2014 she carried out approximately 430 engagements, including visits to schools, factories, hospitals, military units, art galleries, local communities and the 600 charities of which she is patron. Events and buildings are opened, commemorative plaques unveiled and speeches are made. Garden parties, of about 8,000 guests, are hosted at Buckingham Palace for people from all walks of life who have made some sort of contribution to society. In 1997 the Queen and Prince Philip hosted a garden party for couples whose golden wedding anniversary fell on the same day as their own. Unlike Victoria, Elizabeth is seen; not heard.

Notes

1 The BEF consisted of four infantry battalions (an infantry battalion is 1,007 men) and one cavalry (549 men). I am grateful to Professor Maggie Andrews for this insight.
2 Longford, *Victoria*, p. 21.
3 Arnstein, *Queen Victoria*, p. 12.
4 Kuhn, 'Victoria's Civil List'.
5 Kuhn, *Democratic Royalism*.
6 Victor Bogdanor, 'The Monarchy and the Constitution', *Parliamentary Affairs*, 49(3), 1996, p. 410.
7 The Queen opened parliament in 1866, 1867, 1871, 1876, 1877, 1880 and 1886. The Lord Chancellor usually read her speech.
8 Quoted in Norbert Gossman, 'Republicanism in Nineteenth-Century England', *International Review of Social History*, 1, 1962, p. 51.
9 *Penny Illustrated Paper*, December 2nd 1871 p. 339.

10 *Daily News*, December 2nd 1871, p. 5.
11 *The Blackburn Standard*, February 28th 1872, p. 3.
12 *The Blackburn Standard*, February 28th 1872, p. 3.
13 Kuhn, *Democratic Royalism*, p. 10.
14 BBC news, September 11th 2014.

Select bibliography

Arnstein, Walter L., 'The Warrior Queen: Reflections on Victoria and Her World', *Albion: A Quarterly Journal of British Studies,* 30(1), Spring 1998, pp. 1–28.

—— *Queen Victoria*, Palgrave Macmillan, 2003.

Aronson, Theo, *Victoria and Disraeli: The Making of a Romantic Partnership*, Macmillan, 1997.

Bagehot, Walter, *The English Constitution*, Chapman and Hall, 1867.

Bartley, Paula, *Life in the Industrial Revolution*, Hodder and Stoughton, 1988.

Basu, Shrabani, *Victoria and Abdul: The True Story of the Queen's Closest Confidant*, The History Press, 2011.

Benson, A. C. and Viscount Esher (eds), *The Letters of Queen Victoria*, First Series, 3 vols, 1837–61, John Murray, 1908.

Blake, Robert, *Disraeli*, Eyre and Spottiswoode, 1966.

—— (ed.), *The Prime Ministers*, George Allen and Unwin, 1975.

Bogdanor, Victor, 'The Monarchy and the Constitution', *Parliamentary Affairs*, 49(3), 1996, pp. 407–22.

Brown, David, *Palmerston,* Yale University Press, 2010.

Buckle, George (ed.), *The Letters of Queen Victoria*, Second Series, 3 vols, 1862–1885, John Murray, 1926–8.

—— *The Letters of Queen Victoria*, Third Series, 3 vols, 1886–1901, John Murray, 1930–32.

Cawood, Ian, *The Liberal Unionist Party: A History*, I. B. Tauris, 2012.

Cecil, Algernon, *Queen Victoria and Her Prime Ministers,* Eyre and Spottiswoode, 1953.

Cecil, David, *Melbourne*, Constable, 1961.

Chamberlain, Muriel, *Lord Aberdeen. A Political Biography*, Longman, 1983.

Charles, Barrie, *Kill the Queen!, The Eight Assassination Attempts on Queen Victoria,* Amberley, 2012.

Connell, Brian, *Regina v Palmerston, The Correspondence between Queen Victoria and Her Foreign and Prime Minister, 1837–1865,* Evans, 1962.

Dennison, Mathew, *The Last Princess,* Wiedenfeld and Nicolson, 2007.

—— *Queen Victoria: A Life of Contradictions,* HarperCollins, 2013.

Duff, David, *Queen Victoria's Highland Journals,* Lomond Books, 1994.

Erickson Carolly, *Her Little Majesty: The Life of Queen Victoria,* Simon and Schuster, 1997.

Eyck, Frank, *The Prince Consort,* Cedric Chivers, 1959.

Farwell, Byron, *Queen Victoria's Little Wars,* Victorian Book Club, 1973.

Fassiotto, Michael Eugene, *Finding Victorias/Reading Biographies,* PhD, University of Hawaii, 1992.

Feuchtwanger, E. J., *Gladstone,* Allen Lane, 1975.

—— *Albert and Victoria: The Rise and Fall of the House of Saxe-Coburg-Gotha,* Continuum, 2006.

Fulford, Roger (ed.), *Dearest Child: Private Correspondence of Queen Victoria and the Crown Princess of Prussia, 1858–1861,* Evans, 1964.

—— (ed.), *Dearest Mama: Private Correspondence of Queen Victoria and the Crown Princess of Prussia, 1861–1864,* Evans, 1968.

—— (ed), *Darling Child: Private Correspondence of Queen Victoria and the Crown Princess of Prussia, 1871–1878,* Evans, 1976.

—— (ed), *Beloved Mama: Private Correspondence of Queen Victoria and the German Crown Princess, 1878–1885,* Evans, 1981.

Gash, Norman, *Sir Robert Peel,* Longman, 1985.

Gosse, E. and Ponsonby, M., 'The Character of Queen Victoria', *The Quarterly Review,* April 1901.

Gossman, Norbert, 'Republicanism in Nineteenth-Century England', *International Review of Social History,* 1, 1962, pp. 47–60.

Greville, Charles, *The Greville Memoirs, 1814–1861,* Macmillan, 1936.

Guedalla, Philip, *The Queen and Mr Gladstone,* Hodder and Stoughton, 1933.

Halevy, Elie, *Victorian Years,* Ernest Benn, 1951.

Hardie, Frank, *The Political Influence of Queen Victoria, 1861–1901,* Frank Cass, 1935.

Hibbert, Christopher, *Queen Victoria in Her Letters and Journals,* Viking, 1984.

—— *Victoria: A Personal History,* HarperCollins, 2000.

Hobsbawm, Eric and Ranger, Terence, *The Invention of Tradition,* Cambridge University Press, 1983.

Hoppen, Theodore, *The Mid-Victorian Generation, 1846–1886,* Clarendon Press, 1998.

Hough, Richard, *Advice to a Grand-Daughter: Letters from Queen Victoria to Princess Victoria of Hesse,* Readers Union, 1976.

Jenkins, Roy, *Gladstone,* Macmillan, 1995.

Kuhn, William M., *Henry and Mary Ponsonby,* Duckworth, 2002.

—— *Democratic Royalism: The Transformation of the British Monarchy, 1861–1914,* Macmillan, 1996.

—— 'Ceremony and Politics: The British Monarchy 1871–2', *Journal of British Studies,* April 1987.

—— 'Victoria's Civil List', *Historical Journal,* September 1993.

Langer, William L., *Political and Social Upheaval, 1832–1852,* Harper Torchbooks, 1969.

Lee, Sidney, *Queen Victoria,* Smith, Elder and Co., 1904.

Longford, Elizabeth, *Victoria,* Abacus, 2000 (first published 1964).

Magnus, Philip, *Gladstone,* John Murray, 1954.

Marshall, Dorothy, *The Life and Times of Victoria,* Weidenfeld and Nicolson, 1972.

Martin, Theodore, *Queen Victoria as I Knew Her,* Blackwood and Son, 1908.

Mathew, H.C.G. and Reynolds, K.D., 'Queen Victoria', *Dictionary of National Biography,* Oxford University Press, 2004–14.

McKinstry, Leo, *Rosebery, Statesman in Turmoil,* John Murray, 2005.

Morley, John, *The Life of William Edward Gladstone,* Edward Lloyd, 1908.

Olechnowicz, Andrezej, *The Monarchy and the British Nation 1780 to the Present,* Cambridge University Press, 2007.

Ponsonby, Arthur, *Henry Ponsonby, Queen Victoria's Private Secretary: His Life from His Letters,* Macmillan and Co., 1943.

Rappaport, Helen, *Queen Victoria: A Biographical Companion,* ABC-CLIO, 2003.

—— *Magnificent Obsession: Victoria, Albert and the Death that Changed the Monarchy,* Windmill Books, 2012.

Rhodes James, Robert, *The British Revolution: British Politics 1880–1939,* Hamish Hamilton, 1976.

—— *Albert, Prince Consort,* Hamish Hamilton, 1983.

Ridley, Jane, *Bertie: A Life of Edward VI,* Vintage Books, 2013.

Robert, Andrew, *Salisbury: Victorian Titan,* Weidenfeld and Nicolson, 1999.

Small, Hugh, *The Crimean War,* Tempus Publishing, 2007.

Strachey, Lytton, *Queen Victoria,* Chatto and Windus, 1921.

Thompson, Dorothy, *Queen Victoria: Gender and Power,* Virago, 1990 (first published 1982).

Vallone, Lynne, *Becoming Victoria,* Yale University Press, 2001.

Van der Kiste, John, *Queen Victoria's Children*, Sutton, 2003.

—— *Sons, Servants and Statesmen: The Men in Queen Victoria's Life*, Sutton, 2006.

Victoria, *Queen Victoria's Journals*, complete journals 1832–1901, Royal archives, available online at www.queenvictoriasjournals.org.

Ward, Yvonne, *Censoring Queen Victoria*, Oneworld Publications, 2014.

Weintraub, Stanley, *Victoria: Biography of a Queen*, John Murray, 1997 (first published Unwin 1986).

—— *Uncrowned King: The Life of Prince Albert*, John Murray, 1997.

Williams, Kate, *Becoming Queen*, Arrow Books, 2009.

Wilson, A. N., *The Victorians*, Arrow Books, 2003.

—— *Victoria, A Life*, Atlantic Books, 2014.

Woodham-Smith, Cecil, *Queen Victoria: Her Life and Times, Volume 1: 1819–1861*, Hamish Hamilton, 1972.

Wyndham, Mrs Hugh (ed.), *Correspondence of Sarah Spencer, Lady Lyttelton, 1787–1870*, John Murray, 1912.

Index

314 *Index*